DANIEL C. ESTY

Greening the GATT:
Trade, Environment, and the Future

Institute for International Economics
Washington, DC
July 1994

Daniel C. Esty, Senior Fellow, formerly served as the US Environmental Protection Agency's Deputy Assistant Administrator for Policy, Planning and Evaluation, as EPA's Deputy Chief of Staff, and as Special Assistant to EPA Administrator William Reilly. He was EPA's chief NAFTA negotiator. He has been a Visiting Lecturer at the Yale School of Organization and Management. He is the author of a number of articles and studies on trade, competitiveness, environment, and development.

INSTITUTE FOR INTERNATIONAL ECONOMICS
11 Dupont Circle, NW
Washington, DC 20036-1207
(202) 328-9000 FAX: (202) 328-5432

C. Fred Bergsten, *Director*
Christine F. Lowry, *Director of Publications*

Cover design by Michelle M. Fleitz
Typesetting by BG Composition
Printing by Automated Graphic Systems

Printed in the United States of America
97 96 95 94   5 4 3 2 1

Library of Congress Cataloging-in-Publication Data

Esty, Daniel C.
    Greening the GATT / Daniel C. Esty.
        p. cm.
    Includes bibliographical references and index.

    1. International trade—Environmental aspects.   2. General Agreement on Tariffs and Trade (Organization)   3. Commercial policy—Environmental aspects.
    4. Environmental policy—Economic aspects.   I. Title.
    HF1379.E88   1994
    382'.92—dc20   93-50830
                                                    CIP

ISBN 0-88132-205-9

Marketed and Distributed outside the USA and Canada by Longman Group UK Limited, London

To Elizabeth,
who contributed directly and indirectly
to every page of this book

Contents

Preface

Throughout its history, the Institute has conducted studies on a wide range of trade policy issues. In particular, we have tried to help set the agenda for such major international negotiations as the Uruguay Round (*Trading for Growth: The Next Round of Trade Negotiations* by Gary Clyde Hufbauer and Jeffrey J. Schott, September, 1985), the NAFTA (Hufbauer and Schott's *North American Free Trade: Issues and Recommendations*, March 1992) and the United States-Japan framework talks (*Reconcilable Differences? United States-Japan Economic Conflict* by C. Fred Bergsten and Marcus Noland, June 1993).

We are now turning our attention to the post-Uruguay Round period with analyses of competition policy, international investment and several other topics that may merit future consideration. One of the most important items on this agenda is the relationship between trade and the environment. The GATT membership has already decided to address the issue but there is, as yet, no clear focus for doing so. This volume aims to contribute to developing such a focus, suggesting both a series of trade-environment linkages that should be addressed and possible responses to each. In addition, it suggests a new approach to managing global environmental problems that would be compatible with the world trading system over the longer run.

Such an analysis could be conducted effectively only by an author, like Daniel Esty, who is well versed on both the trade and environmental dimensions of the issue. Dr. Esty was an honors graduate in economics from Harvard before receiving a Rhodes Scholarship at Oxford and taking a law degree at Yale. He was a practicing trade lawyer and subsequently represented the Environmental Protection Agency in the negotiations on the environmental provisions of the NAFTA (and at the Earth Summit in Rio de Janeiro in 1992). His ability to blend the several aspects of the problem will, I believe, provide a valuable contribution to its future understanding and resolution. A major part of this study was conducted while Dr. Esty held an International Affairs Fellowship from the Council on Foreign Relations, whose support he and I deeply appreciate.

The Institute for International Economics is a private nonprofit institution for the study and discussion of international economic policy. Its purpose is to analyze important issues in that area, and to develop and communicate practical new approaches for dealing with them. The Institute is completely nonpartisan.

The Institute is funded largely by philanthropic foundations. Major institutional grants are now being received from the German Marshall Fund of the United States, which created the Institute with a generous commitment of funds in 1981, and from the Ford Foundation, the William and Flora Hewlett Foundation, the William M. Keck, Jr. Foundation, the C. V. Starr Foundation, and the United States–Japan Foundation. A number of other foundations and private corporations also contribute to the highly diversified financial resources of the Institute. The Rockefeller Foundation provided substantial support for this project. About 16 percent of the Institute's resources in our latest fiscal year were provided by contributors outside the United States, including about 7 percent from Japan.

The Board of Directors bears overall responsibility for the Institute and gives general guidance and approval to its research program—including identification of topics that are likely to become important to international economic policymakers over the medium run (generally, one to three years), and which thus should be addressed by the Institute. The Director, working closely with the staff and outside Advisory Committee, is responsible for the development of particular projects and makes the final decision to publish an individual study.

The Institute hopes that its studies and other activities will contribute to building a stronger foundation for international economic policy around the world. We invite readers of these publications to let us know how they think we can best accomplish this objective.

C. FRED BERGSTEN
Director
June 1994

Acknowledgments

I have benefited from the assistance of an enormous number of people in carrying out this project. C. Fred Bergsten made the study possible by broadening the ambit of the Institute for International Economics beyond familiar trade matters to include environment and development issues and their relationship with trade. His guidance has shaped this book from its earliest days. Bill Long of the OECD also contributed fundamentally to the project, having provided me with a research base and many helpful suggestions about how trade and environment policies might be woven together. The Institute for International Economics, the Rockefeller Foundation, and the Council on Foreign Relations provided substantial funding for this study; additional research support came from the European Community Visitors Programme.

Close readings by colleagues have sharpened this work considerably. I am particularly grateful for the careful attention and detailed comments I received from Kenneth Berlin, William R. Cline, Richard Cooper, Steve Charnovitz, Aaron Cosbey, Terry Davies, Kimberly Ann Elliott, Ian Fletcher, Hillary French, Damien Geradin, Alex Hittle, John Jackson, Robert Keohane, Winfried Lang, Patrick Low, Konrad von Moltke, Robert Morris, James Murphy, William Pedersen, Patti Petesch, Robert Repetto, J. David Richardson, Charlie Ries, Carol Rose, Nevin Shaw, Peter Uimonen, John Williamson, Paul Wonnacott, and Edith Brown Weiss.

I also benefited from comments, suggestions, and guidance from Senator Max Baucus, Thomas O. Bayard, Jagdish Bhagwati, Gordon Binder,

Giles Briatta, Laurens Brinkhorst, Tom Burke, Frances Cairncross, James Cameron, Josephus Coolegem, Killian Delbrucke, I.M. Destler, Elizabeth Dowdeswell, Gilbert Dubois, Richard Eglin, Jeremy Eppel, Geza Feketekuty, Robert Fisher, Ellen Frost, Sandy Gaines, Edward M. Graham, Joseph Greenwald, Jay Hair, Scott Hajost, Rebecca Hanmer, Jurgen Henningsen, Carla A. Hills, Rob Housman, Gary C. Hufbauer, Nancy Kete, Benedict Kingsbury, Peter Lallas, Brice Lalonde, Grant Lawrence, Claas van der Linde, Mikael Lindstrom, Daniel Magraw, Warren Maruyama, Ann McCaskill, Michael McCloskey, Jacques de Miramon, Richard Morgenstern, Alastair Newton, Risaburo Nezu, Robin Pedler, E. U. Petersmann, Michael E. Porter, Michel Potier, Disiano Preite, Cornelia Quennett, William K. Reilly, Michael Reiterer, Rubens Ricupero, Freider Roessler, James Salzman, Anya Schoolman, Jeffrey J. Schott, David Shark, Takashi Shinohara, Andrew Shoyer, Mike Smith, William Snape, Tom Spencer, Candice Stevens, Yasuo Takahashi, David Van Hoogstraten, Rene Vossenaar, Timothy Wirth, and Durwood Zaelke.

A number of other people provided materials, support, and help of other kinds including Mario Aguilar, Penny Allen, Ken Andrasko, Richard Ayres, Pep Fuller, David Harwood, Karl Hausker, Stewart Hudson, Ted Krauss, Angus Macbeth, Monica Medina, Janet Nuzum, Joel Scheraga, Steve Seidel, Elizabeth Sherwood, Dennis Tirpak, and Richard Weiner.

Daniel Rosen offered tireless research assistance and enormous creativity in tracking down all the facts, figures, and references required. I am very appreciative for all his efforts and contributions to this study. Lisa Heredia typed, retyped, and re-re-typed the manuscript more times than either of us would care to count. I am particularly thankful that her boxing training was never brought to bear on me. Christine F. Lowry and Valerie Norville provided superb editorial help, Brigitte Coulton shepherded the book through production, and Faith Hunter assisted them with great skill. Coleen McGrath organized study groups and publicity for this project with energy and style. Jay Dick, Sabrina Wood, and Clavel Hunter all played important roles in keeping the words flowing. I am also thankful for the help of Janet Saunders, who found books that seemed to be impossible to get, and Donna Becraft who made sure that the effort stayed on track in a dozen different ways.

Introduction

"Trade and environment" is a hot topic in political circles. The issue loomed large in the North American Free Trade Agreement (NAFTA) debate. It also emerged as a concern in efforts to bring the Uruguay Round of global trade negotiations under the General Agreement on Tariffs and Trade (GATT) to an end. It has become a central focus of discussions aimed at setting a course for future multilateral trade talks. And it is the source of numerous bilateral tensions as the United States squabbles with Norway over whaling, China and Taiwan over tiger bones and rhinoceros horns, Mexico over tuna fishing and dolphin deaths, Japan over protection of endangered sea turtles, and Brazil over rain forest preservation. It represents, furthermore, a key issue in environmental policy debates from climate change to hazardous waste exports to ozone layer depletion, as well as a central element of efforts to promote "sustainable development" and to advance the policy agenda approved at the 1992 Earth Summit in Rio de Janeiro.

Unfortunately, trade and environment policy encompasses not a single issue but a multiplicity of related (and unrelated) concerns that have been bundled under the "trade and environment" rubric. The debate over the NAFTA alone raised a number of trade-related environmental concerns, including: fears that expanded trade would result in pollution spillovers into the United States from increased industrial activity in Mexico; lower US environmental standards and a loss of US sovereignty as laws and regulations were "harmonized" at compromise or baseline levels; limitations on the ability of the United States to use trade measures in support of international environmental agreements; and marketplace disadvantages for US facilities competing against plants located in "pollution haven" Mexico—resulting in job losses or downward pressure on US environmental standards.

Trade liberalization viewed through the environmentalists' lens seems to invite increased pollution, lost regulatory sovereignty, an anti-environmental counterforce driven by the desire for jobs and profits, and policymaking by obscure, unaccountable, business-oriented international bureaucrats. Similarly, free traders regard the agenda of some environmentalists with distrust (box 1). In particular, the trade world sees a danger that new forms of protectionism—blocking foreign producers from entering markets and reducing the efficiency gains from trade—will emerge in the guise of politically attractive environmentalism. Moreover, many free traders fear that the use of trade penalties to enforce environmental agreements or, worse yet, to promote unilaterally determined environmental choices will break down the already-fragile international trading regime. They particularly object to efforts to adjust for differences in environmental standards (or, more troubling, environmental compliance costs) to address competitiveness concerns, fearing this will undo differences in comparative advantage that form the basis for the economic gains from trade.

This study seeks to untangle these separate strands of concern, analyze their validity and seriousness, offer ways to respond to the critical issues, and find means for improving the coordination of trade and environmental policymaking. The overarching goal is to reconcile two important policy pursuits: the promotion of economic growth through trade and protection of the environment.

Chapter 1 identifies the trends in world affairs that have brought the formerly distinct worlds of trade and environment into contact and, all too frequently, conflict. Chapter 2 reviews the possible effects of trade liberalization on the environment and the impact of environmentalism on international trade. It identifies four core propositions of environmentalists that are related to trade:

- Trade may cause environmental harm by promoting economic growth that, without environmental safeguards, results in the unsustainable consumption of natural resources and waste production.

- Trade rules and trade liberalization often entail market access agreements that can be used to override environmental regulations unless appropriate environmental protections are built into the structure of the trade system.

- Trade restrictions should be available as leverage to promote worldwide environmental protection, particularly to address global or transboundary environmental problems and to reinforce international environmental agreements.

■ Even if the pollution they cause does not spill over onto other nations, countries with lax environmental standards have a competitive advantage in the global marketplace and put pressure on countries with high environmental standards to reduce the rigor of their environmental requirements.

The first two propositions constitute the "defensive" environmental agenda. In this regard, the environmentalists' goal, which many free traders share, is to ensure that trade liberalization does not harm the environment. Of course, in some circumstances trade liberalization may actually enhance environmental quality. For example, the elimination of agricultural subsidies that distort trade also reduces the incentive to use environmentally damaging, chemical-intensive farming practices. Although more attention should be paid to these cases where trade and environmental interests are coterminous, the trade and environment debate centers on cases where these two policy goals appear to be in conflict.

The second two propositions represent the environmental "offensive" agenda. Of course, the term "offensive" in this context does not mean obnoxious or distasteful (although some free traders do find this agenda to be offensive in this sense). Instead, the term reflects the interest of the environmental community in using trade as a point of leverage to advance environmental goals.

Without safeguards, there can be no guarantee that trade will make people better off. It may make them richer, but at what environmental price? The critical issue—and the heart of the first environmentalist proposition—therefore becomes, what safeguards are required to ensure that freer trade has a net positive effect on the environment and thus on social welfare broadly defined? Most environmentalists see the onus for such environmental protection falling on the trade regime and requiring a "greening" of GATT rules and procedures. But many free traders, as good economists, argue that, if markets are working properly and appropriate environmental policies are in place, trade can be pursued without hurting the environment, and little reform of the GATT is required. In particular, they note that if the costs of environmental spillovers or "externalities" (e.g., the harm imposed on the public through air pollution from smokestacks, water pollution from waste pipes, or the dumping of toxic substances or other waste products) were factored into the prices consumers and producers pay—that is, "internalized"—then market forces would limit environmental harms while increasing society's financial well-being. Chapter 3 explores this "economic" basis for resolving trade and environment conflicts.

This book, in addition to laying out a program for "greening" the GATT, traces part of the trade and environment tension to two aspects of a broad-based failure of environmental policymaking: (1) an economic failure to internalize environmental costs and to make consumers and producers pay the full price for the environmental harms they cause and (2) a political failure to override special interests and adopt cost-internalization policies that protect the environment while encouraging trade. Indeed, if environmental regulations relied more on economic incentives and all environmental harms were fully internalized, the scope for trade and environmental policy conflict would be considerably reduced. Not only would the safeguards necessary to address the first environmental proposition be in place, the issues raised by the second, third, and fourth propositions would also be largely resolved.

Recognizing the essential problem of collective action that underlies these failures, this study calls for creation of a Global Environmental Organization or GEO (see chapter 4). Creating a comprehensive international environmental management structure would protect environmental policies and values from competitiveness-driven government actions; promote environmental policymaking that is in step with trade, development, and other potentially competing goals; and help to coordinate global environmental efforts. A GEO would put the environment on equal footing with trade in the international realm and facilitate the reconciliation of trade liberalization and environment protection on a basis that permits simultaneous pursuit of both of these important contributors to social welfare.

Establishing a new environmental regime faces serious practical obstacles. Thus, although the idea of a GEO, with an overarching management structure that would ensure a systematic and comprehensive worldwide response to global environmental issues, offers the optimal way to integrate trade and environmental policymaking, a new international environmental regime must be considered a long-run prospect at best.

It is possible that environmental cost internalization could be accomplished without an international regime of this type. Yet it has been difficult to persuade nations to impose costs—and potential competitive advantages—on their own industries, that face global competition. Cost internalization would therefore be politically much easier to adopt in the context of joint action among a broad group of nations. The political dynamic of competitiveness thus makes a GEO an important, or even perhaps an essential, tool for advancing cost-internalizing environmental policies.

Absent coordinated environmental cost internalization, each of the environmentalist propositions must be addressed individually and woven into a comprehensive GATT reform package. Thus this book analyzes the key propositions in turn and develops a program of procedural and substantive GATT reform to ensure systematic consideration of environmental factors within the GATT and in trade relations more broadly.

The second proposition highlights the tension between traditional trade and environmental goals. Trade liberalization often takes the form of agreements to open markets to imported products, and in doing so, nations accept limits (or to use trade terminology, ''disciplines'') on their own freedom to set national standards. Such agreements to limit nontariff trade barriers address not only environmental regulations but standards governing the size, shape, labels, safety testing, and many other features of products as well. These agreements, backed by GATT rules and review mechanisms, are designed to separate legitimate ''high'' regulatory standards from trade barriers masquerading as environmental (or other) regulations and from restrictions that disproportionately and unduly burden imports. Chapter 5 will explore how to balance these competing needs.

The third proposition, concerning the necessity of using trade measures as environmental leverage, highlights the fact that few options exist in real-world international relations to respond to pollution that spills over borders or to coerce nations that fail to abide by international environmental agreements into compliance. In the absence of financial inducements or other effective policy tools, the GATT must find ways to accommodate and to manage the use of trade restrictions as an environmental ''enforcement'' mechanism, especially in response to global and transboundary issues. Chapter 6 will propose a system of bounds designed to permit the use of trade as leverage in appropriate circumstances (where a trade partner's environmental standards are too low—resulting in pollution harm to others) and to discourage it elsewhere.

The fourth proposition—addressing competitiveness concerns—is the most problematic. It raises questions about who decides what constitutes proper environmental standards and whether it is appropriate for one country to try to dictate to another environmental policies addressing localized problems. At its logical extreme, such actions threaten not only to undermine traditional notions of national sovereignty but also to unravel the advantages of trade derived from different national circumstances—that is, comparative advantage. As an empirical matter, moreover, environmental standards have not proved to be a very significant competitiveness factor. In addition, economists observe that exchange rate adjustments can eliminate the trade balance effects of differential environmental cost structures.

But as this study explains, when viewed more broadly, competitiveness concerns relating to environmental standards have some validity. In particular, the traditional "environment and competitiveness" analysis has focused rather narrowly on pollution control expenditures rather than on broader factors such as energy pricing policies. Moreover, the ability of exchange rate adjustments to accommodate policy differences in environmental standards on the macroeconomic level without affecting a nation's balance of trade does not obviate potentially significant microeconomic or sectoral effects. Competitiveness analysis may also need to evolve to accommodate a business world that is increasingly global and highly cost-conscious. Beyond any economic impact, low standards in some countries create "political spillovers" or "political drag" that can be an important obstacle to the adoption of optimal environmental policies in other nations. And unquestionably, competitiveness concerns have great potency as a political matter and can threaten ongoing support for trade liberalization. Thus the environment and competitiveness relationship deserves serious analysis and is the focus of chapter 7.

Chapter 8 offers an analysis of the significant North-South dimension of the trade and environment conflict. Notably, environmental policy–based trade restrictions are often invoked by developed countries in the absence of resources to coax developing countries into joining global environmental efforts or to adhere to specified environmental standards. Unfortunately, environmental protection programs adopted at the point of a gun almost never work. More importantly, this use of the trade "stick" in the absence of financial support or other "carrots" raises fundamental questions of fairness. These questions can become particularly acute in light of the perceived historical responsibility of the North for many of the planet's environmental problems—and the sense that the developed world enriched itself in the past by ignoring environmental harms. This study therefore tries to change the terms of the trade and environment debate, identify new sources of funds for environmental investments, and establish new bases for North-South cooperation.

Chapter 9 offers a blueprint for "greening" the GATT. It identifies specific procedural and substantive reforms that should be considered as the GATT moves to absorb environmental considerations into the workings of the international trading system. This chapter also reviews various strategies for amending or refining GATT rules.

Ultimately, the goal of this book is to reconcile the various interests that must be brought together to achieve both continued trade liberalization and effective environmental protection. The need to pursue these two policy goals simultaneously is clear; both contribute in important ways to public and individual welfare.

Achieving agreement on a trade and environment policy among all the interested constituencies within each country (and especially within the United States) will not be easy. There is a constant tension within the trade community between those who will benefit from freer trade and those who would like to use the trade system to protect their markets. Within the environmental community, there exists perhaps an even greater range of views and goals. Indeed, while one could, within certain bounds, get some agreement about what trade liberalization means, no such consensus would emerge over what constitutes environmentalism. Beyond the disagreement over environmental goals, an even greater divergence exists over how one should achieve whatever ends are chosen.

Moving the policy process forward internationally can be seen as requiring widening circles of consensus. Given the spectrum of trade and environmental opinions that must be consolidated to develop a national position, it is no wonder that efforts to resolve trade and environmental conflicts often appear to be moving slowly. In particular, the United States—whose leadership is crucial for action—has not been able to articulate a clear vision of how to advance the issue.

Once the US government settles on a direction, there remains a difficult series of issues that must be resolved between the United States and the world's other largest trading bloc—the European Union—and then, more broadly, with other industrialized countries, in particular the 24 developed nations that make up the Organization for Economic Cooperation and Development (OECD). A final level of intense negotiation will be required to bring together the views of the developed nations (the North) and the developing world (the South).

To achieve consensus at all of these levels at one time will require better understanding of the trade and environment problem, compromise on all sides, and considerable creativity. This study seeks to advance the process, building on two fundamental bridges between the trade and environmental communities: the opportunity to advance both environmental protection and trade liberalization by promoting regulations that internalize environmental costs, and the recognition that the goals of both freer trade and environmental protection are enhanced by international regimes that facilitate cooperation and support mutual adherence to agreed-upon standards of behavior.

1

Origins of the Trade and Environment Conflict

Environmental protection was not a major issue when the General Agreement on Tariffs and Trade was drawn up just after World War II (see appendix A for background on the GATT). Indeed, the GATT does not explicitly reference the "environment." Until recently, trade policymakers and environmental officials pursued their work on separate tracks, rarely perceiving their realms as interconnected. Today, environmental protection has become a central issue on the public agenda—and trade and environmental policies regularly intersect and increasingly collide. This reflects the fact that the norms and institutions of international trade remain rooted in the pre-environmental era and that there exists no international environmental regime to protect ecological values, to reconcile competing goals and priorities, or to coordinate policies with institutions such as the GATT.

The growing clash between trade and environmental policymaking can be traced to a number of social and political trends. Several high-profile recent events have recently brought simmering tensions to a boil.

Rising Environmental Interest

Although the environment comes in and out of fashion as a political priority, the long-term growth in interest in environmental issues has been dramatic over the last several decades. Eight out of 10 Americans now call themselves environmentalists (*Wall Street Journal*/NBC News Poll, 2 August 1991, A1). Membership in environmental organizations has grown dramatically. Members of Congress and senators pay great attention to the environmental issue ratings they receive from groups such as the League of Conservation Voters, a Washington-based advocacy group that monitors political progress on environmental issues. Without a doubt, the environment has become a first-tier public-policy concern (Gore 1992), challenging long-standing issues of "high politics" such as national security for attention on the political stage. As Moran (1990) notes: "Low politics is becoming high politics."

The rise of environmentalism reflects, in part, a "wealth" effect (Wildavsky 1988). Specifically, in affluent societies, quality of life issues become more salient, and people feel that they can afford higher environmental standards (Hahn and Richards 1989). Perhaps more importantly, the public refuses to believe it must choose between economic growth and environmental protection.[1] Although interest in the environment is greatest in the richest countries (e.g., the United States, Germany, the Netherlands, and the Scandinavian countries), the trend extends across the world (Gallup International Institute 1992).

Environmental consciousness played an important role in the recent revolutions in Eastern Europe, and the issue has taken root in much of the developing world, where the effects of environmental degradation are often acutely felt. In fact, the environmental history of Eastern Europe and the republics of the former Soviet Union—cities choked with soot, abandoned waste pits teeming with toxic chemicals, water not only unfit to drink but also so corrosive it is unusable in industrial processes—has made clear the price that is paid in reduced life expectancy, increased cancer rates, and other public health and ecological effects for the blind pursuit of economic growth without environmental safeguards. While they may have trouble defining it, politicians everywhere now respond to the call for "sustainable development,"[2] acknowledging the need to pursue economic growth and environmental protection simultaneously.

---

1. Only 25 percent of the American public now believes that we must choose between environmental protection and economic growth (Roper 1992).

2. See the World Commission on Environment and Development (1987) (hereinafter the Brundtland Commission). The Brundtland Commission's definition of sustainable development—economic growth that "meets the needs of the present without compromising the ability of future generations to meet their own needs"—is widely regarded as a useful starting point for understanding the concept. Stephan Schmidheiny (1992, 10) translates the sustainability challenge for business into the concept of "eco-efficiency," meaning optimal reduction of wastes generated and resources consumed. Gifford Pinchot's (1987, 505) definition of conservation offers another good point of departure: "The foresighted utilization, preservation, and/or renewal of forests, waters, lands, and minerals, for the greatest good of the greatest number for the longest time."

Interest in addressing the environment has been driven not only by greater affluence, which makes a response to environmental problems possible, but also a growing sense of the seriousness as a public health matter of exposure to chemicals or pollutants.[3] As scientific understanding of these effects improves, the public's tolerance for contaminants falls.

The expanding interest in the environment further reflects a threshold effect, as ecological problems that have been building for some time become visible (Brown, Flavin, and Postel 1991; Dasgupta 1990). While the "Club of Rome" or "limits to growth" theories predominant in the environmentalism of the 1970s (Meadows 1972)—arguing that the world risked running out of critical resources—have been largely dismissed as overblown,[4] environmentalists today focus instead on pollution concerns and the buildup of waste in critical ecosystems. Specifically, there is now a widespread recognition that the Earth does not have an unlimited capacity to absorb pollution (MacNeill, Winsemius, and Yakushiji 1991; Cairncross 1992; Schmidheiny 1992).

The environmental threats to the planet should not be overstated. The Earth does have a powerful ability to cleanse itself. Many environmental wounds do heal—in some cases with amazing speed. For example, unlike the 1989 *Exxon Valdez* calamity, the massive 1993 *Braer* oil spill in the Shetland Islands produced very little immediate impact and was virtually unnoticeable within a few months (Crookston 1994).

But the limits of the Earth's assimilative capacity can be reached over time either because pollutants cumulate or because emissions levels rise beyond the capacity of the relevant ecosystem to process waste. Thus, fish in the Great Lakes are showing increasing numbers of deformities

---

3. See, for example, "An Association between Air Pollution and Mortality in Six US Cities," in the *New England Journal of Medicine* 9 December 1993, (vol. 329, no. 24, 1753), suggesting that air pollution, even at levels that meet federal air-quality standards, may increase the risks of cancer and cardiovascular disease. Recent issues of this and other public health journals reveal an enormous number of articles identifying possible environmental links to a range of health problems. See also "Cancer Risk Up Sharply in this Era," *Washington Post*, 9 February 1994, A1 (reporting on a new study showing significant environmental cancer risks and quoting Devra Lee Davis of the US Department of Health and Human Services as saying "there are preventable causes out there that remain to be identified").

4. These theories failed to credit sufficiently the powerful force of technological advancement in helping to reduce "input" needs and to generate substitutes for diminishing resources. Furthermore, while population growth remains a critical environmental issue, the population "explosion" on which the theories were predicated did not occur (see, e.g., "Poor Lands' Success in Cutting Birth Rate Upsets Old Theories," *New York Times*, 2 January 1994, Al). For a recent defense of the "limits to growth" perspective, see Goodland, Daly, El Serafy, and Von Droste (1992).

Figure 1.1 Differing patterns of harm

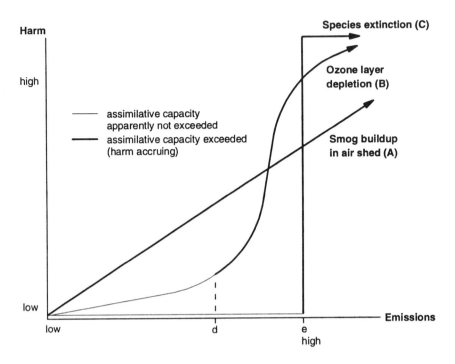

Different types of environmental problems result in varying patterns of harm, depending on the affected ecosystem's assimilative capacity. Curve (A) represents a linear function. Harm rises directly with an increase in air emissions; no critical threshold exists. Curve (B) shows a logarithmic function that occurs as the ozone layer's ability to assimilate CFCs is overwhelmed: while seemingly unimportant at low emission levels, rapid harm results past the critical threshold at point (d). The most dramatic threshold effect is demonstrated by curve (C), a "step" function: drastic harm—such as species extinction—occurs with little or no warning once the critical threshold at point (e) is passed.

because toxic substances are building up in their systems. And although automobile emissions dissipate relatively quickly into the atmosphere, Los Angeles has so many cars (and a geography that limits natural dissipation of exhaust fumes) that smog builds up. The critical issue is, when does pollution result in environmental harm that goes over the line from self-regenerating to nonsustainable or even irreversible?[5] (figure 1.1)

---

5. Pezzey (1988) usefully distinguishes between ''effluent'' and ''pollution.'' Pollution is effluent that causes a loss of environmental value. Effluents (i.e., emissions) are not considered to cause environmental harm if they are within the ''assimilative capacity'' of the relevant ecosystem.

Environmental issues often reflect the "tragedy of the commons," where harmful (or even benign) actions by one individual or a small number of people will have no noticeable effect on a public resource, but the same behavior by larger numbers destroys the resource (Hardin 1968). Similarly, any one person's or group's effort to address the problem alone will be of little value in the face of the ongoing harm caused by others—creating an incentive not to act. For example, one individual's use of a wood-burning stove seems harmless, but when everyone heats his or her home with a crackling fire, even small towns or remote valleys can become choked with smoke. In fact, serious winter air pollution problems now exist in seemingly pristine but wood stove–intensive areas such as Klamath Falls, Oregon.

From the well-known smog of Los Angeles to toxic-laden groundwater in New Jersey to the Antarctic ozone hole, environmental indicators suggest that the Earth's assimilative capacity has been passed in a number of areas. Critical thresholds are being exceeded not only in the United States but around the world (McKibben 1989; Brown 1994). In the 50 years since World War II, land clearing for agriculture and other human activities have degraded almost 5 billion acres of land area worldwide, about 17 percent of all vegetated space on the planet (Brown 1994, 10). This leaves, for example, many nations trying to squeeze more food production out of less and less productive soil.

The United Nations Food and Agriculture Organization (FAO) estimates that all 17 of the world's major fishing areas have reached or exceeded natural replacement levels (Brown 1994, 11; *The Economist*, 19 March 1994, 21). As a result, fish yields have fallen sharply. In some traditionally rich fishing grounds, such as Georges Bank off the East Coast of the United States, strict fishing controls have had to be instituted.

The perceived limits of the natural environment to serve as a dump is a driving force behind today's interest in environmental protection. The recognition that environmental problems require collective action—cooperation among people to avoid overuse or destruction of common resources—has also increased the focus on the environment as a matter of public policy. In examining the tie to trade, the political or geographic level at which collective action is required becomes important. Some critical environmental problems are local in effect; others are global in scope. The broader the problem, both geographically and politically, the more difficult is the coordination required to overcome the collective-action problem and to protect the environment. The link to trade is, of course, much clearer in the context of global problems. From an environmental perspective, trade presents an attractive policy tool that is inherently international and therefore commensurate in scale with global environmental problems.

Over the last 30 years, governments around the world have taken the first steps toward addressing environmental problems, challenging the fundamental assumption that the planet's land, air, and water are available for free for waste disposal. By asserting "property rights" over natural resources, governments signaled the end of the free-dumping era. In the United States, first-generation air and water pollution laws were adopted beginning in the late 1960s and early '70s. In effect, society recognized that the natural environment is a valuable public good, and governments moved to reclaim it as community property (box 1.1).

Dispute over the Ends and Means of Environmentalism

The distress of discovering that we are approaching or have exceeded the critical threshold of the Earth's assimilative capacity in a variety of areas has been compounded by a recognition that our pollution control tools are by and large grossly inadequate. The weakness of those tools and the heavy economic burden of some approaches to environmental regulation have heightened the tensions between environmentalists and free traders. Specifically, to the extent that some environmental regulations are economically irrational (the most basic definition of which would be that the social costs imposed by the program exceed the benefits obtained), welfare-maximizing free traders question the wisdom of blindly protecting the regulations, particularly when the result is a barrier to trade that also reduces the economic benefits of open markets.

Many environmentalists are also frustrated by the high cost and modest benefits of some environmental programs. These environmental analysts would be the first to agree with economists (e.g., Hahn 1993) who note that environmental regulation is not the same thing as environmental protection. But environmentalists worry that judgments about the efficacy and value of environmental regulations are best made by environmental officials, not trade experts. Thus, while a revolution is now under way to redirect environment regulation toward risk-based analysis backed by more efficient and effective "market mechanisms" (EPA 1990b; Carnegie Commission 1993), most environmentalists are nervous about scrutiny of environmental regulations in the context of trade liberalization.

To date, environmental regulation in the United States (and other industrialized countries) has primarily focused on nationally established waste, air, and water pollution rules aimed at reducing emissions from the smokestacks or effluent pipes of big factories. These "command and control" programs, which allow fixed amounts of emissions or mandate certain pollution control technologies, have produced dramatic progress in some industrial sectors. But today we see the limits of this blunt regulatory approach. Fixed emissions limits backed by criminal or civil penalties are an ineffective response to dispersed sources of pollution. Moreover, the command and control system is expensive to implement and administer, produces environmental progress too slowly, discourages process and technology innovation, and invites litigation, foot dragging, and calculated noncompliance.

To achieve further increments of environmental progress, attention must shift from big industries to smaller facilities and to the environmental behavior of individuals. Additional progress also requires attention to a broader set of problems, ranging from global issues such as climate change to stubborn aspects of traditional concerns such as fertilizer runoff and other hard-to-track sources of water pollution. Effectively attacking these more diffuse, complex, and subtle problems often entails changing the behavior of not just a few thousand companies but millions or even billions of people. This requires a major reorientation of environmental regulation toward incentive-based programs and the use of market forces to support environmental protection.

Environmental regulation today increasingly builds on market mechanisms designed to internalize the costs to society of environmental harms and the use of economic incentives to guide people's actions (Hahn and Stavins 1992). While the goal of these new programs is to ensure that polluters pay the full bill for their emissions from society's point of view, uncertainties over who is responsible for pollution and how much compensation should be required for various kinds of emissions have made the shift to incentive-based regulations that internalize pollution externalities a slow process. In sum, although the environment has become an important public priority and environmental policymakers recognize the need to apply market forces as a regulatory tool, our ability to "price" environmental resources is still relatively primitive.

The polluter pays principle—the idea that emissions impose environmental costs on society for which a price should be paid—has become well established in theory (see, e.g., OECD 1972; Pearson 1994; Gaines 1991). But policymakers have just begun to incorporate this economic concept into the structure of commercial relations in practice. For example, despite the emergence of many high-technology alternatives for power generation, the use of coal (a relatively dirty energy source) has risen, not fallen, in recent years. Today, 55 percent of America's electricity comes from coal-fired power plants. The reason is simple: coal is cheap. But coal is cheap because the substantial costs of mining, transporting, and burning this fuel are only partly reflected in the price consumers pay directly.

A recent analysis (Cullen 1993) estimated that if the costs of mining accidents, black lung, other health effects on miners, water pollution from mine runoff, other environmental damage around mine sites, air pollution, and greenhouse gas emissions from the transportation and final combustion of coal were factored in, the price per ton of coal would be over $200, not the current average of about $46. The difference between $46 and $200 is the environmental and other social costs, which the public pays indirectly. For instance, the cost of mine accidents is, at least in part, paid for through welfare, social security, and other support payments to widows and their children. The costs of air pollution are borne by the public in terms of higher incidence of lung and respiratory disorders.[6]

Because these costs are neither precisely calculable nor indisputably attributable to burning coal, they have not been incorporated in the price

---

6. The American Lung Foundation puts a price tag of $50 billion a year on the health effects of air pollution from all sources (Cannon 1990).

consumers pay for coal-based electricity. As a result, alternative (less polluting) sources of power cannot compete on a price basis and are not used (Kozloff and Dower 1993). Some sophisticated policymakers are beginning to recognize the need to account for such externalities. The California Public Utilities Commission, for example, has indicated that in analyzing the economic viability of any new proposed power plant designed to burn coal, it intends to factor in a "shadow price" of $24,490 for every ton of sulfur dioxide to be emitted, $31,448 for each ton of nitrogen oxides, and $33 per ton of carbon dioxide (Cullen 1993). With these costs internalized, new coal-fired power plants are much less likely to be built.

This new generation of environmental policy mechanisms faces many constraints (Pedersen 1994a). Notably, using market forces cannot eliminate political controversies in the environmental realm. Better economics—and better science—can narrow the range of appropriate answers, but how much value to put on environmental amenities and harms remains a quintessentially political problem.

Movement away from technology standards toward market-based, performance-oriented environmental regulation can improve the efficiency of environmental regulation and help the public get the maximum bang for its environmental buck and, at the same time, narrow the scope for conflict between trade liberalization and environmental protection. But to the extent that politicians and government officials reach out for politically feasible, second-best policy tools (e.g., mandated pollution control technologies and ad hoc limits on emissions of certain chemicals), they will continue to run head-on into the demands for an open economy advanced by free traders. Thus, a commitment to cost-internalizing environmental regulations offers a key bridge between the environmental and free trade camps. Indeed, economists (and liberal traders) and environmentalists virtually all agree on the value of the polluter pays principle as a way to ensure that prices accurately reflect costs, including environmental harms otherwise "externalized," and therefore as a means to both better environmental protection and more efficient markets.

Ecological Interdependence

In addition to the general rise in public interest in environmental protection, the international political scene has been changed by the emergence of global environmental problems such as deforestation, loss of biological diversity, climate change, and ozone layer depletion (National Research Council 1992).[7] As the National Commission on the Environment (1993,

---

7. To this list of global threats one must at least add ocean pollution, environmental

60) concludes: "The natural systems that provide the living conditions for humans and other species know no political boundaries." The rules of international trade have not caught up with this development. Characterized by the fact that the emissions from one country spill across borders and in some cases blanket the Earth, these issues have demonstrated the "ecological interdependence" of the planet (e.g., Schneider 1976; Myers 1989). Thus, for example, even if the United States were to stop all releases of chlorofluorocarbons (CFCs) and other chemicals that harm the Earth's protective ozone layer, if other countries continue to produce and to use CFCs, the ozone layer would still be destroyed.

Not only have we recently become aware of the existence of indivisibly global issues, but a number of these problems appear to be at a potentially critical stage. The ozone hole is expected to cause thousands of additional cases of skin cancer and cataracts in the United States over the next 20 years—though the EPA projects these would increase by tenfold were it not for the Montreal Protocol, phasing out the production and use of CFCs.

From 1980–90, on average 15.4 million hectares of forests were lost each year (UNFAO 1993a), an annual compound deforestation rate of 0.8 percent. The destruction (often by burning) of these tropical trees is estimated to release 1.6 billion tons of carbon (with a ± 0.4 billion ton margin of error) into the atmosphere yearly and eliminates the capacity for the "uptake," or absorption, of millions of metric tons of carbon dioxide. This absorption process is essential to keeping the planet's natural carbon cycle in equilibrium and preventing the buildup of greenhouse gases in the atmosphere (Dixon et al. 1994).

The loss of forest cover also threatens the biological diversity of the planet. More than half of all known species live in tropical rain forests (Brown 1994, 28). Harvard biologist Edward O. Wilson (1992, 278) calculates that some 50,000 of these species are becoming extinct annually, largely due to human activity. If current trends continue, 5 to 10 percent of all species now on the planet may disappear in the next 25 years (Brown 1994, 195). Reduced biodiversity could have serious consequences: loss of a counterbalance against new strains of plant and animal diseases, fewer new medical treatments—half of which in recent years have come from tropical plants—and loss of the basic balance in the Earth's ecosystems.

While the implications are not yet fully clear, the level of carbon dioxide in the Earth's atmosphere has risen steadily over the last several decades.

---

management of Antarctica, protection of outer space, and the spread of radioactivity. Moreover, scientific advances continue to broaden our understanding of the connectedness of the world's ecosystems, making the identification of new global issues a near certainty. For example, DDT uncovered in the Great Lakes of the northern United States has been traced to use of the product in Mexico, suggesting that airborne chemicals can be transported thousands of miles by high-level winds (Rapaport et al. 1985).

In its widely read climate change study, the National Academy of Sciences (1991, xv) concluded that carbon dioxide levels today were 26 percent higher than in the preindustrial era. According to the UN-sponsored Intergovernmental Panel on Climate Change (IPCC 1990, xxii), this trend of increased greenhouse gases, if it were to continue, could lead to a 1.5 to 4.5 degrees Celsius rise in average temperatures over the next century or sooner. This seemingly small change (don't people in Atlanta already live with warmer weather than in Boston?) could mean a rise in sea levels, losses of arable land to desertification, destruction of valuable wetlands, more severe storms, and changes in rainfall patterns (IPCC 1990, xxv; Cline 1992; Smith and Tirpak 1989, xxx; Mintzer 1992, 4).

Cline (1992) notes that the potential harm may be much greater than the conventional analysis shows because the warming process could well go beyond the usual benchmark (a doubling of the carbon dioxide buildup in the atmosphere).[8] Cline argues, moreover, that in analyzing the climate change issue the correct policy time frame should be 200 to 300 years—not the 35-year scenarios that are predominant. Cline (1992, 130–32) estimates that for the United States potential damage from a 2.5°C warming (a midpoint in the range of prevailing estimates) could total close to $60 billion annually or about 1 percent of US GDP. Factoring in intangible losses, Cline's estimate rises to 2 percent of GDP, and if greater levels of warming (4.5°C) are contemplated, the damage could reach 4 percent of GDP. The losses in other developed countries would be comparable to those of the United States. The losses in developing countries might well be much greater in percentage terms (Topping 1992). Over the very long term and with pessimistic assumptions, Cline's analysis suggests the price for global warming might hit 20 percent of world product.

Not only have global issues loomed larger in the last several years, but the inability of the world community to systematically address these matters has become more apparent. Domestically, adherence to environmental rules can be assured by designated government officials authorized to impose penalties on violators. In fact, in the United States, the federal Environmental Protection Agency (EPA) and its state counterparts bring thousands of enforcement actions every year. But in the international context, no such enforcement mechanism exists (Chayes and Chayes 1991; Hahn and Richards 1989). Coordinated, multilateral environmental programs are required to address global problems. Thus,

---

8. Cooper (1992) offers a cautionary note in the opposite direction, observing that the uncertainties surrounding climate change are so significant that drastic and costly policy responses are not warranted. Nordhaus (1992), using narrower time frames than Cline, puts a much lower dollar figure on the potential costs of climate change, observing as well that there is broad scope for mitigation before climate change effects become severe. Mendelsohn, Nordhaus, and Shaw (1992) further argue that adaptation may reduce the economic impact of potential climate change.

the parties to international environmental agreements have begun to use market-access and other trade measures to encourage broad participation in the agreements and to penalize cheaters. For example, the Montreal Protocol, phasing out the production of CFCs and other ozone layer–damaging chemicals, bars trade in certain goods with countries that are not complying with the agreement.

As the number of global environmental issues has multiplied and agreements incorporating trade measures as tools to encourage participation and compliance have proliferated, trade officials have looked on nervously. With no guidelines to ensure that trade restrictions are applied in a limited, consistent, and appropriate manner, the trade community sees a danger that the trying task of preserving an open world market will be made more difficult by the indiscriminate (and perhaps even the discriminating) use of trade penalties to promote environmental policies. Moreover, powerful countries such as the United States appear willing to impose trade measures unilaterally to discipline countries that it alone determines to be damaging the "global commons." Such actions threaten not only to unravel the delicate balance of mutual commitments to freer trade but risk breaking down international harmony more broadly.

Economic Interdependence

Another trend driving trade and environmental policymaking together derives from the growing economic interdependence of the world's major economies (Cooper 1968; Ostry 1990). World trade in merchandise and services amounted to almost $4.7 trillion in 1992 and accounts for an ever-growing share of global economic output. In many countries, exports represent a significant element of the economy and account for many jobs. Even the United States, with its huge domestic economy, has significant trade interests. US annual combined merchandise and services exports amount to about $600 billion, and imports total more than $650 billion. In fact, America has become reliant on export sales as an engine of economic growth and domestic prosperity (box 1.2; Drucker 1994; Bergsten 1993; Davis 1992).

The increasing intensity of global economic competition has transformed formerly "local" environmental issues such as waste management and air and water pollution into international concerns, as industries that export or face import competition (potentially almost all manufacturers) monitor closely any differential between their costs of production and those of producers elsewhere (EPA 1990a; OTA 1992; *Wall Street Journal*, 11 June 1992, B1). Thus, while there are legitimate reasons for environmental standards—and therefore pollution control expenses—to vary, countries that pursue dramatically less stringent (and

Box 1.2 World trade: What's at stake?

- World trade in merchandise approached $3.7 trillion in 1992, more than doubling in a decade and equaling 16.4 percent of the world's total 1992 output. Additionally, trade in services approached $1 trillion in 1992 (UN 1993; IMF, *International Financial Statistics* 1993).
- Trade barriers in the United States cost American consumers about $70 billion annually, 1.3 percent of GDP (Hufbauer and Elliott 1994).
- Trade has been estimated by Hufbauer and Schott (1992, 55) to create about 14,500 jobs per billion dollars of national exports, and increased trade has supported a significant proportion of all job growth in the United Stats since 1986 (Davis 1992).
- The recently concluded Uruguay Round of GATT negotiations produced liberalization agreements expected to generate $270 billion in global gains from trade (OECD 1993b).
- In 1992, international trade represented about 10 percent of American and Japanese GDP, 23 percent of France's, 38 percent of Germany's, 27 percent of Indonesia's, and 8.5 percent of Brazil's (IMF, *International Financial Statistics* 1993).

Trade between selected countries and regions by export destination, 1992 (billions of dollars)

Exporter	US	Japan	EU	Developing world	OECD
US	–	47.8	110.9	181.4	261.8
Japan	96.7	–	68.8	155.1	183.4
EU	95.3	26.5	–	251.0	1175.9
Developing world	213.4	108.5	261.8	–	603.1
OECD	315.7	97.8	1231.0	653.8	–

therefore less costly) approaches to air, water, or waste problems are perceived in segments of both the business and environmental communities to have seized an unfair competitive advantage.

Environmentalists, in particular, see competitiveness pressures as a threat to high US environmental standards and fear that trade liberalization in an open global marketplace adds to these pressures (French 1993a; Mead 1992).[9] The long-term international trend toward greater emphasis on trade liberalization and economic integration adds to their nervousness.

The seriousness of the competitiveness issue has been much debated (Krugman 1994). Economists have traditionally found little effect on competitiveness from spending on pollution control requirements (Kalt 1988; Leonard 1988; J. David Richardson 1993). This received economic wisdom does not, however, comport with political reality, where com-

---

9. There are many definitions of "competitiveness." This study follows the definition provided by the Competitiveness Policy Council (1992, 1), which identifies the economic competitiveness of a nation as its ability to produce goods and services that meet the test of international markets while its citizens earn a standard of living that is both rising and sustainable over the long run.

petitiveness concerns arising from environmental standards are a major issue (Baucus 1991; Gephardt 1992). One response to this political argument is simply to assert that the politicians do not know what they are talking about and that their huffing about environmental competitiveness is a smoke screen for trade protectionism.

But such back-of-the-hand treatment is not fair. First, although spending on environmental compliance amounts to less than 2 percent of value added for 85 percent of American industries, some industries (petrochemicals, refining, cement, steel) do have significant pollution control expenditures and thus potential environmental competitiveness issues (US Trade Representative 1992, 166). Moreover, the traditional economic analysis has largely focused on the overly narrow category of spending on pollution controls. When other aspects of environmental costs (e.g., energy pricing) are factored in, serious competitiveness questions emerge. More importantly, few of the competitiveness studies are recent enough to account for the increasingly cost-sensitive, trade-oriented, dynamic business world of today.

Those who deny that environmental compliance requirements affect competitiveness in any serious way are also overlooking the US experience of competition among its states for new investment during the 1940s, '50s, and '60s. Throughout this period, states sold themselves as attractive sites for new industrial facilities at least in part because they offered low costs, including lax pollution control requirements. While recent commentators (Revesz 1992) have tried to debunk the "race to the bottom" line of reasoning, this pattern of interstate competition contributed significantly to the drive for national environmental standards in the United States in the late 1960s and '70s.[10] With the globalization of the world economy, there is every reason to believe that a similar pattern of international competition will plague environmental policymaking (Richard B. Stewart 1993b).

---

10. As Angus Macbeth, one of the founders of the Natural Resources Defense Council (NRDC), recalls, "Competitiveness concerns were a very big theme" in the drive for national environmental standards (interview with the author, 14 April 1994). Senator Edmund Muskie, for example, insisted that the Clean Water Act contain federal technology requirements so that West Coast lumber mills would not be able to discharge pollutants and gain a competitive advantage over mills in Maine that were facing tighter environmental requirements (CRS 1973, 168–70). Richard Ayres, a leading participant in the early battles for national clean air standards, reports a similar line of reasoning running through the 1970 Clean Air Act debate (interview with the author, 15 April 1994). Jack Sheehan of the United Steelworkers Union, another major figure in the debate leading to national air pollution standards, also remembers competitiveness concerns playing a central role in building a consensus for action (interview with the author, 13 May 1993). See, for example, Senate Report 91-1196, 91st Congress, 2nd session (1970). The congressional hearings leading up to this report also sound the state-versus-state competitiveness theme. See, for example, the hearings before the Subcommittee on Air and Water Pollution on S.3229, S.3466, S.3546 (16–18 March 1970, 75, 99, 115).

Perhaps most importantly, *environmental* concern over competitiveness has little to do with how companies fare economically in the international marketplace. What is of concern is the possibility that industries will try to improve their competitive position by externalizing pollution costs. In addition, environmentalists worry about the "political drag" created by the low environmental standards of trading partners. Specifically, they fear that lax environmental regulations elsewhere give credence to business arguments about competitive disadvantage and can be significant in debates over the rigor of new environmental laws, leading to weakened support for strong environmental standards.[11]

The internationalization of capital markets and investment flows heightens corporate sensitivity to differences in environmental policies.[12] While there are limits to short-term business mobility, many companies do in fact threaten to take their production elsewhere if they are faced with environmental compliance costs significantly greater than their competition's. For example, several major multinational companies operating in the Netherlands recently threatened to shift their new capital spending abroad and forced the Dutch government to scale back plans for increased energy and environmental taxes (Arden-Clarke 1992b).

Additional competitiveness concerns arise from the fact that programs to attack global environmental issues can vary widely in the costs they impose on individual countries. For instance, a number of US critics of aggressive greenhouse-gas emission reductions have noted that Europe is better-positioned to reduce emissions than the United States since Germany and England are trying to scale back use of subsidized, expensive coal in favor of cheaper Eastern European and Russian natural gas, which happens to produce lower greenhouse-gas emissions.

Evolving Threats to Freer Trade

From a trade perspective, environmentalism looms large on the horizon of new issues—and is viewed with some trepidation ("Green Gang's GATT Holdup," *Journal of Commerce*, 10 December 1993; "Greening the

---

11. In the 1989–90 debate over the Clean Air Act amendments in the United States, US companies argued that the added regulations would be extremely costly and seriously disadvantage them in international markets (e.g., "Politics in the Air," *National Journal*, 6 May 1989, 1098). Similar arguments were made in opposition to President Clinton's 1993 proposal for a BTU tax (e.g., "Merits of Increased U.S. Energy Taxes at Issue," *Oil and Gas Journal*, 1 February 1993, 15).

12. A countervailing factor, as noted earlier, is the ability of exchange rates to adjust for across-the-board policy cost effects without affecting trade balances. Of course, this adjustment does come at the expense of a nation's standard of living, an element of competitiveness as defined here.

GATT," *Financial Times*, 23 February 1994). This reflects, in part, evolution in the focus of trade liberalization efforts. Some 120 "contracting parties" now subscribe to the GATT rules regulating trade, and the GATT has made great progress in its original goal of reducing tariffs. As a result, attention has shifted to nontariff barriers to the free flow of international commerce (Jackson 1969; 1992b). In fact, Cowhey and Aronson (1993) argue that the international trading system has become a market access regime that goes well beyond concerns about border controls to cover international and domestic economic issues that require at least partial harmonization of a variety of national policies.

The Tokyo Round of GATT negotiations in the 1970s consolidated the assault on nontariff barriers and produced a series of GATT codes to combat some of these obstacles. The recent Uruguay Round of negotiations advanced this process further, adding new nontariff concerns such as intellectual property to the GATT agenda. Trade experts see a pattern: as one field of nontariff barriers is cut down, another one springs up as protectionist interests find new ways to bend the rules of the trading system for their own benefit.

Environmental protection is, in fact, just one of many social policy issues affecting trade; two other examples are antitrust policy and labor standards. In fact, the international trading regime will likely struggle to address these concerns along with issues of "competition policy" for some time to come (Graham 1993). As a subset of the competitiveness policy debate, trade experts see special dangers in protectionism masquerading as environmentalism. It is particularly difficult to challenge policies cloaked in environmental garb because of their popular appeal and the skittishness of politicians and government officials at the prospect of being cast as anti-environmental. Moreover, environmentalists often add potency to their arguments by distilling complicated issues for the public into black and white choices or, more precisely, "brown" and "green" positions. The hostility of some parts of the environmental community to economic growth as a goal and therefore to trade as a tool for achieving growth, gives added intensity to the fears of those who see misguided and narrowly focused environmental initiatives as derailing trade liberalization.

Changing International Scene

The rise of environmental concerns in general, global issues in particular, and competitiveness-based interest in environmental policies has taken place in a time of rapid change in international affairs (Bergsten 1990 and 1992; Rizopoulos 1990). The Cold War has ended, and market-based capitalism now stands triumphant. The move to a "new world order" has raised new strategic issues, including environmental concerns.[13]

Ironically, at this moment of victory, the relative power of the United States seems to be declining. In particular, chronic budget deficits have sapped the United States' willingness to use money to induce others to resolve international disputes in ways that protect US interests. But the US public's expectations, and even more fundamentally congressional attitudes, have not adjusted to these new strategic realities. This makes compromise and cooperative efforts to address critical international questions much more difficult. Moreover, to the extent the United States uses its market muscle to impose its views on the world, others can and will rebel and refuse to cooperate on the issue in question or other unrelated matters. Concern about US environmental "bullying" is especially significant in the developing world, and denunciations of US "ecoimperialism" now regularly rain down upon US environmentalists.[14]

Another element of the changing political scene is a shift in the axis of international tension and conflict from East-West (communist versus capitalist) to North-South (developed versus developing nations). This trend is particularly marked in the environmental realm, breaking apart the traditional alliance between northern environmentalists and developing-country interests (Speth 1992). When asked to forgo development options or bear additional costs to meet international environmental goals, developing countries feel entitled to compensation not only on the basis of economic equity and ability to pay but more fundamentally on their sense of who bears the moral responsibility for environmental harms. In fact, many global problems reflect the accumulated emissions of industrialized nations and represent an ecological by-product and unfunded liability of the hundreds of years of economic activity that have provided the developed world great wealth.

Given these differences, collaboration on global environmental problems often breaks down. When developing countries refuse to divert limited resources from other fiscal priorities and the industrialized world declines to subsidize the developing world's mitigation programs, the conflicts spill over into the trade realm. Specifically, short on "positive" leverage (i.e., financial aid), the North turns to the "negative" leverage of trade measures to reinforce its environmental priorities.[15] Many US

---

13. Mathews (1989) argues that the concept of national security would need to be expanded to include resource and environmental issues even if the Cold War had not ended.

14. Similar tensions exist in the trade realm, where the "aggressive unilateralism" of the United States is widely condemned (Bhagwati and Patrick 1990; Bayard and Elliott 1994).

15. There are some examples of the use of carrots—Montreal Protocol funding of CFC substitutes and Global Environment Facility support for biodiversity projects to name two—but there are more uses of the stick: the Greenpeace-led boycott of Icelandic products in response to Iceland's whaling, Austria's tropical timber labeling and tax scheme,

environmentalists, frustrated at the lack of funds available to assist developing countries but equally impatient with the South's implied threats not to cooperate in efforts to tackle global problems, have called for even broader use of consumer boycotts and trade restrictions to support environmental policies.

Not only do developing countries dispute who should bear the financial burden of meeting international environmental goals, they also view the North's environmental interests with suspicion. They fear that new environmental requirements are being structured to block their exports and to protect the markets of industrialized-country producers. They also object to environmental programs that ignore the urgent environmental priorities of the South (e.g., sewers, drinking water, the alleviation of poverty) in favor of what seem to them to be the longer-term and therefore less-pressing projects of the North (e.g., climate change, ozone layer depletion).

The failure of the 1992 Earth Summit in Rio de Janeiro to bridge this North-South divide adds to the difficulties that trade and environmental policymakers now face (Esty 1993b). Despite a great deal of hoopla and a grueling series of preparatory sessions over two years, the convocation in Rio did almost nothing to solidify the concept of sustainable development.[16] No major new program of environmental financial assistance emerged. No plan materialized to encourage developing countries' economic growth so that resources for environmental investments would be generated. And the Earth Summit delegates failed to advance any initiative to restructure international environmental institutions to bring coherence to the management of global environmental issues.

Despite the failure to accomplish much on the "official" agenda, the Earth Summit was a great success in other regards, foreshadowing changes that are transforming the international milieu in which future environmental efforts will take place.[17] Notably, the Rio conference showed the array of new nonstate actors that now play on the international stage—environmental groups, private development agencies, business associations, international organizations, corporations, and foundations—and which shape policy at the local, national, and interna-

---

and US trade penalties imposed on Taiwan for failing to control illicit trade in endangered rhinoceros and tiger body parts.

16. Admittedly, the concept of sustainable development is inherently difficult to make concrete. But the chance to develop a practical program to integrate environmental protection and economic growth was lost due to a lack of interest in parts of the US government and a preoccupation among a number of developing countries with using the Earth Summit as a vehicle to extract new foreign aid commitments from the developed world (Esty 1993b).

17. Gardner (1992) offers an interesting review of the Earth Summit and challenges ahead for future ecodiplomacy. Speth (1992) provides an upbeat assessment of the Earth Summit and identifies some of the new forces (e.g., nongovernmental organizations) at play in Rio.

tional levels.[18] As Nye (1992) notes, transnational entities (e.g., corporations) and transnational forces (e.g., the spread of technology or the danger of global warming) now contend with the nation-state as influences on world politics. Indeed, led by a dynamic Swiss industrialist, Stephan Schmidheiny, the international business community played a major role in the events in Rio, demonstrating worldwide corporate interest in pursuing prosperity with new sensitivity to environmental considerations.

The Earth Summit's Global Forum brought together thousands of environmental groups and other nongovernment organizations (NGOs), provided another vivid demonstration of this transnational phenomenon, and helped to hardwire environmental NGOs into a global network. These new cooperative relationships facilitate "information arbitrage," permitting rapid dissemination of data and ideas. Indeed, the information revolution (fax machines, computer linkages, etc.) reinforces the shift away from a nation-state focus in global affairs. For as Peter Drucker (1994) says of worldwide information flows, they "do not fit into any theory or policy. They are not even transnational; they are nonnational." At least some of the GATT's problems stem from the fact that its structure reflects the nation-state focus of the post–World War II international order. This translates into rules and procedures that do not easily accommodate nongovernment actors (Bergsten and Graham 1994) and that become a source of tension in the handling of environmental matters in which a wide array of nongovernment organizations take great interest.

Triggering Events

Two recent events—the debate over NAFTA and a GATT dispute settlement panel recommendation against the US imposition of a trade ban against Mexican tuna imports to support US dolphin protection efforts—have catapulted the previously arcane trade and environment linkage onto center stage in American politics. Before NAFTA, environmentalists paid little attention to trade issues. But the US government's announcement in the fall of 1990 of plans to negotiate a trade agreement with Mexico rang alarm bells in the environmental community in North America and launched trade and environment as a prominent issue. US environmentalists in particular saw potentially serious ecological harm arising from expanded trade with a developing country.

At the same time, some politically shrewd members of the environmental community perceived an opportunity in NAFTA. Specifically, they saw a chance to use the negotiations with Canada and Mexico as

18. Bramble and Porter (1992) discuss the role of nongovernment organizations in environmental policymaking. Pearson (1985) examines the role of multinational corporations in environment and development policymaking.

leverage to advance environmental issues on which it was otherwise hard to sustain political attention (e.g., pollution problems along the US-Mexico border). The difficulty of achieving a pro-NAFTA congressional majority and the existence of a sizable bloc of generally pro–free trade, pro-environment senators and congressmen who appeared to be NAFTA swing votes ensured the environmental community an ongoing high profile in the NAFTA debate.

Drawing on their experience in the 1980s in building environmental sensitivities into the World Bank and other multilateral development institutions, the environmentalists used their time in the NAFTA spotlight to demand not only a "green" US-Canada-Mexico trade deal but broad changes in international trade policymaking and the GATT ("Greens Talk Trade," *National Journal*, 13 April 1991). The environmental provisions of the NAFTA and the existence of a special environmental side agreement are testament to the environmental community's success.

The NAFTA debate also exposed the often unnoticed fact that the environmental community is not monolithic. Indeed, the issue sharply split US environmentalists.[19] One fissure separated those who believe that economic growth is a positive environmental force that generates resources that can be invested in pollution control and resource conservation from those who see growth as inextricably linked to increased industrial activity, which creates pollution. A second divide set "national" groups—those that feel powerful enough to affect federal government decisions, that see their role as shaping policy from the "inside," and that are therefore comfortable with the environmental policymaking process NAFTA puts in motion—against grass-roots groups. These local groups have no confidence in national policies (never mind international policy efforts), and their agendas often include a commitment to "grass-roots democracy" with the maximum degree of decision making delegated to the local level.

---

19. Six major environmental groups—National Wildlife Federation (NWF), Environmental Defense Fund (EDF), Natural Resources Defense Council (NRDC), Audubon Society, World Wildlife Fund (WWF), and Conservation International—endorsed the NAFTA with great fanfare, calling the free trade pact a "watershed," "an unprecedented tool for reconciling ecological and economic objectives," and "a solid institutional framework" for protecting the environment of North America (see 14 September 1993 press releases of EDF, WWF, and NRDC). Anti-NAFTA environmental groups including the Sierra Club, Friends of the Earth, and many grass-roots environmental organizations, rallying under the banner of the Citizens Trade Campaign, accused the pro-NAFTA environmental groups of "selling off the North American environment" and of being "too cozy with their corporate funders." Jay Hair of NWF attacked the anti-NAFTA groups, declaring that they were "putting their protectionist polemics ahead of concern for the environment" and "feeding off misinformation." Other pro-NAFTA environmentalists denounced the anti-NAFTA organizations for being more interested in finding an issue to support their fund raising than in good public policy ("The Free Trade Accord," *New York Times*, 16 November 1993, B11).

The trade community also reflects a spectrum of opinions—from those who see the GATT as a finely tuned instrument that already balances competing needs and is at risk from major reforms designed to accommodate environmental interests, to those who recognize the value of building into the GATT new environmental provisions and other reforms so as to preserve the credibility of the institution and to maintain its central role in managing international economic relations. But while there remain deep disagreements within the environmental community and between environmentalists and trade experts over whether and how the international trade regime should be reformed, everyone now agrees that the environment is on the trade agenda.

While the NAFTA drew attention to the trade and environment issue, a 1991 GATT dispute panel decision on US-Mexico tuna trade turned interest into fury. The panel concluded that the United States was in violation of its GATT obligations for instituting a ban, as required by the US Marine Mammal Protection Act, on the importation of Mexican tuna caught using ''purse seine'' nets, which killed large numbers of dolphins in the Eastern Tropical Pacific Ocean (Housman and Zaelke 1992b).

Although the GATT has never formally adopted the dispute panel's recommendation, this now notorious ''tuna-dolphin'' decision seemed to put trade obligations on a higher plane than environmental protection and raised the specter of environmental laws and regulations being routinely challenged and overridden by an obscure international trade tribunal with no environmental sensitivity or expertise. Consequently, the decision touched a raw nerve in the US environmental community. The fact that the US law was structurally defective, setting Mexico's dolphin kill limit retroactively based on the number of dolphins killed by US tuna fishermen, was forgotten. Instead, the tuna-dolphin decision became a symbol for far deeper issues than the survival of America's beloved TV dolphin, ''Flipper.'' In environmental circles, the case has come to stand for the proposition that countries may not use their market power to influence the environmental practices of foreign governments or producers (box 1.3).

In the minds of many environmentalists, the tuna-dolphin decision casts doubt on the consistency with the GATT of the trade provisions of any international agreement aimed at influencing environmental activities outside a country's own borders. This broad interpretation of the tuna-dolphin ruling leaves in GATT limbo such important international environmental agreements as the Montreal Protocol phasing out CFCs and other chemicals that destroy the ozone layer, the Convention on International Trade in Endangered Species of Wild Fauna and Flora (CITES), and the Basel Convention on the export of hazardous waste. Although the panel decision notes that there existed no international

Box 1.3 The tuna-dolphin case

The tuna-dolphin case arose because the US Marine Mammal Protection Act (PL 92–522, 86 Stat. 1027), enacted in 1972, required the US government to curtail the incidental killing of marine mammals by commercial fishermen. In addition to imposing limits on US fishermen, the MMPA required the secretary of commerce either to certify that foreign governments were taking steps to prevent the killing of marine mammals or else to prohibit the importation of tuna products from the offending countries.

In 1988, believing that dolphins in the eastern tropical Pacific Ocean, where tuna swim together with dolphins, were being killed by fisherman in violation of this law, a California environmental group, Earth Island Institute, sued to enforce the congressional mandate (*Earth Island v. Mosbacher*, 746 F. Supp. 964). The federal court agreed that the administration was not upholding the law and ordered Mexican tuna imports banned from the United States. At the time the ban was imposed, the US tuna fleet had largely abandoned fishing in this part of the Pacific Ocean, so the dolphin protection provisions of the MMPA did not apply to them.

Mexico, believing that its GATT-guaranteed right to sell tuna in the United States had been violated, challenged the US ban and asked for a GATT dispute settlement panel to adjudicate the matter. The GATT panel concluded:

■ The US ban on Mexican tuna inappropriately discriminated (in violation of GATT Article III's "national treatment" requirement) against the imported product based on production practices that were not legitimate as a focus of US regulation.

■ The US standard for incidental dolphin kills, which depended on the number of dolphins killed by US fishermen in any given year, was retroactive and variable, and thus inappropriate. In fact, Mexican fishermen could not know their limits until the results of the American harvest were announced.

dolphin protection agreement—implying that the US action might have been justified if there were such an accord—the panel suggests in other parts of the decision that any extrajurisdictional environmental trade measure would violate the GATT. In doing so, the tuna-dolphin decision can be read as undermining the fabric of all international environmental efforts and making more difficult the already-challenging task of getting broad adherence to global environment programs.[20]

In addition to the NAFTA and the tuna-dolphin controversies, a number of other, less well-known matters have helped fan the flames of the trade and environment fire. The list of such issues includes the European Union's[21] market integration program, including the issuance of

---

20. In the Tuna Dolphin II Case—the European Union's challenge to the US tuna embargo law—the GATT panel focused not on the extraterritorial aspect of the US action but on a more sound basis for challenging the embargo, the unilateral nature of the US policy.

21. Upon the entry into force of the Maastricht Treaty on 1 January 1994, the European Community (EC) formally became the European Union (EU). In this study, reference to the EC indicates a consideration of pre-1994 matters.

- The US claim of justification under GATT Article XX(b) for actions necessary to protect human or animal life was inapplicable on the grounds that this exception does not encompass harms occurring outside the jurisdiction imposing the trade measure and because less-restrictive means were available to the United States to achieve its objective.

- The US claim of justification under GATT Article XX(g) for the conservation of exhaustible natural resources could not be unilaterally pursued outside the national context.

- The United States had a right to maintain its "dolphin safe" tuna labeling program (see chapter 5, box 5.6) because the program had no discriminatory effects.

The three-member panel's findings have not been adopted by the GATT Council, and so under pre–Uruguay Round GATT rules technically have no precedential value. Yet the analysis has provoked heated debate over the GATT's ability to resolve trade and environment conflicts in a balanced manner. The sweeping nature of the panel recommendations—broadly condemning unilateral trade actions with an extraterritorial reach—went well beyond the scope of the facts. The decision provoked full-page newspaper advertisements across the United States from a broad-based coalition of environmental groups deriding the GATT as a threat to American sovereignty and virulently anti-environmental.

Because Mexico declined to get the tuna-dolphin panel report "adopted" by the GATT Council, the European Union brought a further GATT challenge—referred to as the Tuna Dolphin II case—objecting to the "secondary embargo" imposed under the MMPA on all countries that trade in tuna with Mexico. The facts of this second case are essentially the same as those in the first case. The second tuna-dolphin panel's decision—again concluding that the US embargo is GATT-illegal—turned on the much more solid ground of the unilateral nature of the US trade action. Appendix C provides more information on this case.

directives harmonizing its 12 member states' environmental statutes and regulations; developing-country claims aired at the June 1992 Earth Summit that the international trading system forces them into unsustainable production practices that slow development and hurt the environment; North-South disputes over compensation, including preferential trade considerations, for participation in international environmental agreements (such as the 1992 Climate Change Convention) that may put additional burdens on development; and the emergence of an increasing number of trade disputes where environmental standards are challenged as hidden trade barriers, such as the US-EC disputes over beef hormones (Froman 1989) and fungicide residues in wine (*International Trade Reporter*, 1 May 1991, 652).

As the tuna-dolphin case demonstrates, GATT efforts to address mixed questions of trade and environmental policy have proved to be highly problematic. Environmentalists decry the GATT's lack of environmental expertise and argue that the rules and procedures of the GATT are biased toward trade values. Even trade experts cringe as the GATT slides beyond its recognized zone of authority and competence, thereby undermining the institution's perceived neutrality and credibility. But the GATT can hardly be blamed for trying to make sense of issues—on its own terms—when there is no established environmental regime with which to share responsibility for managing global trade and environment matters.

How to address this institutional gap and to balance competing interests is a central focus of this study. The goal, recognizing both the value of free trade as a boost to economic growth and the need to safeguard the environment, is to ensure that environmental sensitivities are built into the international trade regime and to guarantee that free trade requirements are respected to the fullest extent possible in environmental policymaking.

GATT IS COMING

What You Don't Know
Will Hurt You

2

Conflict or Convergence

In the wake of the tuna-dolphin decision, the international trade regime came under withering attacks from elements of the environmental community both in the United States and abroad. Papering Washington with posters of "GATTzilla" (see opposite) and running newspaper advertisements under the headline "Sabotage!" pro-environment free trade critics painted an unflattering and inaccurate portrait of the GATT as a secretive cabal of "faceless bureaucrats" in Geneva carrying out "sneak attacks" on democracy and American sovereignty. In a colorful if analytically contorted article haunted by visions of international conspiracies, Walter Russell Mead (1992, 37) offered the readers of *Harper's* magazine his view of the world according to GATT:

> . . . a kind of free-trade World Government . . . all Bottom Line: a global corporate utopia in which local citizens are toothless, workers' unions are tame or broken, environmentalists and consumer advocates outflanked . . . regulations of all kinds will be lax: factories will be dangerous and their waste will be toxic. . . .

Ross Perot turned the attention of the anti–free trade chorus from the GATT to the North American Free Trade Agreement. In *Save Your Job, Save Our Country: Why NAFTA Must Be Stopped Now!* (1993), he disparages the NAFTA as a "secret deal" likely to result not only in a "giant sucking sound" of jobs flowing to Mexico but also "back-door deregulation of US health and environmental standards." In trying to explain NAFTA's "Technical Barriers to Trade" section, Perot baldly asserts that "NAFTA will lower US standards," and without any explanation or support he goes on to suggest that the agreement will destroy "the American system of checks and balances." Perot concludes that "one of Mexico's principal economic attractions has been the government's lax enforcement of its environmental laws." To address this supposed unfair commercial advantage, Perot recommends that Mexican goods be barred from entering the United States unless they are produced under conditions that meet US environmental standards.

A Clash of Cultures

The uninformed nature of attacks of this sort and the level of misinformation they reflect has led some observers to conclude that the origins of the trade and environment conflict could be traced to a clash of cultures between free traders and environmentalists, reflecting differences in goals, assumptions, procedures, and traditions. No doubt progress toward mutually supportive trade and environmental policies has been slowed by the fact that the trade and environmental communities approach similar problems in different ways (Magraw 1994). Even the language of the two communities can be a source of confusion. For example, the word "protection" warms the hearts of environmentalists but sends chills down the spines of free traders.

Trade negotiators are generally outcome-oriented, utilitarian, and willing to compromise. Their goal is to lower trade barriers and increase economic welfare. They are comfortable with the diplomatic practice of working in secret and rarely seek public attention, particularly since they understand that trade liberalization produces diffuse benefits—lower prices, broader consumer choice, and future export opportunities—that may fail to rouse sufficient public support in the face of special interests.[1]

In contrast, environmentalists, although interested in results, tend to be process-oriented as well. They come from a tradition of openness and put great stock in public participation in decision making as a way of ensuring that business interests do not dominate decision making (see Shabecoff 1993 for a history of the environmental movement). These traits reflect, in part, the nature of ecological problems: understanding of them evolves as scientific understanding advances, they benefit from broad review and critique, and they demand continuous refinements in policy. Stereotypical environmentalists see the world in Manichaean terms, with clear "white hats" and "black hats," and are uncomfortable with compromise. They often perceive themselves to be pursuing moral imperatives that cannot easily be traded off in an economist's cost-benefit or welfare-maximizing calculus (Housman 1992). They reject the pursuit of economic growth as an end, fearing that it often fails to fully incorporate environmental degradation costs, through which economic

---

1. It is again important to recognize the range of views within each "camp" as well as between the two. For example, many true free traders, as opposed to neomercantilists, are comfortable with more "sunshine" in the trade negotiation process, recognizing, as environmentalists do, that special interests find it easier to contort the policy process to their advantage under the cover of darkness.

"success" translates into environmental "failures"—including polluted air, fouled waterways, lost species, and climate change.

This cultural divide may also reflect the fact that the environment is a latecomer to the policy party. Modern trade theory has been understood for the better part of two centuries; the GATT has been in existence for nearly 50 years. Environmental efforts have not yet jelled into a coherent theory, and there is no overarching international environmental regime. It is always hard to assimilate new participants or new ideas into a mature policy structure. The task of integrating environmental considerations into the trade realm (and vice versa) is made all the more difficult by the unformed nature of environmental protection as a policy discipline and the still-evolving theories of optimal modes of environmental regulation.

Some progress has been made in bridging the trade-environment gap through education of the trade community about environmental protection and the environmental community about trade liberalization.[2] Unfortunately, the root cause of the conflict is not differences in approaches or language. The rift runs much deeper and is tied to assumptions about the future and questions of philosophy, political theory, and priorities (Sagoff 1988).

A Clash of Paradigms

The trade and environment debate can also be seen as a clash of paradigms: the environmentalists' law-based world view versus the trade community's economic perspective. Environmental policy in the United States has deep legal roots. Beginning in the late 1960s, the United States moved into the modern environmental era with broad-based national environmental standards established under path-breaking statutes such as the Clean Water Act, the Clean Air Act, and the Comprehensive Environmental Response, Compensation, and Liability (Superfund) Act and with precedent-setting lawsuits brought by environmental groups.[3] Many US environmentalists are therefore strong believers in the power of laws and rules, and punishment for those who fail to meet established stan-

---

2. Beginning in 1991, the Organization for Economic Cooperation and Development (OECD) in Paris convened a joint experts group on trade and the environment designed to build an analytic foundation for GATT reform (OECD 1994c). In both the United States and Europe, a great number of academic, think tank, and foundation study groups are discussing trade and environmental policy linkages. The GATT itself has reinvigorated a long-dormant working party on the environment. But developing countries insisted upon a very narrow initial agenda for the GATT working party for fear that concerns about the environment and unsustainable resource depletion would be used to limit their development options. Thus, while some work has been done to link trade and environmental policymaking, serious confusion and misunderstandings remain.

3. Percival et al. (1992) provide a thorough review of the evolution of US environmental law, including case histories of the path-breaking lawsuits.

dards. They have traditionally been uncomfortable with incentive-based regulation for fear that this approach puts a price tag on pollution and lets big business buy its way out of cleanup obligations.

Thus much of the US environmental community entered the trade and environment debate with a bias toward restructuring the rules and procedures of the GATT to advance environmental priorities. Since environmentalists often bring to their work a conviction (the future of life on Earth is at stake!) that the environment represents a higher-order concern than trade (which is just a question of money), many environmental groups believe the use of trade penalties to enforce environmental standards, whether embodied in multilateral agreements or unilaterally imposed, is justified without regard to the disruption to trade or any cost-benefit analysis.

The trade world's economic paradigm puts great stock in the prosperity that freer trade stimulates and the opportunity this creates to devote additional resources to environmental protection. In this regard, they worry that excessive deference to environmental regulations or standards will result, in some cases, in barriers to trade not justified by real environmental results. They also believe that indiscriminate use of trade as leverage will result not in broad conformity to high environmental standards but in international chaos and lost economic opportunities for those whose environmental policies are deemed inadequate and who therefore are subject to environmental trade measures (see box 5.5 for further discussion of these measures). Economists fundamentally see the trade and environment issue as a matter of weighing the relative costs and benefits of trade and environmental policies to maximize social welfare.

Economists and free traders also believe that trade policy goals and environmental policy needs can be made largely compatible by ensuring that environmental resources are properly priced. Many environmentalists recognize the value of cost internalization and increasingly understand the potential of the polluter pays principle[4] for making trade and environmental policies mutually reinforcing. In fact, as environmental regulations become more incentive-based, the scope for clashes with free trade goals is sharply reduced. Although some environmentalists have been slow to recognize the power of the market as a tool for ecological and public health protection, there is a growing emphasis on market mechanisms in the "next generation" of environmental programs now being developed and implemented.

Despite the incipient prospect of collaboration based on adherence to the polluter pays principle, each paradigm finds fundamental faults with

---

4. While the polluter pays principle is not the only way to internalize costs, it is a critical tool for moving toward full-cost pricing in the environmental realm. Unless otherwise specifically differentiated, references in this study to the polluter pays principle imply cost internalization generally.

the other. Free traders believe that environmentalists systematically undervalue the real-world economic consequences of their inflexible command-and-control policies and the growth-stunting impact of environmental trade measures. They also see environmentalists as preoccupied with the use of coercion, rather than positive incentives, and as inattentive to whether this "negative reinforcement" approach to difficult issues actually delivers environmental quality improvements.

Free traders, moreover, see the application of environmental trade measures as a threat to the trading system and to international harmony more generally. They argue, consistent with traditional public policy theory, that *trade* measures are never the best *environmental* policy tool (e.g., Anderson and Blackhurst 1992b; Eglin 1993c).[5] Even if the threatened countries do agree to change their environmental policies in the face of punitive trade measures, they do so without enthusiasm. Thus, there is little commitment to the required policy. Poor performance, backsliding, or cheating are the likely results.

The free traders have a point. As chapter 1 noted, there is a broad gulf between environmental regulation and environmental protection. The concern about the ineffectiveness of coercive trade measures as an international environmental policy tool mirrors the raging debate in the national context over the effectiveness of various threat-based environmental policy approaches and the potentially greater efficacy of market-based mechanisms.

Environmentalists believe the economic paradigm is equally flawed. They see free traders living in a world of economic theory that distracts them from environmental realities. Thus they argue that the trade community is too focused on a welfare-maximizing calculus that encompasses only impacts that can be easily reduced to a monetary value. Specifically, environmentalists believe the trade and environment clash is inherently over "values" and that such disputes are not amenable to solutions based on economic algorithms.

As the last chapter made clear, the environmentalists also have a point. Yellowstone National Park could be converted into the Disneyland of the Rockies with high-tech rides weaving in and out of the geysers, dozens of new restaurants, and hotel and condominium complexes sprawling across the land. This would, no doubt, raise property values and increase the return to the US government on Yellowstone as an economic asset. But the fallacy of this pure economic value analysis is evident. Nevertheless, the problem of properly valuing environmental resources and harms and the broader issue of reconciling the trade community's economic approach to the world with the environmentalists' political-legal *weltanschauung* remains an underlying source of tension in the trade and environment debate.

---

5. For a ranking of trade policy tools, see Roessler (1992).

A Clash of Judgments

The nature of environmental problems exacerbates the valuation problem and thus the tension between environmentalism and free traders. In particular, ecological problems are characterized by threshold effects; time lags between emissions and detection; biological, chemical, and physical interactions that are not well understood; and sometimes substantial scientific uncertainties over the source, scope, and magnitude of public health or habitat damage. These characteristics make the costs of environmental harm and the benefits of emissions reductions or cleanup hard to calculate. These uncertainties can lead economists (and their trade community colleagues) to dismiss environmental values and to ignore environmental variables in their analyses. Although there exists a rich economic literature (e.g., Diamond and Rothschild 1978) on dealing with uncertainty, economists, in their desire for analytic rigor, may say, "If you can't put a number on it, leave it out of the equation." Unfortunately, this bias toward quantifiable data results in systematic underattention to frequently hard-to-quantify environmental concerns in trade policymaking.

In dealing with environmental harms that will arise in the future, there is an additional problem of determining how much weight to put on these issues. Specifically, there is a serious debate over the "discount rate" that should be applied to future costs (Cline 1993; Birdsall and Steer 1993). Building on the time value of money, traditional economic theory "discounts" future burdens. For example, an economist (using a 10 percent discount rate) would prefer to pay $1 million in 200 years than one cent today, arguing that if one invests the penny it will yield more than $1 million in 200 years. Environmentalists—building on a strong base of political reality—fear that society is not setting aside resources to pay for future cleanups. In other words, we are leaving unfunded environmental liabilities to our progeny. On this basis, environmentalists reject the discount rate analysis. From an economic perspective, Cline (1992, 240–43) argues that, in analyzing long-term environmental problems, one should use a lower-than-traditional discount rate. He comes to this conclusion not only because of concerns about intergenerational equity but also the fact that being richer may not adequately compensate future citizens for being endowed with a degraded environment because the "price line," or trade-off, between environmental amenities and all other goods may shift over time. Nordhaus (1992) rejects this conclusion, seeing no basis for treating future environmental burdens differently from any other future economic cost.

In addition to these economic debates, the conflict between environmentalists and free traders is, in part, a dispute over the relative scientific seriousness of the environmental issues the world faces. In analyzing how the world responds to global environmental issues, Porter and Brown (1991, 69) identify four elements of policymaking: issue definition, fact finding, bargaining, and regime strengthening. As Susskind (1994, 62) notes, scientific investigations have an integral role in each of these areas. The combination of scientific and economic uncertainty make policy consensus hard to achieve in the environmental realm. If one accepts that the global problems outlined in chapter 1—ozone layer depletion, climate change, deforestation, loss of biological diversity—are large, pressing, and potentially irreversible, then minor intrusions on the trade system are a fair price to pay to facilitate an effective worldwide response. For example, if one were to believe the upper-bound estimates of the economic impacts alone of climate change—20 percent of world GDP (Cline 1992)—then even a substantial decline in the gains from trade over some period would be worth accepting if it were to help head off climate change.

If, however, one assesses the probability of real climate change to be zero or calculates the damage from such change to be low, then little or no interference with trade can be justified on these particular environmental grounds. More broadly, the enormous spectrum of uncertainty that surrounds almost all global environmental issues makes policy reconciliation hard to achieve. Ecoskeptics will always be able to discount the seriousness of environmental threats. Ecofanatics will similarly be able to find "evidence" that the sky is falling so that all commercial interests should be subjugated to environmental needs.

This study rejects both extremes and proceeds from a middle ground. It accepts that some global environmental issues pose relatively well-established threats such as CFC depletion of the ozone layer. For other matters, the probability, magnitude, and speed of the risk of harm are not as certain, as with climate change. But as long as some of the global risks are real (and most credible scientists accept that they are) and the potential costs are nontrivial (again, most credible analyses show possibly serious ecological, economic, and social burdens) a sensible "precautionary"[6] approach to protection of the environment is appropriate.

This study also works from an understanding that many pollutants are the by-products of valuable activities and therefore that there is an optimal amount of pollution control that is unlikely, in most cases, to reach a zero emissions level. At the extremes, there will be pollutants for which zero discharge should be the goal (e.g., bioaccumulative toxics). Similarly, there are sources of pollution (e.g., diaperless babies swimming in the ocean) that cause such low-volume and low-level harm that we are far from reaching the assimilative capacity of our ecosystems (figure 1.1), making it justifiable to treat the problem as though it had no cost and to have no system of pollution control.

---

6. The "precautionary principle" suggests that in the face of scientific uncertainty and potentially great environmental harms, policymakers should skew their actions so that errors of too much protection are more likely than errors of too little (O'Riordan and Cameron 1994, Bodansky 1991; Cameron and Abouchar 1991; Schneider 1976).

The Environmental Challenge

While the vituperative nature of some of the assaults on the international trade regime has been excessive, the charge that trade and trade liberalization can be environmentally counterproductive is accepted even by the most ardent free traders (Anderson 1992c). Stripped of its ad hominem aspects, the environmentalists' challenge to free trade boils down to four central propositions:

- Without environmental safeguards, trade may cause environmental harm by promoting economic growth that results in the unsustainable consumption of natural resources and waste production.

- Trade rules and trade liberalization often entail market access agreements that can be used to override environmental regulations unless appropriate environmental protections are built into the structure of the trade system.

- Trade restrictions should be available as leverage to promote worldwide environmental protection, particularly to address global or transboundary environmental problems and to reinforce international environmental agreements.

- Even if the pollution they cause does not spill over into other nations, countries with lax environmental standards have a competitive advantage in the global marketplace and put pressure on countries with high environmental standards to reduce the rigor of their environmental requirements.

The first proposition is the essence of the debate—in some senses encompassing the other three propositions. Environmentalists argue that if trade causes environmental degradation, then either it must be stopped or environmental safeguards must be built into the rules that guide trade relationships. The fear that the transportation of goods from one country to another will result in environmental harm (e.g., oil spills or air pollution from the engines powering trucks, planes, and ships) is one aspect of this issue.

But the core environmental concern arises from what are often called scale effects. Specifically, to the extent that economic activities cause pollution, promote consumption of nonrenewable resources such as oil, and use renewable resources such as water above the rate of natural replenishment, then promoting more of such activities is harmful. The damage can arise both from increased production (causing air or water pollution) or from consumption (using up resources or generating waste). Lallas (1993) identifies, in addition, "indirect" effects of trade on the environment such as the redirection of investment flows and changed patterns of economic growth. For example, the NAFTA created the prospect of new manufacturing facilities in Mexico with potential increased environmental stress to the Mexico-US border region.

Of course, the underlying issue here is really not trade but economic activity per se. The expansion of this activity is largely driven by the fact that the Earth's population has grown by more than 40 percent over the last 25 years, adding 1.6 billion consumers of resources and generators of garbage to the planet. In fact, in an overarching sense, trade helps society to be more efficient in its modes of production and use of resources—allowing more output to be produced with fewer inputs, including fewer natural resources. Nevertheless, in the more immediate and tangible context, trade liberalization creates new market opportunities for exporters and therefore leads to new economic activity, which, in the absence of properly priced environmental amenities and harms, can result in more pollution. Trade also generates wealth, which allows consumers to acquire more goods and gives environmentalists who are concerned about exhausting limited resources another reason for worry.

The second proposition focuses on trade liberalization and trade rules designed to promote market access. The issue turns on how to ensure that the trade regime reinforces legitimate environmental regulations but prevents hidden trade barriers masquerading as environmental rules and regulations that disproportionately and unfairly burden imports. This entails a trade-off between the commercial benefits of *uniformity* in standards—the ability to achieve scale economies in production, testing, labeling, and distribution of goods—and the environmental and economic benefits of regulatory *diversity*—namely, the freedom to tailor environmental standards to local needs and preferences.

The commercial value of uniform environmental standards is straightforward. With easier access to overseas markets, producers can achieve scale economies and reduce costs. Moreover, if importers can enter a market relatively easily, consumers get the benefits of competition: lower prices, a broader selection of goods, and better service.

Divergent environmental standards may, however, be justified where conditions vary. Differences in climate, weather, population density, existing levels of pollution, risk preferences, levels of development, and environmental priorities all could result in nations making different political choices about the stringency of environmental regulations. For example, countries with slow-moving rivers that do not break down organic pollutants quickly may need tighter water pollution requirements than nations with fast water flows. Similarly, windy communities may not need as strict air pollution controls as places with little or no breeze, where emissions build up. In fact, such differences underlie the theory of comparative advantage on which the gains from trade depend.[7]

---

7. The principle underlying the theory of comparative advantage is that different nations will be relatively better at producing different goods and services—and that by trading

But permitting regulatory diversity exposes the world to two opposite risks. From the trade perspective, there exists a danger that countries will set environmental regulations that are "too high," blocking trade.[8] From the environmental viewpoint, the fear is that nations will set their standards "too low," externalizing harms onto others. Separating legitimate high standards from illegitimate trade barriers is the essential challenge underlying the second environmental trade agenda item. Determining when and how the low standards in other countries may be appropriately challenged using environmental trade measures is the essence of the third environmentalist proposition.[9]

In some sense, environmental standards cannot really be too high. What constitutes an appropriate level of protection will vary with economic and environmental conditions and is thus a political judgment that should be left largely to national governments (so long, as is explained below, as the choice made does not have spillover effects on others). When environmental rules and regulations are attacked for being set too high in the trade context, what is really at issue is the environmental legitimacy of the measure or the appropriateness of the means by which the environmental goal is pursued.[10]

---

among countries, consumers will benefit by access to a wider variety of goods at lower prices. For example, if Connecticut had to produce its own oranges, the crop would be very limited and expensive, but trade with Florida allows for a more plentiful and cheaper supply of oranges. Similarly, Florida benefits by not trying to specialize in goods made in Connecticut (e.g., helicopters). The prevailing refinement of this basic concept can be found in the Heckscher-Ohlin model of trade, named for the two Swedish economists who developed it (see Krugman and Obstfeld 1991, 68; Caves, Frankel, and Jones 1990, 126).

8. Repetto (1994) argues that the fear of "green protectionism" is overblown. He sees little burden on trade from environmental regulations, even discriminatory ones.

9. Note that the standards that are likely to be too high are product standards, with which the GATT is well prepared to deal. The standards that might be considered too low will probably be process standards, for which the GATT has no structure, thus creating a systemic bias within the trading system to address the "trade" problem—product standards blocking trade—but not the "environmental" problem—process standards so lax that they result in environmental harms being externalized.

10. Environmentalists fear that some "trade" attacks on environmental standards are really an attempt to lower standards or to deregulate, with anti-environmental interests trying to achieve through international trade procedures what they could not accomplish directly through the national political processes related to environmental policymaking. Senator Max Baucus has, for example, challenged the Clinton administration's decision to revise its "reformulated gasoline" regulations in the face of a GATT challenge from Venezuela. Charnovitz (1994e) discusses this and other cases where trade rules have been used to lower environmental standards or to "chill" environmental regulation. Use of the trading system to refine environmental policies to make them more consistent with free trade goals is legitimate. Trade challenges brought primarily for the purpose of changing environmental standards are, however, improper—and the rules of international trade should be structured to filter out actions of this sort.

Specifically, environmental standards can be crafted chiefly to benefit domestic producers, not to protect the environment. For example, France's February 1994 "health" inspections of imported fish (which took so long to arrange that the fish all rotted) had nothing to do with public health or the environment and much to do with appeasing French fishermen angry about low-cost imports (*Inside US Trade*, 18 February 1994, 17).

Alternatively, nations with legitimate environmental goals may choose means of implementing them that disproportionately and unfairly affect foreign producers. For instance, the US Corporate Average Fuel Economy (CAFE) standards setting fleetwide average mileage requirements for automakers selling cars in the United States have a valid underlying motive: to improve the fuel efficiency of US automobiles. Unequivocally, however, the means chosen to carry out this environmental goal, the CAFE standards, are disproportionately burdensome to foreign high-end niche automakers that sell only expensive, heavy, and not very fuel-efficient cars.[11] Notably, Ford, Chrysler, and General Motors, all of which make small as well as large cars, can meet the fleetwide average requirements, but Volvo, BMW, and Mercedes cannot. The US Congress could have selected other less trade-distorting mechanisms for improving fuel efficiency—for instance, a higher gasoline tax or a "sipper-guzzler" fee system on all cars, subsidizing the purchase of cars that get good mileage and penalizing owners whose cars do not. But Congress intentionally selected the CAFE mechanism to protect the US auto industry jobs and the automobile market share of the Big Three US automakers.[12]

Thus, there is a danger that environmental regulatory processes will be "captured" by protectionist interests, who will use environmental standards as a guise for erecting barriers to imports. The political difficulty of attacking environmental regulations makes them especially attractive as a tool for preserving a special position in the marketplace and enables the protectionists, in the absence of foreign competition, to extract extra profits or wages—what economists call monopoly "rents." But environmentalists fear that opening up the ends and means of environmental protection to review in a trade context does not provide a fair

---

11. The European Union has a pending GATT case against the United States on this matter. Appendix C provides more details on this action.

12. As the House Ways and Means Committee 1975 report on the CAFE legislation explains: "The Committee considered heavier taxes on fuel-inefficient automobiles, as well as the possibility of providing tax credits for fuel-efficient cars. It was decided not to impose a heavier tax because of the danger of a major loss of jobs in the automobile and related industries. Currently, many fuel-efficient cars are imported, and your Committee did not want the auto efficiency tax to provide a stimulus to increased imports of autos in view of the depressed state of the US auto industry" (H.R. Rept. no. 94–221, 94th Cong., 1st Sess., p. 14).

basis for decisions. Specifically, they worry that legitimate environmental programs will be found to be GATT-inconsistent because trade-oriented GATT dispute panel members will not give appropriate deference to environmental goals and programs.

The risk on the opposite side is that low environmental standards will result in producers not internalizing environmental costs. In fact, absent regulation, producers have an incentive not to handle their own wastes but rather to send them up a smokestack or out an effluent pipe, "externalizing" costs they would otherwise have to bear. In some cases, these pollution spillovers affect only local citizens. In other instances, however, the spillovers can affect neighboring countries or the shared resources of the global commons, such as the atmosphere. The critical issue, in this regard, is the legitimacy of one country using trade measures to force its own or internationally agreed environmental standards on another sovereign nation. This study argues that determinations concerning the use of environmental trade measures should turn on the nature and locus of the pollution spillovers or environmental injuries at issue.

If the pollution effects are localized and affect only the environment of the foreign producer, low standards may well be a legitimate political decision reflecting economic and environmental trade-offs appropriate to that country.[13] But where the low standards create global or transboundary environmental problems, claims to sovereignty or the right to exercise one's comparative advantage do not hold up. Unfortunately, GATT's current structure of trade rules does not differentiate between cases of local and global harm. Indeed, GATT's mandate covers neither the problems of low environmental standards nor the potentially unfair cost advantage that can be obtained by externalizing environmental harms.

GATT's Existing Rules

The heart of the existing trade regime is the nondiscrimination requirements of GATT Articles I and III, which obligate parties to treat imports from any GATT party no less favorably than other imports (the "most-favored nation" requirement) and no less favorably, after border duties are paid, than domestically produced "like products" (the "national treatment" requirement).[14] Appendix A offers more details on these GATT obligations. Although the environment is not mentioned explic-

---

13. There is a further layer of complexity to the "low standards" problem, involving the recognition that scientific advances are constantly identifying new physical pollution spillovers and that psychological or political spillovers may also justify attention. These issues are discussed in chapter 7.

14. Thus the GATT permits discrimination insofar as foreign products may be subject to duties up to agreed-upon levels. GATT Article III(8)(b) also exempts subsidies from the national treatment requirement.

Box 2.1 GATT Article XX: general exceptions

Subject to the requirement that such measures are not applied in a manner which would constitute a means of arbitrary or unjustifiable discrimination between countries where the same conditions prevail, or a disguised restriction on international trade, nothing in this Agreement shall be construed to prevent the adoption or enforcement by any contracting party of measures:

(a) necessary to protect public morals;
(b) necessary to protect human, animal or plant life or health;
(c) relating to the importation or exportation of gold or silver;
(d) necessary to secure compliance with laws or regulations which are not inconsistent with the provisions of this Agreement, including those relating to customs enforcement, the enforcement of monopolies operated under paragraph 4 or Article II and Article XVII, the protection of patents, trade marks and copyrights, and the prevention of deceptive practices;
(e) relating to the products of prison labour;
(f) imposed for the protection of national treasures of artistic, historic or archaeological value;
(g) relating to the conservation of exhaustible natural resources if such measures are made effective in conjunction with restrictions on domestic production or consumption;
(h) undertaken in pursuance of obligations under any intergovernmental commodity agreement which conforms to criteria submitted to the contracting parties and not disapproved by them or which is itself so submitted and not so disapproved;
(i) involving restrictions on exports of domestic materials necessary to ensure essential quantities of such materials to a domestic processing industry during periods when the domestic price of such materials is held below the world price as part of a governmental stabilization plan; *Provided* that such restrictions shall not operate to increase the exports of or the protection afforded to such domestic industry, and shall not depart from the provisions of this Agreement relating to nondiscrimination;
(j) essential to the acquisition or distribution of products in general or local short supply; *Provided* that any such measures shall be consistent with the principle that all contracting parties are entitled to an equitable share of the international supply of such products, and that any such measures, which are inconsistent with the other provisions of this Agreement, shall be discontinued as soon as the conditions giving rise to them have ceased to exist. The contracting parties shall review the need for this subparagraph not later than 30 June 1960.

itly, GATT Article XX provides exceptions to these general rules, including provision for some environmental regulations (box 2.1 and box 2.2).

Environmentalists fear that the disciplines accepted by each country to implement the nondiscrimination principles of Articles I and III will result in a loss of regulatory freedom, diminishing environmental protection. Notably, Article XX has been narrowly interpreted to limit the scope of trade restrictions undertaken for environmental purposes (Housman and Zaelke 1992a; Lallas, Esty, and Van Hoogstraten 1992; Shrybman 1989). In particular, environmental policies with trade im-

---

Box 2.2 Making sense of GATT Article XX

GATT Article XX provides "general exceptions" to GATT obligations.[1] It excuses otherwise GATT-illegal actions designed to protect public morals, preserve national heritage, and limit commerce in goods made with prison labor. Although it does not mention the word environment, Article XX—particularly sections XX(b) and XX(g)—also offers a basis for deviating from GATT principles in support of environmental policies.

Specifically, Article XX holds that the GATT should not prevent contracting parties from taking actions:

- necessary for the protection of human, animal, or plant life or health; or

- relating to the conservation of exhaustible natural resources—provided trade measures are joined by restrictions on domestic production or consumption.

GATT provides, therefore, considerable scope to countries to pursue their own environmental programs—even if those programs have trade effects. Parties invoking Article XX face a number of hurdles, however, before their claim of exception to GATT's other obligations will be accepted:

- "Chapeau" requirements. Article XX does not excuse arbitrary or unjustifiable discrimination. Nor may Article XX be used to justify disguised restrictions on international trade.

- Limited scope. Article XX expressly covers only health issues relating to the conservation of exhaustible natural resources. It does not explicitly mention the environment, and thus may not cover policies designed to protect the atmosphere, oceans, forests, or other resources outside the "exhaustible natural resources" category. Indeed, then–Senate Finance Committee Chairman Lloyd Bentsen once purportedly observed that Article XX was designed to deal only with rabid dogs and sick plants.

- "Necessary" test. To be justified under Article XX(b), environmental measures must be "necessary." Recent GATT cases have defined this term to mean

---

pacts must be shown to be "necessary to protect human, animal, or plant life or health" under Article XX(b) or "relating to the conservation of exhaustible natural resources" under Article XX(g).

The "necessary" provision has been restrictively defined to justify environmental policies only if no "less GATT-inconsistent" policy tool was available to achieve the established goal.[15] This sets an almost impossibly high hurdle for environmental policies because a policy approach that intrudes less on trade is almost always conceivable and therefore in some sense "available." The Uruguay Round rules on tech-

---

15. A "least GATT-inconsistent" or "least trade-restrictive" test could work as an efficiency precept, forcing attention to the means chosen to pursue environmental goals, without threatening the goals chosen. Unfortunately, the GATT jurisprudence has developed without regard to this ends-means distinction and without regard to the political difficulty of adopting optimal environmental policies that serve both trade and environmental purposes, effectively eviscerating Article XX (Charnovitz 1991).

"least GATT-inconsistent" (see the *Thai Cigarettes* Case in appendix C). This creates a high hurdle for invoking Article XX because some less GATT-inconsistent policy can almost always be conceived.

- "Relating to conservation" test. Article XX(g)'s stipulation that an environmental policy must only "relate to" a conservation goal offers a more balanced requirement. GATT panels have interpreted this language to mean that a questioned environmental policy should be "primarily aimed" at addressing a conservation goal (and invoked in conjunction with comparable restraints on domestic production) in order to be justified. This permits "mixed motives"— which are almost always the case in political processes—so long as the main purpose of a measure was environmental (see the *Salmon and Herring* case, appendix C).

- Extrajurisdictional or extraterritorial measures. The 1991 tuna-dolphin decision concluded that Article XX may not be invoked in defense of extrajurisdictional actions—that is, policies addressing environmental harms outside the country using trade measures. This interpretation of the GATT seems inappropriately narrow (Charnovitz 1993c) given the absence of an effective supernational body to address global and transboundary environmental harms (see the *Tuna-Dolphin* case in appendix C, and chapter 5, footnote 5 explaining the distinction between extrajurisdictional and extraterritorial).

- Limitation on unilateral actions. The tuna-dolphin panel also suggested that unilateral environmental actions with trade impacts generally may not be excused under Article XX. Again, this narrow reading of Article XX seems unnecessarily rigid and renders the GATT insufficiently sensitive to legitimate efforts to address global environmental needs (*Tuna-Dolphin* case, appendix C).

---

1. For a more complete discussion of Article XX, see Lallas, Esty, and van Hoogstraten (1992, 275–85), on which this summary is based.

---

nical barriers to trade and its sanitary and phytosanitary rules refine this hurdle and other related disciplines on standard setting—lowering the environmental burden in some senses, but raising it in others (box 2.3).

The requirement "relating to conservation of exhaustible natural resources" has been interpreted somewhat more leniently, permitting policies that have as their predominant purpose a conservation goal. But it too has serious limitations. The scope of Article XX fails to cover important natural resources such as the atmosphere, the oceans, the ozone layer, and other elements of the global commons. Indeed, the tuna-dolphin decision implies that Article XX cannot be used to justify environmental trade measures aimed at harms outside the jurisdiction of the nation imposing the measures.

The most fundamental problem with Article XX is that it makes the legitimacy of environmental regulations turn on what is produced, not how it is produced. Specifically, GATT's existing rules focus on the

Box 2.3 Uruguay Round

The Uruguay Round agreement (GATT 1993b) expands, refines, and to some extent narrows the GATT Article XX general exceptions. Specifically, the revised rules apply a "least trade-restrictive" test for standards (known in GATTspeak as "technical barriers to trade," or TBT). This new discipline requires that environmental regulations "not be more trade-restrictive than necessary to fulfill a legitimate objective, taking account of the risks non-fulfillment would create" (TBT Article 2.2). The new GATT rules also mandate that national regulations be revised if circumstances or environmental goals change and the "changed circumstances or objectives can be addressed in a less trade-restrictive manner" (TBT Article 2.3). In addition, the TBT agreement requires that national regulations be based on "relevant international standards" except where these would be "ineffective or inappropriate means for the fulfillment of the legitimate objectives pursued" (TBT Article 2.4). Finally, the new rules make clear that nations are free to select their own levels of risk without fear of a GATT challenge.

The Uruguay Round results also refine the rules relating to food, plant, and animal health standards (known as sanitary and phytosanitary or SPS measures). The new provisions grant each nation the right to determine its own "level of protection" so long as the resulting SPS standards are not "arbitrary or unjustifiable distinctions" (SPS paragraph 20). Moreover, SPS standards must be:

- "necessary"
- "based on scientific principles"
- "not maintained without sufficient scientific evidence"
- based on a risk assessment "appropriate to the circumstances"
- avoided if "there is another measure reasonably available, taking into account technical and economic feasibility, that achieves the appropriate level of protection and is significantly less restrictive to trade"

"Necessary" is a term of art in the GATT, traditionally meaning "least GATT-inconsistent." The requirement that standards be based on scientific principles is a compromise between those who wanted a "sound science" requirement that would allow trade authorities to override any environmental regulation that did not reflect the preponderance of scientific thinking and those who argued that environmental science is always in flux and that nations should, within the bounds of reason, be able to rely upon their own analyses and judgments. The risk assessment language is meant to provide each nation with a right to determine as a political matter the level of risk to which its citizens will be exposed. The phrasing, however, limits this regulatory freedom so that countries cannot structure their risk analyses in ways that create systematic and unsupportable biases against foreign products.

The final requirement reflects an important refinement on the traditionally "necessary" test. The new GATT language requires parties to consider less trade-restrictive means of achieving their environmental goals in the sanitary and phytosanitary context but leaves the choice of goals up to the nation setting the standards. In addition, the word "significantly" narrows the obligation to search for less trade-restrictive means to those cases where an alternative policy will be clearly superior. The new language also limits the hurdle over which environmental policies must go by clarifying that parties need only consider alternatives that are "reasonably available." This phrase is qualified to indicate that the availability issue is meant to focus on economic and technical variables. Thus, it remains unclear whether political difficulties in pursuing an alternative environmental policy are an acceptable excuse for GATT-inconsistent behavior.

concept of "like products," barring environmental discrimination against imports that are physically similar to domestic products no matter how damaging the production process used to make or obtain the good. Thus GATT permits regulation of the physical or chemical makeup of products—rendering, for example, auto emissions standards, pesticide safety requirements, and toxic labeling rules GATT-legal—but forbids environmental standards aimed at how goods are produced, constructed, gathered, grown, or caught.

This differentiation between products and production processes cannot be sustained in an ecologically interdependent world. For example, to say that a nation must accept an imported semiconductor because it physically resembles a domestically produced semiconductor is absurd if the product was made in violation of the Montreal Protocol, restricting the use of chemicals harmful to the ozone layer.

It is this shortcoming of the current trade regime that lies at the center of the third and fourth environmental propositions. The ability to use trade as leverage to address global and transboundary issues seems fundamental to environmentalists. In fact, most free traders acknowledge the need to protect the shared resources of the global commons. Although some may wonder why trade restrictions must be invoked for environmental purposes, many accept the fact that there are few civilized ways to exert power internationally and thus that trade should be available as a tool for promoting participation in and the enforcement of international environmental agreements aimed at addressing global or transboundary pollution spillovers.

Indeed, many free traders place great weight on international cooperation and the prevention of harmful behavior. They recognize that unfair trade practices or spillover pollution harms that break down the mutual respect and forbearance the GATT is designed to promote may undermine the cooperative international system, trigger retaliation, and risk a downward spiral of tit-for-tat responses. Indeed, the central role international cooperation and mutual forbearance play in achieving collective goals creates a second fundamental bridge between free traders and environmentalists (the first being support for the polluter pays principle).

The use of trade restrictions to address competitiveness concerns presents the most controversial element of the environmental trade agenda. As discussed in the last chapter, where overseas producers gain a competitive advantage by adhering to lower (and presumably cheaper) ecological or public health standards, environmentalists fear degradation of the environment in the low-standard country. They also worry that producers will use the presence of environmental compliance cost disadvantages vis-à-vis overseas competitors to lobby for more relaxed environmental standards or at least to hold off further tightening of requirements.[16]

16. Some observers (Smith 1992) believe that environmental regulations in "high" stan-

Most free traders reject the competitiveness argument and the use of trade measures to adjust for environmental compliance cost differentials. They argue that countries have varying conditions that justify sovereign political authorities coming to different conclusions about environmental standards.

But as discussed earlier, when low standards result in pollution that harms neighboring countries or the global commons, the claim to comparative advantage and national sovereignty does not hold up. The key issue thus becomes whether the variation in environmental standards derives from a legitimate difference in national priorities or conditions—or reflects an inappropriate attempt to externalize environmental costs. Efforts to harmonize standards or to promote more modest programs of policy convergence will be justified to address global or transboundary issues. But this, in turn, raises the question of just how widespread global environmental problems are. Those who do not believe that pollution spillovers are common will see little reason to worry about developing baseline environmental standards to address competitiveness concerns.

Those who believe that global and transboundary environmental problems are extensive will be much more likely to accept the logic of the environmentalists' competitiveness argument. Moreover, as chapter 7 discusses, harmonization efforts may be useful in discouraging a competitiveness-driven "race to the bottom" in environmental policymaking and in encouraging cooperation in adopting cost internalization and other optimal pollution control policies.

The GATT-Specific Environmentalist Critique

The generic environmentalist propositions about trade and trade liberalization translate into two specific criticisms of the GATT and the existing multilateral trade regime:

- GATT procedures reflect a systematic bias toward trade concerns and fail to provide an appropriate (open, democratic, technically competent, and fair) forum for setting the rules of international economic

---

dard countries such as the United States are systematically too burdensome and thus should be held in check by competitiveness concerns. Richard Stewart (1993b) and Hahn (1993) have argued in a less doctrinaire fashion that competitiveness is a useful discipline on environmental regulation—forcing attention to industry complaints and to the cost-effectiveness of regulatory programs. But whether competitiveness pressures force government officials to produce less cumbersome, time-consuming, red-tape-entangled rules and procedures that truly internalize environmental costs is unclear. The political result may simply be to roll back existing environmental requirements or hold off on new (potentially more effective and streamlined) programs. More troubling from a trade perspective, environmental competitiveness concerns may provide a justification for actions that are fundamentally trade protectionism in green garb.

interaction or for adjudicating disputes that affect environmental policies;

- GATT's substantive rules, which predate the emergence of the environment as a critical issue, are too narrowly focused on the commercial benefits of trade facilitation and must be updated to reflect environmental considerations.

The GATT-specific critique is hard to deny. Resolving trade disputes through closed-door reviews by panels of GATT experts fails to produce results with perceived legitimacy, particularly if the dispute overlaps into environmental questions that fall outside the competence of the trade gurus who sit on panels. In addition, the impression that "insiders" manipulate GATT negotiations and decisions and that business interests wield undue influence—effectively advanced by some environmental groups and ineffectively rebutted by GATT officials, who failed until recently to take the charges seriously—has corroded the GATT's public image and political support, at least in the United States.

The substantive rules of the international trade regime are also unequivocally in need of being updated to respond to the environmental critique (Jackson 1992a; London 1993b; Hittle 1992; European Parliament 1994). The GATT, for example, currently has no provision that permits a party to use trade actions to act against another nation's low environmental standards and resulting pollution spillovers or degradation of the global commons. Nor does it provide a safe haven for parties imposing trade restrictions required by international environmental agreements such as the trade controls on CFCs mandated by the Montreal Protocol. In addition, as discussed earlier in this chapter, the GATT's rules for analyzing cases where one country's environmental regulations have been challenged by another as a barrier to trade are imbalanced and insufficiently attentive to environmental considerations.

But the GATT is not as misguided as some environmentalists would have the public believe. In fact, many environmentalists have failed to appreciate that the GATT's singular mission, insular style, and seeming rigidity are neither evidence of ossification of the trade regime nor historical accidents. As the next chapter explains, the GATT's narrow focus and insulation from political pressures were designed into the institution to help it sustain its long-term perspective and trade-liberalizing mission in the face of challenges from special-interest politics and protectionist demands. In some ways, the trade regime's environmental problems reflect the fact that the GATT has been too successful. Specifically, in its enthusiasm for freer trade and a desire not to be distracted by competing policy considerations, the GATT has ignored changes in society's priorities that should have been observed and absorbed. Notably, the GATT way of thinking failed to recognize the public's growing appetite for environmental protection and to adapt its rules or procedures accordingly.[17]

Prospects for Convergence

On some issues, free trade interests and concern for environmental protection line up quite closely. For example, agricultural subsidies both distort trade flows and hurt the environment. Specifically, the tens of billions of dollars paid to European (and American) farmers in price supports create incentives to farm on marginally productive land (often using chemical-intensive production methods to boost yields) and on environmentally sensitive land (e.g., alongside rivers and streams). These practices result in severe environmental harm in the countries offering subsidies (for example, pesticide and fertilizer "loadings" have rendered all of the groundwater in the Netherlands polluted) and pose a significant trade barrier to nations that might otherwise have found new markets for their agricultural products. The burden is especially severe for developing countries for which agricultural exports represent a major element of their economies (Mhlanga 1993, 264–65).

More generally, how one reconciles trade and environmental goals and what specific changes in the GATT are required depend entirely on how one responds to the four central environmentalist propositions about trade enumerated above. In somewhat oversimplified terms, there are three basic answers to the question of how to reconcile trade and environmental policymaking. The hardline "economic" view is that trade liberalization and environmental protection are fundamentally not inconsistent because both aim at rationalizing the use of resources and thus no changes to the GATT are needed. The "no-growth environmental" view, which starts from a premise that economic growth is bad and therefore trade is bad, concludes that no convergence of trade and environmental interests is possible. The middle-ground conclusion—accepted by environmentalists who support sustainable development and by many free

---

17. This raises an important question: what is the GATT? Or more precisely, who is the GATT? The answer is, nothing more than the collectivity of the nation-states that are parties to the GATT accord. Thus one can argue that GATT staff members are simply international civil servants and should not be expected to try to update trade rules. But this line of reasoning lets the GATT Secretariat off the hook too easily. The GATT is, of course, dependent on the willingness of its member nations to make changes. The GATT staff, however, can and should alert the government representatives to the GATT when issues arise that require reconsideration of existing trade rules or procedures. Similarly, the government representatives to the GATT must share responsibility for not having seen environmental issues as sufficiently important to merit real attention, backed by a GATT reform game plan. But in defense of both groups, it is only fair to note that the depth of interdependence between trade liberalization and environmental protection has only recently been recognized. Moreover, how the GATT should respond to the environmental challenge is controversial—and no clear path of reform has yet become visible.

traders as well—is that trade and environmental goals are in some tension but trade-offs can be made to make these competing public aspirations more mutually compatible. Specifically, changes to GATT rules and adjustments to environmental policies can ensure an appropriate balance between trade benefits and environmental virtues.

Within this "balancing" or "trade-off" category, a variety of refinements—small and large—to the GATT might be considered. Some observers, such as Jagdish Bhagwati (1993c), would make modest changes to the existing rules to accommodate internationally agreed environmental standards aimed at global pollution spillovers. Other analysts, such as Steve Charnovitz (1994b), would dramatically refashion the GATT to give nearly complete deference to nationally determined environmental policies. This study argues for a middle course—broader reform of the international trade regime than Bhagwati might want and greater control over unilateral environmental action than Charnovitz advocates.

The problem with the view that GATT needs no reform is it relies too heavily on "trickle down" theories and assumes that because trade generates new resources, money will be devoted to environmental projects. The more sophisticated version of this economic line of reasoning, represented by Bhagwati, argues that the cause of environmental protection can be served by trade liberalization if appropriate environmental policies (specifically ones that internalize environmental harms) are in place—and that the GATT, with some minor adjustments, can fulfill this role. In fact, as a matter of economic theory, trade economists note that if environmental harms are properly "priced," there is no reason to believe trade or economic growth will worsen pollution (GATT 1992c, 30). Or put the other way around, if matched with proper environmental policies (in particular, the polluter pays principle), free market forces and open trade can serve to protect the environment.

The validity of this economic argument strikes at the heart of the critical first environmental proposition offered above. If, in fact, trade liberalization accompanied by proper cost-internalizing environmental policies helps rather than hurts the environment, then the core of the environmentalists' critique of free trade is upside down. This conclusion would mean not only that radical GATT reform is not justified but also that much of the real trade and environment problem should be addressed by environmental policy reform. This basis for trade and environmental policy convergence is explored in chapter 3.

Chapter 4 takes this line of analysis one step farther, examining the possibility that rather than ' greening" the GATT, trade liberalization and environmental protection might be made mutually supportive by "GATT-ing" the greens. It proposes establishing a new international environmental regime to facilitate market-based environmental regulation (particularly implementation of the polluter pays principle as a fundamental guideline) that meshes more easily with free trade. Such a structure would also be positioned to manage global environmental issues in parallel with the GATT's coordination of trade matters.

On the environmental side of the spectrum, even if one puts aside the uncompromising opposition of no-growth environmentalists, there exists a large group of "greens" who see a healthy environment as an end in itself while trade is simply one means to the end of economic welfare. Adherents to this "traditional" environmental view want GATT recognition and reinforcement of both the defensive environmental agenda (propositions 1 and 2)—ensuring that trade and trade liberalization do no harm to the environment—and the offensive agenda (propositions 3 and 4)—guaranteeing that trade measures will be available as leverage to support environmental policy goals. Purists from this school argue that trade should be made subordinate to environmental ends. The reform implications of this perspective are dramatic. In its extreme form, this viewpoint might be used to argue for broad limitations on trade (Lang and Hines 1994; Batra 1993). Even a more temperate version would require a thorough overhaul of the GATT to ensure that the advancement of environmental values becomes a priority of the trade regime.

This environmental critique of trade proffers insights into the reform that is required of the GATT but, in its strict form, cannot provide a foundation for both trade liberalization and environmental protection. Redesigning the trade regime to serve environmental ends alone risks sacrificing the contribution to well-being in general and to environmental protection in particular that sustainable, trade-generated growth promises. Building environmental safeguards into trade relations and the trade liberalization process makes a great deal of sense. Subjugating trade to environmental goals in every circumstance is irrational unless one believes that environmental regulations always translate into environmental protection and that the environmental harms from trade will always be greater than the economic benefits—propositions that seem highly unlikely. Moreover, insofar as legitimate differences of opinion exist about how to handle environmental issues, permitting broad scope for the offensive use of environmental trade measures invites further disputes and a potentially serious threat to international harmony.

An important offshoot of this environmental view is what might be called the "sovereignty school" (Charnovitz 1994b). Adherents to this line of thinking believe that environmental policymaking should be left entirely to national politicians and the GATT should be stripped of all authority to challenge nationally determined policies. Some supporters of the sovereignty school would accept review of environmental policies by the GATT to determine if they are really disguised protectionism. Others would permit no international oversight whatsoever. Charnovitz (1994b, 24), for example, concludes: "Trade-offs are appropriate for a government's internal policy making, but inappropriate for an international institution. . . . Any international supervision of national values leads GATT down a slippery slope."

The value of the sovereignty line of reasoning is that it highlights the inappropriateness of having international authorities routinely second-guess domestic decision makers who are acting within the spectrum of legitimate environmental policies. It also suggests that care should be employed in questioning the means that national political leaders and environmental officials have selected to carry out their goals. These principles are good ones and should inform the structuring of GATT rules to weigh the commercial benefits of trade against competing environmental ends.

But the sovereignty school leaves far too much leeway for environmental guises for trade protectionism. Indeed, if the GATT were to avoid judging the merits of all "environmental" policies and to cede jurisdiction over the review of any policy that a country claims is part of its environmental program, designing environmental excuses for protectionism would quickly become an art form around the world. For example, the Japanese might define grass-fed beef as environmentally superior to grain-fed beef—a not wholly implausible claim because of the energy consumed in producing grain. This would provide an excuse to block US cattle producers from the Japanese market and thus protect Japan's domestic grass-fed beef business. The French would certainly find a reason to deem US grains and oilseeds "environmentally unsound." Thus, it is not the trade-off approach to trade and environmental problems, but the sovereignty school, that leads the GATT down a slippery slope.

The sovereignty school does nothing, furthermore, to address global problems or to facilitate international environmental cooperation. The emphasis on unilateral, inherently noncooperative approaches is unlikely to produce good environmental results (Hoel 1991). Specifically, punitive single-country trade actions have a very limited record of success (Hufbauer, Schott, and Elliott 1990). This is especially true if one looks at environmental improvements as the critical measure of progress. In fact, the US tuna embargo of Mexico has done little to end Mexico's dolphin killing.[18] Blocking access to the US market, moreover, can only affect foreign-generated global environmental harms if the product happens to be exported to the United States. Environmentally damaging products sold only in the foreign producer's domestic market or in third-country markets go untouched.[19] Thus, in promoting unilateral approaches to environmental protection, the sovereignty school

---

18. Mexico has taken a number of steps to reduce dolphin deaths, but these appear more related to its interest in advancing the NAFTA than an effort to lift the tuna trade embargo, which remains in place.

19. This same "limited effectiveness" problem also exists in the application of countervailing duties to attack domestic subsidies available to foreign producers.

lets countries that illegitimately set low environmental standards that adversely affect global resources off the hook too easily.

In short, the theory that the trade-environment clash can be reconciled by GATT rules that grant each country free reign over environmental policies no matter what their effect on other countries fails to take seriously the lessons of history regarding the temptation to slip into protectionism, the dynamic of trade retaliation, and the need to promote international cooperation both to promote environmental protection and to maintain open markets.

Fundamentally, the sovereignty school relies on the wise exercise of power by individual sovereign states both to protect the environment and to preserve the international trading system. But this faith is misplaced; abuses of power are common and the risk that the wolf of trade protectionism will be hidden in the sheep's clothing of environmentalism is too significant to ignore. Just as American democracy and most other successful democracies are built on a system of checks and balances, GATT rules, if working properly, can limit abuses of national regulatory power. Thus, as noted earlier, the political judgments of national governments should be given considerable deference—but not absolute deference.

The reciprocity of the international trading system is, furthermore, central to its success. Each nation, in return for accepting modest limitations on its own exercise of sovereign power over environmental regulations, gets guarantees that other countries will not run roughshod over its interests on their home turf. Specifically, in exchange for participating in the trade regime and accepting GATT rules, countries get protection for their significant export markets and opportunities. And if the rules of international trade were structured properly, they would also get support for their interests in protecting the planet's environment and the shared resources of the global commons.

The sovereignty school also misunderstands the realities of trying to exercise power unilaterally in the post–Cold War era. The United States can no longer dictate policies to the world without repercussions, no matter how wise and moral those policies seem to Americans. In fact, the sense of moral superiority that sometimes permeates unbridled US unilateralism engenders deep hostility abroad. In condemning those who see themselves as the "custodians of a superior civilization" and who seek to "transfer it to more benighted lands and climes," Lal (1993, 356–57), for example, argues: "There is a contemporary movement of idealists in the West—the global environmentalists—who might trigger another round of imperialism in the name of saving spaceship Earth."

This study thus argues for a balancing of trade and environmental interests, building on two fundamental points of policy convergence: the use of the polluter pays principle to internalize environmental harms and the creation of a functioning international environmental regime to operate in parallel with the GATT. Such a regime would make more coherent and systematic the world's response to global environmental problems and would be able to channel and to regulate efforts to use trade measures to advance environmental goals.

Although cost internalization in the environmental realm would profoundly improve the mutually reinforcing nature of trade liberalization and environmental policy, a commitment to incentive-based environmental regulation cannot put to rest all trade-environment disputes. Nor does an international environmental regime to enforce the polluter pays principle seem politically realistic as a short-term policy option. Thus, peace in our time between the trade and environmental communities must be built on refining GATT rules and procedures to better balance competing commercial and environmental goals and to provide a system of checks and balances to prevent both trade and environmental abuses emanating from national policy choices. Examining the specific trade-offs that must therefore be made and outlining rules to facilitate this process are the focus of much of the rest of this book.

3

Making Trade Work for the Environment

The proposition that trade harms the environment and that more trade harms it more (that is, trade liberalization is bad) has two separate environmental perspectives embedded within it. First, some environmentalists adhere to a "limits to growth" philosophy and are opposed to economic development and thus to almost all trade. Adherents to this no-growth world view have little interest in building environmental safeguards into the GATT. For them, no trade is good trade. Other environmentalists accept "sustainable development" as a goal and see economic growth as positive if it is achieved in ways that are sensitive to the environment. These "pragmatic" environmentalists seek to ensure that some of the gains from trade are in fact devoted to environmental purposes and that environmental safeguards put the economic activities promoted by trade on a sustainable course.

The elements of the environmental community that are convinced that trade and environmental protection are in inexorable conflict want to gut the GATT (Lang and Hines 1993). Adherents to a "small is beautiful" philosophy see trade liberalization resulting in unchecked development and economic growth resulting in more pollution, unsustainable resource use, and a buildup of waste in critical ecosystems. As Batra (1993, 245) bluntly declares: "Since trade pollutes the earth, it is essential that it be kept to the minimum."

In fact, this line of criticism has nothing really to do with trade. It reflects the affinity of a vocal antigrowth minority in the environmental community for a nonmaterialistic world where individuals live simply with what they or others nearby can produce. From this point of view, international trade is not much worse than domestic exchange of goods. As one wag joked, adherents to this "deep ecology" philosophy support trade only to the extent possible by bicycle.

Although simplicity and less materialism may be virtues, this neo-Luddite vision of Nirvana holds little attraction for most people in the United States or around the world. Despite the underlying truth that unending population growth and the increased economic activity that accompanies it are not sustainable in the long run, the question is, when will the long run come and what will happen in the intervening time?

Herman Daly argues that the world is already 40 percent "full" (Goodland et al. 1992, 30) in the sense that nearly half of all arable land has been put into use for food production. He therefore concludes that the "limits to growth" are near. Others see population curves dipping down and foresee technological advances forestalling the Malthusian crisis[1]—making economic growth a positive force for centuries to come. Based on this latter view, the majority of environmentalists today have adopted a credo of sustainable development that supports economic growth so long as it builds in protection for public health and ecological resources.

But pro-growth environmentalists share their no-growth colleagues' concern with the concept of pure free trade (Lallas, Esty, and Van Hoogstraten 1992). There is, they argue, no a priori reason in the absence of environmental safeguards to be confident that free trade will produce benefits that exceed its costs and therefore improve social welfare. A richer society is not necessarily a better society. If environmental problems are not properly accounted for, today's prosperity may be acquired under false pretenses that make society worse off over the long run. In pure economic terms, if the cost of addressing future environmental harms caused by today's economic activities is great enough, then the wealth acquired now and endowed to our progeny will not adequately compensate them for the environmental debts we also leave them.

Thus, sustainability cannot be assumed; it must be expressly provided for in trade agreements. Economists concede that to maximize social welfare, the benefits of trade must be weighed against the costs of ecological degradation from expanded economic activity (e.g., Anderson 1992b). They recognize that, to be fully appropriate, this calculus must

---

1. Thomas Malthus first predicted the world's demographic demise based on a growing population and limited availability of food in his famous *Essay on the Principle of Population*, published in 1803 (available as *T.R. Malthus*, Donald Winch, ed., from Cambridge University Press, New York).

factor in all costs, including those that have traditionally not been part of the analysis because they were externalized and never translated into a price that someone paid. In fact, most economists would acknowledge that a number of assumptions about the functioning of the market must be fulfilled to be confident that market forces will produce an efficient social outcome.[2]

The "Trade Is Pro-Environment" Case

GATT officials and others in the trade world do not perceive themselves or the international trade regime to be anti-environmental. Thus, the trade community was initially caught off guard by the force of the anti-trade green onslaught. As good economists, most free traders see both trade liberalization and environmental protection directed toward more efficient use of resources and thus fundamentally compatible. Their confidence in this convergence of interests stems in particular from a conviction that trade generates wealth that can be used to address environmental problems and from a belief that market forces, if properly channeled, will protect the environment in the context of trade liberalization. Thus, free traders seemed taken aback at the outset of the trade and environment debate that their studious environmental agnosticism was viewed as heresy by environmental true believers.

Trade Generates Resources That Can Be Devoted to Environmental Protection

GATT experts are often puzzled by the failure of many environmentalists to see the links between trade, economic growth, and the availability of resources to invest in environmental protection. As Palmeter (1993, 69) suggests: "Any dispassionate study of the issue reveals . . . not only that the areas of potential conflict are limited and manageable, but also that expanded trade, by increasing overall world wealth, itself can contribute to the cause of a better environment." GATT officials frequently make the same point. In its sharply argued 1992 Trade and Environment Report (GATT 1992c, 19), the GATT Secretariat observes that the international trade regime supports environmental protection by increasing the efficiency of resource use and raising incomes, making possible increased expenditures on the environment. Similarly, both the Bush and Clinton administrations argued that the North American Free Trade Agreement would advance the cause of environmental protection in

---

2. Environmental issues are, moreover, only the latest in a long list of "new" considerations such as the special needs of developing countries that have been folded in the trading system. Cooper (1972) reviews some of the earlier refinements.

Mexico by providing new funds through economic growth for much-needed environmental investments (USTR 1992 and 1993b).

In building on this pro-growth, pro-environment proposition, the free traders are in good company. The widely heralded Brundtland Report, for example, argues that environmental protection supports long-term economic growth—that is, sustainable development—and that prosperity, promoted by trade liberalization, enhances the prospects for sustained support for environmental protection. In fact, the Brundtland Report can be read to make an even more fundamental point: poverty per se is a form of environmental degradation, and thus economic well-being is an environmental plus, regardless of its effects on pollution control or environmental protection efforts.

The correlation between prosperity and environmental protection seems logical (rich countries can afford higher environmental standards), appears consistent with observed data (despite higher levels of emissions, air and water quality is generally higher in OECD countries than in developing nations) and has some empirical support. Notably, Grossman and Krueger's (1993) study of pollution levels and national wealth concludes that although poor countries suffer increased pollution as they begin to industrialize, when they reach middle-income levels (about $5,000 GDP per capita), they invest more in pollution controls, and emission concentrations begin to fall (figure 3.1).

In response, environmentalists observe that the correlation between economic conditions and pollution levels reflects only a theoretical relationship, not necessarily a causal connection (Lee 1992). Environmentalists remain suspicious that the invisible hand of market forces is attached to an insufficiently environmentally conscious body. They argue that, in the trade liberalization context, the economic growth/environmental progress link should be made explicit, with environmental funding provisions accompanying all free trade agreements. Express environmental commitments are needed, they suggest, because political forces tend to neglect environmental considerations, and the time lags between economic growth and increases in environmental spending may be substantial. In addition, environmentalists point out that many studies, including Grossman and Krueger's, show increases in pollution in the short to medium run. Thus how growth takes place matters a good bit.

In light of this reality, trade liberalization efforts should be accompanied by environmental analyses designed to identify environmental harms that might be exacerbated by freer trade and to spot opportunities to advance environmental protection. These environmental impact assessments need not be exhaustive studies but should be designed to alert trade negotiators to the environmental variables they face and to alternative ways of dealing with them. Further consideration will be given to this policy recommendation in chapter 9.

Figure 3.1 Income and pollution

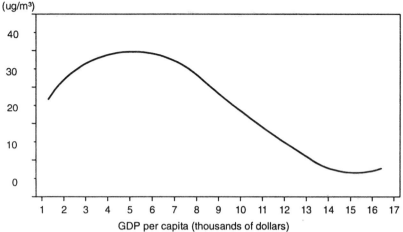

Additional units of sulfur dioxide (ug/m³)

GDP per capita (thousands of dollars)

Concentrations of sulfur dioxide rise with income at low levels of per capita GDP, fall with income at middle levels of GDP, and eventually level off in the most advanced economies. The estimated turning point comes at a per capita income level of about $5,000 (1988 dollars).

Source: Grossman and Krueger (1993), MIT Press. Reproduced with permission from the authors and publisher.

The Economic Congruence of Trade Liberalization and Environmental Protection

The free traders' more dramatic argument is that trade liberalization ought to directly help protect the environment. At least in theory, the scope for environmental harm arising from liberalized trade can be greatly reduced or eliminated by ensuring that prices fully reflect environmental costs. In fact, Robert Repetto (1993a) and others (Richard Stewart 1992; Anderson and Blackhurst 1992b) argue that there is no inherent trade and environment conflict since both trade liberalization and environmental regulation have similar aims—to make more efficient use of resources. Stephan Schmidheiny, chairman of the Business Council for Sustainable Development, makes the same point in arguing for businesses to become "eco-efficient." Specifically, Schmidheiny (1992, xxiii) observes: "Conservation of the environment and successful business development should be opposite sides of the same coin—the coin being the measure of the progress of human civilization."

From this perspective, the key to reconciling trade and environmental policy goals is implementing the polluter pays principle and internalizing environmental harms. If environmental externalities are internalized,[3] free trade will increase welfare both nationally and globally.[4] Moreover, market forces, including free trade, result in more efficient resource use (reducing the stress on natural resources), encourage technological innovation, and lower the cost of environmental protection by improving productivity and permitting the same levels of output to be produced at lower costs both in monetary and environmental terms. As Young (1994) argues, if "social costs and nonmarket considerations could be factored into global markets, then the gains from trade liberalization would be unambiguously positive in a social and an economic sense."

The key issue, in laymen's language, is whether the prices that businesses and the public see reflect the full costs of producing and consuming goods, including burdens currently unaccounted for that are imposed on others through environmental spillovers such as pollution. In this regard, the tension between trade and environmental policies can be traced to pervasive market failures to which environmental policies have not adequately responded. Many environmentalists recognize the value of cost internalization both as a way of improving environmental protection per se and as a means of reconciling trade and environmental policies (Repetto et al. 1989; Meyer 1993). As Pearson (1994, 5) argues: "By allocating abatement costs to the private sector, market prices would more closely reflect the social cost of production. This would tend to encourage pollution abatement by reducing consumption of pollution-intensive products. . . . Thus the [polluter pays principle] supports improved efficiency in the allocation of natural and environmental resources (i.e., helps correct externality-distorted product prices). At the same time, it helps prevent a *trade* distortion."

But even economically minded environmentalists worry about the difficulties of putting this line of reasoning into practice. They note that the obverse of this argument is that market forces may not protect the environment if pollution effects and natural resources are inappropriately priced or given no value at all. They recognize that uncorrected market failures are the rule, not the exception, in the environmental realm (and other) areas and thus that trade liberalization does

---

3. Baumol and Oates (1975) provide the classic analysis of the problem of environmental externalities more broadly.

4. Of course, when professed free traders, particularly in the business community, are faced with the reality of cost internalization, they often demur, citing competitiveness concerns or other arguments why, in the case in question, internalizing costs will not work. The business community's broadly negative reaction to President Clinton's proposed energy tax offers a classic example of this behavior. This argues that resolution of the trade and environment conflict cannot rest on the polluter pays principle alone but must also build on an international regime that ensures worldwide adherence to cost internalization.

not now generally work to reduce environmental harms.[5] More specifically, because so many resources are improperly priced, market forces cannot today be relied upon to allocate scarce natural resources efficiently or to guarantee that polluters will face real incentives to minimize their emissions.[6]

Economists also recognize the difficulty of implementing the polluter pays principle. Pearson (1994, 3) notes: "Although durable and widely referenced, the [principle] is not without its ambiguities and idiosyncratic interpretations." He identifies a number of issues: who pays internalized costs, how much polluters should pay, which economic instruments are compatible with the principle, and how equity and fairness considerations are taken into account.

In addition to the ease with which pollution travels, another difficulty with getting environmental prices right is that natural resources tend to be communal property, or what economists call public goods—no one owns them exclusively. Air, for instance, is a public good; anyone can breath it or emit pollutants into it. Because of the difficulty of charging people for using or excluding people from taking advantage of these resources, they tend to be overused or exploited.

Economic theory offers two solutions to the public-goods problem. First, Pigou (1918) suggests that where free market competition systematically undervalues a resource, government intervention to correct this market failure through fees, taxes, or subsidies is required. Coase (1960) offers another approach based on the assignment of property rights in the overexploited resource. He argues that once resource ownership is established (no matter whether rights are assigned to the polluters or those affected by emissions) and assuming no transactions costs, the polluters and others who have an interest in the resource will negotiate a price and other terms for the use of the resource that will result in an optimal (sustainable) level of exploitation.

Society already relies on both of these mechanisms to regulate environmental amenities and natural resources. For example, escalating taxes have been placed on chlorofluorocarbons (CFCs) in the United States to protect the ozone layer—a public good. These fees have created an incentive not to use products that damage the ozone and have in fact resulted in a sharp drop in CFC consumption, ahead of the schedule

---

5. Some trade experts respond to this point by asking why, if these market failures are pervasive, the trade realm should be held responsible and singled out for special environmental rules. One answer to this question is that trade, by increasing the number of transactions at improper prices, may exacerbate pollution problems.

6. Kozloff and Dower (1993) provide an excellent discussion of how market prices fail to capture the environmental and other social costs of energy—and the market-distorting effect of this mispricing on society's mix of energy supplies. There is, of course, no agreed method for actually determining the correct value of environmental externalities (National Commission on the Environment 1993).

mandated by the Montreal Protocol and its amendments. The assignment of property rights has also been used to improve environmental protection. For instance, the issuance of a limited number of permits to set lobster traps has stopped overharvesting and helped to stabilize the lobster population in Long Island Sound.

Most environmental regulation builds on both the assignment of property rights and efforts (albeit often crude) to adjust prices to reflect social costs. As noted in chapter 1, one of the critical forces shaping the trade and environment conflict is the reassertion of public ownership over air and water, which had previously been viewed as a free good. With the property right established, the government can reduce exploitation by controlling access with permits or by charging emissions fees. Nevertheless, there are many resources over which property rights remain in doubt and an even greater number of cases in which pollution burdens or natural resources remain unpriced or underpriced.

Beyond the problem of externalities and the public-goods nature of environmental amenities, there is a third element of market failure that requires government intervention to ensure optimal attention to environmental protection: the intergenerational aspect of many environmental problems (Brown Weiss 1989). Specifically, because environmental problems often have long lead times and show threshold effects, it is possible for one generation to ignore issues at the expense of future generations, who will have to face the problems as they become visible and acute. In these circumstances, the market fails to produce an optimal outcome because future generations are not able to cast their market "votes" and bequest motives may not be strong enough to ensure optimal long-term outcomes (Diamond 1977; Brandts and de Bartolome 1988).

These market failures result in a sometimes significant divergence between private marginal costs and social marginal costs in the environmental realm—throwing off the price signals that would otherwise work to promote environmental efficiency (i.e., supporting long-term optimal consumption of natural resources and limiting use of the natural world as a waste dump). Cairncross (1992, 89) observes in *Costing the Earth*:

> . . . in environmental affairs, the invisible hand of the market fails to align the interests of the individual or the individual company with those of society at large. Individuals may drive their cars to work rather than take a bus; companies may use CFCs to insulate and cool refrigerators. In both cases, the costs to the environment and thus to society at large exceed any private cost to individual or company. That is inefficient. Governments need to step in to align private costs with social costs.

Increasingly, economists and environmentalists agree that the way to respond to this failure is through full-cost pricing and adherence to the polluter pays principle. Moving in this policy direction would align economic forces and environmental protection needs. It would, more pointedly, help to ensure that the market incentives brought to bear by freer trade would also help to protect ecological values.

Policy Implications

Several policy implications follow from the notion that the polluter pays principle and better cost internalization would not only correct the recognized market failures that plague environmental protection but also improve the environmental consequences of trade liberalization. First, efforts to convert environmental regulation from command-and-control requirements to market-based mechanisms ought to gain added impetus. If environmental regulations were market-based (not ad hoc emissions limits or technology requirements) and "monetized" (i.e., reduced to a price paid for the harm caused), then their scope for conflict with market access agreements and disciplines on standards would be much reduced. For example, if the United States sought to discourage gasoline consumption with a higher gas tax rather than the Corporate Average Fuel Efficiency (CAFE) fleetwide mileage requirements, Volvo, BMW, and Mercedes would have no basis for complaining about unfair treatment in the US market. Broad-based commitment to cost internalization would also reduce the need for using trade as leverage, except to ensure adherence to the polluter pays principle. Countries might still disagree over how much must be charged to internalize environmental costs, but such disputes would be a matter of degree.

Second, less-radical revision of the GATT would be required if progress were made in shifting from standards-based environmental regulation to cost internalization. In other words, GATT reform and environmental policy conversion are in some senses fungible. Even if one concludes (as this study does) that environmental cost internalization does not provide a "silver bullet" for integration of trade and environmental policymaking in the short term, it should remain a long-term priority.

A corollary of the "get prices right" proposition and the observation that trade restrictions are a poor substitute for proper environmental policies is the conclusion that the use of trade penalties to enforce environmental agreements or to promote environmental goals constitutes a second-best (or third- or fourth-best) policy mechanism. Environmental trade measures can easily become counterproductive from either an environmental or economic standpoint or both.[7] Thus, in crafting such trade measures, policymakers should attend to the effectiveness of the programs they put in place and be aware of the danger that the mea-

7. For an example of this phenomenon see the discussion of tropical timber trade restrictions in appendix B.

sures may backfire.[8] When evidence of deleterious environmental results from environmental trade measures is found, officials should move quickly to reshape the policy in question.

Attacking the Market Failure

The insight of economists—that important elements of the trade and environment conflict have arisen because the costs associated with environmental harms are not internalized—is significant. Unfortunately, having identified this market failure, trade analysts tend to believe the burden of resolving the conflict and implementing the polluter pays principle rests on the environmental community.

A spate of recent articles from trade experts (e.g., Palmeter 1993; Jackson 1992a; Bhagwati 1993b) and even some environmental economists (Repetto 1993b) have therefore suggested that the dispute between trade and environmental interests is a "false conflict" and "much ado about little." In leaning too heavily on the conceptual opportunity presented by the polluter pays principle, economists and their trade colleagues tend to overstate the prospects for convergence. The real challenge lies in the practical obstacles to making trade and environmental policies mutually reinforcing. Disputes would still exist over what our environmental goals should be and how to value environmental amenities and harms. Valuation controversies are inevitable in the face of substantial scientific and risk uncertainties, variations in political priorities and judgments, and differences based on geography and level of development. As chapter 1 explained, market mechanisms are clearly not a panacea for all environmental problems, never mind all trade and environment issues.

Even where goals can be agreed upon, consensus on means is often elusive. Powerful political forces frequently intervene to prevent the internalization of costs in deference to industries or other policy actors with deeply entrenched interests in the status quo. The need to internationalize any commitment to the polluter pays principle adds further practical complexities. Moreover, society does not know how to get what it wants from environmental regulation. Science cannot say with certainty what is ecologically safe. Defining the dimensions and magnitude of environmental externalities—putting a price on pollution—therefore has an irreducible political element. Perhaps to a larger degree than in the trade realm, environmental regulation has a significant noneconomic dimension.[9]

---

8. For instance, some observers have questioned the efficacy of the African ivory ban—arguing that limited sales of ivory on a sustainable basis would do more to protect elephants (Bonner 1993).

9. As pressures to consider issues such as human rights and labor standards gain currency as legitimate trade concerns, this noneconomic or "values" dimension of trade policymaking may expand.

In addition, in contrast with environmental regulation, trade liberalization is backed by a relatively coherent and well-accepted economic theory about what leads to greater social welfare. This theory has furthermore been translated into international rules.[10] Although there is a growing recognition of the conceptual power of cost internalization as the cornerstone for future programs to protect ecological resources and public health, environmental policymaking remains hobbled by the lack of a broadly accepted theoretical foundation. Thus, despite efforts to build in more analytic rigor through the use of better science, risk analysis, and economic tools, environmental regulation retains an important dimension that is art or philosophy. In this domain, political judgments are required, and experts disagree. It is in this zone of politics that the interests of free traders and environmentalists often clash.

We cannot hope to establish a common social welfare metric that will resolve all trade-environment strife unless we have answers to critical questions: How much is it worth to save a human life? What risk of cancer are we willing to accept? What is the value of a pretty view? Nonetheless, cost internalization, and particularly adoption of the polluter pays principle, offers a conceptual beacon on the horizon that should be followed for both the environmental and trade benefits it offers.

In the meantime, to the extent that environmental policies continue to obstruct the free flow of commerce, as they inevitably will, GATT reform is needed because the current system of trade rules and procedures lacks the balance necessary to adjudicate the relative merits of environmental and trade policies. How and when trade leverage should be employed to ensure compliance with a cost-internalization obligation or other principles will also continue to be controversial. Finally, the prospect of internalizing environmental harms does not fully address the offensive agenda of environmentalists who want to use trade measures to address competitiveness concerns.

Thus, even if one grants that full environmental cost internalization would significantly reduce the scope of trade and environment clashes, the suggestion that these disputes are "much ado about little" makes for an intellectual diet that is awfully rich on theory and rather thin on immediate policy application. In fact, this attitude belies the hard question that should be asked: why is it so difficult to get good environmental policies that internalize costs adopted?

10. Perhaps the contrast is between a single discipline field (economics) with a compelling theoretical foundation and a highly complex, multidisciplinary policy domain (biology, chemistry, economics, ecology, etc.) largely driven by observable natural reality.

4

GATTing the Greens

In their exchange of slings and arrows, both environmentalists and free traders have missed a critical point: sound environmental policies are hard to advance politically for the same reason free trade is difficult to sell to legislatures—that is, a "political failure" in our system of government[1] that allows special interests to influence the policy process at the expense of the long-term public interest.[2] The benefits of both environmental protection and trade liberalization are diffused so widely across society that individuals do not see their value, and relatively few groups are organized or motivated to systematically defend either.[3] The short-

---

1. This "defect" afflicts nondemocratic governments as well. In fact, special interests may find it even easier to gain preferred treatment from governments that face no public scrutiny or from officials who are corrupt.

2. There is a long political science and economics literature addressing the role of interest groups (e.g., Downs 1957; Olson 1965; Buchanan and Tullock 1971; Lowi 1969). For a classic study of the special interest manipulation of environmental policymaking see Ackerman and Hassler (1981). Destler's (1992) study of trade politics in America offers an insightful and provocative view of Congress's vulnerability to protectionist pressures.

3. The explosion of environmental legislation in the United States over the past 25 years might seem to belie the suggestion that environmentalists are disorganized and thus politically weak. But as Elliott, Ackerman, and Millian (1985) explain, these developments may actually be attributable to other factors, such as the desire of polluters to preempt disjointed state actions, the reelection-maximizing behavior of Congress, and the political entrepreneurship of aspiring presidential candidates. Rose-Ackerman (1981) furthermore identifies the strategic incentives for national legislation created by federal political structures, which may explain the adoption of several rounds of clean air acts, clean water statutes, and other federal environmental laws.

term costs of trade liberalization (e.g., dislocation of uncompetitive producers and their workers) or environmental protection (e.g., the expense of meeting pollution control requirements) are often concentrated on well-organized groups (e.g., companies or unions) with political power.[4] As David Mayhew (1974, 137) observes: "Congress will be reluctant to legislate new programs benefiting the unorganized over the opposition of the organized." This problem is not new. Nearly a century ago, Gifford Pinchot decried the "special interests" operating in the political realm that "nullify the will of the majority" with regard to conservation and environmental goals (cited in Shabecoff 1993, 279).

Even when environmental groups are politically effective, their successes may be narrowly focused and may not translate into a comprehensive program of environmental quality. In the United States in particular, Congress often reacts to media-inflamed environmental scandals (e.g., toxic chemicals seeping into homes along Love Canal, residue of the pesticide Alar on apples), skewing priorities to the hot issue of the moment and rendering long-term, risk-based priority setting and coordinated policy responses difficult. This additional element of political failure has given the United States (and other countries as well) a somewhat incoherent and haphazard environmental protection regime that in many cases undercleans but in some cases overcleans—and in most cases falls short of delivering the maximum bang for the environmental buck.[5]

Lack of attention to this political failure has contributed to the breakdown of efforts to identify mutually reinforcing trade and environmental policies (Dasgupta 1990). As noted in the last chapter, many trade experts have become consumed with the theoretical opportunity to make trade and environment policies compatible by means of economically "appropriate" environmental policies that force polluters to pay for the damage they cause. Their relative disinterest in the real-world political difficulty of getting such measures adopted seems particularly ironic since the creation of the General Agreement on Tariffs and Trade (GATT) was sparked by the inability of national governments to maintain appropriate trade policies in the face of political pressures.

---

4. The passage of the North American Free Trade Agreement and the success of the United States in eliminating import barriers (Hufbauer and Elliott 1994) might also seem to belie the suggestion that pro–free trade interests will be inevitably weak. But the level of opposition to the NAFTA, despite the demonstrable benefits to the country, make clear the difficulty of organizing the "dispossessed."

5. As Shabecoff (1993, 279) observes: "For much of this century, the [environmental] movement has been functioning as an ecological emergency squad, responding to crises . . . [but environmentalists must now] acquire the *power* necessary to achieve fundamental change."

For their part, environmentalists, while accepting the need to internalize pollution costs and even conceding the value of proper resource pricing as a way to reconcile trade and environmental interests, have become fixated on changing the rules and procedures of the GATT. As a result, they have largely overlooked the possibility that restructuring environmental policy mechanisms and establishing a parallel international environmental regime alongside the GATT offers a more sound basis for protecting environmental values than does "greening" the GATT. In this regard, the GATT should be seen as a potential model for advancing environmental interests—not an object of scorn to be torn down.

In sum, it appears that both free traders and environmentalists have gotten off track. Environmentalists have been thrown off the scent by their preoccupation with the GATT. Free traders, having tracked down an important economic failure (lack of cost internalization) that underlies the conflict, stopped hunting and missed the real quarry—the political failure that makes adopting economically efficient, free trade–consistent environmental policies so difficult.

The GATT's Role in Fixing the Trade Policy Political Failure

The GATT is a central pillar of the post–World War II international order. Its rules, norms, and dispute settlement procedures are designed to prevent governments from pursuing "beggar-thy-neighbor" policies that limit imports and promote exports to establish a competitive advantage in the international marketplace at the expense of other countries. Such policies are likely to generate significant economic costs, invite retaliatory actions, and lead to a downward spiral into global economic chaos, as occurred in the 1930s in the wake of the Smoot-Hawley tariffs. Nevertheless, national governments find protectionist policies difficult to avoid because of the substantial political clout of "rent-seeking" economic interests.

The architects of the Bretton Woods economic order[6] saw that the international noncooperation on trade and the economic failure it produced was really a function of domestic political pressures. As Sylvia Ostry (1990) observes: "No policy is as domestic as international trade policy." So these leaders set up the GATT as a government-to-

6. The GATT, the World Bank, and the International Monetary Fund were launched in 1944 after a conference in Bretton Woods, New Hampshire, among the Allied leaders. Looking for ways to establish postwar stability, peace, and prosperity, the leaders concluded that the world needed better international economic management and cooperation. Solomon (1977) provides a full history of the Bretton Woods system.

government contract centered on principles of mutual forbearance in support of freer trade, eventually encompassing an international system to reinforce the agreed-upon rules promoting trade liberalization.[7]

By enshrining the principles of liberal trade in an international regime, the creators of the GATT not only built a mechanism for reducing friction among nations, they also elevated the commitment to freer trade to a nearly ''constitutional'' level, thereby limiting the power of governments around the world (and legislatures in particular) to give in to the pleadings of domestic interests—both producers and labor groups—seeking shelter from the rigors of global competition (Petersmann 1992). In moving free trade principles to a higher plane of authority and providing a buffer against protectionist pressures, the GATT provides a mechanism for addressing the collective-action problem that plagues domestic trade policymaking and thereby enhances society's overall economic well-being, promotes international stability, and serves the long-term public interest.

No comparable system exists to shield environmental protection policies. Notably, governments tend not to require polluters to compensate society fully for the environmental damage they cause because these interests can effectively lobby the government for relief.[8] As with the losses from protectionism, the costs of environmental degradation are spread widely across society, making it difficult to organize those affected systematically in response.

The existence of threshold effects and sometimes substantial time lags between emissions and the detection of environmental problems further reduces the apparent urgency of limiting environmental harms or of charging polluters for their actions. Environmental issues are often marked, moreover, by substantial scientific uncertainties, which make the damage from environmental degradation and the benefits of pollution control easy to dismiss as too distant or speculative. In contrast, the price of pollution controls in the form of higher costs or taxes is often easily calculated and visible to the affected interests; it is thus relatively easy to mobilize opposition.

---

7. The GATT was meant to be (and now finally has been) superseded by a more fully developed international institution, the International Trade Organization (ITO), but the US Congress refused to ratify the ITO. This left the GATT as the central element of the international trade regime. Appendix A offers a brief history of the GATT, including the final chapter of the ITO story—the 1994 creation of the World Trade Organization.

8. This is not to deny that environmental groups wield power and can be an effective policy force (Schuck 1981). But as Elliott, Ackerman, and Millian note (1985), environmentalists have a limited and more subtle ability to influence policy outcomes than traditional groups. Moreover, as noted earlier, some environmental organizations are themselves special interests with their own narrow perspectives and focus on maximizing their own power, influence, and fund-raising prospects.

The defeat of President Clinton's 1993 energy tax proposal offers one example of this phenomenon.[9] The difficulty of getting the Congress to adopt real cost internalization in the 1990 Clean Air Act and the special treatment given numerous industries (e.g., the coal industry, steel producers) in the legislation offers another example. This distribution of political costs and benefits leaves governments with a nearly irresistible temptation to push pollution burdens onto the ultimate inactive and unorganized interest group—generations yet unborn.

Global environmental issues offer the additional opportunity, as in the trade context, to transfer burdens to foreigners. Where the pollution from one country spreads across the entire planet, as occurs with greenhouse gas emissions, only a small fraction of the harm actually affects the citizens of the polluting country. In such cases, governments recognize that burdening their own domestic industry with cleanup costs, the benefit of which would redound largely to others around the world, cannot be justified based on the relevant political calculus (i.e., domestic costs compared with domestic benefits) and might disadvantage their own producers competing in the global marketplace against companies whose governments are not requiring similar spending on pollution abatement. When all nations make the same calculation and engage in the same behavior, the cumulative results can be disastrous for the environment. This collective-action problem and the public goods nature of environmental programs lie at the heart of some elements of the trade and environment conflict.

Institutional Imbalance

The lack of an institutional structure to protect the environment the way the GATT guards free trade lies at the heart of the antagonism between trade and environmental interests. With its established rules, norms, and procedures, GATT defends an open (or at least relatively open) global marketplace against encroachments. GATT's focused mission and relative success make environmentalists both angry and envious. On the one hand, environmental activists see the GATT as insular, rigid, and narrow. They find its procedures impenetrable and fault its decision making for failing to take account of environmental concerns. But simultaneously, they recognize the efficacy of the GATT, which is in part a function of its narrowly tailored mission and ability to shield itself from

---

9. Although cast as a budget measure, not a pollution control program, the failure of President Clinton's 1993 energy tax proposal in the face of multiplying "carve-outs" for certain affected industries and intense opposition from some energy industry representatives and their congressional allies demonstrates the challenge to environmental interests. The near defeat of the NAFTA offers a parallel case study of the vulnerability of free trade policies to special interest pressures.

political forces advancing other priorities. Thus, while denouncing the GATT, environmentalists admire its power and would like to remold it to serve "green" purposes.

In contrast to the international trade regime centered in the GATT, the management of international environmental affairs has little structure and is marked by policy gaps, confusion, duplication, and incoherence (Wirth 1992a). A dozen different UN agencies, the secretariats to a number of environmental treaties and conventions, the World Bank, regional political groups, and the world's 190 countries acting individually try to cope with the planet's environmental problems. For example, at least five separate organizations are developing methodologies for greenhouse-gas emissions inventories to follow up on the 1992 Climate Change Convention signed in Rio de Janeiro: the UN Environment Programme, the Global Environment Facility, the Organization for Economic Cooperation and Development, the Intergovernmental Panel on Climate Change, and the International Negotiating Committee that put together the Climate Change Convention. Collaboration occurs, if at all, on an ad hoc basis.

The difficulty with existing international institutions that address environmental issues, such as the UN Environment Programme and the recently created UN Commission on Sustainable Development, is that they have been given narrow mandates, small budgets, and limited support. No one organization has the authority or political strength to serve as a central clearinghouse or coordinator, nor does any organization have the mission of establishing broad GATT-like principles as the basis for norms in international environmental relations.[10]

In addition, the management of international environmental problems suffers from what Edith Brown Weiss (1993b, 697) calls "treaty congestion." With more than 900 legal instruments addressing international environmental issues now in place (Brown Weiss, Magraw, and Szasz 1992), it cannot be surprising that disconnects arise in the handling of environmental matters. Moreover, this multiplicity of institutions makes systematic analysis of risks across problems, budget priority setting, and other aspects of coordination nearly impossible (Hajost 1990; Wirth 1989). The difficulties of fixing this institutional problem are further discussed later in this chapter.

Building a Global Environmental Organization

To make the best environmental policies politically feasible and to defend the long-term interests of all humankind in a healthy biosphere,

---

10. There, nevertheless, have been some successes in achieving agreements in specific international environmental niches (Haas, Keohane, and Levy 1993).

the world needs GATT-like rules of mutual forbearance to protect the environment and a supporting international body to manage global environmental relations. Such a regime would contribute to international harmony. Specifically, it would help to ensure that environmental values are not overwhelmed by more established interests such as trade liberalization. It would respond to the "tragedy of the commons" problem and the difficulty of overcoming the collective-action problem to achieve mutually protective policies in the international environmental realm. And it would provide a bulwark against the tendency of governments to transfer environmental burdens to those who are outside their borders or politically weak.

From the perspective of economic theory, the case for a strong and comprehensive Global Environmental Organization (GEO) is overwhelming. The presence of global environmental externalities, the public goods nature of environmental programs,[11] and the intergenerational trade-offs inherent in environmental policy choices necessitate an overarching regulatory structure. Such a system is needed to limit self-serving (focused on local or national costs, not global consequences), irresponsible, and destructive behavior and to ensure that all of the relevant environmental actors participate in a unified regulatory program (Sprinz and Vaahtoranta 1994). Without global cooperation and collective action, there is a serious, ongoing risk of "market failure" in environmental protection, as some countries and some companies free ride on the pollution control efforts of others.

As discussed in chapter 3, tradeable emissions permits, effluent fees, or subsidies can be used to overcome this market failure and to align the incentives private actors face with a socially optimal allocation of resources. But to make the market work, there must be a recognized authority to enforce property rights and to regulate behavior. In the international realm, however, no such coordinating mechanism exists. As long as it is absent, the world will suffer pollution damage, perhaps even to the point of threatening the sustainability of vital ecosystems.

An international environmental regime could help to alleviate both the market failure and the corresponding political failure that makes adoption of appropriate environmental policies on a national basis difficult. Specifically, it would allow countries to cooperate in developing cost-internalizing environmental regulations so that no one country would be competitively disadvantaged. The benefits of joint action are significant because environmental policymaking in the global context

---

11. The nonexcludability that characterizes the environmental amenities created makes it hard to get full cooperation. In addition, in dealing with public goods, there exists a tendency for some actors to free ride on the efforts of others. Olson (1965) describes public choice, public goods, and free riding in the international context.

reflects an element of the "prisoners' dilemma." In fact, there are considerable incentives to "cheat" on pollution control, since noncooperative behavior allows producers to free ride on the environmental investments of others, often gaining a cost advantage in the global marketplace (Barrett 1990). The presence of an institutional structure would help reward cooperation, discipline misbehavior, remind participants of the ongoing nature of the issue, and increase the chances of producing a "win-win" result (Dixit and Nalebuff 1991).

A GEO would also address the lack of parallelism that now undercuts public and political support for GATT management of trade and environment issues. As they are currently structured, the rules of international trade are fundamentally asymmetrical vis-à-vis the environment. Specifically, the GATT addresses environmental standards that are argued to be too high, potentially deeming them unacceptable barriers to trade. But the GATT provides no mechanism for deeming environmental standards to be too low, creating an unfair trade advantage based on the externalizing of environmental costs. The best the GATT can do is permit trade measures to be used to punish environmental bad actors. The GATT cannot, however, tell a nation that it has violated environmental standards it is obligated to uphold.

A GEO would be positioned to make "positive" determinations concerning environmental obligations.[12] In doing so, it would provide a balance to the GATT's market access–oriented rules and a more coherent and comprehensive management structure for international relations. Not only would a GEO ensure symmetry in handling trade and environmental issues, it would relieve the pressure on the GATT to be an environmental body as well as the cornerstone of the international trading system.

Just as the GATT was built on a few central concepts such as nondiscrimination, negotiations to establish a Global Environmental Organization might initially focus on defining general environmental principles to guide the world community.[13] For example, universal acceptance and application of the polluter pays principle—forcing governments, industry, and individuals alike to bear the full costs of the environmental burdens they impose on society—would create powerful incentives for pollution prevention and environmental care, consistent with the long-

---

12. A critical issue, discussed in chapter 6, is on what basis such determinations should be made or, in other words, whose standards should be applied.

13. By helping nations to frame broad-based policy principles in the context of reciprocal long-term commitments, a GEO, like the GATT before it, would enable decision rules to be established in the abstract, not in the face of short-term political pressures. Constructing a "veil of ignorance" (Rawls 1971) about the specific circumstances under which the principles will be applied facilitates consideration of intergenerational equity and optimal long-run policy prescriptions.

term interest of the public in a healthy environment and ongoing economic growth.[14] Other principles that might be developed include:

- a commitment to good science and to life-cycle analysis of environmental issues (OECD 1993a and 1994b; Moss 1993) so that policies are based on a comprehensive view of environmental effects from production through consumption to disposal of a product;

- a "precautionary" approach to environmental regulation that skews policymaking errors toward protection of public health and ecology, especially in the face of potentially great environmental harms (Bodansky 1991; Cameron and Abouchar 1991);

- an emphasis on "pollution prevention" rather than end-of-pipe treatment (EPA 1993b).[15]

Framing cardinal principles in the environmental realm that are also implementable as decision rules no doubt presents a more complicated challenge than the drafters of the GATT faced. In particular, an environmental regime entails a potentially more intrusive effort to prescribe certain behavior for governments (e.g., cost internalization) whereas the trade regime simply proscribes government actions that would disrupt the free flow of commerce.[16] Moreover, cost internalization and the other environmental principles that might be advanced all have serious practical problems.[17] Getting universal agreement on how to address uncertainties and to quantify incalculables would be no mean feat.

But the limits on our current knowledge and methodologies should not be crippling. A GEO need not begin life all-powerful. It would be appropriate for the new organization to have a sliding scale of authority depending on the global reach, severity, scientific certainty, and time urgency of the various environmental problems it took up. Some issues might initially merit no more than discussions at the international level

---

14. Gaines (1991) discusses the evolution of the polluter pays principle and its possible role in future international environmental protection efforts. Stevens (1993a) argues the case for a "GATT for the environment."

15. A good review of several possible principles can be found in Feketekuty (1993). Roht-Arriaza (1992) discusses some of the principles—e.g., precaution, participation, access—that are essential for good environmental policymaking but currently missing from the GATT structure.

16. While the traditional GATT may have been more narrowly focused, the GATT and the future World Trade Organization now have substantial prescriptive aspects regarding such issues as intellectual property rights.

17. For example, the Train Commission Report (National Commission on the Environment 1993) reviews the complexity of internalizing environmental costs. Arnold (1993) shows how difficult life-cycle analysis can be.

(e.g., approaches to cleaning up toxic waste dumps). At the other end of the scale would be issues that demand compulsory international rules with clear sanctions for violators (e.g., ozone layer depletion). Such a structure would allow the GEO to grow into its job—with a mandate that expands (or contracts) as our understanding of environmental issues and analytic capacity evolves.[18]

Over time, a GEO might add to the existing body of international environmental law and develop a cohesive set of norms, rules, methodologies, and procedures for countries to follow in carrying out a shared commitment to the protection of the planet.[19] The organization would provide a forum for negotiations to address global environmental problems or transboundary pollution spillovers. And to the extent that countries might want to reduce the competitiveness pressures that create political tensions among nations and anti-environmental sentiment in the business community, a GEO could facilitate the development of baseline environmental obligations. Clearly, any work on the harmonization or convergence of environmental standards would better be done in a GEO than in the GATT.[20] The organization would also provide a single, recognized forum for settling environmental disputes with established technical competence and neutrality.

A GEO could also serve as a focal point for work to improve the scientific understanding of ecological problems, gather data on environmental trends, refine analytical tools, and develop environmental "indicators" to track the success of different policies. In addition, the organization would be in a position to facilitate the exchange of environmental information and data and to promote the transfer of pollution control technologies, particularly to developing countries. It would also help broaden the link between different international policy spheres such as trade and development as well as trade and environment (Lallas 1993). In doing so, the GEO would expand the scope for trade-offs across a wider range of issues in pursuit of global environmental protection (Susskind 1994).

---

18. Even those observers of the international environmental scene who deny the existence of or significance of global problems justifying action should be willing to consider a narrowly tailored GEO as an insurance policy, guaranteeing that there is a structure in place to handle global issues if they become more portentous.

19. Wirth (1992b) highlights the need for advancing international legal processes in support of the environment. Dunoff (1994) also analyzes the need for better international environmental legal structures and concludes that such needs can best be handled in a new international environmental institution.

20. As chapter 1 noted, the environment represents just one of a series of social issues over which there is likely to be pressure for future GATT negotiations to delineate what constitutes a legitimate basis for competitive advantage in the global marketplace and what is "unfair." The GATT is ill-suited to making such social policy judgments and should not be asked to do so.

If the environment had its own effective international body, the narrow focus of the GATT on trade principles would not seem so oppressive to environmentalists. A GEO with an appropriate mandate would counterbalance GATT's international stature and influence. It would be able to work with the GATT to establish a functional division of responsibilities where trade and environmental policies intersect, as well as rules and procedures for weighing and balancing trade and environmental goals and programs when they fell into conflict. The goal should be for environmental policy judgments to be made by the GEO and trade policy determinations by the GATT. Where an issue contains elements of both, each organization should play a role.[21]

The GATT already has provisions that require it to incorporate into its legal framework decisions made by other international organizations. Specifically, Article XXI requires the GATT to take cognizance of certain actions required by the United Nations, Article XV mandates that the GATT accept findings of the International Monetary Fund, and Articles XII–XIV provide for GATT acceptance of balance of payments safeguards undertaken by countries in coordination with the IMF.

These provisions are of considerable value to the GATT, relieving the trade regime from responsibility for assessing the legitimacy, for example, of a nation's claim of a balance of payments crisis as justification for trade-restrictive actions. Similarly, the presence of a GEO with authority to adjudicate the validity of environmental claims that result in trade-restrictive policies would be of great benefit to the GATT. Such a decision-making structure would relieve the GATT of the burden of trying to make policy judgments outside its established realm of expertise and recognized legitimacy.

Institution Building on the Regional Level

The importance of institution building in the environmental realm is increasingly being recognized. The European Union recently established an environment agency in Copenhagen to facilitate the coordination of environmental efforts and the harmonization of environmental standards among its 12 member states. The goal is to facilitate collaborative efforts in data gathering, testing, risk analysis, and other areas in support of the unified European market.

Environmental institutions tied to regional trade agreements may, in fact, offer the best mechanism for moving in the short run toward a new international environmental regime (Esty 1994a). The Commission on

---

21. Where the two institutions come to conflicting conclusions and cannot resolve a policy dispute, there would need to be a recourse to some outside arbiter. This might be a yet-to-be-established UN Economic Security Council or it could be the International Court of Justice. Postiglione (1990) reviews other options for settling international environmental disputes.

Environmental Cooperation set up under the North American Free Trade Agreement (NAFTA) environmental side agreement has many of the powers a GEO might possess (Esty 1994a). It is charged with examining cases where poor environmental performance has become a trade issue. It contributes to dispute settlement where environmental issues are at stake. And it has a mandate to try to harmonize environmental standards (upward) over time. Because the NAFTA countries are neighbors, the incentive to find cooperative solutions to environmental problems, as well as the potential for trade-related problems, is at a maximum (Johnson and Beaulieu 1994). Extending this regional model to other parts of the world, such as to the Asia-Pacific Economic Cooperation (APEC) forum would be fruitful.[22]

Carrots as Well as Sticks

Theoretically, a GEO could implement the polluter pays principle and equate the social and private marginal costs of polluting activities through a system of global pollution charges such as carbon taxes, CFC fees, and ocean dumping charges. The prospect, however, of sovereign nation-states surrendering to an international bureaucracy the responsibility for environmental regulation, including the imposition of taxes or fees, seems remote. Fortunately, as Coase (1960) has demonstrated, as long as transactions costs are minimized, the same results—optimal pollution reductions—can be obtained by paying polluters to reduce their emissions. Although this policy appears to reverse the polluter pays principle and create a ''victim pays'' scheme, which many environmentalists find distasteful, the prospect of ongoing environmental degradation and unsustainable resource use is far worse.

In fact, subsidizing the acquisition of more environmentally benign products, technologies, or production processes can, if done properly, reinforce the cost-internalization goal. Specifically, by lowering the cost of the less-polluting alternative, one raises the *relative* price of the polluting product, technology, or production process—sharpening the incentive for consumers and producers to choose the environmentally preferable course of action. For example, by subsidizing CFC substitutes purchased by refrigerator producers in developing countries, one can induce them not to use environmentally harmful CFCs as refrigerants and help to ensure that consumers will prefer the CFC-free product because it is less expensive than the CFC-based competition.

Budget limitations and competing spending priorities make it difficult for poor countries to justify devoting limited development funds to envi-

---

22. Since much of the progress in the trade realm is being made at the regional level (European Union, NAFTA, APEC, etc.), it makes considerable sense to explore regional environmental initiatives at the same time.

ronmental problems, particularly to global issues that pose distant and somewhat speculative risks in comparison with pressing public health needs. Getting developing countries to take on new environmental mandates that add to the cost of their development programs will therefore be nearly impossible unless the financial burdens of global environmental programs are subsidized. Thus, to be successful, a GEO would need a source of revenues to help meet the incremental costs it imposes on developing countries.

GEO Funding

The prospect of having to raise funds to make a GEO effective seems daunting. The environmental needs of the planet are virtually limitless. Finance ministers and other government officials around the world fear that funding of new global environmental projects could become a black hole in the budgets of governments everywhere, absorbing endless billions of dollars. But unless one discounts entirely the market failures that threaten environmental protection efforts in response to global harms, it makes sense to invest something toward putting the world economy on a sustainable growth path.[23] As economists' marginal utility analysis suggests, initial investments offer the prospect of high returns. Moreover, from a philosophical and moral perspective, almost nothing is more important than ensuring that we endow a healthy biosphere to our progeny.

From an economists' point of view, we should invest funds in environmental protection today to the extent that the benefits (including the discounted present value of future environmental resources that would otherwise be lost) exceed the costs from a global perspective. Unfortunately, funding decisions are largely made at the national level, meaning that benefits that accrue outside the nation contemplating an environmental investment do not factor into the analysis. For example, China plans to build as many as a hundred coal-fired power plants over the next decade. In determining what pollution controls, if any, will be required, China has almost no incentive to consider the global climate change effects of increased carbon dioxide emissions.

Consequently, many projects with substantial global benefits (such as efforts to improve Chinese power plant efficiency) are not funded or are not carried out so as to optimize overall (worldwide) welfare. In addition, countries assess not only whether the project will pay them a positive return in the sense that the ecological or public health benefits are greater than the costs but also whether there are alternative investments (e.g.,

---

23. Some observers (Smith 1992) believe that the welfare losses from environmental externalities are small and that government efforts to address them are likely to be counterproductive, resulting in an argument for no environmental action.

economic development projects) that will yield a higher return. Thus, even if China were to consider efficiency projects as part of its power sector development program, such investments might well not be funded in favor of road building deemed likely to contribute more to economic growth. The difficulty of calculating environmental benefits—which leads many economic decision makers to put a zero value on them—presents a further obstacle to optimal environmental funding.

Earth Summit conference director Maurice Strong estimated that the developing world's environmental needs totaled about $625 billion per year.[24] He called on the developed countries to pick up $125 billion of this tab. This figure includes both the national environmental needs of developing countries and the funds they would need to address global environmental problems. Similar estimates of global needs are found elsewhere. For example, Lester Brown (1988) calculates that the additional expenditure required to achieve sustainable development would total $149 billion over the period 1990–2000.

Perhaps the best place to start is in addressing the developing-country role in global environmental issues since it is here that the market failure that plagues environmental policymaking has its most profound spill-overs. Notably, to protect the citizens of the United States and other developed countries from the ill effects of ozone depletion, climate change, deforestation, ocean pollution, and other global problems, industrializing countries must be enabled to undertake development programs that address these global environmental problems. This argues for a fund (based on the estimates above) with approximately $15 billion to $20 billion to disburse annually. Although it could offer only limited support for developing countries to address their own national or local environmental problems, such a fund would provide a sufficient mechanism for protecting the US environment (and that of every other country) from global harms.

Other Funding Options

Global Environment Facility

The World Bank, United Nations Development Programme (UNDP), and the UN Environment Programme (UNEP) have established a fund—the Global Environment Facility (GEF)—to finance global environmental

---

24. Strong estimated that the developing countries would need $500 billion to $625 billion per year to implement Agenda 21 during 1993–2000. He observed that most of the resources would have to come from domestic sources but suggested that $125 billion in foreign assistance would also be needed. Of this total, only $15 billion to $25 billion would be required for global issues such as climate change, the balance would go to domestic environmental problems such as providing drinking water (Petesch 1992).

projects (El-Ashry 1993). Launched with $1.2 billion for an initial three-year period running through 1993 and made permanent with a four-year, $2 billion commitment of funds in March 1994, the GEF supports projects in four areas: climate change, biological diversity, pollution of international waters, and stratospheric ozone depletion. The largest donors to the GEF, which depends on voluntary contributions, have been France and Germany. Italy, Britain, the Netherlands, Austria, Switzerland, and the Scandinavian countries have also made significant contributions to the GEF's "core fund." The United States declined to contribute directly to the GEF in its pilot phase but offered $150 million through the US Agency for International Development to "parallel finance" projects consistent with GEF objectives.[25] The Clinton administration has, however, committed to a contribution of just over $400 million for 1994–98.

The GEF aims to address the public goods nature of global environmental problems and the market failure that hampers efforts to respond to them. It specifically tries to fund the incremental costs of environmental projects where "domestic costs are greater than domestic benefits, but global benefits are greater than domestic costs" (World Bank 1993a). The GEF has also been designated as the interim financing mechanism for the international environmental conventions on climate change and biological diversity.[26]

The GEF has helped to frame the critical questions that must be answered if funding for global environmental efforts is to be managed in a rational manner. The GEF suffers, however, from serious limitations. Notably, the fund is far too small to reverse negative cost-benefit analyses (from a national perspective) and ensure that projects go ahead in every case where global benefits exceed costs. Given the budget deficits of major donor countries including the United States and the recent worldwide economic slowdown, there appears to be little prospect of substantially expanding the GEF anytime soon. Replenished in 1994, the GEF now has just over $2 billion to disburse in the four-year period from 1994–98. In addition, some of the GEF's early projects were not well vetted and seemed to reflect funding proposals that had previously been rejected by the main World Bank review process.

---

25. As part of its effort to move the 1992 Climate Change Convention negotiations to conclusion, the Bush administration committed $50 million to the GEF "core fund" for 1993. The Congress trimmed the contribution to $30 million and conditioned the funding on the GEF being restructured. Because some of the congressional conditions were not met, no US funds were ever provided.

26. For more details on the scope, legal framework, decision-making procedures, membership, and governance of the GEF, see Esty and Koehler (1993). For a critique of the GEF pilot phase, see Bowles and Prickett (1994).

Filling the Green Gap

Although many developing-country officials and some developed-country observers argue that the industrialized world should accept its historic (some would say moral) responsibility for global environmental problems and adequately fund the GEF, it would be unwise to wait for such voluntary financial contributions. All nations, moreover, have prospective, if not retrospective, responsibility for addressing environmental problems and maintaining the habitability of the Earth. A global Green Fund should therefore be created. The primary purpose of the fund should be the protection of the global environment from ecological harms emanating from developing countries.[27]

Ideally, monies would be raised by fees imposed on activities with negative worldwide environmental effects.[28] But given the complexity of calculating what these fees should be and the administrative difficulty of collecting them, it may be easier to support the Green Fund with a small tax (perhaps 1/100th of a percent) on global trade and capital flows.[29] Imposing the fee worldwide on all international economic activities would be progressive since the developed world is responsible for a disproportionate share of global trade and financial activity. Moreover, a green tax would be neutral in its effect among countries and, at the small scale proposed, virtually unrecognizable from a business point of view. To the extent there were any effect on capital flows, which total more than $800 billion per day, the fee would provide a disincentive (however small) to currency speculators and arbitrageurs.

The obvious response to this suggestion is that it opens up a Pandora's box. If we have a Green Fund, why not an education fund, a health fund, and a drug enforcement fund? Although the lines are not entirely clear, a distinction can be drawn. Specifically, none of these other activities is as directly linked to economic activity as the environ-

---

27. The fund should be sold in the industrialized world as the most cost-effective way for developed countries to protect their domestic environments from global environmental harms. Of course, given the indivisible nature of global environmental problems such as climate change, the developing countries would also benefit.

28. Poterba (1991) offers a thoughtful discussion of how to tax greenhouse gas emissions. See Stavins (1988) for a discussion of Project 88, an important survey of ways to use market forces to internalize environmental harms. Nordhaus (1992) and Oates and Portney (1992) have also examined global environmental externalities. Repetto et al. (1993) survey a wide variety of possible "green fees."

29. The idea of such a transactions tax has already been pushed by Yale economist and Nobel laureate James Tobin (*Financial Times,* 22 December 1992) for the purpose of creating a disincentive to currency speculators. In his 26 January 1994 farewell address at the GATT, long-time EC GATT Ambassador Tran Van Thinh called for a Solidarity Fund for the global environment financed by a 0.25 percent levy on all imports except those of the least-developed countries.

ment is, and none suffers from the potential market failure problems that the environment does.

Such a fund would generate approximately $10 billion to $20 billion per year,[30] which could make a significant contribution to protecting the planet. It also presents serious management challenges. Tight fiscal and policy controls would be important to the fund's credibility. Concessional lending or grants should be limited to subsidizing the incremental costs of projects with global environmental benefits. Although defining "incremental costs" has proved to be difficult in the context of the Global Environment Facility, it is analytically the appropriate formula for addressing global problems and a necessary element of financial restraint. To address "local" environmental needs and to win developing-country support, a separate revolving fund with monies available at market interest rates should be established. This fund would finance projects that return *national* environmental benefits but that otherwise might not be undertaken due to capital limitations and competing priorities.

Not Another International Organization!

The proposal for a Global Environmental Organization is certain to elicit groans from many quarters. At the very least, the list of legitimate queries will be long. Why add another ineffective organization to the already troubled UN bureaucracy? What's wrong with existing international environmental organizations? Can't the UN Environment Programme (UNEP) or the UN Commission on Sustainable Development (CSD) play the global coordinating role? Shouldn't environmental decisions be made at the national or even the local level? What rules could a GEO agree upon and enforce? Wouldn't UN-style, one-country, one-vote decision principles lead to worse rather than better environmental policies? Could the GEO be set up, like the World Bank, somewhat outside the ambit of the UN? Isn't it unrealistic to expect nations to surrender sovereignty over their natural resources and environmental policy to a GEO? Can a GEO function without leadership from a strong nation? Is the United States willing to lead? Is anyone else?

Separately, one can question whether the analogy to the GATT is apt. Doesn't the fact that the GEO must prescribe behavior, not simply proscribe government actions, render the GATT comparison meaningless?

---

30. The baseline data used to generate these figures are drawn from the International Monetary Fund's 1993 *Balance of Payments Statistics Yearbook*. Recognizing that the proposed tax would have very little effect on trade flows but a more substantial impact on currency movements, some adjustment has been made for a reduction of the tax base after the fees begin to be imposed. The level of the global green tax could be adjusted up or down over time as the level of ongoing needs is clarified. Obviously, there will be significant administrative issues that will need to be resolved to make such a tax feasible, particularly on capital flows.

Moreover, the GATT exploits exporter interests to overcome the domestic political clout of those who might seek protection from import competition. What comparable interplay of interests will allow the GEO to transform the domestic political landscape vis-à-vis environmental policy-making? Isn't the success of the GATT due to the fact that trade is inherently international while most environmental issues are actually local?

These questions raise serious issues. The prospect of another low-productivity international organization providing sinecures for do-nothing global bureaucrats is both unattractive and unacceptable. Moreover, the powers of skepticism and inertia are great. But the starting point for a serious analysis of a prospective GEO must be a reiteration of the fact that the international environmental status quo is not working. The environmental "indicators" cited in chapter 1 concerning the potentially serious effects of unsustainable economic activity must alone give pause for thought. As the trends continue, the impacts are likely to become ever more visible.

There is nevertheless understandable skepticism about adding another international organization at a time when there already exist so many dysfunctional UN bodies. But it is illogical to argue that because there are so many organizations that do not work, we should stick with them and not add another one. Rather, we should dismantle the ones that are not performing or do not reflect current international policy demands. Many of the multilateral organizations that populate Geneva, New York, and other international centers have outlived or outgrown their mandates (Roberts and Kingsbury 1993; Williams and Petesch 1993). At the same time, the need for a broad and coordinated management structure for international environmental issues has only recently emerged with the recognition that some of today's ecological problems are inherently global in scope and must therefore be addressed on a multilateral basis.

To respond to the concern about the multiplicity of international organizations, it might be useful to eliminate or consolidate three or four existing groups at the time the GEO is established (National Commission on the Environment 1993, 65).[31] It would also be a step in the right direction if the GEO were to be set up with a "sunset" clause, putting the organization out of business in 20 years unless it were then deemed

---

31. Every observer of the international organization scene will have his own list of existing bodies ripe for consolidation, redirection, or elimination. At the creation of the GEO, it might make sense to eliminate or fold into the new organization the following UN bodies: the UN Environment Programme (UNEP), the UN Development Programme (UNDP), the UN Industrial Development Organization (UNIDO), the UN Conference on Trade and Development (UNCTAD), the World Meteorological Organization (WMO), the UN Institute for Training and Research (UNITAR), and the Commission on Sustainable Development (CSD).

to be serving a useful purpose and the world community affirmatively voted to extend its mandate.

Unlike the GATT, the GEO would have to be created against the backdrop of existing UN organizations with environmental mandates, particularly UNEP and the CSD. These organizations are not, however, fulfilling today's international environmental needs. UNEP has far too narrow a mandate to coordinate the critical global issues that require unified management. Its budget is small, and its staffing is inadequate. Despite the valuable political signal sent by having the organization in a developing country, there is growing sentiment that UNEP's ability to succeed is compromised by its location in Nairobi, where communications too often break down, political instability disrupts work, and crime and other quality-of-life issues make it hard to attract and retain a first-rate staff. Thus, the option of operating within the current institutional structure and strengthening UNEP is probably a nonstarter.

The institutional legacy of the Earth Summit—the UN Commission on Sustainable Development—has an attractive dual mandate to promote both environmental protection and economic growth. But the CSD has even more limited authority than UNEP, suffers from a lack of political and financial support, and is further hobbled by its unwieldy charge to follow up on Agenda 21, the 700-page Earth Summit compendium of environmental concerns and needs. Since Agenda 21 covers every imaginable environmental issue without differentiating priorities and often reflecting contrary points of view, this mission is a bit like being told to follow up on the Bible. In addition to weak political support and lack of focus, the CSD suffers from the belief in many developed countries that it has been "captured" by developing countries and as a result will not act with the economic and analytic seriousness requisite for a major role on the world scene.

Despite the manifest inadequacy of the existing, utterly decentralized institutional structure, some critics of a GEO still argue for issue-by-issue management of global environmental problems, with individual international agreements and separate secretariats for each. Many "old school" environmentalists are attracted to this model as well, since it mirrors the local decision-making tradition embedded in the philosophy of America's grass-roots environmentalism. But to slaughter a sacred environmental cow, decentralized issue-by-issue decision making is not always the right answer. As Carol Browner, administrator of the US Environmental Protection Agency, recently told a business audience (speech to Chamber of Commerce, Washington, 19 November 1993): "The old piecemeal approach . . . doesn't work for me as a regulator, and it doesn't work for you." And long-time environmental policy observer Terry Davies (1994) notes: "As the deficiencies of the current environmental laws become ever more obvious, the chances for a new integrated approach steadily improve. Such an approach is urgently needed."

There are a number of reasons to avoid reliance on ad hoc environmental policymaking. Notably, a central aspect of today's understanding of environmental issues is the connectedness of problems. Deforestation is of concern not only because of the loss of trees as a "sink" for carbon dioxide but also because forests are essential for species preservation and biodiversity. CFCs are a problem not only because they deplete the ozone layer but also because they are a greenhouse gas and cause global warming. Without a comprehensive approach to environmental problem solving, opportunities for efficiency and synergies across issues will be lost.

Efforts to protect the environment are always plagued, moreover, by competing issues and limited resources. The result is often haphazard decision making without any clear sense of priorities or understanding of which issues pose the greatest risks and deserve attention first. Ad hoc international environmental policies that promote separate conventions for every issue exacerbate this policy confusion. With a single, coordinated international environmental regime, risks across problems could be compared, budgets could be rationalized, and priorities intelligently set.

There is, in addition, growing evidence that the patchwork of US national environmental laws is a source of many shortcomings in US environmental protection.[32] The result is overlapping issue coverage, regulatory gaps, limited ability to set priorities, inconsistent treatment of risks, reliance on conflicting and noncomparable data bases, a failure to update policies comprehensively as scientific knowledge advances, redundant activities, and inefficient spending of scarce environmental resources. To quote the report of the Train Commission (National Commission on the Environment 1993, xxvi), a blue-ribbon panel set up to reexamine America's environmental agenda: "Efforts to halt pollution should become more integrated and holistic." Similarly, replicating internationally the US issue-by-issue approach to environmental regulation is an invitation to long-term policy failure. Again, as the Train Commission suggests (1993, 65): "The proliferation of complex international agreements on the environment and resources will lead to a crazy-quilt of laws and policies. . . ." The overlaps and disconnects evident in the international efforts on the related topics of climate change, ozone layer depletion, deforestation, and funding through the Global Environment Facility make clear that this problem already exists.

Some objections to a GEO reflect general hostility to all international organizations as forerunners of a world government and as potential threats to American sovereignty. Such calls have an attractive political ring, appealing as they do to individuals' sense of national identity.

---

32. One of the earliest articulations of the problems with ad hoc environmental policymaking is Davies (1970). For more recent developments of this theme, see Irwin (1992) and Haigh and Irwin (1990). The United Kingdom has recently moved to an integrated approach to environmental regulation with some early signs of success.

While chauvinism and xenophobia make for good politics, these attitudes do not produce good policy outcomes. But many politicians cannot resist an opportunity to play to the public's fears. For example, Newt Gingrich, minority whip of the US House of Representatives, raised the sovereignty argument in opposing the new World Trade Organization (*Inside US Trade*, 6 May 1994, 19), decrying the specter of a "Third-World dictatorship-dominated" international organization. As Joe Cobb of the Heritage Foundation notes (1994), such concerns are unfounded. He cogently argues: "The World Trade Organization will expand the sovereignty of American citizens by reducing the power of interest groups to manipulate trade policy."

Strictly speaking, sovereignty is simply a question of who has the liberty to do what and who has the authority to set rules. Governments must always regulate liberty—ensuring that individual freedoms are neither trampled by majoritarian rule nor exploited at the expense of others.[33] Indeed, one person's unfettered freedom may result in severe restrictions on the choices available to others. For example, a smoker who insists on lighting up in a crowded room has exercised sovereignty at the expense of many others who lose the freedom to breathe fresh air. Similarly, pure majority rule can result in "sovereignty" that crushes the freedom of individuals or minority groups within the voting jurisdiction—and perhaps even deprives a majority of some subset or larger set of voters of its ability to make sovereign choices.

National sovereignty, furthermore, is by no means inherently good. In the environmental realm, there is no guarantee that optimal pollution control programs will be achieved by decision making at the nation-state level. As noted above, it is quite clear that some environmental policy decisions are best made at the local level; others require broader perspectives and are thus best made at the national or international levels. Just as the smoker's "sovereignty" threatens others in the same room, unbounded national sovereignty would be devastating to worldwide efforts to address global environmental problems. Such sovereignty would, for example, free countries to ignore the CFC controls of the Montreal Protocol, destroying the ozone layer for everyone. Thus, in dealing with global environmental problems, it is only by surrendering a bit of national sovereignty and by participating in an international regime that we can ensure our freedom from environmental harms and protection of our own natural resources.[34]

---

33. Isaiah Berlin's (1969) path-breaking essay explaining the difference between "freedom to" act and "freedom from" interference helps make such concepts clear.

34. Indeed, the relative success of the Bretton Woods institutions—the World Bank, International Monetary Fund, and the GATT—in managing global economic affairs and in helping to discourage self-serving and internationally harmful national behavior demonstrates the value of a multilateral regime.

Calls to blindly protect national sovereignty are therefore a red herring. While the public often feels a strong sense of national identity, allegiance to a particular flag does not necessarily translate into an iron-clad principle about the optimal governmental level at which to set environmental policy. To the contrary, one can be a loyal American (or a loyal citizen of any other nation) and still want effective environmental protection, which may at times require decisions made by authorities at other than the national level.

Ultimately, while shared values sometimes make the national level the most appropriate for environmental policymaking, ecological problems rarely correspond to political boundaries. There is therefore no intrinsic basis for assuming that environmental policymaking should take place at the national level. Instead, it is important to have an array of policy-making structures and to tailor environmental decision making to the particular issue at hand. A GEO would help to ensure that, where appropriate, international decision-making mechanisms would be available and that global environmental programs would be as scientifically sound, economically efficient, and environmentally effective as possible. In some cases, no other basis for action will do. Thus, as economists have long bemoaned John Maynard Keynes's unfortunate remark that "in the long run, we are all dead," forward-looking environmentalists express equal distress at the narrow vision of the oft-quoted slogan: "Think globally; act locally."[35]

There is a more serious question about how democratic international institutions are and thus how decisions might be made in a new GEO. The GATT, for instance, has been severely criticized for its closed decision-making processes. More pointedly, legitimate questions are often raised about ceding political judgments to international bureaucrats who are not readily answerable to elected officials.

There are several ways to address this issue in the context of a new GEO. First, it is important to recognize that all international organizations are run by their member governments, not by their secretariats. Given this reality, it is critical that decision making in the new body be made transparent to increase governments' confidence that the interests of the general publics they represent are being served. All reports and analyses should be public documents. Most meetings should be open to the public. Nongovernment organizations should be provided access to decision makers and should be able to submit views on any matter under discussion. Second, there should be more regular reporting on work and accountability to national elected officials, who in turn should be held responsible for seeking the removal of interna-

---

35. To be fair, René Dubos, to whom the slogan is often attributed, had a very far reaching view of the world and its environmental problems. Indeed, another of his famous maxims was "trend is not destiny" (Dubos 1981).

tional officials who are not performing adequately. Finally, oversight hearings on GEO staff performance would be useful, perhaps conducted by GLOBE, the international group of legislators interested in environmental issues.

A second question relating to democracy is the form of voting to be used in the GEO. Existing UN bodies suffer serious credibility problems because one-country, one-vote procedures do not reflect the realities of power on the international scene.[36] One of the strengths of the GATT is its consensus decision making without formal votes but with an unspoken recognition that the views of the biggest trading nations will be given particular weight and that objections by small nations will not hold up progress. In this regard, too, the GATT may provide a useful model for the GEO.

There are, of course, limits to the GATT analogy. The decision rules the GATT applies, such as nondiscrimination, are relatively straightforward. How the GEO would assess, for example, whether environmental costs were fully internalized presents a much greater challenge. In important respects, as noted earlier in this volume, defining the boundaries of environmental externalities is inescapably a political problem and one ill-suited to multilateral decision making by ''nonpolitical'' officials. For the GEO to work, norms would need to be set through negotiation by governments. These international commitments would then be translated into decision rules, reducing to a minimum the need for political judgments by GEO officials. Indeed, the more clear the rules, the smaller the scope for interpretation—and thus for dispute. In fact, one of the critical reasons for moving the trade and environment debate forward is to narrow the enormous existing uncertainty over how trade versus environmental policy clashes will be handled.[37]

The GEO could also serve as a forum for governments to meet and to make common political judgments about appropriate environmental standards. With regard to this goal, the International Labor Organization (ILO) may be a more apt model than the GATT.[38] In fact, the ILO's tripartite structure, drawing on business, labor, and government repre-

---

36. Past environmental negotiations have at times suffered from this disconnect from the realities of power. The Law of the Sea Treaty, which has elements that the United States refuses to accept, offers an example of this sort of breakdown (*New York Times*, 29 March 1994, C1).

37. At the very least, behavioral rules and procedural guidelines to facilitate nation-to-nation environmental cooperation could be developed and applied. While such a role may seem relatively unimportant, it is not. In helping to ensure the legitimacy of environmental policy processes, particularly as they relate to the use of trade measures, a GEO would serve to protect the interests of small countries, as do GATT rules in the trade context.

38. Steve Charnovitz (1993c) has called for an International Environmental Organization modeled on the International Labor Organization and focused on establishing environment and trade rules.

sentatives, might be followed in the GEO with structured roles for business, environmental groups, and governments.

If competitiveness concerns continue to increase in political intensity, the standard-setting function of the GEO may emerge as critical. Moreover, as environmental regulations become more sophisticated, pressures to coordinate regulatory approaches to ease market access restrictions will become stronger. Such efforts need not mean harmonization of standards themselves. For example, considerable benefit would be obtained by coordinating chemical testing methodologies and protocols—allowing mutual recognition of environmental safety data. Not only would such international data exchange facilitate regulatory approvals, it would ease the administrative burden on environmental officials, thus freeing up resources for other activities and reducing the chances that an unsafe product could get to market.

As noted earlier, competitiveness concerns dramatically broaden the scope of the trade and environment conflict, giving even local environmental problems international implications. In fact, some critics of a GEO suggest that few environmental issues have physical spillover effects that extend internationally, and thus that a new international environmental regime is unnecessary. But this discounts the significance of the different approaches to local environmental problems. First, there are a nontrivial number of global and transboundary problems already recognized. More importantly, as our scientific understanding advances, new pollution spillovers are constantly being uncovered. Second, most countries (if not the United States) live in proximity to their neighbors; thus local environmental problems often have transboundary effects. Third, wide divergences in pollution control requirements, even if limited to domestic problems, create political pressures for unilateral action to "level the playing field" and thus argue for creation of an international forum to set baseline standards (as chapter 7 explains in more detail).

In constructing a functioning GEO, lessons might also be drawn from the experience of the World Intellectual Property Organization (WIPO), set up in 1967 to respond to the thicket of intersecting patent and trademark agreements and other bilateral and multilateral intellectual property accords and "unions" that had grown up around the world. WIPO helped to rationalize the global protection of intellectual property and to unsnarl the "treaty congestion" that had plagued this realm.

Clearly, the GATT is not a complete or sufficient institutional model for a GEO. But in one critical respect, the GATT analogy is important: the elevation of long-term values above the pressures of special interest domestic politics. Just as the GATT, to use Petersmann's term (1991a), "constitutionalizes" the commitment to freer trade, a successful GEO would establish and protect the principle of environmental cost internalization and other environmental norms. Specifically, the new organization would provide a mechanism for identifying appropriate long-term environmental policy goals abstracted from the distortions and short-run focus of interest-group politics.[39]

Just as the GATT is an imperfect defender of trade liberalization and governments often falter in their commitment to open markets, the GEO could not guarantee the internalization of all environmental externalities. But it would provide a systematic reminder of the goal. Even if governments chose to ignore GEO decisions, there would be a certain shaming effect on those whose blatant disregard for appropriate environmental policymaking attracted GEO scrutiny.

Perhaps most importantly, a GEO, like the GATT, would support government-to-government cooperation. Since governments acting collectively often can do more to address a problem than any government can do alone, a GEO would facilitate proper long-term treatment of environmental issues. Obviously, such an organization could not be established overnight. Nor should it emerge, as Athena did, full blown from the head of Zeus. Building a functioning international environmental regime would require establishing norms, extracting rules from these norms, refining dispute settlement mechanisms, and other activities that will take years, or even decades, to develop. This study's proposal to establish a GEO must be seen in this extended time context.[40]

Whether even the first steps toward a GEO can be taken without strong leadership from the United States is a serious question. The answer is, probably not. Even in the unipolar world we now live in, the United States does not always get its way. It remains difficult, however, to advance major initiatives affecting the world order without US support. The failure of the Earth Summit to address institutional issues despite the interest of many countries in updating the mechanisms of international governance relating to the environment reflected the difficulty of moving forward without the United States.[41] Since the summit,

---

39. Some may argue that to shield certain values from day-to-day politics is antidemocratic. But this is the case only to the extent the US Constitution, defending fundamental rights against majoritarian political whims, is antidemocratic. Rawls (1971) makes clear the benefits of establishing overarching policy principles outside issue-specific politics.

40. Richard Cooper's (1985) analysis of the time (nearly 70 years) it took to mobilize an effective worldwide response to contagious diseases such as cholera and smallpox demonstrates both the difficulty of coordinating action internationally—and, at the same time, the importance of doing so in the context of problems that are inherently global in scope.

41. White House Chief of Staff John Sununu, whose environmental antipathies were well known, made it very clear to the Earth Summit organizers from the start of their endeavors that the United States was unwilling to consider any new international environmental institutions. Thus, although the June 1992 Rio conference brought worldwide attention to environmental issues and highlighted the importance of sustainable development, little effort was made to update the management of international environmental affairs.

the United States elected an administration with a decidedly more environmental cast. Doubt nevertheless remains about the interest of the United States in exercising bold international leadership on environmental matters.

Even with US backing, creation of a GEO will not occur without support across the spectrum of OECD countries and among developing nations as well. Ideally, momentum for a GEO would arise from outside the United States to ensure that many nations can buy into the idea as their own—and not simply as something forced upon them by the United States.

A Reality Check

Despite the many advantages of a global environmental regime, the prospects for the creation of a new international environmental entity with a comprehensive and coherent mandate in the near future are dim. Lacking a major trauma to the international system to highlight the need for a new institutional structure (as World War II provided the impetus for the GATT regime) and having missed the opportunity for change offered by the 1992 Earth Summit,[42] there appears to be little momentum for a Global Environmental Organization.[43] Unfortunately, this guarantees ongoing confusion and incoherence in the management of international environmental affairs and further degradation of potentially critical elements of the Earth's ecosystem. It also means greater pressure on the GATT to inculcate environmental values and to establish structures that will permit the trade regime to reconcile internally competing trade and environmental policies. Political reality therefore dictates a careful inquiry into ways to modify the existing trade rules and legal structures to achieve these goals.

---

42. As noted earlier, the United States blocked any consideration of institutional reform at Rio in 1992. The multiple-year preparatory process in advance of the Earth Summit and the enormous amount of work that went into developing the products of UNCED, the Rio Declaration, and Agenda 21 have exhausted environmental policymakers around the world. It would, therefore, require US leadership to reignite international enthusiasm for a new environmental reform initiative.

43. Although he did not endorse a GEO specifically, in his NAFTA signing speech (8 December 1993) President Clinton promised to seek "new institutional arrangements" to protect the worldwide environment in the context of expanded trade.

5

New Rules for Trade and Environment Disputes

Because an international commitment to internalizing environmental costs and a Global Environmental Organization to enforce it appears not to be imminent, the conflict between environmental goals and trade liberalization principles must be settled within existing institutions, particularly the international trading system. Some free traders fear that building environmental safeguards into the international trade regime will derail the General Agreement on Tariffs and Trade's focus on trade liberalization. But as trade expert Gary Hufbauer (1989, 73) notes, "Trade policy has never been pursued with single-minded attention to economic gain." Other goals—such as national security—have always played a role in the structure of the trade regime. As new issues emerge, the trading system should be refined to accommodate them as well.

Environmentalists have developed long lists of amendments to the GATT they would like to see adopted (e.g., Patterson 1992; Arden-Clarke 1993a; Lallas, Esty, and Van Hoogstraten 1992; Prudencio and Hudson 1994). In parallel, free traders have honed their arguments in response to these suggestions and have added some counterclaims (e.g., Bhagwati 1993c; Sorsa 1992; GATT 1992a).

Indeed, taxonomies of trade and environment problems abound (Dean 1992; Fletcher and Tiemann 1992; Sistema Económica Latinamericano 1992; Vander Stichele 1992; Pearson and Repetto 1993; Feketekuty 1993; Charnovitz 1994c). The standard menu of concerns usually includes GATT Article XX reform, import prohibitions, export restraints, product standards, restrictions on production processes and methods, taxes and subsidies, unilateral and extraterritorial actions, and the use of trade penalties to enforce international environmental agreements.

Unfortunately, analysis of these issues often leads into a convoluted debate over abstruse GATT concepts, dispute panel precedents, and trade terms of art. Rather than sorting out the trade and environment problems along lines of analysis that reflect this traditional thinking and follow GATT's legal structure, this chapter and the next two track the environmental propositions laid out in chapter 2 and propose a new set of rules to guide the use of environmental policies with trade effects.

The starting point for this effort is the environmentalists' fear that the current set of trade rules and the processes of trade liberalization will be used to override legitimate environmental regulations (Daly 1993). This chapter also attempts to address the countervailing concerns of free traders that illegitimate ''environmental'' standards might become a serious obstacle to freer trade. Specifically, it spells out a new balancing test to weigh competing trade and environmental values.

The analysis here begins with an assumption that a broad-scale shift of environmental regulation to market-based mechanisms, which would minimize the conflict with trade policies, is not immediately forthcoming. It also builds on the recognition (explained in chapter 2) that environmental values are not scientifically reducible to a single standard and thus political judgments will always be required. Consequently, there is no strict algorithm or set of absolute decision rules that can yield clear answers every time trade and environmental interests appear to be at loggerheads. Fact-specific, case-by-case analysis will be required, and judgment calls will be needed to settle conflicts.[1]

The proposals laid out here also proceed from a belief that by clarifying trade rules and building greater attentiveness to environmental considerations into the GATT, the breadth and depth of trade-environment clashes can be reduced. Thus, the central goal of this chapter is to establish a new, more balanced basis for weighing competing commercial and environmental principles when such disputes are taken to the GATT.

Does Trade Liberalization Threaten Environmental Regulation?

Many environmentalists worry that the structure of trade rules and trade liberalization make it more difficult to stop ecological harm and

---

1. Where no other decision criteria are specified, a ''rule of reason'' should be applied, asking what a reasonable, environmentally well-informed, economic growth–supporting person with special sensitivity to the world her great-grandchildren will live in would do. Of course, even this traditional concept in Anglo-American law (and embodied in the European Court of Justice's jurisprudence [see the *Belgian Waste* case in appendix C]) glides over a critical question in the global context: where does this putative reasonable person live? After all, what seems reasonable to a North American or European may not be at all reasonable to an Asian or an African. Nevertheless, some ''default'' decision criterion is required, and none better than the ''rule of reason'' exists.

reduce pollution-based health risks (Zaelke, Housman, and Stanley 1993). They particularly fear that market access agreements and rules to enforce them (i.e., negotiated restrictions on the scope and effect of national regulations, called "disciplines" in trade parlance) will effectively force harmonization of environmental standards at the lowest common denominator or at average levels. Environmentalists therefore demand that trade rules not inhibit countries from setting their own environmental requirements above established norms, and they want to ensure that countries that use trade restrictions to protect their own markets from environmentally substandard imports are not exposed to GATT scrutiny and countermand. In fact, many environmentalists believe that international trade rules and dispute settlement procedures should give great deference—some ecoadvocates would say total deference (Charnovitz 1993a)—to highly protective environmental policies.

Free traders worry about the flip-side of the environmentalists' concerns. They want to protect international commerce and the economic benefits it provides from ill-considered environmental policy intrusions. Specifically, the trade community worries, first, that protectionists will use contrived environmental standards to disguise barriers to trade and, second, that poorly crafted environmental programs with minimal ecological or public health benefits will impose unjustifiable burdens on the free flow of commerce (Bhagwati 1993a).

France's imported fish "inspections" designed to assist French fishermen (discussed in chapter 2) offer an egregious example of covert protectionism in the form of a food safety program. The European Community's decision to bar the sale of beef from cattle injected with growth hormones, benefiting European beef producers to the detriment of US exporters, may be another example.[2]

Even if domestic regulations are not intentionally crafted as hidden trade barriers, they may impede the free flow of commerce. If the burdens imposed significantly outweigh any environmental benefits, some doubt must be cast on the appropriateness of the regulatory program. The US Environmental Protection Agency's decision to ban all uses of asbestos despite the fact that the material has never been shown to present any health hazard in some applications would be an example of a legitimate environmental goal (protecting the public from cancer due to asbestos exposure) pursued by an inappropriate means (an overly broad ban).[3]

---

2. The decision was made despite the fact that there was no scientific evidence of risk to public health from the presence of the hormones at the levels detected in the US beef. Indeed, European beef accepted for sale had, and continues to have, comparable naturally occurring hormones.

3. In fact, the EPA asbestos ban was overturned as inappropriate in a court challenge brought by importers of Canadian asbestos (*Corrosion Proof Fittings v. EPA*, 947 F. 2nd 1201 [1991]).

Germany's "packaging" initiative, requiring merchants to take back from their customers all boxes, wrappers, and containers in which their products are sold, may be a second example (Brisson 1993; Fishbein 1994). Designed to reduce solid waste disposal problems, the German law mandates that packaging materials be recycled or reused in certain fixed percentages. These requirements create, in many cases, a much heavier burden on importers, who have a more difficult time arranging for reuse of their packaging waste and much longer distances to back-haul their packaging materials, than on domestic producers. For instance, Kenyan flower producers have been driven out of the German market because it is not economical to fly empty flower crates back to Africa, and incinerating the boxes in Germany (which can be done in modern facilities with almost no environmental impact) is not allowed. It is not unreasonable to ask whether, for very modest (perhaps nonexistent) environmental benefits, Germany should be permitted to destroy an important export market for Kenya (box 5.1).

While environmentalists see the GATT as narrow and rigid, trade experts argue that the agreement is relatively unobtrusive and flexible. The truth is that almost all environmental regulation is in fact GATT-consistent. As Schoenbaum (1992) notes:

> Contrary to the alarmist claims of some environmentalists, there is no inherent conflict between international free trade as it has evolved under the aegis of the GATT and protection of environmental quality. The GATT recognizes and contains policy instruments that can be used to protect domestic and global natural resources; the GATT and environmental protection are largely compatible.

Many others echo this point (Eglin 1993c; Charnovitz 1992b; Jackson 1992a), arguing that GATT rules actually permit broad latitude in pursuing environmental goals and proscribe only policies that are unjustifiably discriminatory or a guise for protectionism.

The GATT does provide broad leeway for countries to pursue *domestic* environmental regulation. As long as the nondiscrimination strictures of GATT Articles I and III are met, governments can impose pollution taxes, enact deposit-refund requirements, set ceilings on emissions, and even bar the production or sale of certain goods. Indeed, in the 45 years of GATT's existence, nations have promulgated tens of thousands of environmental regulations affecting domestic production and the consumption of products, whether domestic or imported.[4] Only a handful of these environmental rules have been found to be discriminatory and judged to be inconsistent with the GATT.

---

4. For an extensive survey of environmental product standards in Western Europe, the United States, and Japan, see Bennett and Verhoeve (1994).

Box 5.1 Sanctions, swords, and shields

In analyzing environmental trade measures, it is helpful to distinguish among different kinds of actions. One important distinction is between measures used on offense—called in this study "sanctions" or "swords"—and those used defensively, called "shields" here. Offensive measures are employed by one country to address environmental harms outside its territory. Such measures target foreign environmental practices or standards that are considered to be too lax. A ban on Mexican tuna imports—aimed at Mexican fishing practices in Mexican or international waters—offers an example of a trade measure used as a sword.

Defensive measures are employed by a country to address the threat of environmental harm within its own borders. In general, defensive trade measures simply require that imported products meet the same environmental standards as domestic products. Indeed, when employed legitimately, such measures are usually not designed with trade in mind, and any trade impacts are an incidental element of domestic environmental regulations or standards. These measures only become an issue when they are perceived by foreign producers to be unfairly disruptive to trade. For example, the EU decision to bar the sale of all beef containing injected growth hormones—despite the lack of any evidence that the hormones used properly presented a health hazard—raised questions because it effectively barred large quantities of US beef from the European market. In contrast, pesticide safety standards—banning the sale of untested products, whether domestic or imported—are generally accepted as legitimate and non-controversial defensive measures.

Of course, one could consider actions to protect the global commons to be defensive. Indeed, as this book explains, whether considered to be defensive or offensive (based on the physical location of the harm), trade measures invoked to protect the global commons may well be justified.

The difference between trade restrictions and trade sanctions in the environmental context also deserves attention (Anderson and Blackhurst 1992b). As used in this study, trade restrictions are conditions imposed on goods in trade based on some element of environmental concern related either to the good or its production process. A requirement for pollution control devices in cars is an example of a restriction related to a good; a ban on tuna from a country that kills dolphins during fishing is a restriction on a process. Trade restrictions may be used as a "sword" to make other countries raise their environmental standards or as a "shield" to protect a country's own environmental protection programs.

Trade sanctions are limitations imposed on goods in trade unrelated to the product's own environmental characteristics but intended to force compliance with environmental policies that the imposing country deems important. In targeting "innocent" products (e.g., no pearl imports will be permitted from Japan because of its whaling), the imposition of sanctions is purely an exercise of power and leverage, which may or may not be used to a worthy end.

Thus, the GATT Secretariat (1992c) argues:

> GATT rules . . . place essentially no constraints on a country's right to protect its own environment against damage from either domestic production or the consumption of domestically produced or imported products. Generally speaking, a country can do anything to imports or exports that it does to its own products, and it can do anything it considers necessary to its own production processes.

As one GATT staff member (Eglin 1993a, 10) adds: "Nondiscrimination is the principal GATT requirement in every case, and it is hard to accept that environmental policymaking needs trade discrimination to be effective."

Even if a country's environmental program has a discriminatory effect, it may still be GATT-consistent. Specifically, it can be justified by reference to the exceptions permitted under GATT Article XX, discussed in chapter 2, which provides for the adoption of GATT-inconsistent measures, including environmental regulations, "necessary to protect human, animal, or plant life or health" or "relating to the conservation of exhaustible natural resources if such measures are made effective in conjunction with restrictions on domestic production or consumption." GATT rules therefore grant considerable scope to countries to pursue their own environmental programs as they see fit, even if their environmental policies have trade effects.

But environmentalists remain unconvinced about the GATT's support for environmental regulations. In fact, the current sweeping interpretation of the GATT Article I and III disciplines and the concomitant narrow view of the GATT Article XX exceptions for the environment are seen as unworkable by many environmentalists (e.g., Shrybman 1993; Housman and Zaelke 1992a; Arden-Clarke 1992b). As noted in chapter 2, there are a number of weaknesses in the current structure of GATT rules. Specifically, in the face of a challenge, the GATT imposes the burden of proof on the country with environmental regulations that affect trade, forcing the party with the environmental interest at stake to defend its policy as an Article XX "exception" to the GATT. In addition, Article XX has been narrowly interpreted. Parties must show that no less GATT-inconsistent policy tool is available for their environmental policies with trade effects.

As explained in chapter 2, the GATT gives countries relatively broad latitude to regulate what products are sold within their domestic markets, but its rules have not been interpreted to allow regulation of environmental variables related to how imported goods are made. This prohibition, based on an artificial distinction between products and production methods, makes no sense in an ecologically interdependent world, where pollution spillovers in the manufacturing process can have global consequences (box 5.2).

Moreover, the GATT has already given up the product versus process distinction in several other contexts. Specifically, the GATT's subsidies code and the Uruguay Round intellectual property provisions both regulate how goods are produced. Since an importing country can scrutinize products at its borders for use of inappropriate government funding or misappropriated intellectual property—in other words, for aspects of production rather than only the goods' physical appearance— it is equally reasonable that the environmental origins of a product be given similar consideration.

Box 5.2 Sovereignty, trade, and the environment

Since the Peace of Westphalia in 1648, comity among nations has been based on a concept of sovereignty that permits each country broad latitude to do as it pleases within its territorial borders. GATT's rules reflect this traditional notion and allow a party to limit trade where a product entering its market is deemed to be environmentally damaging or dangerous. But where the product itself is environmentally benign, GATT rules do not permit trade restrictions, no matter how polluting or ecologically unsafe the process for making the product.

The emergence of global environmental issues renders this traditional approach to sovereignty outdated. Today, we recognize that *how* products are produced can be of vital importance. Pollution and other environmental harms arising from production or manufacturing can have important transboundary or global consequences. Thus GATT rules, which focus on "like products" defined in terms of the physical characteristics of goods as they appear at the importer's border, are environmentally inadequate. For example, goods produced in violation of the Montreal Protocol and its controls on chemicals that destroy the ozone layer may appear to be exactly like other competing products made in compliance with the global chlorofluorocarbon (CFC) phaseout. But just because one semiconductor looks like another does not mean that it should be accepted in international trade. If one is made in violation of the Montreal Protocol, GATT rules should permit countries to bar the product.

Global interdependence is actually a phenomenon that extends beyond the environmental realm. As Paul Kennedy (1993) has observed, today's "trends from global warming to twenty-four-hour-a-day trading are *transnational* in character, crossing borders all over our planet, affecting local communities and distant societies at the same time, and reminding us that the earth, for all its divisions, is a single unit." International environmental law (to the extent that there is such a thing) has begun to catch up with the implications of ecological interdependence. Both the Stockholm Declaration (1972) and the Rio Declaration (1992) establish obligations not to harm the global commons and to avoid transboundary pollution (Brown Weiss 1992; Hurrell and Kingsbury 1992). But this more complex understanding of modern life and its implications for political sovereignty—and, in particular, the shared ecological destiny of the nations of the planet—has not yet transfused the rules of international trade.

Trade Measures as Leverage

Many environmentalists believe that trade measures, beyond their use in protecting domestic markets from environmentally unsound products, can be an effective way to exert leverage on other countries where environmental standards or practices are considered to be too lax. Trade measures aimed at changing the behavior of foreign producers and imposed extraterritorially[5] are not permitted under the currently prevail-

---

5. Charnovitz (1992c, 208–09) has highlighted the difference between extraterritoriality, which implies the imposition of domestic standards on transactions occurring abroad (e.g., applying US antitrust laws to Japanese corporations' activities in Japan) and extrajurisdictionality—a term invented by the GATT tuna-dolphin panel to condemn the

ing interpretation of GATT rules.[6] Free traders argue that the high standards forced by one nation on another may not produce "optimal" levels of environmental protection. Specifically, they observe that environmental conditions and assimilative capacities vary from country to country, and thus "proper" pollution control strategies and requirements should be expected to vary. Not only do countries have different national resource endowments, they also have different demands for environmental amenities based on variations in income levels and tastes.

Indiscriminately penalizing countries that have chosen "low" standards may therefore be unfair (Blackhurst 1992). Can poorer countries such as Mexico afford, for instance, the same strict controls on air emissions (in some cases focused on visibility concerns) required in the United States when the Mexican public faces far more serious environmental risks and the Mexican government has limited resources to devote to environmental protection? Free traders further note that strict harmonization of environmental standards undermines the theory of comparative advantage and overrides legitimate differences in environmental policies that may derive from variations in climate, weather patterns, resources, existing pollution levels, economic needs, population densities, risk preferences, and environmental priorities (e.g., Richard Stewart 1993b).

Free traders particularly object to unilateral determinations of environmental priorities when these national values are "exported" by means of trade measures imposed extraterritorially. Such actions, they fear, threaten the international cooperation among nations on which open trade depends.

Chapter 6 of this volume examines in detail the legitimacy of using trade as leverage for environmental policies with overseas effects. The

---

US trade ban on Mexican tuna. The latter term, although not defined, appears to concern attempts to regulate behavior abroad through controls on transactions at the border (e.g., barring Mexican tuna from entering the United States based on Mexican fishing methods deemed inappropriate by US standards). Under Charnovitz's distinction, the substantive issue for the trade community is extrajurisdictional actions, which are much more common than truly extraterritorial ones. A better distinction—but clearly not consistent with the tuna-dolphin panel report—would recognize that harms to the global commons while outside the territory of any nation and therefore extraterritorial in a strict sense are not beyond the jurisdiction of countries who indivisibly share these resources; thus these actions to protect the global commons are not extrajurisdictional. For example, protecting dolphins on the high seas would be extraterritorial but not extrajurisdictional. Baker (1992) addresses this jurisdictional argument.

6. See, for example, the 19 November 1992 New Zealand GATT Statement objecting to extraterritoriality in the form of efforts to use trade measures to shape the behavior of parties outside the jurisdiction of the party applying the trade measure. See also USCIB (1992), EC (1992b), and Canada's (1992) submissions to the GATT Environmental Measures in International Trade group.

analysis focuses on whether the standards applied are unilaterally or multilaterally developed and on the nature and locus of the harm being targeted. In particular, it argues that there is an important distinction between global and transboundary issues and purely local environmental problems. Trade measures used as a sword to address issues with physical spillover effects around the world or across borders can much more readily be defended. The use of trade measures to force other countries to meet one's own environmental policy standards—in the absence of pollution spillovers—is problematic. However, even when the environmental harm is confined to another nation's territory, there may be psychological and political spillovers that make some uses of trade leverage appropriate.[7]

Many trade experts acknowledge the need for new GATT rules to accommodate global and transboundary environmental issues. Most recognize specifically that, where pollution spillovers occur, the trade regime should support international agreements aimed at limiting the environmental damage. But a number of free traders fear that environmentalists conflate the local and global issues and will insist on sweeping environmental changes to the GATT to address a very small number of truly international issues.

Of course, the line between protecting "high" domestic standards with trade restrictions used defensively and attacking another country's "low" environmental standards with trade measures used offensively blurs at the margins. Is the US ban on Mexican tuna caught using dolphin-unsafe fishing methods a shield, protecting the US market (and US tuna producers, who bear higher costs to catch dolphin-safe tuna) or is it a sword aimed at forcing Mexico to change its tuna fishing practices? As a GATT issue, the matter arose as a challenge to US tuna standards considered by Mexico to be too high and an obstacle to trade. But the intent of the US law was to protect dolphins and therefore was aimed at environmentally lax Mexican fishing practices. One can view the harm as occurring on the high seas, outside the United States, and thus as an example of offensive use of trade leverage. But one could also argue that the dolphins on the high seas are part of the global commons—in which

---

7. Psychological spillovers (Blackhurst and Subramanian 1992) are concerns based on moral judgments about another's behavior or that arise over harms to resources outside of one's own country. Thus, dolphin deaths, no matter where they occur, may distress Americans and have a psychological spillover effect. Similar psychological spillovers arise in the context of human rights violations and other issues. Political spillovers relate to the fourth element of the environmental critique discussed above. Specifically, where a country with low environmental standards is perceived as having established a competitive advantage for its producers based on lower environmental compliance costs, companies competing in the global market against these producers may pressure their own governments to lower standards to "level the playing field." Thus, the low standards create a "political drag" that may translate into reduced environmental protection in other jurisdictions.

the United States has an indivisible interest—making the US action defensive.

For the sake of analytic clarity, this study makes the physical locus of the harm the determinative factor in separating offensive from defensive environmental trade measures. But as chapter 6 examines in greater depth, the offensive use of trade measures to respond to transboundary or global harms may be justified and worthy of GATT support. In any case, in the tuna-dolphin matter, the United States acted on its own without an international agreement on dolphin protection. As the analysis that follows explains, environmental trade measures invoked unilaterally in defense of the global commons should have a very firm grounding based on a significant threat to the sustainability of an important global ecosystem or species.

Using the locus-of-harm criterion to separate offensive from defensive uses of trade measures, the rest of this chapter defines new basic GATT environmental rules—particularly focused on the regulation of defensive environmental trade measures. Chapters 6 and 7 of this study will consider potential GATT approaches to the use of offensive environmental trade measures.

The Value of International Standards

Most trade and environment disputes arise over environmental standards that differ from one country to the next. These differences stem from divergent judgments about environmental goals and priorities as well as approaches to problems. Where standards are harmonized, the scope for conflict is markedly reduced. Indeed, internationally accepted standards greatly facilitate multilateral cooperation in general and enhance commercial interaction in particular. (The issue of what constitutes an international consensus and how one achieves an international agreement will be dealt with in the next chapter.) A point that is often overlooked is that standards may assist environmental protection efforts. The value of universal traffic signals such as ''go on green, stop on red'' can hardly be overstated. The failure to harmonize important rules often leads to confusion and clashes (if not crashes): witness the difficulties of American visitors to Britain entering left-hand driving traffic.

Common rules make it easier to achieve scale economies in production and distribution. Equally importantly, common standards, or at least joint approaches to problems, facilitate efficient and effective environmental regulation. For example, the United States now spends approximately $100 million per year safety testing and regulating pesticides. Other major nations spend significant sums on their own pesticide safety programs, with different testing protocols and data requirements.[8] Rather than making pesticide companies submit separate data to every separate national regulatory authority, it would be more efficient to have unified international pesticide-testing protocols, at least for purposes of gathering safety data. Countries might ultimately choose different pesticide residue standards, based on different risk preferences or food consumption patterns, but there is no reason such decisions could not be built on a common data base. A joint testing program or at least a process for reciprocal recognition of data would save money, potentially allowing the United States, for example, to redirect some portion of EPA's pesticide regulation budget to other pressing environmental problems.

Common standards also help to avoid slipups in enforcing restrictions on environmentally unsound products. For instance, there has been considerable concern in the United States about the "circle of poison," in which pesticides barred in the United States are sold abroad and then slip through border inspections, returning to the US market as residues on imported fruits or vegetables.[9] If common standards were in place, the scope for such problems would be dramatically reduced; a pesticide would either be fit for international commerce or it would not.

The lack of uniform environmental standards within the United States has also recently been recognized to have serious adverse effects on the development of new pollution control technologies.[10] Because of the multiplicity of regulatory authorities (California alone has 191 environmental regulatory boards and agencies by one count) and the diversity of standards imposed, it is impossible to get new cleanup technologies certified and approved for use in an economically efficient and environmentally effective way.

Dag Syrrist, a California venture capitalist, recently told the US Senate Environment and Public Works Committee that the lack of uniformity in US environmental regulation "penalizes innovation and repels capital" (hearing of the Committee on Environment and Public Works, 21 May 1993). Syrrist's study of the US environmental industry found major barriers that inhibit rapid commercialization of environmental technologies, most notably a daunting regulatory maze. As Syrrist explained, "It is not only the federal permit requirements that can destroy a [startup] company, but also the multiple state and local regulations that have effectively partitioned a national market into several

---

8. A number of governments do, however, piggyback on US safety regulations, permitting any product meeting US standards to be sold in their countries.

9. Senator Patrick Leahy proposed legislation (S. 898) in the 102nd Congress to address the "circle of poison" problem.

10. Not only is the development of new technologies helpful in addressing environmental problems, it is an important aspect of national competitiveness (Inman and Burton 1990).

hundred regional and local markets, each with unique permitting requirements.''

This fragmentation of the market is even more severe on the international scale. The price paid for regulatory diversity, Syrrist argues, is staggering. Every year, hundreds of young environmental companies with potentially important new pollution control and prevention technologies fail to reach financial viability and die on the vine because of a regulatory process that lets separate environmental authorities force companies to re-prove the effectiveness of their products. EPA's own studies confirm this conclusion (EPA 1991b). The argument against regulatory fragmentation within the US market applies with equal or greater force to the world market for environmental products.

But uniform standards do not always improve social welfare. Where conditions vary, different standards may well be justified. For example, where the number of pedestrians is limited, the ''right turn on red'' rule makes good sense—improving traffic flow, reducing gasoline consumption, and cutting emissions from vehicles idling at stop lights. But on the crowded streets of Manhattan, for instance, where large numbers of pedestrians would be put at risk, the rule does not make for higher social welfare. In addition, where the political views, unique culture, or traditions of a community are strong, the desire to conform to broader norms may well be low (e.g., driving on the left in Britain or refusal to use the metric system in the United States). Finally, there may be benefits in having different jurisdictions applying a range of environmental policy approaches as a way of testing alternative courses of action. In fact, US federalism is often touted as providing 50 state ''laboratories'' for policy development.

The issue becomes one of trading off the benefits of uniformity against the virtues of diversity—the commercial and environmental value of market access against the ability to tailor regulations to local needs and preferences. This balancing act is complicated by the fact that those who pay the price for uniformity (in sacrificing their own regulatory choices) may perceive the commercial benefits that result as largely accruing to those outside the community. For instance, if the United States were to accept an international pesticide residue standard, not only would US citizens forgo the right to set their own standard based on unique US risk preferences, but US pesticide makers might lose sales in the face of new competition from foreign products that can more easily enter the US market. Attention must therefore be paid to the broad benefits of freer trade, including the consumer gains, environmental advances from new technologies at lower costs, and the reciprocity of the process (opening new markets for exporters) as all nations conform their standards to international norms.

Creating a system to weigh these competing interests is an essential prerequisite to trade and environmental policy integration—and a central focus of this book. One specific question is how much scope nations should have to diverge from established international norms. Defining bounds for legitimate environmental policies where no international standards are available is a second key issue.

Uniformity versus Diversity

The challenge in integrating trade principles and environmental policy goals is to accommodate, on the one hand, the legitimate interests of nations and their political subdivisions in setting environmental policies to protect their resources and the public health according to local circumstances and preferences with, on the other hand, the value to all nations collectively of a healthy global environment and of free trade. This balancing of interests raises very fundamental questions about political control and sovereignty and thus can appear to create trade-offs between efficiency and growth and local environmental regulations as well as other public desires such as maintaining a sense of community or national identity.[11] Neither absolute uniformity of environmental standards nor total regulatory diversity serves the public interest.

In some circumstances, international standards are an essential component of effective environmental policies. Common approaches are especially important in responding to global problems and can be useful in reducing the temptation to establish competitive advantage based on degrading the environment. Internationally accepted environmental rules can also clarify the requirements for market access, simplifying and strengthening environmental regulation and at the same time opening up opportunities for producers to achieve scale economies.

Regulatory diversity can, however, produce better results if environmental conditions, risk preferences, or policy priorities diverge. What matters—and cannot be determined *a priori*—is whether the divergence in baseline conditions and desires is founded on legitimate differences and is significant enough to justify tailoring regulations to local demands. Specifically, a calculation must be made as to whether people are enough better off as a result of locally (or nationally) determined standards to offset the economic losses due to the inefficiency of varying market-entry requirements and the disadvantages of decentralized and fragmented regulatory programs.

US Environmental Federalism

The intersection of state and federal environmental regulation in the United States offers a working example of how to strike the balance

---

11. See Patrick Buchanan, "NAFTA," *Washington Post*, 7 November 1993, who rejects free trade as requiring too high a price in terms of the lost sense of community. Daly (1993) also stresses the community values of regulatory diversity.

between uniform requirements and regulatory diversity. The right of US states and localities to set their own environmental standards is always in tension with the power of the federal government to regulate interstate commerce both to prevent low standards, which might permit environmental harms to be externalized or present an unfair competitive advantage, and high standards that would be an unjustified burden on interstate trade.[12] The reach of the US Constitution's commerce clause (Richard Stewart 1977)—the focal point of federal trade authority—has been the subject of a number of US Supreme Court cases. Although the US commerce clause jurisprudence does not yield any precise formula for adjudicating competing trade and environmental claims (Geradin 1993a; Richard Stewart 1992), it does offer a valuable starting point for analyzing how environmental considerations might be woven into the fabric of the GATT.[13]

In the United States, federal environmental laws can preempt state regulation or can apply concurrently with state statutes, in which case, the federal rules establish a floor that states may exceed so long as they do not intrude excessively on the free flow of interstate commerce.[14] In the absence of federal legislation, states are free to determine their own environmental standards, constrained only by the "dormant" federal interest in free trade among the states. By analogy, international environmental agreements could preempt national standards[15] or run con-

---

12. The additional layer of checks and balances provided by the GATT should as well be seen as protecting not only the free flow of commerce but also, if the rules of the international trading system are properly structured, guarding against trade advantages established by degrading the environment. Petersmann (1991a) discusses the role of the GATT in subjecting the exercise of national regulatory power to oversight and limits that enhance individual and social welfare.

13. The European Union has a similar jurisprudence that has emerged from cases involving environmental obstacles to the single market imposed by member states and brought to the European Court of Justice. The EU analysis is quite similar to, although less coherent than, the US case history (Geradin 1993a; Demaret 1993). Most notably, the EU balancing test incorporates a more strict proportionality requirement (i.e., cost-benefit test) than the US Supreme Court has applied. See the EU case histories presented in appendix C. French (1991) analyzes the European Union as a model for global environmental decision making.

14. The state's freedom to adopt its own environmental standards is always constrained by the "dormant commerce clause," which establishes the federal authority to regulate interstate trade and to protect it against interference from inappropriately burdensome state regulation.

15. Given the hesitancy to surrender regulatory sovereignty to international entities, preemptive regulations are unlikely to be useful policy tools on the international scene. Indeed, recent efforts to make international environmental agreements preempt national authority have failed entirely. The refusal of the US Congress to ratify the International Oil Spill Convention because of provisions waiving local jurisdiction over liability and damage assessments demonstrates this point ("Congress Renews Debate Over Oil Spill Liability,"

current with national authority and thus simply provide a floor beneath which states may not fall.

Whether nations are regulating in the absence of international standards or based on concurrent authority, they should be given leeway to set their own policy goals and to determine their own levels of protection. But they should be obligated to consider carefully the means they employ to avoid excessively burdening international trade. The US experience again provides a useful point of departure for efforts to strike this balance. In the United States, considerable deference is given to state efforts to ameliorate environmental harms (e.g., *Huron Cement Co. v. Detroit*, 362 US 440 [1960]). There is, in addition, an implicit recognition in US jurisprudence that a "precautionary" approach to environmental issues is appropriate (e.g., *Palladio v. Diamond* 321 F. Supp. 630 [S.D. N.Y. 1970]). But the deference granted is not absolute—ensuring that checks and balances exist.

The Commerce Clause Standard

Where an argument is made that a state's environmental regulation has crossed the line into protectionism, the US courts consider several factors. The court first examines whether the state environmental standards discriminate overtly. Where the regulatory scheme appears to apply evenhandedly, the court applies a "light" balancing test, examining whether the statute in question is rationally related to a legitimate state interest and whether the burden imposed on interstate commerce is "clearly excessive in relation to the putative local benefits" (*Pike v. Bruce Church*, 397 US 137 [1970]).[16] This light review appropriately gives great deference to the state regulations.

If, however, a state regulation is discriminatory on its face, overtly burdening trade, the court applies a more stringent balancing test with strict scrutiny of the "purported legitimate local purpose and of nondiscriminatory alternatives" (*Hughes v. Oklahoma*, 441 US 322 [1979]; see also *Philadelphia v. New Jersey*, 437 US) that might have provided a regulatory mechanism to achieve the established goal with a less negative effect on interstate commerce. The court is not fooled by clever legislative drafting. Where the language is superficially neutral but "plainly discriminates" in effect, strict scrutiny is applied (*Dean Milk Co. v. Madison*, 340 US 349 [1951]).

National Underwriter: Property and Casualty Edition, 2 July 1990, 1). Even greater hostility is mounted to trade-based efforts to preempt environmental policy options. Indeed, environmental opposition to several potentially preemptive provisions in the GATT Dunkel text led to a number of changes in the final Uruguay Round text (Charnovitz 1993a).

16. Geradin (1993a) provides a complete and thoughtful analysis of the commerce clause jurisprudence and the European Court of Justice's parallel case decisions.

The basic balancing test, as developed in the seminal case of *Pike v. Bruce Church*, seeks to determine whether the regulations in question:

- effectuate a legitimate local public interest;

- have only an incidental effect on interstate commerce;

- impose a burden on interstate commerce that is clearly excessive to the putative local (i.e., environmental) benefits; and

- could be structured to achieve the same ends with a lesser impact on commerce.

As noted above, the Supreme Court does not always apply this balancing test strictly. When the challenge is to a statute that is facially neutral, the Supreme Court has sometimes shown a more permissive attitude, requiring only a "rational" relationship between the environmental regulations employed and the state's policy goal (*Huron Cement Co. v. Detroit*, 362 US 440 [1960]). In an attempt to articulate this more lenient standard, one court declared: "If the burden on interstate commerce is slight, and the area of legislation is one that is properly of local concern, the means chosen to accomplish this end should be deemed reasonably effective unless the party attacking the legislation demonstrates the contrary by clear and convincing proof" (*Procter & Gamble v. Chicago*, 509 F. 2d. 69 [7th Cir], cert. denied 421 US 978 [1975]). In effect, this invokes the *Pike* balancing criteria but does so with a strong presumption in favor of the environmental standards in question.

This US experience in balancing trade and environmental interests can be distilled into an analysis of:

- the intent or effect of the challenged regulations;

- the legitimacy of the underlying environmental policy or claim of environmental injury;

- the justification for the disruption to trade.

A New International Trade-Environment Test

With some modest adaptation, this three-pronged analysis provides a solid foundation for adjudicating trade and environmental disputes in the international context.[17] Specifically, a review of intent and effect

---

17. Although designed for dispute settlement, the criteria proposed would also be useful as guidance to nations in advance of disputes as to when and where environmental trade measures would be appropriate. Support for a revised GATT trade-environment analysis derived from the US commerce clause is growing (USCIB 1993; OECD 1992).

should determine the level of scrutiny to be given to an environmental trade measure. An environmental "legitimacy" test should be employed to assess the underlying environmental injury or interest of the jurisdiction whose standards or regulations are in question and whose use of trade measures in support of its environmental policy has been challenged. Finally, an "unjustified disruption to trade" inquiry should be used to judge whether the trade restriction or sanction employed was clearly disproportionate to the environmental harm at issue and whether equally effective alternative policies were reasonably available.

This new set of rules could replace the existing GATT Article XX analysis and should be employed to review any case where an environmental policy is challenged as a trade restriction. A finding of discrimination (that is, a violation of the "national treatment" or "most-favored nation" obligation)—which must be affirmed before Article XX can be invoked—would continue to be relevant. The Article XX headnote regulating arbitrary actions and unjustified discrimination would be folded, along with the "necessary" test, into the third-prong "unjustified disruption to trade" analysis. The Article XX screen for "disguised restrictions on international trade" would be part of the first-prong intent and effect analysis.

Who Decides

Who applies the proposed balancing test is of considerable significance.[18] GATT's demonstrated success in trade dispute settlement carries little weight outside of the trade realm. Environmentalists question the GATT's legitimacy, technical capacity, and neutrality in cases that involve environmental issues.

In an ideal world, environmental authorities would make environmental judgments, and trade authorities would render trade decisions. But in the absence of a recognized environmental dispute settlement

---

18. It is notable that the US Supreme Court has a long history of adjudicating trade and environmental disputes among the US states and has regularly overturned state environmental standards as unduly burdensome to interstate trade (e.g., *Oregon Waste Systems v. Department of Environmental Quality*, slip opinion 93–70 [1994]). Like the GATT, the Supreme Court has no special environmental expertise. Yet, the Supreme Court has never been the object of environmentalists' wrath or protests, as has the GATT. In brief, the Supreme Court has legitimacy. It is accepted as a neutral forum applying balanced rules, with opportunities available to any interested party to submit "friend of the court" briefs offering their views on issues under consideration, with arguments that are open to the public. Perhaps more importantly, the Supreme Court holds a special place in America's political structure that every school child learns to revere. The GATT can never expect to obtain comparable legitimacy, but new structures can be established to improve the public's image of international dispute resolution in general and the GATT in particular. Indeed, the Uruguay Round GATT agreement includes a number of dispute settlement reforms.

body, or a Global Environmental Organization, available for this purpose, the GATT is the sole candidate for applying the proposed test. However, to do so effectively it must much more aggressively recruit environmental experts for its dispute panels. Indeed, these new trade and environment rules should be implemented along with reform of the GATT dispute resolution process (as discussed in chapters 2 and 9).

At the same time, it should be recognized that shifting responsibility for environmental judgments out of the GATT would relieve the international trading system of a major burden and a serious source of strain on the system's legitimacy. Such a shift should be welcomed by trade authorities as well as environmental officials. Chapter 6 will analyze this issue further.

The First Prong: Intent and Effect

To begin the analysis, a determination should be made about the intent and effect of the trade measure employed. The purpose of this inquiry is to unmask hidden trade barriers and to identify environmental policies that disproportionately burden foreign interests, perhaps unreasonably. Where an intent to discriminate is uncovered, strict scrutiny of the environmental legitimacy and of the justification for the disruption to trade should be applied. Provisions that "facially discriminate"—that is, plainly treat foreign products less favorably than domestic ones—are not hidden barriers but should be examined closely to see if the discrimination is justified. The Montreal Protocol, for example, overtly calls for discriminatory trade treatment of nonparties—but for a good reason: protection of the ozone layer.

Even if there is no apparent discriminatory intent, there must be an examination of the *effect* of the measure to smoke out cleverly disguised efforts to protect domestic producers. For example, the European Community's ban on beef injected with growth hormones was not plainly discriminatory on its face insofar as it prohibited the sale of hormone-treated European beef as well as imported beef. But the effect of this restriction was clearly discriminatory, protecting European cattle producers for whom the use of growth hormones is not a standard practice and blocking beef exports from the United States and Australia, where cattle producers use growth hormones as a matter of course. In such cases, the discrimination may in the end be deemed justified, but the restriction should be subject to strict scrutiny.

If there is no discriminatory intent or effect, there is little basis for a trade challenge to an environmental policy or program. Environmental regulations that are neutral on their face and that have only an incidental effect on trade should be presumed to be legitimate and appropriate. They should be subject only to a light review of the underlying environmental policy and the reasonable availability of equally effective alternative policies that would make even the incidental trade burden "clearly disproportionate" in light of the putative environmental benefits.

In reviewing cases under this standard, a dispute settlement panel should question the environmental program only if it determines that environmental protection is not the primary purpose of the challenged program or that the burden imposed on the free flow of commerce is clearly disproportionate to the environmental interest at stake. Legislators and regulators should be granted broad leeway in structuring environmental policies so long as their efforts are not a smoke screen for trade protectionism. The "clearly disproportionate" test should be used only to cull poorly crafted statutes and regulations where all or part of the environmental policy results in serious trade burdens but little or no environmental benefit.

Most domestic environmental standards, which use trade restrictions simply to ensure that competing imported products meet the same standards as local goods, would fall into this light-scrutiny category. Thus, for example, pesticide regulations limiting the public's exposure to chemical residues on fruits or vegetables should be given only a light review unless evidence is advanced of an underlying intent to block imports or the standards have a clearly disproportionate and unfair effect on imported products.

The Second Prong: Environmental Legitimacy

The use of trade restrictions to reinforce environmental standards should generally be seen as appropriate if they are used in response to an environmental injury in which the country using the measures has a legitimate interest. To avoid ad hoc determinations of environmental harm, the international trading system needs an environmental injury or legitimacy test. Where a country is trying to prevent environmental harms within its own territory, broad deference to its political choices should be granted. Where, however, the injury it seeks to confront is outside its borders, or extraterritorial, more care should be taken in examining the legitimacy of the underlying environmental policy.

As a general matter, the international trading system should presume the legitimacy of any environmental standards or policy established by international convention. Chapter 6 will discuss the bases for such environmental agreements. In the absence of a multilateral agreement, the legitimacy of an environmental policy or goal as the foundation for a unilateral trade action should be established on the basis of:

- the presence of a bona fide environmental harm or issue; and
- the nexus of the party claiming the right to use trade measures to the harm they wish to stop.

The rights mentioned here are what might be called strong rights, entitling a party to impose trade measures commensurate with the seriousness of the environmental harm it faces and to have its action supported by the international trading system. Parties should always retain, however, what might be considered basic rights to impose trade restrictions in support of their policy choices and in contravention of GATT dictates so long as they are willing to compensate those whose trading opportunities are impaired.

Where a party acts under its basic rights and imposes a trade restriction that harms others, it should be required to pay compensation or to accept withdrawal of equivalent trade benefits. This "rebalancing" might occur through a process analogous to the existing Article XXIII "nullification and impairment" mechanism. By requiring compensation to be paid, countries would be forced to weigh how strongly they feel about their value preferences. Of course, product labeling requirements, educational efforts, financial assistance programs, and other GATT-consistent policy tools can often be employed to effectuate environmental goals without creating any basis for a GATT case.

Many free traders worry that granting such basic rights would fundamentally break down GATT disciplines. As an alternative, Hudec (1989) argues for "self-help" and selective disregard for GATT mandates in a political gesture akin to civil disobedience. In practice, self-help would be indistinguishable from the exercise of basic rights as described above. In both cases, a party with strong environmental convictions that contravene its trade obligations would be able to stick to its environmental guns—with compensation owed (perhaps paid and perhaps not) to others whose trading opportunities have suffered. Thus, for example, the United States could retain its marine mammal protection laws regardless of their GATT consistency, and the European Union could still ban the sale of furs from animals caught in leg-hold traps.

Bona Fide Environmentalism

There can be no absolute litmus test for the bona fides of environmental policies. There are, however, two aspects of *real* environmental concerns that separate them from ones that do not merit unilateral trade actions: scientific underpinnings (versus value judgments) and significant (versus incidental) harm or threat of harm.[19] Environmental policies should be based on efforts to address harm or risks to public health or ecological resources identified through scientific methods.[20] Legitimate

---

19. To accommodate the need for a "precautionary" approach to environmental policymaking, even a threat of harm should be actionable.

20. This test is not meant to impose a "sound science" requirement that actions be based on the preponderance of scientific belief, nor should it be seen to dictate what level of risk

environmental programs should have as their primary purpose addressing such issues.

Some guidance in determining whether a program has scientific underpinnings can be found in the recent US Supreme Court *Daubert* decision (113 US 2786 [1993]), which addressed the admissibility of scientific expert evidence in US federal courts. The Court rejected the contention that only scientific views that are generally accepted may be considered. The justices recognized that "[s]cience is not an encyclopedic body of knowledge about the universe. Instead, it represents a *process* for proposing and refining theoretical explanations about the world that are subject to further testing and refinement. . . . [I]n order to qualify as 'scientific knowledge,' an inference or assertion must be derived by the scientific method." Similar criteria should be applied in evaluating the bona fides of environmental policies.

Of course, the line between science and politics or ethics is fuzzy. Thus, some policies called "environmental" really reflect ethical preferences or cultural norms. For example, many animal welfare concerns (e.g., protection for nonendangered dolphins) are based on moral choices, not scientific data. The fact that some environmental trade measures derive from moral choices should come as no surprise. Moral choices can and should play a role in determining what behavior is acceptable in the international realm in general and in the trade world in particular.[21] "Psychological spillovers"—the harm caused by knowing that others are not living up to one's own ethical standards—can be very real. The desire in the United States to protect whales and dolphins, regardless of whether they are on official endangered species lists, runs rather deep (Day 1987).

But what constitutes a legitimate basis for moral judgments and thus trade action must be spelled out. Without clear rules, unilateral trade actions, reflecting cultural preferences that may not be broadly shared, could undermine the international trading system. As Jagdish Bhagwati (*Wall Street Journal*, 19 March 1993, A10) suggests: "If a nation's trading rights can be suspended simply because it refuses to accept another

---

a society must accept. This "scientific method" standard is meant simply to require analytic rigor in making environmental decisions. The GATT Uruguay Round results move some distance in this direction by requiring sanitary and phytosanitary standards to be based on "scientific principles" rather than the "sound science" requirement proposed earlier in the negotiating process. The NAFTA standards chapter first advanced this scientific methods approach.

21. GATT's rules already reflect a number of explicit and implicit moral judgments. For instance, the products of prison labor may be banned or subject to other restrictions under Article XX(e). However, the GATT does not forbid the use of forced labor; it simply condones unilateral imposition of trade measures against those who export goods produced by prisoners. Thus, while it may not be GATT's place to make moral judgments, GATT should accept and enforce moral bounds derived elsewhere.

nation's idiosyncratic values, everyone could insist on 'morality-driven' trade restrictions, and the whole international trading system would head down a slippery slope.''[22]

Despite Bhagwati's argument, it is also true that nations should not be forced into complicity with trade they consider morally repugnant. Being required to open one's market to ethically tainted products is fundamentally unsatisfactory. If a society collectively feels strongly about the products of dolphin sacrifice, it should be able to bar such goods. The issue is simply whether it gets to impose the ban with an international blessing from the trade system or without it—and thus whether compensation is due to the party whose product is blocked from the market.

The test for imposing "moral" environmental policies must be whether the values are widely shared, as measured by whether the ethical position at issue is reflected in an international agreement. Without such a restriction, Bhagwati's concern becomes salient. Japan might choose to bar grain-fed beef, claiming a cultural and value preference for grass-fed meat and thereby blocking US beef exports to Japan. Or India could choose to block any product made by people who eat the sacred cow.

The touchstone for legitimacy in the case of "moral" environmental policies must therefore be international agreement.[23] Deference should be given to—and the trade system should uphold—widely held values reflected in multilateral agreements whether or not they are fully justified scientifically. Thus, the scientific validity of the International Whaling Convention's whaling moratorium is irrelevant since the preponderance of interested nations have agreed to a common standard, reflecting a widely held view of what constitutes the appropriate moral baseline for behavior in the modern world vis-à-vis whales.

The significance of the harm or threat of harm should be judged by reference to:

- the importance of the environmental resource affected;[24]

- the strength of the scientific assessment of injury;

---

22. The same issue of values-driven trade restrictions arises in the context of human rights. In the current debate over China's human rights record and whether this should be linked to trade, Lardy (1994) argues against withdrawing China's most-favored nation trade status.

23. One variation on this rule, requiring moral judgments to be backed by international agreements, would be to permit countries to impose trade restrictions unilaterally in support of moral environmental policies but only for a limited period, say two years. This would give the nation time to get an international agreement negotiated—thus demonstrating that its moral judgment is widely shared.

24. The importance of the ecosystem or species should be determined by the uniqueness of the threatened resource and role of the resource in supporting other species or life on the planet.

- the speed at which the harm is occurring (i.e., the urgency of the situation);
- the irreversibility of the potential damage;
- the breadth of the threatened harm.

As a general matter, the greater the harm, the stronger is the claim to a right to respond and to use strong trade remedies as an element of the response. Actions to protect the life-sustaining ozone layer would fall at one end of the spectrum. Policies focused on protection of a subspecies of the snail darter might fall at the other end.

Incidental harm should not give rise to trade measures. Every country, like every person, must accept some amount of minor nuisance from others' behavior. Where, however, the injury suffered goes beyond incidental or relatively trivial harm, a right to respond should be considered possible.

Nexus to the Harm

The more clearly the source of the harm can be identified and the more directly the harm affects a party, the stronger is that party's claim of right to invoke trade measures unilaterally in response to the environmental injury. Thus, where an upstream country is poisoning a river with toxic chemicals lethal to all forms of life, a downstream country has a strong case for redress. A country whose claim rests on an environmental injury that is small in magnitude or from a source that cannot be pinpointed or which has only an uncertain or indirect causal connection with its injury has a much less clear basis for invoking trade restrictions.

In determining the circumstances under which the GATT should condone the use of unilaterally determined environmental trade measures, the location of the harm therefore becomes a critical factor. Five categories of injuries should be differentiated in descending order of justification for the use of trade measures to combat environmental injuries or threats of harm:

- domestic harm (harm to the public health or natural resources of the nation imposing import restrictions);
- transboundary harm (where pollution spills over from a neighboring country);
- global harm (cases such as ozone layer depletion where harmful effects spread across the planet);
- foreign harm with a loss of transboundary or global ''positive externalities'' (where the direct harm or pollution does not go beyond the

foreign nation's borders but an environmental resource providing transboundary or global benefits to the country imposing the trade measures is diminished or harmed);

- purely foreign harm (limited to the country whose low environmental standards are the target of the trade measures in question).

Purely Domestic Where the harm arises within and directly affects the country setting the challenged environmental standard, the legitimacy of using trade restrictions to respond to environmental injuries is at its maximum. As long as the causation and scientific underpinnings of the environmental harm are established, countries should be generally free to determine appropriate levels of environmental protection within their own territories and to choose whatever reasonable means of regulation they deem most suitable. For example, countries should be able to set domestic automobile emissions standards as part of a program to combat air pollution. Unless a challenger can establish that environmental protection was not the primary purpose of the regulatory scheme or that the trade measure is not rationally related to the environmental goal, the legitimacy of the chosen policy should be assumed.[25]

There may well be cases where the motives behind ostensibly environmental regulations are a mix of legitimate environmental concern and protectionism. For example, the US Corporate Average Fuel Economy (CAFE) requirements, the subject of a recent EU challenge in the GATT, have a very real environmental goal—reducing gasoline consumption and the attendant air pollution. In this case, however, the means chosen (requirements on fleetwide average miles per gallon) were clearly discriminatory in effect and were, in fact, specifically selected to benefit domestic auto producers at the expense of some foreign car makers. Such "mixed motive" cases must be decided on the terms of the third prong of analysis—whether the disruption to trade is justified.

---

25. This does not guarantee that the standard will be upheld. It must still clear the "unjustified burden to trade" test under which it might be found to produce benefits clearly disproportionate to the burdens imposed on international commerce. These lines will not always be sharp. In some cases, a policy's shortcoming could be seen as either failing to meet the environmental legitimacy test or failing the "unjustified burden to trade" test. For example, the US ban on asbestos in all forms and uses was so overly broad and scientifically insupportable that it was overturned by a US court upon a challenge brought by the importers of Canadian asbestos. In that case, using the decision rules offered here, a panel could have rejected the EPA asbestos regulations either because they were overly broad and not rationally related to the scientific risks from asbestos or because of the grossly disproportionate effect on asbestos trade in its benign applications.

Transboundary Where the harm results from transboundary pollution spillovers, the threshold for establishing a legitimate environmental interest should be relatively low. Acid rain resulting from a neighboring country's coal-burning power plants might well qualify for action if bona fide injury and causation can be shown. Indeed, the right not to be harmed by transboundary pollution is well established in international law.[26] Any scientific evidence of injury beyond de minimus or transient effects should therefore constitute grounds for a demand that:

- the polluter stop the offending emissions;

- compensation be paid for the harm caused; or

- trade restrictions to induce the polluting nation to stop the emissions or to pay compensation be accepted.

It is worth noting that the right to use trade restrictions in cases of transboundary pollution derives from the environmental harm; it does not emanate from a trade relationship. The right to redress in such circumstances has little to do with whether the nation suffering the harm trades with the polluter nation in the product that causes the pollution. Such cases are not primarily trade and environment matters but rather more general international environment problems, with trade restrictions or sanctions simply providing possible remedies. Obviously, when the polluter does export the pollution-causing product to the country suffering transboundary harm, the imposition of measured trade restrictions on that product would be particularly justified. But even if there is no trade in the offending product, the polluted country would still have a right to be recompensed for its environmental injury and should be eligible to impose trade sanctions in the absence of such compensation.

Since these cases focus on environmental injuries and may or may not involve trade in the products resulting in the transboundary pollution, any disputes over the claim of injury should be heard by international environmental or legal authorities, not the GATT. Moreover, the GATT should recognize the decisions of such authorities, including judgments that permit trade retaliation for transboundary environmental harms, and should ensure that the international trading system

---

26. Principle 21, Report on the UN Conference on the Human Environment, UN Doc A/CONF. 48/14/Rev. 1 (1973) (hereinafter "Stockholm Declaration"); Principle 2, Rio Declaration on Environment and Development, UN Doc E.93.I.11. See also the Corfu Channel Case (*US v. Albania*) 1949 I.C.J.4; Lac Lanoux arbitration, (*France v. Spain*) 12 R.I.A.A. 281 (1957); Trail Smelter Case (*US v. Canada*), 3 R.I.A.A. 1905 (1941). For a complete discussion of these cases see Dunoff (1992).

upholds them.[27] Of course, in the absence of alternative environmental or legal forums for adjudicating these cases, the GATT may be called upon to review trade measures invoked in response to transboundary environmental harms.

Global Harm to the global commons is almost invariably somewhat indirect in its effect on a single country. Thus, a more rigorous showing of injury should be required before trade measures based on harm to shared global resources are accepted as justified.[28] To establish environmental legitimacy in these circumstances, a party should demonstrate that its actions are based on an environmental policy or program designed to protect against a *significant threat to the integrity or sustainability of an important species or ecosystem in which the party has an interest*. The importance of the threatened resource and the significance of the harm or threat of harm should be judged according to the criteria laid out earlier in this chapter.

The greater the significance of the potential harm and the importance of the threatened resource, the stronger the basis for asserting a right to invoke trade restrictions or sanctions. But under this structure, unless there is a threat specifically to the sustainability of a global resource,[29] no right exists to unilaterally impose trade bans or other severe trade actions.[30]

---

27. GATT's legal framework needs to be expanded to ensure that environmental decisions of this kind are automatically incorporated into the international trading system, as are decisions made by the United Nations (see GATT Article XXI(c)) and the IMF (see GATT Article XV).

28. The obligation not to harm the global commons can be found in the Rio Declaration, Principle 2 and the Stockholm Declaration, Principle 21; see also the Vienna Convention for the Protection of the Ozone Layer, the UN Convention on the Law of the Sea; the Convention for the Prevention of Marine Pollution from Land-Based Sources. The American Law Institute's *The Restatement (Third) of the Foreign Relations Law of the United States* (1988) suggests that "certain offenses recognized by the community of nations as of universal concern" may legally give rise to a responsive action even though the nation taking action "has no links of territory with the offense" (Section 404). For a thoughtful review of the bases for jurisdictional claims that extend beyond one's own territorial borders, see Baker (1992).

29. The word "threat" is used to reflect the fact that the evidence of harm need not be definitive and to suggest that countries may pursue policies based on the "precautionary principle" of skewing errors in the direction of safety in the face of incomplete data or scientific uncertainty.

30. The "right" that would not be available is that of having a recognized justification for imposing trade restrictions; the party retains the basic right, in a softer sense, to impose trade restrictions if it is willing to pay compensation for the policy choice this represents. As discussed earlier, the sustainability requirement would not apply where trade actions are taken pursuant to an international agreement.

Applying these principles in the tuna-dolphin case, the environmental legitimacy of the US policy would be judged on the basis of whether scientific data would show a threat to the sustainability of the dolphin species at issue. If so, the trade restrictions on Mexican tuna would be justified. If not, the United States would have to obtain international agreement in support of its dolphin conservation program, demonstrating that dolphin protection was a widely held moral value (and not merely a peculiar US predilection). Alternatively, the United States would be encouraged to use other less trade-intrusive forms of persuasion—labeling, education, technology transfer, financial assistance—to persuade Mexico and other countries to follow its environmental standard. As in every case, the United States would always be free to exercise its basic rights, maintaining the US law and the value choice it represents, and paying compensation to those whose trade opportunities are impaired.

Undoubtedly, this scheme will not satisfy those who view as reprehensible individual animal deaths or other second-order environmental harms, even where there is no suggestion of a threat to the sustainability of a species or ecosystem. But agreement on a defining moral principle for *unilateral* trade actions other than sustainability is unlikely.

Those who object to all unilaterally determined standards will also find the proposed approach unwise. They will argue that even this carefully confined window for individual country actions in defense of the global environment opens a can of potential protectionist worms. The response to this criticism is straightforward. As things currently stand, countries are free to make up their own rules and frequently do so, often to the detriment (but sometimes to the benefit) of trade flows. The structure proposed here is carefully designed to delimit unilateral imposition of environmental trade measures.

Loss of Positive Externalities The fourth case—harm limited to a foreign country but which indirectly affects the global commons or resources shared with other countries—presents an awkward basis for action. Two examples may help to illuminate the circumstances in which such a loss of ''positive'' spillovers can arise. Imagine a country that does not regulate pesticides rigorously and allows the use of chemicals such as DDT that degrade the quality of its wetlands, which serve as a bird habitat. These weak regulations may cause indirect harm to migratory birds that depend on the wetlands during part of the year but which spend some months in another country. Although the direct harm is confined to the country with the lax pesticide standards, a claim of environmental injury by the country that shares the migratory birds might be justified.

Similarly, if a country with tropical forests chooses to cut down timber at a fast pace to achieve its cash-flow goals for development, other nations may complain that they are losing a rich source of biological diversity[31] and the carbon sequestration benefits[32] of the forests, which are critical elements of the planetary ecosystem.

The issue in these cases is whether one country has the right to dictate to another how it should manage its natural resources. In economists' terms, migratory bird habitats and extant rain forests offer "positive externalities," which others enjoy without paying for them. To demand that another country provide global benefits without compensation seems morally dubious, no matter how environmentally desirable.

The obvious policy answer—and the one economists would argue is the most efficient solution to the problem of markets underproviding these public goods—is for the owners of migratory bird habitats, rain forest services, and other positive environmental externalities to be paid for the benefits they provide (Dasgupta 1990). Such an obligation provides an important corollary to the policy emphasis on internalizing costs discussed earlier. Given the weak moral position of those wishing to coerce others into providing uncompensated global benefits, trade restrictions or sanctions should be invoked in these cases only on a multilateral basis, after fair compensation has been offered, and in the face of ongoing intransigence on the part of the nation whose resources are at issue.

Purely Foreign Harm   Where the environmental injury is completely contained within the borders of a foreign country, there is little direct environmental justification for the use of trade measures to coerce a change in the foreign country's behavior. In such cases, any standards enforced must be developed by international agreement to meet the legitimacy test (box 5.3). Some environmentalists may be distressed by rules that permit countries to be "dirty." To the extent this concern is based on a belief that no environmental problem is really "local," evidence that the problem does result in a physical spillover immediately moves it out of this category and into the categories of transboundary, global, or foreign harm with loss of positive externalities described above, which may provide a basis for trade actions.

If the issue is the psychological spillover of knowing that someone else's policies are environmentally lax and that animals or other resources are being harmed, this concern can be addressed by international agreement, at which point violation of the agreed-upon standards becomes a legitimate basis for trade measures. Concern about the "political drag" of low standards in one country creating a competitiveness-based argument against high standards elsewhere poses a more serious

---

31. More than half of all species are found in tropical forests (Brown 1994, 28).

32. Green plants absorb significant quantities of carbon dioxide during photosynthesis, thereby helping to maintain equilibrium in the planet's carbon cycle. Fast-growing tropical forests are particularly efficient at "sequestering" carbon.

Box 5.3 US policy on environmental trade measures

The US government recently announced a new policy on the use of environmental trade measures (US Government 1994; Timothy Wirth, testimony before hearing of the US Senate Subcommittee on Foreign Commerce and Tourism, 3 February 1994), identifying four general categories where "the consideration of trade measures may be appropriate":

- when trade measures are an obligation under an international environmental agreement, assuming nondiscriminatory treatment of nonparties and other conditions (in this category of cases, there is almost a presumption that trade measures will be used, as the country has presumably determined that such measures are appropriate before undertaking the obligation to apply them);

- when the environmental effect of an activity is partially within a country's jurisdiction;

- when a plant or animal species is endangered or threatened, or where a particular practice will likely cause a species to become endangered or threatened;

- where the effectiveness of an international environmental or conservation standard is being diminished (for example, a fisheries conservation regime or the moratorium on drift nets).

The fact that the United States has developed a policy is notable and must be welcomed after several years of internal policy squabbling. Unfortunately, the new policy is not very illuminating. It indicates only when consideration of environmental trade measures may be appropriate, not when such measures should or will be used.

The first category is, moreover, confined to cases where an international agreement obligates trade actions and fails to provide guidance when trade measures are permitted but not required. The second category fails to spell out whether the effect must be a physical spillover or whether psychological harms or political impacts (e.g., competitiveness effects) are a sufficient basis for action. Nor does it make clear whether the global commons are within the jurisdiction of a country and thus within the purview of this category. The third category does little to help separate out important cases that really justify action from less significant ones. The fourth category, drawn from existing US law (the Pelly amendment) provides the most useful demarcation but would be more clear if it were combined with the first category in a straightforward statement that trade measures should be considered whenever a party fails to meet the terms of an international environmental agreement.

problem. As chapter 7 explains in greater detail, the best response to this issue is multilaterally agreed standards.

The Third Prong: Unjustified Trade Disruption

Once a policy with trade implications has been established as environmentally legitimate, the remaining inquiry is whether the specific sanctions or restrictions that have been imposed to support it are appropriate vis-à-vis the burden imposed on trade flows. The issue here is whether the means selected to achieve the designated environmental goal are reasonable. In all cases, an international review body should give substantial deference to the means selected by the national authorities whose policy is in question. Exactly how far this deference extends should be a function of the severity and location of the harm and the degree to which other less trade-disruptive measures have been employed or are available.

As a general rule, a body reviewing environmental policy–based trade sanctions should consider whether the trade burden from the measures imposed was clearly disproportionate to the putative environmental benefits.[33] This test should be applied with the greatest deference when the harm in question is local to the jurisdiction whose environmental policies are under review.[34] Thus, the judgment about how to approach local environmental problems should be largely left to the discretion of political officials and environmental authorities, unless they are clearly ignoring serious trade impacts of their policy choices.

In practice, the "clearly disproportionate" review standard would likely result, for instance, in the US CAFE fuel economy regulations being found to be GATT-illegal. Chosen specifically for political expedience, the benefits of this awkward means of improving the fuel efficiency of cars driven in the United States are modest and likely to be deemed clearly disproportionate to the significant trade impacts on European automakers, estimated at as much as $100 million per year.[35] On the other hand, the US proposal to require foreign oil refiners to use US average gasoline composition data (in the absence of their own data) in meeting the clean fuels provisions of the Clean Air Act would probably survive under the "clearly disproportionate" standard since it provides environmental benefits that are significant and administrative conveniences that are substantial. Taken together, these benefits would not likely be deemed demonstrably less important than the burden on foreign refiners.

Under this new set of GATT rules, there would be no "necessary" test, no requirement that the policy chosen be the "least trade-restrictive" or the "least GATT-inconsistent," and no strict proportionality requirement implying that the benefits of the environmental

---

33. In an ideal world, the judgment on appropriateness, which requires balancing noncommensurate environmental benefits against trade benefits, would be made by trade and environmental authorities jointly.

34. For example, "harm" in these circumstances should be valued using local "prices" and preferences. In contrast, harm to global resources should probably be weighed using international values.

35. While environmentalists may be distressed by this result, a GATT judgment against the CAFE standards would likely put pressure on the US Congress to adopt more trade-neutral—and more environmentally effective—fuel efficiency standards.

regulation must outweigh the costs. The "clearly disproportionate" test would work like the "arbitrary and capricious" standard for the review of government regulations under US administrative law. Close calls are not second-guessed; only obviously off-base decisions are overturned.[36]

One specific criterion in making the "clearly disproportionate" judgment would be whether equally effective alternative policy mechanisms were reasonably available. The political difficulty of winning approval for a superior policy option would be another factor.

Some environmentalists will undoubtedly object to even this light scrutiny of the putative benefits of environmental policies employing trade measures. No balancing, they will argue, is possible or appropriate when environmental values are at stake. This narrow (efficiency-be-damned) perspective, while a time-honored tradition in some parts of the environmental community, is dangerously counterproductive. Whenever society undertakes environmental investments that provide ecological or public health returns dramatically short of the costs imposed on producers and consumers, public support for environmental protection programs falls. Thus, without trying to impose a rigid cost-benefit or proportionality requirement, it is not only reasonable but essential to long-term environmental progress to screen for poorly conceived policies that yield benefits completely out of proportion to their negative impact on trade. The "clearly disproportionate" standard ensures that environmental regulations are given every benefit of the doubt but provides a check on policy errors or regulations that unfairly burden foreign interests.

Some free traders will object that the "clearly disproportionate" standard tips the scales too far in the direction of condoning trade-disruptive environmental policies. Indeed, some free traders would like the GATT rules to more aggressively screen out inefficient environmental programs and standards and have argued for a strict proportionality test like that employed in the European Court of Justice in trade and environment cases (appendix C). Such a proportionality test would allow GATT panels to find environmental policies GATT-inconsistent if they failed to provide benefits greater than the trade losses they produced.

But a pure cost-benefit test of this sort makes no sense in the GATT context. Judgments about how to weigh the costs and benefits of environmental policies in particular will vary from country to country. It is therefore neither practical nor appropriate for international authorities

---

36. It is unlikely that very many US environmental standards would be rejected by the GATT on this basis. Once regulations have cleared the court challenges they almost invariably face in the US administrative law process, they likely have a sufficiently rational basis to pass GATT muster. Other nations with less rigorous legal screening processes might, however, find themselves more often at odds with GATT judgments.

to substitute their judgments for that of the original political decision makers. More importantly, national sovereignty should not be overridden lightly. Fundamentally, the role of the international review should be to control flagrant abuses of national regulatory power at the expense of foreign producers that threaten to unravel international comity and reciprocal trade cooperation.

What Remedies Are Appropriate?

Trade restrictions are the essence of some international environmental agreements. For example, the substantive focus of the Convention on International Trade in Endangered Species of Wild Fauna and Flora (CITES) is a bar on trade in endangered species. Other environmental agreements specify trade restrictions to be imposed for noncompliance. The Montreal Protocol, for instance, mandates a trade ban on certain products with nonparties to the protocol.[37] But many international environmental agreements lack a schedule of penalties, and thus even when international standards are available, unilateral judgments about appropriate trade remedies in the face of noncompliance may be required. Furthermore, trade restrictions employed to support domestic environmental standards are by definition unilaterally set. As a result, the severity and kind of environmental trade measures employed varies from country to country and even from issue to issue.

A threshold question is why trade measures should ever be used to enforce environmental policies. The answer, of course, is that trade actions should not be used to pursue environmental goals; environmental policy tools should be. In fact, in public policy schools, it is standard learning that policy tools should be tailored to the problem at hand (Tinbergen 1952) and thus that trade measures should be applied only in response to trade problems. But lacking a global authority for managing environmental issues that makes cost internalization and other environmental policy mechanisms feasible and effective, the use of trade measures becomes politically attractive, if not strictly necessary.

In some cases, where the restrictions are employed as a shield to ensure domestic environmental regulations apply with equal force to imported products, trade measures are incidental to government efforts to protect public health or ecological resources. In such cases, the legitimacy of using trade restrictions is not really in doubt so long as the regulations treat imports no less favorably than domestic products. But trade purists do question the use of environmental trade measures as a sword or sanction to force another country to change its behavior within its own territory or the global commons. They argue that a range of

---

37. A number of other environmental agreements contain trade provisions (appendix D).

other interventions, from diplomatic warnings to withdrawal of financial assistance, could be and should be employed.

This argument is valid; other tools for exercising influence should be tried before trade penalties are invoked. The tools of traditional diplomacy in particular—notes, demarches, and consultations by diplomats—have a role to play. In fact, before resorting to trade measures, parties should be required to demonstrate good-faith efforts to resolve their environmental concerns through diplomacy. But in the end, very few options exist in the international realm for disciplining misbehavior. In other areas of international affairs, truly bad actors face military action. But air strikes and similar interventions would likely be viewed as overkill in the environmental context and in any case would likely do more environmental harm than good. Trade blockades or embargoes are another possibility for penalizing outlaw states and might be justified in the face of extreme ecological harm (Kelly 1992).

Ultimately, if no other way of rectifying an environmental injury produces a satisfactory result, trade measures must be available. What is important—and what the GATT review process should focus on—is whether a particular measure is roughly commensurate to the harm that has been suffered. Without guidance as to what trade measures are appropriate under various circumstances, some countries invariably leap to severe restrictions.[38] Specifically, trade bans—the nuclear weapon of trade restrictions—are invoked indiscriminately. To avoid overkill, parties should have available a spectrum of trade measures so they can match their policy responses to the severity of the environmental harm they face.

A range of trade measures commonly available, in roughly decreasing order of intrusiveness on trade flows, are identified in box 5.4.[39] Some

---

38. The choice of trade penalties can often be explained by the domestic politics of the country imposing trade measures to reinforce its environmental policies. Countries such as the United States are relatively impervious to the threat of retaliation and therefore are much more willing to "go ballistic" in support of even minor environmental preferences. The US ban on Mexican tuna in response to the death of a small number (relative to the total population) of nonendangered dolphins and the inability of the Bush administration to get any congressional support for Commerce Secretary Robert Mosbacher's promise to the Mexicans that the United States would change the Marine Mammal Protection Act to relieve Mexico of the tuna embargo demonstrates this principle. Secretary Mosbacher expressed great incredulity that the environmental "tail" could wag the trade "dog." But with little sense in Congress that Mexico (or anyone else) could or would retaliate in response to the US tuna ban, there was no incentive for action to relieve Mexico. Smaller or more trade-dependent countries dare not impose heavy trade restrictions in support of their environmental policy preferences. Austria's failed tropical timber restrictions offer a cautionary tale in this regard.

39. For a more complete discussion of these trade measures, including examples of each kind, see appendix B.

Box 5.4   Measures to Affect Environmental Behavior

1. Trade sanctions on "innocent" products
2. Import bans on environmentally harmful products
3. Import restrictions short of a ban
4. Differential tariffs or taxes
5. Labeling requirements
6. Diplomatic warnings
7. Informal consultations
8. Environmental educational programs
9. Technology transfer to polluters
10. Financial assistance to polluters

Items 6 through 10 fall outside the trade sanction–restriction spectrum. Items 6 and 7 are pre–trade measure actions, and 8 through 10 are actually inducements to act in response to environmental harms. The last four items are, moreover, the only unequivocally GATT-consistent measures on the list. Further explanation of each trade measure may be found in appendix B.

environmental agreements do specify the trade measures to be employed for noncompliance, but the mandated action is almost always top-of-the-line sanctions or an import ban. Rather than moving straight away to such severe trade actions, an escalating scale of measures would be more appropriate, starting with nontrade actions (e.g., written warnings) and moving up the spectrum of trade measures only over time. Moreover, rather than immediately resorting to threats and negative incentives, parties should consider the potentially greater efficacy of positive inducements for changing behavior, such as technical or financial assistance.

How far up the spectrum a party is entitled to go should depend on the seriousness of the environmental injury it has suffered, which in turn is a function of the intrinsic seriousness of the injury and where the harm occurs (see appendix E for an illustrative matrix of appropriate remedies). How much effort has been applied to make lesser measures work should also be considered.

In assessing the appropriateness of a particular trade measure, some consideration should also be given to the likely effectiveness of the chosen action. In this regard, Hufbauer, Schott, and Elliott (1990) have examined dozens of case histories of economic sanctions. They observe that trade leverage is likely to be effective in only a limited number of circumstances. Specifically, they conclude:

- political pressures often overshadow economic deprivations;

- the more parties needed to implement restrictions, the less likely they are to succeed;

- the smaller and weaker the target country, the more likely it is that economic pressure will succeed;

- economic pressure works best against erstwhile friends and trading partners;

- restrictions that impose high costs on the countries effectuating the penalty are unlikely to succeed;

- objectives and means should be carefully assessed to ensure the "right tool for the job" is selected.

To ensure that unilateral trade actions remain focused on motivating change in environmental behavior and do not become an element of protection for domestic competitors, such trade restrictions should be time-limited. After a fixed period, perhaps three years, countries should be required to review any trade bans or other unilaterally imposed trade restrictions and to recertify that the measures are achieving an environmental purpose. This would help to spur negotiations on international standards and would help to weed out trade actions that are ultimately counterproductive from an environmental point of view.

Another refinement that should be considered is the traditional use of trade measures by one country on another. Actions taken against all companies from a targeted nation make little sense in today's world. Indeed, the "nationality" of particular companies is often hard to determine (Grunwald and Flamm 1985).[40] It might be more appropriate to target specific "bad actors" and to apply trade restrictions on a company-by-company basis. A more refined company-specific approach to trade measures would permit restrictions to be aimed directly at the real environmental culprits and reward competing companies whose activities conform to the environmental norm in question. For instance, a trade ban narrowly targeted on Mexican tuna caught using purse seine nets that are dangerous for dolphins might have been more effective than a complete ban on Mexican tuna imports to the United States.[41] Specifically, a partial ban, barring only the tainted product, creates an incentive for individual Mexican fisherman to fish in a dolphin-safe manner so they can sell their product in the lucrative US market.

---

40. Not only is the nationality of companies getting harder to determine, identifying the nationality of products is also now very problematic. See, for example, the 1988 USITC antidumping case on forklifts from Japan, in which the US International Trade Commission struggled with the issue of how to handle a multinationally produced product.

41. One of the strongest policy precepts to come out of the Hufbauer, Schott, and Elliott study (1990) is the suggestion that the more narrowly tailored the economic penalty, the greater the odds of its efficacy.

Ecolabeling

In almost all circumstances, labeling offers a useful "default" trade restriction. Permitting products to be sold but giving consumers information about possible environmental harms related to the product strikes a useful balance between trade and environmental goals in many situations where the appropriateness of more severe restrictions is uncertain. Labeling can, in fact, be a powerful tool for environmental policy advances. For example, the GATT battle over the US ban on Mexican tuna really took place after the war was already over. Specifically, almost no Mexican tuna caught using the dolphin-killing purse seine nets was being sold in the United States at the time the ban was put in place because the US tuna canners had begun a "dolphin safe" labeling program that had made it nearly impossible to sell dolphin "unsafe" tuna in America.

The potent combination of labeling and consumer market power can also be seen in the success of California's Proposition 65, which requires consumer warnings at the point of sale for any product known to produce more than a de minimus risk of cancer or birth defects. This law has resulted in the reformulation of many products to make them safer. For example, canners stopped using lead solder. And the makers of White Out typewriter correction fluid eliminated trichloroethylene (TCE), a dangerous carcinogen, from their product (Roe 1989).

It is worth noting that the GATT has accepted the appropriateness of voluntary ecolabels and expressly approved the US dolphin-safe labeling scheme in the tuna-dolphin case.[42] The use of labels therefore provides a valuable approach to some of the more troubling trade and environment disputes. For instance, concerns about the sale of tropical timber and rain forest deforestation (Myers 1992) might effectively be dealt with through a well-structured labeling program (box 5.5). This would permit consumers to signal tropical timber producers of their interest in sustainable forestry and avoid the potentially counterproductive effects of a timber ban.

Policy Recommendations

- GATT should move away from its traditional differentiation between environmental standards aimed at products (acceptable) and production processes (unacceptable).

---

42. Indeed, then–GATT Director General Arthur Dunkel called for expanded ecolabels and greater consumer sovereignty in response to the trade and environment pressures brought to bear on the GATT in the wake of the tuna-dolphin case (Cairncross 1993).

Box 5.5   Ecolabeling

A well-structured labeling program must include several elements. First, it needs to reflect the spectrum of issues related to the product at hand. In the case of tropical timber, this would mean attention to the role of forests in carbon sequestration to mitigate climate change, soil erosion, water pollution, and loss of biodiversity. The process of setting environmental criteria should furthermore be open to all interested parties, including foreign producers that will be affected.

Second, despite the difficulties inherent in simultaneously analyzing different environmental values, labels should consider the life-cycle impact of products, not simply a single pollution or conservation criterion. The difficulty of making apples-to-oranges comparisons can be reduced by using multiple scales (e.g., one ranking for air pollution, another for climate change effects, another for water pollution) and not trying to reduce all the variables to a common metric. To the extent possible, the criteria should be scientifically derived and quantifiable.

In addition, the criteria chosen should be sensitive to differences in natural endowments among countries. Requiring Swedish paper producers to meet high recycled-fiber content requirements for paper (as Germany is) may not be fair or environmentally sound in light of Sweden's tree-rich, people-poor (and thus recycled paper–poor) condition. In these circumstances, standards based on levels of recycling in the producer's domestic market might be a more reasonable market-entry requirement. Of course, Germany will argue that unless it can require all paper to have 50 percent recycled content, it will not be able to address its waste problem.

Finally, draft standards should be made available for comment by all interested parties, and label standards should only be finalized after the regulating authority has considered and responded to all substantive criticisms. Special scrutiny should be given to the environmental legitimacy of any criteria that yield commercial benefits to domestic producers at the expense of imported products.

■ In separating legitimate environmental regulations from trade obstacles, GATT's rules should focus on the nature and locus of the environmental injury at issue, recognizing that this will legitimize some production process standards.

■ In an ecologically interdependent world, a blanket prohibition on unilateral or extraterritorial environmental trade measures cannot be sustained. Where parties are responding to global or transboundary harms, their use of reasonable trade restrictions should, under defined circumstances, be reinforced by the GATT.

■ The rules of the GATT should be clarified to guarantee that parties invoking trade restrictions consistent with international environmental agreements are not vulnerable to trade challenges.

■ The GATT rules used to weigh competing trade and environmental values should be "rebalanced" to give greater deference to the judgments of national decision makers about environmental goals and the means chosen to pursue them.

- GATT should develop an illustrative list of available trade measures and circumstances when their use might be appropriate.

- Parties should be encouraged to use the full spectrum of tools available for promoting their environmental policies and to avoid resorting to trade bans as an opening gambit.

- Environmental judgments should be made by environmental officials, and GATT should seek to build new dispute structures that accommodate this principle.

Wielding Swords: The Offensive Use of Environmental Trade Measures

Recalibrating GATT's balancing test for trade and environment conflicts, as suggested in the last chapter, will make it easier to defend legitimate environmental policies against GATT challenges that they are "too high" and constitute trade barriers. By focusing on the environmental injury in question and substituting the more deferential "clear disproportionality" review standard for the current "necessary" test, which results in excessive second-guessing of national environmental policy approaches, the proposed rules put GATT on a greener tack. Fundamentally, however, the reforms advanced would simply fine-tune the existing balancing scheme.

In contrast, the new three-pronged test to replace Article XX, and especially the environmental injury focus, would quite dramatically reconfigure the GATT handling of "offensive" environmental trade measures. The GATT rules as applied today forbid extraterritorial measures, effectively making the use of trade as leverage GATT-illegal. As this study has made clear, these rigid rules cannot be maintained in an ecologically interdependent world, and they are practically unworkable in the absence of an international environmental regime. This chapter examines how and why the GATT prohibitions on extraterritorial and unilateral trade actions might be softened, thereby reducing the clash between trade and environmental policy goals while legitimizing and controlling limited use of offensive environmental trade measures.

The proposition that trade leverage should be available to promote global environmental protection is the third core element of the environmental critique of the international trade system, spelled out in chapter 2. At the same time, concerns about unilateral and extraterritorial trade actions go to the heart of many free traders' fears about the harm environmentalism might do to trade liberalization. In fact, from the point of view of much of the world, the importance of the tuna-dolphin decision (chapter 1, box 1.3) was that it enunciated clearly the GATT ban against countries acting alone and using trade mechanisms to address environmental issues arising outside their jurisdiction.[1]

As this chapter will explain, the focus on the evils of unilateralism and extraterritoriality makes little sense. We do not have established international rules to protect the global environment, nor do we have mechanisms that permit a multilateral response to environmental harms. Without a Global Environmental Organization to play this role, it should come as no surprise that the trade regime, perhaps supported by the web of existing international environmental agreements, must fill the vacuum—at least in the short run.

More importantly, the terms "unilateralism" and "extraterritoriality" are used far too loosely in most trade and environment debates. Specifically, in deciding when the use of trade measures—sanctions, swords, or shields—is appropriate, three questions must be answered:

■ Who sets the environmental standards?

■ Who decides if the standards are being met?

■ Who determines what trade measures are appropriate?

GATT dispute settlement procedures simultaneously address these three questions. Cases arise as a result of challenges by countries facing environmental trade measures. For example, Country B brings a GATT case against Country A after A has imposed trade sanctions or restrictions on B to advance A's environmental policies. GATT dispute panels muddle through all three questions simultaneously in determining whether the trade measures employed by Country A violate A's GATT obligations to Country B.

When, for instance, Mexico brought a GATT claim against the United States claiming discrimination against its tuna exports to the United States, the GATT dispute panel rejected the US right to set standards for Mexican fishing practices. Having determined that the US dolphin-protection standard was inappropriately "extrajurisdictionally" applied to Mexico, the GATT panel had no need to decide whether Mexico had

---

1. When Mexico refused (in the shadow of negotiations for the North American Free Trade Agreement) to present its tuna-dolphin victory to the GATT Council for ratification, the European Community launched its own challenge to the US tuna embargo to drive home the points about unilateralism and extraterritoriality.

in fact violated the standard set or to determine whether the remedy employed by the United States was reasonable.

In addition to conflating the three "who decides" issues, GATT's existing structure of rules makes no provision whatsoever for the use of environmental trade measures as sanctions or swords. That is to say, it is considered improper under the GATT to use trade measures to try to shape behavior abroad. As noted earlier, the GATT does permit countries to use trade measures to protect their own domestic environmental standards so long as the restrictions imposed are aimed at products, not foreign production processes.

This chapter argues for a more refined GATT structure to manage the use of environmental trade measures aimed at behavior and harms occurring outside the country imposing the sanctions or restrictions. Specifically, four separate circumstances—which are increasingly problematic from a GATT perspective—need to be considered:

- trade restrictions or sanctions expressly authorized by international agreement and imposed multilaterally;

- unilaterally imposed trade measures employed in support of internationally agreed standards (and thus at least tacitly internationally condoned);

- unilaterally imposed trade measures invoked without the benefit of any multilateral agreement but aimed at global or transboundary harms affecting the country imposing the measures;

- unilaterally imposed trade measures invoked without any multilateral agreement and aimed at extraterritorial harms with no direct physical impact on the country imposing the measures.

Extraterritoriality Is Not the Issue

The GATT's "product" focus is tied to dated concepts of sovereignty (box 5.2). Today, nations have interests in the environmental effects of activities that take place outside their own territory, both because pollution may spill over borders into their physical space and because environmental harms to the global commons can be seen as an injury to the environmental interests of every country and therefore to each nation individually as well.

As Baker (1992) argues, trade actions to defend the global environment should not be considered extrajurisdictional. Rather than making GATT legality turn on the issue of where the trade measure is aimed—barring extraterritorial actions—the critical determination should be the presence or absence of a bona fide environmental injury[2] and an assessment of who applies an environmental standard.

Fundamentally, the GATT is asymmetrical; its rules only permit a decision that particular environmental standards "excessively" intrude on trade prerogatives. The GATT provides no comparable process for declaring a nation's economic activities (and related trade) to be environmentally "inadequate"—and therefore an unfair basis for trade. Thus, the GATT fails to satisfactorily accommodate environmental protection in defining the ground rules for trade.

The key question is, how are baseline environmental standards to be defined? There is no consensus on this point. In fact, each of the four cases identified above might, to some observers, define the appropriate multilaterally determined threshold of "adequacy." The clearest case is where international standards have been agreed upon, a violation is adjudged multilaterally, and trade measures set by international agreement are imposed. There is little doubt in such a case about the multilateral foundation for action. For example, a country found by the parties to the Montreal Protocol to be in violation of the protocol's CFC phaseout and thus subject to a trade embargo should have no cause for complaint—no matter that its GATT rights have been infringed by extraterritorial trade actions on the part of other GATT parties.

Multilateral approaches to global issues are undoubtedly superior to unilateral action. But getting worldwide cooperation in response to ever-pressing environmental problems can be a trying exercise. There are thus other cases where the imposition of environmental trade measures appears somewhat more unilateral but still has elements of multilateralism. The second and third cases listed above are examples of this sort of "multilateral unilateralism." To give an example of the second situation, when the United States imposed trade restrictions on Norway for violation of the International Whaling Commission's whaling moratorium, the standard (no whale killing) had been set multilaterally, but the trade measures were imposed unilaterally. In this case, the trade actions were taken in the context of a multilateral environmental program and were therefore condoned in some sense by the other parties to the accord. If they wished, these parties could have disagreed with the US trade pen-

---

2. In effect, the issue boils down to a battle over the nature of the environmental problems the world faces and can be seen as a tussle between two fundamental philosophies. In John Donne's view of the world ("no man is an island"), the interdependence of nations and the continuity of the biosphere is salient, making the need to carve out new GATT rules addressing global environmental issues and other pollution spillovers critical. If, however, the great modern thinker and former Speaker of the US House of Representatives Thomas P. "Tip" O'Neill Jr. ("all politics is local") is correct—and truly global problems are few and far between (Subramanian 1992) and political judgments about how to respond vary widely—then the emphasis on developing new GATT rules to respond to global and transboundary environmental issue is overdrawn.

alties, rejecting either the judgment about Norway's noncompliance or the severity of the measures imposed by the United States.

In the third case, as in the environmental injury or legitimacy judgment spelled out in chapter 5, adequacy is defined unilaterally, at least with regard to the specific instance at hand. But the unilateral environmental trade measure is backed up by the multilaterally agreed principle that causing global or transboundary environmental harm is unacceptable.[3] Thus, the trade action is carried out within a multilateral legal structure and is therefore somewhat confined. In such cases—at the outer edge of multilateral unilateralism—it would be appropriate for GATT to examine the judgment of the party imposing trade actions regarding the legitimacy of the environmental injury suffered (i.e., the goal of the environmental policy that resulted in the imposition of trade measures) and the appropriateness of the trade penalties imposed (i.e., the means used to carry out the environmental policy) according to the balancing test laid out in chapter 5.

Thus, for example, if the United States were to limit Brazil's US exports because the Brazilian government failed to mandate the use of "turtle excluder devices" by all of its shrimp fisherman (*Inside U.S. Trade* 6 May 1994, 13), the US trade action would have no direct multilateral authorization. Yet, because the sea turtles in question do migrate into US waters, the United States has some basis for claiming a transboundary environmental harm—and thus some justification for its judgment concerning the inadequacy of Brazil's turtle protection standards and its actions under established international law.

A GATT review would appropriately examine the legitimacy of the US environmental goal and the means chosen to implement it. This would ensure that the US unilateral action was subject to bounds set multilaterally. Such oversight, if conducted properly, would protect Brazil from overreaching by the United States and simultaneously reinforce the use of environmental trade measures by the United States if employed in a defensible manner.

There is ample precedent in the trade realm for the use of environmental trade measures under the condition of multilateral unilateralism. In fact, trade actions based on a unilateral injury determination in conformity with established international standards are a familiar aspect of the existing trade system in the context of antidumping or countervailable subsidy cases. Adding environmental injuries to the list of actionable harms should therefore not be too disruptive, particularly if uni-

---

3. The obligation not to cause transboundary or global pollution harms is spelled out in the Stockholm Declaration, Principle 21, and the Rio Declaration, Principle 2, among other places. It is also well-established in international case law. See, e.g., the Corfu Channel case (*US v. Albania*) 1949 I.C.J.4; Lac Lanoux arbitration (*France v. Spain*) 12 R.I.A.A. 281 (1957); and the Trail Smelter case (*US v. Canada*) 3 R.I.A.A. 1905 (1941).

lateral imposition of environmental trade measures are subject to multilateral review.

Of course, to avoid abuse of the power to make unilateral determinations concerning the environmental harms they face, multilateral action in response to environmental problems should be encouraged. In fact, unilateral actions should be avoided unless international efforts to address the problems have failed. In any case, all environmental trade measures employed "offensively" should meet the chapter 5 criteria of a bona fide environmental issue presenting a "significant threat to the integrity or sustainability of an important species or ecosystem in which the party has an interest." Application of these tests of seriousness and scientific underpinning will ensure that countries do not act willy-nilly on the basis of their own predilections or whims, or worse, in response to domestic protectionist pressures.

The final case presents the most severe strain on the multilateral system. Where there exists no physical spillover—and thus not even a broadly defined multilateral obligation—unilateral trade sanctions or restrictions should not be accepted. Some environmentalists (and US politicians) would like to define any divergent standard that is lower than, for example, US standards as inadequate, even when the matter involves only local harms. But, as chapter 5 made clear, there is no environmental justification for such actions. Fears about competitive disadvantage should not, under these circumstances of limited harm, be dealt with unilaterally. The threat of psychological spillovers or competitive pressures creating "political drag" may be serious, but these harms must be dealt with through standards set by international agreement.

In sum, when international environmental agreements are violated or demonstrable transboundary or global environmental injuries result, a strong case can be made that environmental standards that permit such harm are "too low" and should be subject to trade disciplines. Ideally, an international environmental regime would exist to make judgments about environmental policies that are too lax.[4] In the absence of a Global Environmental Organization, however, enforceable environmental standards should be set internationally (first choice) or unilaterally with reference to established multilateral obligations (second choice).

Unilateralism: Evil or Necessity?

As chapter 5 indicated, there are enormous benefits—both economic and environmental—to international coordination of environmental regula-

---

4. In an ideal world, after a nation's environmental policy was deemed to be too lax—perhaps by a determination that its standards or environmental enforcement practices failed to uphold the polluter pays principle—those harmed by environmental problems whose costs are not internalized would be able to seek compensation for the impairment of their rights under GATT Article XXIII's compensation provisions.

tions. But is unilateral action in pursuit of environmental policy outcomes, particularly "multilateral unilateralism" as defined above, the bogeyman that it is often made out to be?

The European Union has made a crusade out of its anti-unilateralism position. Not only did it put the Tuna Dolphin II case on the GATT docket, it has made its "no unilateralism" stance all but nonnegotiable in its proposals to reconcile trade and environment conflicts. The EC official GATT statement (EC 1992b) on the issue suggests:

> The basic rule according to which a country should not unilaterally restrict imports on the basis of environmental damage that does not impact on a country's territory needs to be upheld. An important application of this rule is that there is no justification to require by unilateral trade restrictions that imported products conform with domestic regulations relating to the production method if production abroad is unrelated to environmental damage caused in the country of importation. . . . Environmental issues of common concern are complex and require discussions and negotiations among countries on environmental priorities and commitments, as well as an equitable sharing of the costs to protect the environment, so as to take into account the common but differentiated responsibilities of countries at different levels of development. This process would be circumvented if a country could take unilateral trade restrictions aimed at changing the environmental policies of another country, while ignoring the costs imposed on that country by trade restrictions. In prescribing such a rule, the GATT is not seeking to impose trade over environmental values, but rather to underline the importance of multilateral cooperation for addressing environmental problems of common concern.

Ironically, other than the United States, the European Union is the entity that has most often used unilateral trade measures. Its unilateral prohibitions on furs caught in leg-hold traps are in place, and its restrictions on cosmetics tested on animals will soon take effect.

The GATT trade and environment report, echoing the 1991 tuna-dolphin panel recommendation, also takes repeated aim at the evils of unilateralism, warning that allowing countries "unilaterally to apply trade restrictions not for the purpose of enforcing its own laws within its own jurisdiction but to impose the standards set out in its laws on other countries" risks endless trade chaos and the breakdown of international cooperation. Other observers have railed against unilateralism as "environmental imperialism" (*Financial Times*, 12 February 1992, 3) and excoriated US unilateral action as tantamount to setting America up as the world's "environmental dictator" (*New York Times*, 3 May 1992, section 3, p. 7). "Multilateralists" argue for decisions to be made by international agreement, fearing that actions by individual countries will break down the mutual cooperation necessary to keep markets open and that unilateralism is inequitable because only a few powerful countries are able to act on their own and get away with it.

Unilateralism is an ugly word almost everywhere but the United States. The Rio Declaration suggests unilateral environmental trade measures "should be avoided." And even in the United States, almost no one admits to being a "unilateralist" by choice.

But the US government (and to some extent the European Union) falls back on unilateral action because there is no established international mechanism to enforce environmental standards or policies. Moreover, the need to achieve unanimity for decisions taken in the international realm can make multicountry agreements bland, inoffensive, and ineffectual. The intrinsic difficulty of multilateral decision making and the lack of existing institutional structures for effective international environmental policymaking therefore makes unilateral action a necessary, if unfortunate, policy option in some circumstances. Even Robert Hudec (1989, 116), a renowned trade aficionado, accepts the inevitability of some unilateral actions, concluding that, under certain circumstances, intentional disregard of GATT obligations may be useful in "breaking legal deadlocks and stimulating improvements in GATT law." Such "justified disobedience" should, in Hudec's view, be conditioned by a requirement that the disobeying country imposes the same standards on itself that it seeks to mandate for others. The US Council for International Business (1994) also acknowledges the inevitability of some unilateral environmental trade measures and argues for a new interpretation of the GATT safeguards rules (Annex 1 A14 of the Uruguay Round text [GATT 1993b]) to accommodate such actions.

A number of observers have argued that the threat of (or actual use of) unilateral trade actions can further progress on multilateral agreements (e.g., Wirth 1992a). In the trade context, Bayard and Elliott (1994) demonstrate, for example, that the US "Super 301" provision, threatening unilateral trade actions, helped to produce major advances in the GATT dispute settlement process during the Uruguay Round negotiations. From an environmental perspective, the US threat of trade sanctions helped advance an agreement to bar fishing with drift nets, a practice environmentalists call "strip mining" the sea (e.g., "South Korea Likely to Follow Japan and Halt Driftnet Fishing," Reuters, 4 December 1991).

Charnovitz (1993a) notes, moreover, that "treaties do not appear like magic spirits. They must be laboriously negotiated. . . . Thus, those arguing that unilateral action is inappropriate have the burden of demonstrating the feasibility of an alternative new dynamic of spontaneous co-operation." While the expectation of spontaneous cooperation may be unrealistic, it is reasonable to ask the proponents of joint action to lead the way in developing effective multilateral policymaking mechanisms. Too often the opposite has been true. For example, it was some of the strongest critics of US unilateralism—the European Community, Brazil, and India—that slowed efforts to launch multilateral GATT talks throughout the early 1980s (Ostry 1990). Moreover, Canada, another leading critic of US unilateralism, has recently questioned the validity of the trade provisions in certain international environmental agreements in statements to the GATT (Canada, GATT delegation 1993).

The Multilateral Ideal

In an ideal, multilateralist world, international environmental agreements would establish environmental standards addressing all matters in which pollution spills across national borders. A Global Environmental Organization or the parties to individual environmental agreements would be called upon to evaluate compliance, and in conjunction with the GATT, determine appropriate trade remedies for noncompliance.

There are, in fact, hundreds of international environmental accords in place. Multilateral agreements, moreover, have broad support as the most reasonable and appropriate basis for determining when GATT should accommodate environmental constraints on trade. Richard Eglin (1993c) of the GATT Secretariat has called multilateral cooperation "the most honorable approach" to setting environmental parameters for trade. The European Community also endorsed "broad international consensus"—that is, multilateral conventions—as the only circumstance under which trade restrictions are appropriate to reinforce environmental policies (EC 1992b). The GATT Working Party on Environmental Measures in International Trade (EMIT) has also developed a broad consensus that transboundary environmental problems should be addressed through international agreements (see Austrian EMIT Summary, reprinted in *Inside U.S. Trade*, 15 October 1993).

But this simple prescription for integrating trade and environmental policymaking elides several important questions:

- How many parties must agree to establish an international environmental agreement?

- Even if there exists an international agreement setting standards, who decides when a country is in noncompliance?

- Can trade restrictions or sanctions be imposed on nonparties to environmental agreements?

- What happens if the agreement does not specify what trade restrictions or sanctions are appropriate?

- When should a party be able to exceed harmonized standards?

What Constitutes a Consensus

How many parties are needed to establish an environmental agreement reinforced by international trading system rules is a matter of some controversy. Where the great majority of GATT parties are members of an accord—such as the Montreal Protocol, with 126 signatories including more than 100 GATT parties—there is widespread agreement that the rules of international trade should be designed to support the accord's environmental goals. Some observers have therefore suggested that participation in an agreement by a majority of the GATT parties would be an appropriate threshold for demonstrating true multilateral consensus. This level of support, however, would be unreasonable in many circumstances. For example, a number of conservation agreements (e.g., those designed to manage declining fish stocks) have only a handful of members but are still important international accords.

With such concerns in mind, the European Parliament has endorsed GATT recognition for any agreement that includes countries representing 80 percent of the production or practices concerned (EC 1992c). Others have called for acceptance of any agreement reflecting membership of a "substantial proportion" of both producer countries and those affected by the practice in question (US Council for International Business 1993). But such rules are unworkable in that they may effectively give veto power over environmental standards to those that may be the problem. For example, if 100 countries were to agree that tropical forests should be managed sustainably, objections by Malaysia and Brazil (representing more than 20 percent of all rain forest land, or a "substantial proportion" of timber production) could block any international agreement on minimum criteria for forest conservation.

Similarly, the International Whaling Convention (IWC) has 31 signatories, most of which are neither "producers" nor "consumers" of whales. While the vast majority of the parties to the IWC have voted for a moratorium on whale killing, the three remaining producing and consuming countries—Japan, Iceland, and Norway—all favor whaling. Indeed, the general requirement that international accords be based on total consensus creates a danger that laggards will dictate the terms of any environmental agreement and argues for a less stringent participation threshold.[5]

Unhappiness with the UN system of giving every country an equal vote has created strong sentiment among the countries with the world's largest economies (and especially within the United States) that small countries should not be able to control international environmental policymaking by forming a "small country" majority. In fact, many economically powerful countries like the weighted voting structures used by the IMF and World Bank, which assign decision-making power based

---

5. For a more complete discussion of international environmental decision making and "leader/laggard" dynamics, see Haas, Keohane, and Levy (1993). The laggard problem also suggests that unilateral action in support of environmental values, in the absence of an international agreement, might be necessary.

on contributions. The current World Bank decision process, for example, gives the United States a 17 percent share of the votes; Japan has a 7 percent share; Germany, France, and Britain each have a 5 percent share, and so on. The Global Environment Facility (GEF), operating under the auspices of the World Bank, the UN Environment Programme (UNEP), and the UN Development Programme (UNDP), has modified this tradition by requiring that any vote of its governing council carry by a "double majority"—reflecting 60 percent of all participants on a one-country, one-vote basis and of countries representing 60 percent of the donations to the GEF. But to avoid the stress that might result from a split decision, the GEF has announced its intention to try to resolve issues by consensus.

Another variant on the economic power versus equity theme can be found in the decision-making rules of the funding mechanism of the Montreal Protocol. Under these rules, decisions are made by consensus among an executive committee of 14 countries (with seats rotating among regional groupings), seven of which are developed countries and seven of which are developing countries. If a vote is required on a proposal, it must receive a majority of both the developed and developing countries to move forward.

In thinking about the participation question in the context of global warming, William Cline (1992) developed a weighting scheme for international decision making that reflects the realities of big-country power (derived both from economic strength and population) and the need to have decisions reflect some sense of equity. Cline allots one-third weight based on population, one-third weight based on current greenhouse gas emissions, and one-third weight based on economic size. Some similar multiple-criteria scale might be useful in assessing the breadth of support for international environmental agreements.

Avoiding votes altogether is, of course, the easiest route to follow. One of the long-standing procedural strengths of the GATT is its preference for decision making by consensus—but reflecting the fact that the powerful countries have more of a say and that opposition by one or more smaller countries does not stop progress. This process, requiring general consensus but not unanimity and granting the most powerful countries an informal veto, may be what is most appropriate for assessing the legitimacy of international trade agreements. Another way to reach a similar result would be to follow the decision process provided in GATT Article XX(h), exempting certain commodity agreements from GATT obligations so long as they are submitted to GATT and not disapproved.[6] This would allow powerful countries to use their muscle to avoid disapproval votes where they felt strongly about the agreement at issue.

---

6. The US Council for International Business (1993) has developed an interesting proposal along these lines drawing on the unadopted Chapter VI of the Havana Charter for an International Trade Organization.

Given the difficulty in specifying precisely what constitutes a consensus among the countries of the world community, it may be more useful to focus on the qualitative aspects of particular agreements in identifying international environmental standards that deserve GATT recognition. As a rule, multilateral environmental standards or policies should be negotiated in a forum open to all interested countries and be open to accession by any country that wishes to join on terms no less favorable than those accorded to any other country. In addition, the opportunity to participate in decisions interpreting the agreement should be available to all interested countries.

To the extent possible, multilateral standards should be set without express voting—relying on the chairperson of a negotiation to find common ground that all participants can live with, if not endorse enthusiastically. Where, however, dissenters cannot be brought on board an otherwise reasonably strong consensus, the standards should not be watered down simply to achieve unanimity. Instead, a vote should be taken on the standards combined with whatever package of inducements can be fashioned to sweeten the deal for hesitant participants. Establishing an affirmative international environmental obligation should require a 60 percent majority of weighted votes—based half on population and half on GDP—of all nations that can demonstrate more than a de minimus connection (as producers, consumers, or guardians of affected resources) to the issue at hand.

Once an international standard has been set, the GATT should recognize as legitimate any trade actions mandated by the agreement. In addition, as explained above, any trade measure invoked in furtherance of internationally agreed standards should also be condoned. Thus, for example, the GATT should not second-guess trade restrictions undertaken in compliance with the Montreal Protocol,[7] particularly if a judgment of noncompliance against a party is undertaken multilaterally.

Who Decides on Compliance?

Setting environmental standards is one thing; assessing compliance with them is quite another, especially in the international realm. Even when there exist recognized common standards, few international agreements specify clearly who judges whether particular countries are in compliance with their obligations. Many environmental agreements make no mention of enforcement whatsoever. This seeming oversight should really be no surprise. Enforcement procedures go to the heart of strongly held beliefs about national sovereignty. Undoubtedly, the prospect of foreigners exercising police powers (whether under the aegis of

---

7. Whether the protocol was in fact violated would be subject to review, as would be the consistency of the penalty with the terms of the international agreement.

international authority or not) and showing up with guns and badges for inspections is, for many countries, fundamentally unacceptable. Thus, glossing over the question of enforcement is often essential to achieving agreement on environmental treaty language. But the decision to duck this difficult matter simply relegates the issue to trade and environmental policymakers, who must face the issue when questions are raised.

Assessing compliance is not always a complicated issue.[8] Some international environmental agreements have straightforward triggers. The Montreal Protocol, for example, bars trade in products containing CFCs with nonparties to the protocol. Who is and who is not a party to the accord is a matter of public record. Some violators of international agreements, moreover, make no effort to hide their disobedience. For instance, Norway issued a press release declaring its intent to continue whaling despite the IWC whaling moratorium and arguing (weakly) that its actions were not in violation of the international accord. There are, however, further layers of uncertainty that can complicate compliance decisions.

Since there is no established verification program for most agreements, catching violators depends on information advanced by the media, nongovernment organizations, or individual countries.[9] Even when information on a possible violation is available, it is often not clear who should act on it. The Global Environmental Organization proposed in chapter 4 could lead the international enforcement charge. Alternatively, parties to a treaty could make compliance determinations for that treaty. Most treaties provide for regular meetings of the "conference of the parties" to the agreement to review the implementation of the accord. This provides at least a forum for assessing compliance, if no guarantee that the parties will have the will to enforce the agreed-upon standards.

Relying on multilateral decision making, as was noted earlier, is almost inevitably cumbersome. International bodies are notoriously slow-moving, and the problems of torpor are compounded in the com-

---

8. The most egregious noncompliance, and the easiest to address, is nonparticipation in an agreement. When countries claim to be in compliance with international standards but are not, either by design or by neglect, more difficult enforcement issues are raised.

9. It would be useful to develop multilateral verification programs similar to those used in the past to verify compliance with nuclear weapons agreements. Certainly in the absence of such programs, and probably in addition to them, it is important for nations possessing the technological capabilities—satellites, infrared sensors, etc.—to monitor compliance with global environmental accords. In fact, reporting on compliance with international environmental agreements could provide a new raison d'être for the world's intelligence agencies, which are in need of a new mission in the post–Cold War era, and at least in some cases have high-technology equipment to bring to bear on the problem. Sophisticated tracking equipment might be used, for example, to monitor compliance with the Montreal Protocol phaseout of CFCs.

pliance context.[10] Countries may not actively participate in all of the ongoing work of the various international conventions of which they are members and therefore may not feel comfortable coming to concrete conclusions on compliance. Other countries may be reluctant to enforce agreements out of solidarity with those who are in noncompliance or out of fear that someday the shoe will be on the other foot.

Given the difficulty of organizing a timely decision-making process by the parties to a convention and until such time that a functioning Global Environmental Organization is available to make prompt compliance adjudications, unilateral enforcement of international environmental standards is not only unavoidable but valuable. Indeed, actions by individual countries or ad hoc groups of countries will in many cases be the only viable mechanism for enforcing international environmental standards or agreements. The focus of the international trading system should therefore be on channeling unilateral trade restrictions and ensuring that any such restrictions meet basic tests of environmental legitimacy and rough proportionality between the trade penalty and the environmental harm targeted. In doing so, the GATT can help to streamline the use of environmental trade measures, minimize collateral damage to trade liberalization efforts, and help to legitimize appropriate unilateral actions while spotlighting overreaching or protectionist abuses.

Recognizing the need for a more effective multilateral compliance assessment process, this study argues that the world community needs a Global Environment Organization. Indeed, an international environmental regime would be able to facilitate multilateral enforcement of environmental standards and, in doing so, minimize the need for unilateral trade measures. In the absence of a GEO, however, some element of unilateral action (or partial multilateral action) by those who believe an international environmental obligation has been ignored or violated, subject to review in a multilateral forum, may be required.

Multilateral environmental procedures should always be pursued first as the preferable policy option. But where such efforts do not succeed, unilateral actions within a multilateral structure of bounds should be considered a policy alternative. The inability to obtain broad support for trade penalties for violations of the endangered species provisions of the CITES agreement, for instance, highlights the need for multilateral unilateralism. The decision of the United States to impose trade sanctions on Taiwan for failing to control illegal trafficking in rhinoceros horns and the body parts of endangered tigers offers an example of this category of trade actions.

If Taiwan were a GATT party and it were to complain to the GATT about the trade penalties they face as a result of the US actions, a GATT

---

10. In contravention of this norm, the GATT Uruguay Round agreement (understanding on Dispute Settlement, paragraph 12.8) commits the parties to complete dispute settlement cases within six months.

panel might be asked to examine first the issue of whether the United States acted in furtherance of an international environmental agreement. If this was in fact the case, the scope of any GATT review should be narrowed to the question of whether the penalties imposed were clearly disproportional to the environmental harm. The broader question of whether the United States was entitled to apply environmental trade measures in the first place would not be relevant.

The international legitimacy of these compliance judgments would be enhanced if the review mechanism were divided between the GATT and an environmental body—if not a new GEO, then the UN Commission on Sustainable Development, the parties to the environmental agreement in question, or UNEP. The participating environmental institution could pass judgment on environmental issues, with any conclusions adopted by reference in the GATT. Adjudication of trade policy issues would remain the responsibility of the GATT. Truly "mixed" issues would be settled by agreement of both institutions. Disputes between the two bodies would have to be negotiated to resolution or, as a last resort, settled by an outside arbiter such as the International Court of Justice. Particularly egregious acts of environmental misbehavior probably should be taken up by the UN Security Council, as was Iraq's "eco-terrorism" in releasing oil into the Persian Gulf.

Nonparties

Another critical issue involves the imposition of discriminatory trade restrictions for noncompliance with international environmental standards on GATT parties (otherwise entitled to nondiscriminatory treatment) that are not parties to the environmental agreement in question. For example, the Montreal Protocol mandates that its signatories limit trade in products containing CFCs with nonparties to the protocol. If a nonsignatory to the protocol that is a GATT member (Morocco, for example) were harmed by such restrictions, that country would have a potential GATT case against those upholding the protocol's discriminatory trade restrictions in violation of the GATT's most-favored nation principle.

This genre of GATT claim should not be accepted. If countries are to enjoy the benefits of the international trading regime, they can reasonably be expected to bear the responsibilities of participation in widely accepted international environmental efforts.[11] The alternative—permitting non-

11. Being a signatory to an environmental accord should not actually be the deciding factor; rather, consistency with the environmental standards laid out for signatories should be the touchstone. Well-drafted environmental agreements already reflect this subtle distinction. For example, the Montreal Protocol's trade restrictions do not focus on party status, but rather on a country's consistency with the substantive requirements of the accord. At the November 1993 meeting of the Montreal Protocol parties, four countries

parties to environmental agreements to assert their GATT rights while in contravention of internationally determined environmental requirements—encourages free riding on the environmental efforts of others and creates a disincentive to join international agreements. Not only does this nonparticipation diminish the effectiveness of the environmental accord, it gives free riders an opportunity to enjoy a competitive advantage in the global marketplace by carrying on environmentally harmful (and likely cost-reducing) practices others have forsworn, creating both environmental and competitiveness tensions.

One important business association, the US Council for International Business (1993), also argues that GATT parties should be permitted, under certain circumstances, to derogate from GATT obligations and to impose trade restrictions pursuant to international environmental agreements on other GATT parties, even if these other countries are nonparties to the agreement. In such cases, however, the council would permit the GATT party subject to trade restrictions to claim compensation for "nullification and impairment" of GATT benefits pursuant to GATT Article XXIII. A GATT panel assessing this claim would examine whether the complaining country had a "reasonable expectation that the conditions of access would not be changed in the future" and whether the effect of the trade measure was "disproportionately concentrated on the country bringing the complaint."[12]

Whether a country is a party to an international environmental agreement therefore should have no bearing on the legitimacy of trade actions under that agreement being applied against the country. The critical variable should be, as discussed earlier, the sufficiency of the consensus behind the international agreement. Adoption of this principle would effectively waive the GATT rights of nonparties to international environmental agreements. But such a precept is essential to a proper balance between competing trade and environmental goals. This "nonparty" rule would also help to reestablish the GATT's broad public credibility and to dispel the fear that the rules of international trade may be used to shirk environmental responsibilities or to override even widely accepted international environmental priorities.

---

that are nonsignatories to the protocol but that are in compliance with the terms of the accord were exempted from the protocol's mandatory trade restrictions.

12. The USCIB compensation proposal is, however, undesirable. First, it is not clear what constitutes "disproportionately concentrated." If the country is the only one not obeying an international environmental agreement and therefore is the only nation facing trade restrictions, does this make the trade measure "disproportionately concentrated?" More importantly, the logic of the "reasonable expectation" language would make any change in environmental regulations a potential basis for a claim of compensation. Such a provision would have an extraordinarily chilling effect on all environmental activity—similar to the proposal in the US domestic political context that any environmental regulation that hurts property values constitutes a government "taking" and should be compensated.

What Remedies Are Appropriate?

As chapter 5 spelled out, nations currently have little guidance as to what trade measures are reasonable under what circumstances. No formulaic response to this question is possible; the severity of the trade action taken should vary with the locus and severity of the environmental harm. Appendix E provides an illustrative matrix showing how these factors might be combined. As a matter of course, parties should move from less severe to more severe measures over time and in the face of ongoing harm. Box 5.4 in chapter 5 provides a range of measures in decreasing order of severity.

Exceeding International Agreements

The proposed new GATT environmental structure outlined in chapter 5 provides guidance on when parties should be able to exceed standards established by international agreement. Again, the answer turns on the locus of the harm. Where a party is addressing a local (domestic) environmental injury, considerable deference should be given to the level and means of protection it chooses. Where, however, the harm at issue lies outside the nation imposing the standards, a more strict basis for any trade restrictions set above international norms should be required.

Policy Recommendations

Although multilateral approaches to environmental policy problems are to be preferred and are in general likely to be more effective, the GATT—and its contracting parties—must move away from the current overly broad ban on unilateralism and extraterritoriality. Judgments about the validity of environmental policies with trade implications should turn on the nature and impact of the environmental harms to which they are addressed. This argues for:

■ dropping the strict prohibition on "extraterritorial" or "extrajurisdictional" environmental trade measures that has been read into Article XX;

■ accepting "multilateral unilateralism" and therefore circumscribing rather that trying to eliminate unilateral and extraterritorial environmental trade measures taken in furtherance of internationally agreed environmental standards or in response to global or transboundary environmental harms;

■ recognizing that in an ecologically interdependent world, some "unilateral" efforts to protect against global or transboundary environmental harms are not "extrajurisdictional" and should not be considered GATT-illegal per se;

■ separating unilaterally invoked environmental trade measures into three categories: those imposed in furtherance of international agreements; those which, while not expressly mandated, are employed in response to global or transboundary environmental harm; and those imposed without the benefit of any international agreement or support—if proportional to the harm, measures imposed under the first two categories should be deemed GATT-legal while those invoked under the latter category should be considered GATT-illegal;

■ encouraging countries with environmental rules that apply outside their own territory to negotiate these provisions internationally in light of the joint jurisdiction of all countries over the global commons;

■ developing a new set of GATT rules on environmental trade measures to ensure both that environmental restrictions do not become a guise for trade barriers and that trade measures are reinforced to discipline countries that fail to meet international environmental obligations or whose lax domestic policies cause transboundary or global harms.

7

More Swords: Competitiveness, Ecoduties, and Harmonization

Although reform of the General Agreement on Tariffs and Trade has been the focus of much of the debate to date over the linkage between trade and the environment, competitiveness concerns, which are likely to be addressed outside the GATT, could soon take center stage. This redirection of attention might well be triggered by the US Congress moving to regulate "unfair" competition based on "low" environmental standards in countries exporting products to the United States. In fact, US House of Representatives Majority Leader Richard Gephardt has promised to push for a "Green 301" provision, permitting ecoduties on imports not produced under conditions meeting US environmental standards.[1]

How Big an Issue?

Politically, no trade and environment issue commands more attention than the potential loss of jobs to overseas producers that can achieve lower production costs because of the low environmental standards or weak enforcement of environmental requirements in the jurisdictions in which they operate. Concerns about competitiveness emerged as the central political issue in the North American Free Trade Agreement (NAFTA) debate, and Ross Perot scored points by calling Mexico a pollution haven and championing a policy of forcing all US trade partners to

---

1. Gephardt's call for a Green 301 provision (*Inside US Trade*, 3 December 1993) refers to Section 301 of the US Trade Act of 1974, which authorizes the US Trade Representative to take unilateral action in response to unfair trade practices by foreign producers.

adopt US environmental (and labor) standards as the price for access to the US market. Competitiveness has become a major policy preoccupation in Europe as well (Paye 1994; EC 1993).

While most of the discussion of competitiveness and environment is cast in terms of the effect on industry and jobs, US environmentalists are actually focused on the environmental policy consequences of competing with nations with lower standards. Specifically, they worry that lax environmental practices elsewhere that result in a cost differential in production will create a "political drag" in policy debates in the United States, making it harder to defend or advance stringent environmental requirements. Thus, they argue for the availability of ecoduties or other trade interventions[2] that penalize countries with low standards in order to break the competitiveness dynamic and thus avoid an anti-environmental "race to the bottom."[3]

The Critical Question

The critical question in deciding whether low environmental standards on the part of a trade competitor raise competitiveness concerns serious enough to justify a GATT-endorsed policy intervention must be: why are the standards low? Several possible reasons must be considered.

The standards may be low because of a lack of information or because the overseas trade partner does not have the governmental expertise to adopt and implement an appropriate environmental policy. In many developing countries, weak environmental performance reflects, at least in part, this lack of capacity. A second, related problem may be resource limitations. Many developing countries face severe short-term crises that consume whatever limited funds the government has available, making it very hard to devote adequate attention to the full range of environmental concerns with which every nation has to deal. In both these cases, punitive trade measures will only exacerbate a difficult situ-

---

2. This is the fourth central environmental proposition on trade, identified in chapter 2.

3. Revesz (1992) dismisses the fear of the "race to the bottom" as lacking in empirical support. He also argues that even if there were a race to the bottom, harmonized standards would not solve the problem but rather simply force the competition for lax standards into other areas of regulation. As noted in chapter 1 and in the further discussion below, Revesz's reading of the situation does not square with history. More significantly, the suggestion that national standards do not address the interstate competition problem (and thus, by implication, that international standards would not address intercountry competition) defies the US federal environmental experience (see the discussion in chapter 1). National environmental laws in the United States have virtually stopped competition among states for investment on the basis of lax environmental standards. To the extent competition has been channeled into other realms, this is a very positive accomplishment, as it protects the environment, which is more vulnerable than almost any other area of regulation to welfare-reducing market failures in the absence of government intervention.

ation, reducing trade-generated income and making future environmental investments more difficult.

Governments may, however, act strategically in setting environmental standards (Barrett 1993). Specifically, they may choose to set low standards with the hope of attracting new investment or of making their own industries more competitive in overseas markets. In such cases, the critical issue becomes, is the strategic behavior legitimate?[4] On one hand, the divergent standards chosen may respond to differences in political judgments by sovereign national authorities or indicate dissimilarities in underlying circumstances that legitimately create comparative advantages. On the other hand, the low standards may represent an attempt to cut costs by imposing pollution burdens on others.

The characterization in any particular case should turn on the distinction that has been at the center of this study—the locus of any environmental harms arising from lax standards. Where differences in environmental policy choices reflect variations in climate, weather patterns, existing pollution levels, population density, economic needs, and risk preferences and where any environmental impacts are confined to local harm, the divergent standards may be considered legitimate—and therefore an inappropriate target for unilateral ecoduties or other efforts to adjust for policy differences.

Where, however, the strategic environmental behavior results in pollution that spills over onto others, the differences in standards should be considered illegitimate, thereby making resort to ecoduties potentially appropriate. In addition, even if there are no physical pollution spillovers, where parties have agreed to multilateral standards, such agreements should be enforceable with trade penalties.[5] This would include existing agreements such as the International Whaling Commission's whaling moratorium (reflecting an ethical judgment that whales should not be hunted and addressing the psychological spillovers that arise from whale killing) or possible future accords setting baseline emissions standards (aimed at narrowing environmental policy differences and reducing the political spillovers such differences can cause).

Responding to Divergent Environmental Standards

There are many ways a nation may choose to respond to differences between it and other nations in environmental standards, particularly

---

4. A separate question, also important, is, will such strategic behavior be effective? Porter and van der Linde (1994) argue that in today's dynamic business world, marked by globalization and advancing technology, the ability to innovate is a much greater determinant of competitiveness than traditional cost advantages, including those derived from low environmental standards.

5. Chapter 6 explores the bases for establishing multilateral agreements.

the less stringent standards that raise competitiveness fears (Barrett 1993; Charnovitz 1993b). The country with the stricter standards may:

- bar substandard imports;

- ignore the differences;

- lower domestic environmental standards to "level the playing field";

- force up the prices of "substandard" imports through countervailing ecoduties or border tax adjustments;

- subsidize domestic pollution control expenditures;

- introduce "ecolabels," flagging for consumers the environmental choices they face;

- negotiate with others to increase the rigor of their environmental requirements by having them meet baseline or minimum environmental standards, harmonize fully environmental requirements, accept a "mutual recognition" system for standards, enforce their own existing laws, or adhere to agreed environmental protection principles such as the polluter pays principle;

- induce other countries to raise their environmental standards through subsidies for their pollution control investments, technical cooperation and assistance, or trade concessions linked to higher standards.

Bar Substandard Imports

The most extreme response to fears about low environmental standards in other countries is to bar imports produced under conditions that do not meet domestic requirements. This is, of course, what the United States did to Mexican tuna in the tuna-dolphin matter. The case for such an extreme reaction to low standards abroad should be based on environmental harm. In general, a trade ban imposed to respond to competitiveness concerns in the absence of internationally agreed standards would be excessive.

Ignore Competitiveness?

At the other extreme, countries could ignore environmental competitiveness issues. Economists (and most free traders) see the competitiveness argument as substantively a nonissue and potentially a protectionist contrivance. Thus they argue against trade measures aimed at addressing environmentally derived competitiveness concerns. In fact, Krugman (1994) recently suggested that the general interest in competitiveness is a "dangerous obsession," distracting attention from the real economic problems in the United States and other countries—particularly low productivity growth.[6]

The GATT Secretariat's *Trade and Environment Report* (1992c) rejects competitiveness concerns as a basis for environmental trade measures. The report asserts that countries have a sovereign right to maintain their own environmental standards and that differences in standards are a legitimate source of comparative advantage.[7] The GATT report further notes, as have many others, that study after study has concluded that differences in environmental compliance costs are rarely a serious competitiveness factor (J. David Richardson 1993; OECD 1991; Leonard 1988; Kalt 1988).

Recent data suggest spending on pollution control amounts to less than 2 percent of value added for 86 percent of US industries, meaning labor costs and other variables swamp environmental compliance expenses in importance (US Census Bureau, *Survey of Manufacturers 1989: Statistics of Industrial Groups and Industries*). Blazejczak (1993) finds similar results in a 15-industry study of environmental spending in Germany. Moreover, empirical studies have shown little propensity of pollution-intensive industries to move to "pollution havens" (e.g., Low and Yeats 1992; Kalt 1988; Tobey 1990). Most of the evidence pointing to migration by dirty industries is anecdotal (e.g., General Accounting Office 1990). Even in industries with high pollution control costs, companies often face other deterrents to relocation, including high fixed capital costs and sensitivity to transportation expenses (Grossman and Krueger 1993).

More dramatically, Harvard Business School Professor Michael Porter (1991; Porter and van der Linde 1994) argues that, in a dynamic business setting, rigorous environmental regulations may actually create a competitive advantage if the regulatory requirements spur innovation. Porter's thesis depends in part on the assumption of a "properly constructed" regulatory program based on performance requirements, not specific pollution-control technologies. Porter observes that under these circumstances, exacting standards encourage companies to reengineer their technologies and production processes in ways that reduce emissions and, at the same time, improve quality and cut costs. Even those who doubt that such "innovation offsets" will improve competitiveness (*The Economist*, 20 November 1993, 19; Oates, Portney, and Palmer 1993;

---

6. While Krugman's basic point has considerable validity, particularly from a macroeconomic viewpoint, he does not focus on North-South competitiveness tensions within industrial sectors, which are emerging as a central focus of concern in the trade and environment context.

7. This is a very standard economic point of view. In fact, the prevailing Heckscher-Ohlin theory of trade (see Krugman and Obstfeld 1991) grounds comparative advantage and thus the source of gains from trade in differences in factor endowments (including variations in environmental preferences and conditions).

Jaffe et al. 1994) acknowledge that high environmental standards do little to make countries or companies less competitive since labor and transportation expenses are so much more significant cost factors.[8]

But these competitiveness arguments all have several limitations. First, the Porter hypothesis of strict environmental regulations enhancing a company's competitive position depends on both the existence of a flexible regulatory scheme that promotes innovation and corporate leadership that sees an opportunity to use an environmental mandate to launch a broader effort to reconfigure production processes and thereby to seize a march on competitors. Oates, Portney, and Palmer (1993) and others argue that such a coincidence of factors rarely occurs in the real world.

Second, while most studies show little competitive impact from environmental compliance expenses, in industries where pollution control costs are above average, some analyses have suggested that companies will factor environmental issues into plant location decisions. For instance, a 1990 General Accounting Office study of the furniture finishing industry (which bears heavy expenses for treating toxic wastes from paints, stains, varnishes, and solvents) found some companies moving out of California to avoid that state's strict pollution control requirements. An OECD analysis (1991) also concluded that some shift of competitive advantage to countries with lower environmental standards in the pollution-intensive textile and leather tanning industries had occurred. In addition, the US International Trade Commission (1994) found that the new US Clean Air Act requirements affected the competitiveness of US producers of metallurgical coke.

As Porter (1990) and Thurow (speech delivered at MIT, May 1993) have noted, the nature of comparative advantage is rapidly evolving, particularly as the traditional factors of production are becoming more mobile. Porter argues that other variables, such as the capacity to innovate and to make use of new technologies, are becoming the predominant determinants of competitive advantage. But his point concerning general factor mobility and the relative equalization of costs of production that this implies could make business sensitivity to wide disparities in other cost elements—for example, environmental compliance spending—more significant over time. Indeed, if other costs are equalized, variations in environmental requirements become relatively more important.

Business concerns about environmental compliance costs may also grow as these expenses rise. The US Environmental Protection Agency (1990a) estimates that US pollution control costs have gone from 0.9 percent of GNP in 1972 to 2.1 percent of GNP in 1990 and will rise to 2.8 percent of GNP by the year 2000. In a McKinsey and Company survey

---

8. Gray and Shadbegian (1993), however, concluded that environmental regulations, as measured by compliance costs, do significantly affect total factor productivity and thus potentially competitiveness.

(1991), senior executives of major corporations worldwide estimated that environmental costs averaged 2.4 percent of total sales. But these business leaders expected environmental spending to rise to 4.3 percent of sales by the year 2000. Thus, even if historically accurate, the traditional conclusion about the minimal competitiveness effect of environmental costs may not be true in the future.

Even when pollution control costs were demonstrably lower, interstate competitiveness concerns played an important role in the history of environmental protection in the United States. Specifically, the establishment of national environmental laws in the United States was aimed at eliminating an environmental "race to the bottom" among the states eager for new investment and willing to compromise their pollution requirements for the sake of jobs.[9] Although some commentators (Revesz 1992) reject the suggestion that low standards in competing jurisdictions really do depress environmental standards, others argue that such pressures are real (Richard B. Stewart 1993b). In setting national minimum standards for air and water emissions and waste treatment, Congress all but eliminated the ability of states to compete on the basis of low environmental requirements. Although the differences in income levels and policy preferences may be greater among nations than among US states, the same logic applies internationally.

Finally, the suggestion that environmental factors do not affect competitiveness (and should be ignored as a policy variable) is demonstrably untrue if one looks beyond the narrow category of pollution control spending. Specifically, broader environmental policies such as energy pricing unequivocally have competitiveness effects.[10] The European Community's decision to postpone proposed energy taxes based on the carbon content and energy content (BTUs) of fuels until the competitiveness implications for European industry could be addressed—by comparable tax increases in the United States and Japan—offers a very concrete example of this phenomenon (*Financial Times*, 25 February 1992, 7). Similar fears about competitiveness impacts led to the demise of President Clinton's 1993 proposal for a new BTU tax in the United States.[11]

---

9. See the discussion in chapter 1 on this point, noting the important role competitiveness concerns played in the legislative history of the early US national environmental standards.

10. As noted earlier, exchange rate adjustments can eliminate any trade balance effect of broad-based cost differences such as energy pricing, but only at the price of a devalued currency and thus a lower standard of living—not an attractive price to pay for environmental protection.

11. To accommodate the competitiveness concerns raised by a number of industries with politically powerful sponsors in Congress, the Clinton administration created exceptions to its BTU tax proposal for certain industries and fuels. As the demands for "carve-outs" mounted, the integrity and the environmental efficacy of the proposed tax were destroyed, and the proposal was dropped.

In addition to the economic impacts on business from competing with companies operating in nations with low environmental standards, the competitiveness dynamic can result in serious environmental impacts. First, where low standards result in transboundary or global pollution, other countries are directly environmentally injured. If, for example, a semiconductor maker were to try to cut costs by using CFCs in violation of the Montreal Protocol, the environmental harm—damage to the ozone layer—would affect all nations. In such cases, the low standards are not a legitimate basis for comparative advantage. Affected trade partners have a strong justification for creating economic incentives to stop these harmful activities. While the use of environmental trade measures in this context does not necessarily eliminate all such pollution, it does mitigate unfair competitive positioning based on the overseas externalization of environmental costs.

Lower Standards and "Political Spillovers"

Even if there are no pollution spillovers and the environmental harm is entirely contained within foreign territory, there is a strong sense among many environmentalists that low standards create "political spillovers," which, combined with fears about competitiveness, put downward pressure on environmental standards elsewhere (e.g., French 1993a; Arden-Clarke 1993b). This "political drag" reflects the perceived vulnerability of environmental regulations to political claims of adverse economic effects, especially competitive disadvantage in the international market and potential job losses at home. While cases of countries lowering environmental standards to gain a competitive edge are hard to find, competitiveness concerns, as noted earlier, have been raised as a major argument against more rigorous environmental controls both in the United States and elsewhere.[12]

Environmentalists of all stripes work hard to avoid having choices posed as jobs versus environmental quality because they recognize that the environment often comes out on the short end of this political divide. To ensure that competitiveness arguments do not loom large, many environmentalists want ecoduties to be available to level the playing field. Ecoduties are, however, a poor policy choice, as explained below.

Alternatively, environmentalists want common standards set at high levels. From an environmental perspective, strict harmonization of environmental policies may be neither necessary nor wise. Less ambitious

---

12. This political dimension of competitiveness is a reality in almost all environmental policy debates. See the discussion in chapter 1 concerning the Dutch government's roll-back of new environmental taxes and the discussion about the competitiveness arguments raised in the US debate over the 1990 Clean Air Act (chapter 1, footnote 11).

efforts at convergence of environmental policies or movement toward a program of baseline standards may suffice. Such efforts would reduce the political drag that puts pressure on environmental standards through the competitiveness channel (Brown Weiss 1993a).

In addition, claims about harm to the environment and about environmental protection programs being undermined can threaten progress toward trade liberalization. Even if many of them are groundless, they can affect the political climate and make winning approval of trade agreements more difficult. Consequently, even when dissimilar circumstances justify differences in standards, it may behoove trade partners to narrow large gaps in standards to blunt environmentally driven, anti–free trade sentiment and to strip protectionists masquerading as environmentalists of an excuse for opposing trade agreements.

Ecodumping

Unfortunately, most "ecodumping" proposals do not exhibit this sort of narrowly tailored focus or any other underlying logic. Unwilling to ignore the political drag of lax standards abroad and outraged at the prospect of having to lower high domestic environmental standards adopted at great political expense, many environmentalists (e.g., Arden-Clarke 1993b) have called for sweeping programs of ecodumping duties to be imposed on imports from countries they deem to have weak environmental programs.[13]

A number of industry officials share the environmentalists' enthusiasm for ecoduties to level the playing field (Trisoglio and ten Kate 1993). Many politicians also believe that lax environmental standards constitute unfair trade, and some elected officials have actually advanced proposals to impose ecodumping duties.[14] In the context of the US congressional debate over the 1990 US Clean Air Act amendments, the US Senate narrowly defeated a proposed resolution urging that special tariffs be imposed on imported goods produced under conditions that did "not comply with the air quality standards prescribed under the Clean

---

13. The term ecodumping is actually a misnomer. What is contemplated are "countervailing" duties to offset an implied "subsidy" to businesses resulting from low environmental standards or weak enforcement of environmental laws. Environmentalists premise that the government's failure to impose appropriate environmental requirements lowers operating costs and provides, in effect, a subsidy (Patterson 1992, 105).

14. In addition to Gephardt's proposal noted at the outset of this chapter, Senator David Boren (D-OK) introduced an International Pollution Deterrence Act; see also Gephardt 1992 and speech by Senator Max Baucus (D-MT), at the Institute for International Economics, 17 September 1991, calling for ecoduties on imported products "to offset any economic advantage gained by producing the product under less stringent environmental protection regulations."

Air Act."[15] In the European Parliament, a resolution has not only been introduced, but adopted, calling on the GATT to forbid "environmental dumping" (Resolution A3–0329/92). US Vice President Gore (1992, 343) has suggested labeling as an unfair trading practice the "weak and ineffectual enforcement of pollution control measures."

Although ecoduties are less intrusive than outright trade bans, trade experts find the prospect of them horrifying. They note that trying to equalize environmental compliance costs runs counter to the theory of comparative advantage. Ecoduties, moreover, are susceptible to "capture" by protectionist interests, open the door to efforts to equalize other intercountry cost differences (e.g., wage differentials), and cannot easily be put into practice (EC 1993; Barcelo 1994; Eglin 1993c). Although these concerns may be somewhat overstated, they are real. As David Palmeter (1993, 57) concludes, offsetting duties are "a practical, if not theoretical, quagmire."

Perhaps with these concerns in mind, the Uruguay Round GATT negotiators, in a little-analyzed definitional provision, appear to have barred "implicit subsidy" ecoduties based on low environmental standards. Specifically, the Agreement on Subsidies and Countervailing Measures defines, for the first time, what a subsidy is and therefore what sorts of subsidies are countervailable. The agreement (Article 1.1) says that a subsidy must reflect "a financial contribution by a government or any public body." The definition goes on to spell out that subsidies arise only if there is "a direct transfer of funds (e.g., grants, loans, and equity infusion), potential direct transfers of funds or liabilities (e.g., loan guarantees)." This language seems to preclude a case brought on the premise that low environmental standards constitute a "brown" subsidy.

There is, however, a further element of the subsidy definition (Article 1.1 [iii]) that leaves the door slightly open to a "brown" subsidy claim under post–Uruguay Round GATT rules. Specifically, a secondary definition of subsidy includes "government revenue that is otherwise due [and] is foregone or not collected." One could thus argue that lax enforcement of environmental standards resulting in penalties not being imposed for noncompliance constitutes forgone revenue. But this reading of the definition seems somewhat tortured. Thus, any attempt to impose countervailing ecoduties premised on an implied subsidy argument would appear to be GATT-illegal.

Ecoduty proposals face not only GATT problems but a series of conceptual difficulties. Notably, what standards should be used? With few exceptions, there are no agreed international environmental standards to apply. Moreover, there is no reason to believe that US environmental

---

15. The so-called Gorton amendment (S. Amend. 1321, 101st Cong. 2d session 136 Cong. Record S3000) was defeated 52–47.

policy choices are optimal. To the contrary, the US regulatory structure is deeply flawed—in some cases undercleaning, leaving serious environmental harms untouched, and in other circumstances overcleaning, wasting limited resources on low-risk and expensive cleanup activities (EPA 1990).[16]

One alternative is to require that countries uphold their existing environmental laws and regulations.[17] Indeed, the NAFTA includes a pollution-haven provision (Article 1114.2) designed to discourage competition for investment on the basis of relaxing environmental standards. The NAFTA environmental side agreement strengthens this commitment and establishes a process by which trade penalties could be applied if one of the NAFTA parties were to be found guilty of a persistent pattern of nonenforcement.[18]

An additional problem with ecoduties is that they only respond to low environmental standards related to imports of the nation imposing the duties. Ecoduties do nothing to address competitive disadvantage in other markets. For example, if the United States were to impose an ecoduty on Korean cars entering the United States (because, for example, Korea's air pollution requirements for auto factories were much less stringent than US standards), this would affect sales in the US market but do little to help US auto producers in their vast export markets. In fact, it could hurt Ford, General Motors, and Chrysler's third-country sales because the Korean car makers might well cut prices in these other markets to make up for lost US sales.

The danger of capture, resulting in countervailing ecoduties becoming a protectionist tool and undermining the open trading system, is well-founded and has ample precedent (Wiemann 1992). For example, the United States pushed for GATT acceptance of antidumping and subsidies codes to ensure fair trade and protect US producers, but these provisions are now frequently used to obstruct US exports (Lipstein 1993). Ecoduties

---

16. This study has cited numerous examples of possible undercleaning, including the basic programs addressing air pollution and water pollution. To give some context to the problem of overcleaning, the US government spends more than $6 billion a year cleaning up toxic waste sites, which often present little ecological or public health risk. This total is matched by private-sector spending of the same magnitude in the face of threatened legal action. These figures dwarf the entire EPA operating budget, which totals just over $2 billion annually.

17. At one point in the NAFTA debate, environmentalists called for the highest standard of any of the three countries in each environmental area to be applied in all three countries. This would, however, have imposed expensive and inefficient hazardous waste cleanup requirements on Mexico and forced all US private development projects to go through the extensive environmental impact statement and government approval processes that are required in Mexico.

18. This provision contains so many steps and hurdles that it will likely never be invoked (Esty 1994a).

might well become another boomerang policy, evolving into a barrier that overseas protectionists use to keep US goods out of their markets.[19]

Worse yet, under some circumstances ecoduties may harm the domestic environment. For example, if a US industry faces an emissions limit regulated by tradeable permits, imposition of countervailing ecoduties on competing imports may allow the protected domestic industry to reap extra profits. This could dull the incentive to attend to the pollution problem, enabling the company to purchase additional emissions rights rather than exploring pollution prevention process changes or investing in lower-emission technologies.[20] The use of ecoduties to protect domestic jobs will also have a negative effect on incentives for environmental protection, retarding movement of workers from dirty industries to cleaner ones. A better approach to the worker dislocation problems caused by changing environmental demands would be direct training and adjustment assistance.

The concern about the slippery slope from ecoduties to equalizing labor costs is specious. Lines must always be drawn as to what constitutes a fair basis for competitive advantage and what is unfair. Moreover, the suggestion that there can be, and should be, thresholds for participation in a trading system is not new. Trade rules and restrictions have been used to prevent the theft of intellectual property without breaking down the international trading system. The use of prison labor has also been deemed unfair, and GATT Article XX(e) permits trade restrictions against any product made by prisoners. There is no reason that similar bounds could not be established for environmental behavior in the trade context.

Setting baseline ethical standards for commerce is also not new. President Franklin Delano Roosevelt, in arguing for the Fair Labor Standard Act in 1937, told the US Congress:

> Goods produced under conditions which do not meet a rudimentary standard of decency should be regarded as contraband and ought not be allowed to pollute the channels of interstate trade.[21]

---

19. If the use of ecoduties were not carefully controlled, many countries would be in a position to impose penalties on US products. For example, the European Union might argue that low US energy prices do not fully internalize the pollution costs of burning fossil fuels, thus justifying a countervailing ecoduty. Other countries might correctly note that the special carve-out granted to coke ovens in the 1990 Clean Air Act is a subsidy to the US steel industry. Extraordinary provisions in the Clean Water Act for feed lots and sugar cane growers might also be seen as targets for foreign ecoduties.

20. IMF economist Peter Uimonen highlighted these potential boomerang effects for the author.

21. This quotation is cited by French (1993a), who argues forcefully that economic integration must be accompanied by environmental integration. Her preferred route to environmentally sound trade policies is through internationally agreed environmental requirements, not ecoduties.

The same principle applies to defining baseline international environmental standards today. The only question is determining the "standard of decency." As noted earlier, producing goods in a manner that degrades some aspect of the global commons is unfair and should not be tolerated in international trade. Ecoduties should also be accepted as legitimate responses to violations of international environmental agreements that establish a global standard of decency.

Ecoduties implemented unilaterally, and particularly those aimed at local as opposed to transboundary or global environmental harms, seem likely to engender endless controversy. In such cases, the valuation problems that make trade and environmental policy disputes hard to settle in the first place would be present in spades.[22] Putting a price on noncompliance or the amount of environmental "slippage" arising in a low-standard country would not be easy. Who determines what the appropriate standard is? How does one measure the gap? Whose prices—US, foreign producer, world—should be employed? Moreover, as noted earlier, since these calculations are inherently subjective, they are likely to be biased in the direction of domestic interests in the country imposing the duties.

In light of these many difficulties, trade experts generally find the concept of ecoduties deeply distressing. The Commission of the European Communities, for example, has called the possibility of environmental dumping duties nonnegotiable (EC 1992b). In particular, free traders see the prospect of unilateral US action under Section 301 of the 1974 trade act as fundamentally incompatible with multilateral cooperation on trade issues. In fact, unilateral action by the United States is unlikely to advance cooperative solutions to the difficult trade and environment issues that must be faced. Thus, applying Green 301 penalties is a bad idea.

The mere threat of ecoduties or a Green 301 provision might, however, have a salutary effect under certain confined circumstances. Specifically, while convergence of environmental standards on a cooperative, negotiated basis offers a more sound approach to addressing competitiveness concerns and to reconciling trade and environmental policy goals, the prospect of unilateral US action might be used to encourage serious negotiation, particularly regarding protection of the global commons. Indeed, if a Green 301 is to be enacted, it should focus initially on environmental problems that result in global or transboundary pollution spillovers and should have a "delayed trigger" of perhaps three years. To mix metaphors, a time-delayed ecoduty provision would place a sword of Damocles over recalcitrant nations and

---

22. Mani (1993), however, calculates potential environmental countervailing duties and concludes that the impact on trade is likely to be very small.

create a powerful incentive to move quickly toward multilateral agreement.[23]

Border Tax Adjustment

Adjusting the prices of imports (or exports) at the border to reflect differences in environmental taxes or fees is another approach to the environmental competitiveness issue. Indeed, the GATT permits border tax adjustments for domestic taxes levied directly on products. Thus an environmental consumption tax may be rebated on exported goods. For example, a tax on coal could be rebated on coal exports. Similarly, domestic taxes may be levied at the border on imported products to ensure that they are treated comparably to "like" domestically produced goods. For instance, US fees on domestically manufactured chlorofluorocarbons (CFCs) may be levied on imported CFCs.

The current rules do not, however, allow border tax adjustments for environmental charges imposed on production processes or inputs, such as energy consumed in manufacturing.[24] Nevertheless, when competitiveness concerns were raised in opposition to President Clinton's 1993 energy tax proposal, a number of policymakers called for a border tax adjustment based on the energy content of imported goods. Such a tax would have maintained the competitive status quo for US manufacturers.

But European and Japanese producers strenuously objected to the proposed border adjustment, noting that such an adjustment would violate GATT obligations. They further argued that they should get credit for the much higher energy taxes they pay in their home markets. The Office of the US Trade Representative, faced with the threat of GATT challenges (and recognizing the strength of the argument that the proposed US border tax adjustment for energy content would be GATT-illegal), advised the White House not to pursue the tax adjustment proposal.

Whether the GATT should provide broader scope for border tax adjustments aimed at compensating for differences in environmental taxes or requirements is a matter of considerable controversy. Pearson and Repetto (1993) argue that the current rules are too narrow because they permit adjustment for taxes on end products but not for more economically

---

23. The specific provision might be that unilateral duties would only be invoked against countries that were not negotiating in "good faith," a definition of which can be found in US law in the Trade Act of 1962 (19 USC 1323). Bayard and Elliott (1994) demonstrate the potential value of a "301 threat" to spur international negotiations.

24. The GATT rules are actually somewhat unclear on energy taxes, but most analysts believe that a GATT dispute panel would not view favorably border tax adjustments on the energy content of imports.

efficient taxes on actual externalities from polluting processes (e.g., taxes on emissions). Thus, taxes on steel are encouraged, but taxes on coke oven emissions are discouraged. To the extent the current rules create an incentive to tax products rather than polluting processes, they discourage pollution-prevention regulatory strategies by making it harder to reward waste reduction efforts with reduced emissions fees.

Charnovitz (1993a) argues that the existing GATT rules are environmentally unsound as well because they do not allow differentiated treatment for environmentally superior products. The GATT, for example, would allow for an adjustment for a tax on all tuna but would not permit adjustment for a tax on dolphin-unsafe tuna. Border tax adjustments are much less intrusive trade measures than outright trade bans and, in this regard, are preferable to the more intrusive trade restrictions that might alternatively be employed.

Border tax adjustments can, however, easily be abused and applied unfairly. For example, most observers, particularly those outside the United States, would have seen a US border tax adjustment on energy as grossly unfair to the extent it were to apply to countries with higher energy taxes. Such taxes in Europe, for example, are often five to eight times higher than US levels (Verleger 1993). Thus care should be taken in expanding the permitted use of border tax adjustments on production processes or inputs.

In opening up the border adjustment mechanism to cover production process charges, equity dictates that provision be made to credit comparable fees and taxes paid by foreign producers. Such a refinement in GATT rules would minimize the unfairness of border tax adjustments and create an incentive for governments to shift environmental regulation toward the use of pollution charges to internalize costs. This would at the same time move environmental regulation toward more efficient and less trade-restrictive market mechanisms.

Green Subsidies

The flip side of an implicit subsidy (a "brown" subsidy) arising from government-authorized lax environmental standards is government funding—an explicit "green" subsidy—of private-sector pollution control expenditures. Such subsidies may be environmentally advantageous insofar as they accelerate environmental cleanups, and they may facilitate movement by industry to new pollution control or prevention technologies and thus to higher environmental standards.

Although the GATT generally takes a dim view of subsidies as a disruption to trade, after the Uruguay Round results are adopted, a window will open up for government assistance to private companies that must make substantial investments to meet mandated environmental standards. Specifically, Article 8.2(c) of the Agreement on Subsidies and Countervailing Measures permits government funding of up to 20 percent of one-time capital investments needed to meet new environmental requirements without running the risk of having the subsidy countervailed by a trading partner. Such nonactionable subsidies cannot cover investments that result in manufacturing cost savings, and any subsidy granted must be "directly linked and proportionate" to the environmental improvement achieved.[25]

GATT rules generally discourage, or in some cases forbid, government assistance to industry, including financial help in meeting pollution control requirements.[26] The reason for this general rule is that subsidies are considered an unfair trade practice. Moreover, they are hard to police and detract from the transparency of commercial transactions. Fearful of such abuses, some US business interests have objected to the Uruguay Round "green subsidy" provision (*Inside US Trade*, 7 January 1994, 8). In particular, manufacturers suspect that some of their overseas competitors will benefit from government assistance that has more to do with productivity improvements than environmental benefits. Other industry representatives have complained that while foreign governments will provide resources to their producers, the US government is unlikely to fund a green subsidy program. Some environmentalists have also raised doubts about the green subsidy rules, arguing that government assistance will unravel the polluter pays principle.

Undoubtedly, ecosubsidies could be abused. One can imagine, for example, the governments in some countries shouldering billions of dollars of costs to help rebuild steel mills on the premise that the new facilities will be environmentally more sound. But the benefits of facilitating environmental protection outweigh the risks of abuse, especially in developing countries.

Indeed, the polluter pays principle must not become dogma. Environmental efficiency—optimal investment in pollution controls—can be achieved either by imposing costs on polluters or by subsidizing their

---

25. An early draft of the Uruguay Round subsidy rules (GATT 1990) defined a variety of types of government support for pollution control investments as nonactionable. At the request of the United States, however, this broad authorization for environmental protection subsidies was withdrawn from later Uruguay Round proposals (GATT 1992c). At the insistence of Mexico and a number of other developing countries, the final Uruguay Round text reopened the green subsidy issue and placed a reasonably significant category of government pollution control expenditures in the nonactionable subsidy category (GATT 1993b).

26. More precisely, under existing GATT rules (Articles VI, XVI, Subsidies Code) all subsidies are countervailable (with the exception now of the nonactionable category under the World Trading Organization). In addition, export subsidies on manufactured goods are illegal, and export subsidies on agricultural products are to be reduced under the agriculture agreement in the Uruguay Round. Production subsidies are legal but countervailable and should not enable countries to acquire more than a suitable share of world trade in the product concerned.

emission reduction expenditures. Thus, the GATT parties should consider widening the category of nonactionable ecosubsidies to include most all domestic subsidies for (true) environmental purposes in developing countries and (carefully controlled) export subsidies from developed countries on the sale of pollution control equipment to developing countries (OECD 1994a). Patterson (1992), for example, would permit green subsidies "to the extent a policy promotes environmental protection," recognizing that the parameters of this category will have to be defined by international negotiation.

Government support for environmental protection investments is particularly important as a transitional tool to enable developing countries to elevate their environmental laws and regulations. Particularly if competitiveness pressures build momentum for common environmental standards, permitting subsidies for producers in developing countries to help them achieve the mandated standards would be very useful. Indeed, agreement on baseline standards to protect vital ecological resources may be impossible in the absence of a subsidy program that would enable developing countries' industries to make pollution control investments without compromising their competitive position in the market.

Ecolabeling

As chapter 5 outlined, ecolabeling can be an effective mechanism for addressing environmentally deficient imports (box 5.5). If used effectively, ecolabels provide the public relevant information about the environmental quality (or lack thereof) of goods and can be a powerful force in channeling consumer purchases.

Rather than blocking all tropical timber sales, for example, an ecolabeling program would simply note whether any timber sold comes from "sustainably managed" forests. While some ecologists reject the possibility of any logging being truly sustainable (Anderson 1989), it is clear that some tree cutting is done with reasonably serious commitments to reforestation that minimize the environmental "footprint" of lumbering operations. Consumers may well be willing to pay a premium for these products.

Ecolabels permit, furthermore, a more refined analysis of the products coming from any particular country. Rather than imposing duties or barring all shipments from a country regardless of how they were produced, ecolabeling schemes permit relatively easy differentiation of environmentally sound products, creating an incentive for individual producers to attend to environmental considerations.

To ensure that ecolabels are accurate and fair, some monitoring will be required. In particular, any differentiation in treatment should be derived from objective criteria that are scientifically testable. Standards should generally be set internationally (or with the participation of foreign producers) and should reflect a comprehensive approach to judging environmental quality (e.g., using life-cycle analysis), not single-variable constructions, which may distort consumer understanding. A regimen for auditing products to be sure that they comport with the claims made on their labels should also be developed, perhaps modeled on the US Federal Trade Commission's regulation of truth in advertising.

Harmonization of Standards

The best long-term response to environmentalists' competitiveness concerns would be multilateral agreement on baseline environmental performance standards.[27] The process should begin with efforts to address issues that result in physical transboundary or global pollution spillovers and that cannot be argued to be legitimate bases for comparative advantage. A second stage, setting standards that relate to production issues that do not result in physical spillovers, might be launched among developed countries with a common interest in reducing political spillovers—both downward pressure on high standards and general anti–free trade sentiment created by fears about loss of competitiveness.

Ironically, many environmentalists object to standards harmonized in a trade context.[28] They fear that standards will sink to baseline or average requirements or that the common standards will preclude individual jurisdictions from adopting more protective standards. The answer to the environmentalists' fear is to negotiate international environmental agreements that set floors that parties are free to exceed so long as they do so in ways that do not unduly burden trade.

The prospect of losing control over environmental regulation to international standard-setting organizations is another major source of concern. Environmentalists worry about this loss of sovereignty because, in many cases, international bodies provide fewer opportunities for public participation[29] than the domestic political process and in some cases are

---

27. For another perspective reflecting the economists' fear that harmonization undermines comparative advantage, see Bhagwati (1993c).

28. The GATT Uruguay Round results, for example, call for international harmonization of environmental standards (Standards Code Article 2.4; Sanitary and Phytosanitary Code, paragraph 9). While the push to common standards is not mandatory, national standards are subject to a "least trade-restrictive" test that derives from recent GATT interpretations of Article XX (see also NAFTA standards chapter; Goldman 1992b, 1296; Charnovitz 1993a).

29. Public participation does not really mean participation of the "public." It refers generally to opportunities for knowledgeable interest groups to participate in decision making. In the trade context, whether the groups participating—both environmental and business organizations—represent the public is a matter of great dispute. Thus it is important to

clearly dominated by business perspectives.[30]

Moreover, as a matter of political theory, some environmentalists argue that decisions should be made at the most decentralized level possible, giving maximum scope to local citizens' priorities and preferences. Of course, their enthusiasm for local decision making wanes when locales choose low standards. Nonetheless, this philosophy has considerable resonance in both the United States, with its strong federalist tradition, and in Europe, where the similar concept of "subsidiarity" has become a rallying cry.[31] Those who argue for decentralized decision making believe that access to policymakers and the ability to hold elected officials accountable for their actions is sacrosanct—and lacking in international bodies.

Environmentalists, in addition, have historically cared very little about the economic efficiencies of standardized market-access requirements. This gives added force to the conclusion to which many environmentalists still cling: that the right to promulgate environmental regulations exceeding international levels is a central element of political sovereignty that should never be surrendered, regardless of the disruption to commerce. The strength of this argument is that environmental conditions and health risk exposures, as well as public priorities and preferences, vary from place to place, particularly with regard to factors such as risk tolerances. If preferences vary considerably and the cost of having varying standards is small, different standards are not only legitimate but welfare-maximizing from an economic perspective.

If, however, every nation and all their political subdivisions have complete autonomy to set their own radically different environmental standards, trade could grind to a halt. Inconsistent production, testing, labeling, packaging, and disposal requirements could become serious

---

differentiate between opening up decision making so interested parties can understand the process and contribute their ideas, and creating opportunities for special interests (be they environmental, business, or other) to manipulate policy outcomes through privileged access to the decision-making process that makes it difficult for the decision makers to advance the true public interest.

30. One example is the Codex Alimentarius, an international organization operating under the auspices of the United Nations Food and Agriculture Organization (FAO). In setting international pesticide residue guidelines, Codex undertakes its deliberations behind closed doors and has no established protocols for ensuring a rational outcome based on scientific evidence (Goldman and Wiles 1994). The Codex process has produced standards—such as the zero tolerance for bovine growth hormones—that do not comport with good science. The International Standards Organization (ISO) has developed rules governing thousands of products, often without controversy. But again, ISO procedures have only limited opportunities for public involvement. More disturbingly, the only representatives at many meetings are invited business representatives from the industry to be regulated.

31. For a more complete discussion of subsidiarity, see "Figuring Out Subsidiarity," *The Economist*, 27 November 1993, 58; also, CEPR 1993.

trade barriers, reducing the opportunities for producers to achieve scale economies and gain market access—economic virtues that translate into broader product choice, better service, and lower prices for consumers.

Environmentalists often overlook the fact that harmonized standards can yield environmental as well as economic benefits. With proper attention to environmental needs, good science, and open decision making, common standards often result in a high degree of environmental protection, not infrequently higher than any individual country would have been willing to adopt on its own.[32] The Montreal Protocol's worldwide phaseout of CFCs is a classic example of upward harmonization beyond the existing regulations of any country. Reciprocal commitments allow nations to escape the ''prisoners' dilemma'' fear that others will take advantage of them if they alone adopt strict environmental standards.

In focusing excessively on their fear of downward harmonization, environmentalists tend to ignore the fact that it is the lack of any coordinated policies that exacerbates competitiveness concerns and depresses the level of standards. The European Community, for example, made implementation of new energy taxes to combat greenhouse gas emissions explicitly contingent on comparable new taxes being introduced in the United States (EC 1992a). Joint action would, in this case, strengthen worldwide environmental efforts. Similarly, as noted in chapter 1, US national environmental standards (e.g., the US Clean Air Act and Clean Water Act) have allowed for rigorous approaches to air and water pollution that might otherwise have been impossible to achieve or enforce if individual states were free to maintain lower standards.

Free traders' concerns about common standards are also frequently misplaced. Specifically, their fears about a ratcheting up of environmental requirements are overblown. The ''environmental federalism'' of the United States is living proof that setting minimum standards and permitting individual states to be more protective, subject to certain constraints to protect the free flow of commerce, can work and work well. The rules developed by the US Supreme Court in balancing environment and trade goals, and refined in chapter 5 for application internationally, can make harmonization work to support both environmental protection and trade liberalization.

Steps Short of Harmonization

In addition to recognizing that efforts at environmental standards harmonization—or, more accurately, policy convergence—should focus

---

32. Some environmentalists insist that harmonization should always occur at the highest level of any of the participants in the process. This is not a sound basis for policy, as ''highest'' does not necessarily mean ''optimal.'' Just because the United States has handled an issue in a particular way does not mean others should follow the same policy path. In fact, any country that let the US Superfund program be its guide for handling abandoned hazardous waste sites would have made a grievous error (Johnstone 1994).

on minimum standards, several other policy recommendations are worth considering. As a first step toward convergence, or in areas where wide variations in standards would be justified (e.g., pesticide exposure limits where food consumption patterns vary)[33] common testing protocols, data requirements, and risk analysis methodologies—not the standards themselves—offer the best initial focus. Harmonization efforts in this context can be undertaken consistent with differences in assimilative capacity, which are legitimate bases for comparative advantage. If and when standards themselves are the focus of convergence efforts, the emphasis should be on environmental performance requirements[34] that address environmental quality levels—not equalization of environmental compliance costs. Common performance standards or agreed methodologies for defining appropriate cost internalization permit countries to address their pollution problems using their own regulatory programs. Such standards also respect variations in national circumstances that justify differences in environmental programs.

Countries and their political subdivisions should retain the right to determine the level of local environmental risk they are willing to accept and thus the level of protection they consider appropriate. This means parties may set standards above international levels. This right to exceed the common standard should be subject only to basic disciplines designed to ensure that a standard does not constitute a hidden trade barrier or impose an unjustified disruption to trade.

Another possible approach is the European Union's mutual recognition principle through which each EU country agrees to accept the environmental standards of other members of the Union with certain caveats. In fact, Nicolaïdis (1993) describes the system as "managed mutual recognition"—states accept each other's standards subject to minimum harmonization of some matters, a monitoring regime designed to ensure appropriate implementation of either harmonized Union-wide requirements or the country's own standards, and safeguards for countries desiring to maintain high standards.

Getting parties to commit to enforcement of their own regulations under a joint review process and to move toward a convergence of their standards over time provides another route toward harmonization.[35] This incremental approach allows differences in environmental priori-

---

33. For example, Japan might want to maintain a more strict limit on pesticide residues on rice than the United States given that per capita rice consumption is much higher in Japan. For an analysis of pesticide standards in industrialized countries see GAO (1993).

34. Performance standards could be defined in terms of human pollutant exposures or ambient levels, both of which could accommodate differences in environmental conditions and assimilative capacity.

35. There is, however, some problem of moral hazard in that countries may choose low standards to avoid any risk of being in noncompliance with their enforcement obligations.

ties, natural endowments, and levels of development to shape the starting point for common environmental programs. It also permits parties to identify together the most promising areas for convergence as part of an ongoing process. This approach is particularly useful when countries at disparate levels of economic development want to advance their trade relationship and at the same time want to mitigate the political tensions created by dramatically different environmental compliance costs for their competing producers. The NAFTA sets up just such a process, establishing a North American Commission on Environmental Cooperation to facilitate the review of each country's environmental enforcement record and to advance progress on the harmonization of standards (Esty 1993a).[36]

Convergence on the Polluter Pays Principle

Rather than actually negotiating common standards, it may be easier to start the process of convergence with agreement on general principles for environmental regulation. The most obvious candidate for initial action would be the cost internalization obligation embedded in the polluter pays principle.

As trade economist Richard Snape (1992) observes: "Efficiency requires that the full costs [of pollution] be brought to bear on the production decision." The trade economics literature is replete with similar statements (Anderson and Blackhurst 1992a; Eglin 1993b). Thus, a nation's failure to internalize environmental costs creates both ecological harm and economic waste. Agreement on a cost-internalization obligation, enforced through the trade regime, would have multiple advantages.

Despite its theoretical attraction, mandating adherence to the polluter pays principle entails serious practical problems. No accepted methodology exists for calculating pollution costs, never mind internalizing them. As this study has repeatedly observed, the uncertainties about how much harm various pollutants cause can be considerable, thus an optimal pollution tax level would be extremely hard to fix. Moreover, many activities generate multiple pollutants with complex effects that often interact with other substances in the air, water, or land. Tracing each individual effect would be nearly impossible, particularly recognizing that, to be strictly accurate, every geographic location would need a separate analysis to account for unique circumstances and consequences. Questions such as whether to give credit for positive effects

36. The NAFTA environmental side agreement adds to this process an enforcement mechanism, designed to put teeth into the commitment to uphold standards by threatening the withdrawal of trade benefits or other penalties for noncompliance. This focus on sticks and not carrots is largely misguided and ironically lacking in real "teeth." But as Charnovitz (1994c, 72) notes, given the provision's "basic mis-orientation, the absence of teeth is not so bad."

(e.g., some scientists believe that sulfur dioxide emissions reduce global warming) would further complicate the appraisal process.

But even if a precise cost internalization calculus is not possible, directionally correct and order-of-magnitude assessments of what policy intervention would be required to meet the polluter pays obligation would often be possible. In any case, establishing a theoretical target for movement toward cost internalization provides a beacon to policymakers as they fashion second-best trade and environment policies.

As a matter of fact, the countries of the Organization for Economic Cooperation and Development have already committed themselves to the polluter pays principle. Thus a good argument can be made that these industrialized nations should simply effectuate the cost-internalization obligations they have already undertaken.

But in addition to the polluter pays principle, the OECD (1972) simultaneously adopted a somewhat conflicting guiding principle:

> In accordance with the provisions of the GATT, differences in environmental policies should not lead to the introduction of compensating levies or export rebates, or measures having equivalent effect, designed to offset the consequences of these differences in prices.[37]

There is, however, a way to square these two obligations. Specifically, the "no equalization of costs" principle (OECD 1972) goes on to clarify that

> different national environmental policies, for example with regard to the tolerable amount of pollution and to quality and emissions standards, are justified by a variety of factors including among other things different pollution assimilative capacities. . . ."

This implies, and the OECD guidelines do in fact promote, harmonization of standards unless legitimate reasons for different standards exist.

Thus by focusing on the convergence of performance standards based on environmental quality, not cost equalization, both OECD guidelines can be met. To make this system work, countries might agree on baseline ambient pollution levels or exposures limits.[38] How a country meets the common standard would then be of no consequence. Countries with dispersed populations and little current pollution, climatic, and other conditions that allow quick dispersal of pollutants may not need any control program. Other countries may need strict controls on emissions.

Under such a scheme, if pollution levels were to exceed the established threshold, the polluter pays principle would be deemed violated,

---

37. Stevens (1993b) provides a more complete discussion of this principle. OECD (1975) discusses the polluter pays principle.

38. Brown Weiss (1993a) argues for minimum environmental standards and proposes criteria for advancing this process.

and an ecoduty would be permitted.[39] The duty should be set at a level that eliminates any cost advantage derived from the producer's failure to meet the established environmental criteria. Calculation of the proper amount might still be difficult, but precision is not essential so long as errors are skewed toward penalties that create an incentive for compliance with the established environmental quality norm.

A system of harmonized minimum environmental performance standards offers significant advantages over unilaterally determined ecoduties or no international environmental standards whatsoever. Specifically, harmonizing standards allows for cooperative action to reduce competitiveness based on environmental degradation and the political pressures this creates. The "job loss" fear and the sense that low standards constitute an unfair basis for comparative advantage make ad hoc ecoduty assessments a real risk in the absence of a structured program to manage environment-based competition. Thus, particularly for countries at a comparable level of development, some effort at convergence of standards should be undertaken.[40]

The GATT is plainly in no position to manage the development of environmental performance requirements. This exercise should be led by an international environmental body, preferably a Global Environmental Organization. In the absence of a GEO, the UN Environment Programme could take up the challenge, but it would need to first bolster its technical expertise. The work of the OECD Chemicals Group (1993) offers a useful model for the sort of harmonization process that could be advanced. In its 15 years in operation, the OECD Chemicals Group has developed testing protocols, risk methodologies, and common data bases on dozens of chemicals (Lönngren 1992, 246).

Policy Recommendations

Responding to competitiveness concerns represents one of the most difficult trade and environment challenges. However, specific policy directions can be identified:

- Policy intervention is most strongly justified in response to competitiveness issues that reflect transboundary or global pollution spillovers. Actions taken to address psychological or political spillovers should be multilaterally negotiated.

---

39. Countries found to be out of compliance with the cost-internalization obligation should be given an opportunity to act on their own to rectify the situation before ecoduties are imposed.

40. Indeed, GATT expert John Jackson (1992a, 1244) endorses the use of trade measures as "a very attractive and potentially useful means of providing enforcement of international cooperatively developed standards, including environmental standards."

- Joint implementation of full-cost pricing, particularly through the polluter pays principle, offers the most sensible long-term target for environmental policy cooperation.

- Convergence on baseline environmental quality requirements, rather than strict harmonization of standards or technology mandates, should be considered among countries at a comparable high level of development. "Mutual recognition" schemes and "enforce your own standards" requirements are a useful step toward convergence.

- Ecoduties should be available as an enforcement tool once internationally agreed standards are in place.

- A Green 301 mechanism is not a constructive tool for dealing with competitiveness concerns. In responding to local environmental problems, unilaterally threatened ecoduties should be used only, if at all, as leverage to get other nations to negotiate seriously—and thus the effective date of any such program should be set for three years from the date of enactment.

- Any nation, state, or locality should be free to determine its own risk preferences and to exceed baseline international environmental standards so long as their rules are not hidden trade barriers and do not impose a burden on trade that is clearly disproportionate to the environmental benefits to be obtained.

- GATT border tax adjustment rules should be refined to encourage environmental cost internalization and to permit adjustment for process-based charges (e.g., emissions fees).

- A broader program of carefully targeted green subsidies should be available to support the efforts of developing countries to raise their environmental standards.

8

The Battle for Sustainable Development

As difficult as it will be to achieve consensus among developed-country free traders and environmentalists on a plan to green the GATT, bridging the gap between North and South on whether and how to build environmental sensitivities into the international trading system will be even harder. Indeed, in more than 100 interviews undertaken for this study, no one defended the existing international trade rules more vigorously than India's ambassador to the GATT (interview with Ambassador B. K. Zutshi, Geneva, 18 May 1993). The GATT representatives from Mexico, Brazil, and the members of the Association of Southeast Asian Nations echoed this support for the trade regime status quo (interviews with GATT representatives from Mexico, Brazil, Philippines on behalf of the ASEAN group, and others, Geneva, 17–19 May 1993).

In fact, a number of developing countries—led by India and Brazil—strenuously fought the 1991 GATT efforts to reinvigorate a long-dormant Working Party on Trade and the Environment. Although the working party was recommissioned, the eco-naysayers succeeded in severely limiting the mandate for the group's work, and in doing so, reinforced the GATT image of environmental callousness. A coalition of developing nations also blocked efforts to establish a permanent Trade and Environment Committee under the new World Trade Organization (*Journal of Commerce*, 16 February 1994). To northern environmentalists, this foot-dragging is unconscionable and has resulted in widening the North-South trade and environment rift.

Refusing even to discuss the greening of the GATT represents a serious tactical blunder on the part of Brazil, India, and others (Esty 1994a). Obstructing debate invites US (and EU) unilateralism on trade and environment issues. However difficult GATT negotiations on environmental issues may be, the results are certain to be worse if the backdrop is a set of US unilateral demands, backed by trade restrictions. Moreover, to outsiders, some of the South's efforts to delay or circumscribe negotiations appear, at best, to bespeak a lack of understanding of the seriousness of the issues, and perhaps represent a cynical attempt to extract concessions from the developed world not based on substance but merely in exchange for opening a dialogue. Unfortunately, the appearance of bad faith undermines developing nations' opportunity to raise legitimate concerns over changes in the GATT to accommodate environmental values.

Notably, for many countries in the South, particularly those emerging from an inward economic focus and trying to develop export markets as part of their development programs, the new emphasis on environmental values in the North presents a potential subterfuge designed to maintain the economic dominance of the industrialized world (Odhiambo 1993). They see northern insistence on rules for sustainability and cost internalization not as a way of building environmental considerations into the trading system but as a process by which they will be required to accept environmental value judgments that conflict with their needs, particularly economic development. They object to upward harmonization of environmental standards to the extent that such efforts force them to invest resources in conservation programs or pollution controls that would not otherwise have been budget priorities and that may crowd out spending on other more pressing social or development needs. They fear that such GATT environmental rules would be used as an excuse to impose penalties on their products and to limit their access to markets in developed countries, whose own producers can more easily afford advanced environmental requirements (Hernandez 1993).

Trade and environmental officials in the South also object to the North's second-guessing of their resource management decisions, and they find international conservation agreements aimed at their natural resources to be highly offensive intrusions on their sovereignty.[1] They see unilaterally determined environmental policies backed by trade measures and market-access leverage—from Austria's tropical timber controls to the US ban on Mexican tuna to Germany's new product packaging restrictions—as even more objectionable and threatening. They find it particularly ironic (and inequitable) that they are being asked to bear costs to address global environmental problems that are the by-product of northern industrialization and the failure of the developed world to internalize environmental externalities. They find requests for action

---

1. The Earth Summit speech of Malaysian Prime Minister Mahathir bin Mohamad (1992) provides an excellent example of the deep sense of outrage in the South about northern political domination and environmental profligacy.

even more outrageous when so little is being done to address the resource-intensive, consumption-oriented life-style of most citizens of the North (Davison 1993; Mahathir 1992).

Finally, leaders in the South vehemently object to the use of environmental trade measures to eliminate any competitive advantage that might arise when their environmental choices differ from northern policy preference. The enthusiasm among so many environmentalists in the North for ecoduties and other environmental trade measures has undercut the long-standing alliance between environmental and development interests. Most developing-country leaders strongly believe, as Patrick Low (1993a) of the World Bank has pointed out, that poverty is "the most aggravating and destructive of all environmental problems." Thus, from a southern perspective, the threat of new trade barriers (particularly ecoduties), which will likely aggravate problems of poverty, seems unfair, economically unwise, and potentially environmentally unsound as well (Ramphal 1990).

Sustainability versus Development

The breach between environmentalists and developing-country officials reflects a deep divide over how to implement the rallying cry of the Earth Summit: "sustainable development." Although there is widespread agreement on the link between environment and development (Strong 1992; Iglesias 1992), it has become clear that one person's vision of development may be another's image of environmental degradation. In fact, just before the Rio de Janeiro conference, a pitched battle was fought over the insistence of developing countries on inclusion of a "right to development" in the Earth Summit summary document—the Rio Declaration. The United States and other industrialized nations objected to this phrase, fearing that it would provide a basis in international law for developing countries to shirk obligations, including environmental duties, by claiming burden to their economic development. Ultimately, a compromise was struck in which a right to development was recognized in conjunction with an obligation to make development sustainable.

In truth, sustainable development is something of an oxymoron. The term derives from two verbs—"to sustain" and "to develop"—with almost opposite meanings. Whether one puts the emphasis on "sustaining" or "developing" can lead to quite different policy prescriptions. In fact, one of the reasons the trade and environment debate has received such broad attention is that it has become a central arena in the contest over what sustainable development means in practice.

Most industrialized-country observers see sustainable development along the lines of the definition developed by the World Commission on

Environment and Development, chaired by Norwegian Prime Minister Gro Brundtland.[2] The Brundtland Commission called for development that "meets the needs of the present without compromising the ability of future generations to meet their own needs." Its report noted that poverty is a central cause of ecological stress, but the commission focused primary attention on the integration of longer-term and broader policy perspectives into economic and environmental decision making. Consequently, the report dealt primarily with issues of intergenerational equity such as resource depletion, biological diversity, and management of the global commons. Others who have picked up the Brundtland Commission torch have also concentrated on creating mechanisms to address global environmental issues such as climate change (MacNeill, Winsemius, and Yakushiji 1991).

In contrast, developing countries tend to stress the importance of alleviating poverty in discussions on sustainable development.[3] Interest in environmental matters centers on short-term human needs and basic public health amenities. Although the impact of soil erosion, deforestation, and other ecological harms can be devastating to their people, officials in many developing countries treat environmental degradation and resource depletion as second-order considerations; global environmental issues are barely a priority at all.

These preferences are not illogical. The World Bank (1992a) estimates that every year more than 2 million people in developing countries die from illnesses attributable to polluted water and billions of people fall ill from waterborne diseases. Moreover, to people who have a life expectancy of 45 or 50 years, the prospects of getting skin cancer or cataracts when they are 70 from sun exposure exacerbated by depletion of the ozone layer seem very remote indeed. Under these conditions, truly long-term problems such as climate change in 50 or 100 years carry almost no weight.[4]

In economists' terms, when daily life is a struggle, people have a high "discount rate," putting great stock in what happens in the next few days or weeks and having little time to fret about whether their choices today will have a negative impact several years into the future. With basic survival not an issue, people in more wealthy countries can afford the luxury of worrying about the planet's longer-term ecological out-

---

2. Historical antecedents of the Brundtland Commission's focus on sustainable development can be found in the writings of Pinchot (1987).

3. For an interesting perspective on the ethical dimensions of sustainable development and the need to transform traditional approaches to development to make them consistent with the "ecological imperative," see Goulet (1990).

4. An interesting exception to this principle is the very active and effective participation in recent climate change negotiations of the island nations of the Pacific and the Caribbean. These small island states recognize that their very existence is threatened by sea level rise.

look. Short-term sacrifices to protect future interests become not only possible but rational. This difference in time horizons profoundly shapes risk calculations and environmental spending choices.

As Frederic Vester (1993), a biologist and systems thinker observes: "We can only get people to behave in an ecological way—compatible with nature—when we give up the idea of making sacrifices and being ascetic. Egoism is one of the strongest forces in the living world." Vester goes on to say that we should appreciate what is important to people and pursue policies that work with, not against, their needs and desires. The failure of industrialized-country environmentalists to build their policies on a foundation that recognizes basic human needs in the developing world is the source of much of the North-South tension over trade and the environment.

Of course, while resource conservation and other sustainable development concepts have no resonance with the very poor, the merely poor can and often do make decisions to trade off short-term gain for longer-term opportunities, particularly if the social structures of their communities (e.g., land tenure policies) give them incentives to do so (Leonard 1989).

Ecoimperialism

To many observers in the South, the North's programs of pollution control and resource conservation smack of paternalism and hypocrisy. From a southern point of view, industrialized countries are rich today because they exploited their resources in the past and continue to do so today. Many developing-world representatives therefore see great unfairness in programs to change the ground rules for natural resource use and wonder whether the modern ecological movement is not driven by a desire to keep poorer countries perpetually underdeveloped and economically dependent on the industrialized world (Khor 1994). Faced with environmental policies and resource protection programs that reflect northern priorities, many developing-country officials now denounce "ecoimperialism" and revile US and European environmentalists as a leading threat to their development.

In addition, environmental officials in the South frequently find the North's ecological agenda to be misguided. They reject the high priority given to nebulous global problems that pose only uncertain and distant risks to the environment. Instead, they want to concentrate their limited environmental resources and whatever development assistance they receive on national priorities such as water systems and sewers that provide direct and immediate benefits to their citizenry. If money is to be spent to address global problems, they insist, it should not be at the expense of the environmental infrastructure needs of developing countries.

In the recent Uruguay Round negotiations, many developing countries felt that their desire to discuss controls on trade in environmental "bads" such as toxic or radioactive waste and chemicals barred from sale in the producing country was ignored. A number of developing countries have complained that multinational companies "dump" on unsuspecting developing-country purchasers products that are not permitted in the developed world or which represent outmoded technologies that no longer meet the standards of sophisticated buyers. Recent horror stories about waste exports resulting in chemical drums breaking open and leaching into water supplies in several African countries have raised awareness about improper disposal practices and the waste trade.

Export bans are, however, controversial. Some developing countries, lacking their own regulatory structures or fearful of regulatory slipups due to skill or capacity limitations (or corruption) want to have developed countries control exports of environmentally questionable products. To respond to these concerns, the Basel Convention on the export of hazardous wastes was negotiated. It tries to prevent improper handling of waste by requiring "prior informed consent" of the importing nation before a potentially harmful product can be shipped.

Other developing-country officials consider such export bans to be paternalistic and inappropriate, arguing that circumstances in developing countries often differ from those in the producer nation and that they should be able to make their own environmental regulatory decisions. They would argue, for example, that antimosquito insecticides banned in the United States for questionable ecological impacts might be appropriate in developing countries where malaria presents a threat to daily life and that any environmental harms are outweighed by the public health benefits.

Concerns about environmentally unsound exports are particularly acute regarding pesticide, fungicide, and insecticide products—banned for sale in the United States or other OECD countries—that companies continue to sell in developing countries. In addition to the potential harm in the purchasing country, such practices worry some US food safety experts, who believe banned products will find their way back into the United States as residues on imported fruits, vegetables, or other products. This so-called circle of poison has prompted several recent congressional efforts to ban the export of products that do not meet US environmental, health, or safety standards.

The GATT has also focused on the issue in the context of negotiations over "domestically prohibited goods." This negotiation was not, however, included in the conclusion of the Uruguay Round due to disagreements of the sort noted above. The issue has now been put on the agenda for the new Environment Committee of the World Trade Organization, to be set up as a function of the Uruguay Round results.

The developing countries' fears about the implications of the northern definition of the trade and environment problem are at least partly right. Equity and ability-to-pay considerations both suggest that the developed world should foot the bill for global cleanup programs that reflect the accumulated emissions of industrialized countries, but this is unlikely to occur. As this study noted earlier, there is little willingness in the North to settle the planet's overdrawn environmental accounts. More importantly, even if the countries of the North should bear a disproportionate share of the burden of dealing with retrospective issues, all countries must share prospective responsibility for protecting the Earth's biosphere.[5]

Equally distressing to developing countries are the North's threats of trade restrictions to force acquiescence to northern environmental priorities over which legitimate disagreement remains regarding the resulting benefits. For instance, in negotiations over the North American Free Trade Agreement, the United States pressured Mexico to install smokestack scrubbers on Carbon II, a coal-fired power plant near the US border. Environmental Protection Agency officials and border area environmental groups leaned on the Mexican government to ensure the facility met not just Mexican requirements but US air quality standards.

Although cognizant of the special pressures created by the negotiation of a broad trade agreement, the Mexicans argued that the hundreds of millions of dollars that would be required to install scrubbers would be better spent in other ways that would do far more to protect public health in Mexico. Specifically, from a Mexican perspective, the desperately dirty air of Mexico City presents a much higher priority than the air of the sparsely populated area near the Carbon II plant. More importantly, Mexican officials noted that the US environmental requirements they were asked to meet focus not on public health threats from pollution but on visibility, an environmental virtue that Mexico is not yet able to afford (interview with Mario Aguilar, Washington representative of the Mexican Ministry of Environment and Social Development, 10 November 1993). They further argued that, in the desert environment, wind-borne dust and dirt affects visibility far more than the Carbon II emissions and that no definitive link had been established between pol-

---

5. Both Agenda 21 and the Climate Change Convention (Article 3) identify "common but differentiated responsibilities" of all nations to protect the planet. In dealing with problems such as climate change, past accumulations of emissions actually represent only a small problem. The real risk lies in potential future CO_2 accumulations. Concentrations of CO_2 in the atmosphere have gone from 290 to 355 parts per million. Over the long term, this level could rise to 1000 or even 2000 ppm (Cline 1992, 50–58). Moreover, less-developed countries already account for 30–40 percent of greenhouse gas emissions. The developing-country share of emissions is expected to rise to nearly 60 percent by 2100 (Cline 1992, 336–37).

lution from the plant and visibility problems on the US side of the border.

Similar North-South disputes arise when the developed world tries to advance through trade restrictions environmental policy judgments or moral values not shared in the developing world. Again drawing on recent US-Mexico experience, the tuna-dolphin dispute presents a classic example of a North-South values clash. From the point of view of the developing world, why should Mexico forgo tuna fishing with efficient purse seine nets, which produce a valuable source of low-cost protein for poor Mexicans and modest export earnings on US sales, just because America has a dolphin fetish? As the Mexicans are quick to point out, the dolphin population in the Eastern Tropical Pacific Ocean is not endangered,[6] and fewer than 30,000 dolphins a year have been killed out of a population that numbers in the millions.

Even more distressing are cases where northern governments have chosen environmental policy tools that disproportionately burden developing countries or which respond at great expense to relatively small environmental harms. Germany's packaging law—requiring wholesalers and producers to take back from their consumers any shipping or packing materials—reflects both of these concerns. The German requirements are much more burdensome to foreign producers. They bear the added expense of returning their packing material longer distances than their domestic competitors if it is to be reused, or paying to join the "green dot" private disposal system, which for some materials can be very expensive.

If this program were addressing a critical environmental risk, most importers into Germany would not begrudge the cost. But waste disposal ranks relatively low on environmental risk lists (EPA 1990b), and more disturbingly, with regard to a number of products, the program is not working (Fishbein 1994). Mountains of yogurt cups, margarine containers, and other packaging materials now mar the landscape in or near the "green dot" waste sorting facilities. Rumors of midnight shipping of waste to Bulgaria and other Eastern European countries are rife. Thus, developing-country exporters to Germany (e.g., Kenyan flower growers) have lost an important export market with minimal environmental benefits accruing to Germany.

Backfiring Trade Restrictions

More dramatically, developing nations point to a number of examples where the threat or use of trade restrictions to advance industrialized-country environmental priorities actually worsened rather than im-

---

6. The eastern spinner dolphin and the northeastern offshore spotted dolphin are, however, listed as "depleted" under the US Marine Mammal Protection Act.

proved environmental quality. The ongoing dispute over rain forest protection illustrates this point. Several countries have proposed restrictions on imports of tropical timber as a way of preserving the rain forests.[7]

Rather than protecting tropical forests, trade restrictions on timber may produce the opposite result (GATT 1992b; Primo Braga 1992). Specifically, by limiting the markets in which tropical timber can be sold, trade restrictions by some countries will reduce demand for the product, thereby lowering the price of tropical timber and potentially forcing exporting countries to cut more trees to maintain much-needed export revenues. Moreover, by driving down the value of standing timber, trade restrictions diminish the incentive to protect remaining forests and to reforest in areas that have previously been harvested. This makes land clearing for alternative uses such as grazing relatively more attractive. In addition, half of all the wood consumed in the world is burned as firewood because the inhabitants are too poor to afford other fuels (Brown 1994, 34). Thus, depriving the people living in or near forests of a chance to make a living in the timber business may increase the consumption of wood for fuel.

This analysis should not be read as justifying deforestation. To the contrary, there is a need to ensure that forest resources are used sustainably and that the global benefits of tropical forests are reflected in logging business decisions. But the potentially perverse effects of blunt trade measures show why developing countries are nervous about the use of trade restrictions to promote industrialized-world strategies for environmental quality improvements. It also argues for more careful study of the environmental implications of policy choices—and perhaps for a trade review mechanism that sends seemingly perverse policies back to national decision makers for review.

A Lack of Carrots

The nub of the North-South trade and environment dispute is the reliance of industrialized countries, and particularly the United States, on "sticks" in the absence of available "carrots" to promote environmental goals. Industrialized countries resort to trade restrictions in their pursuit of environmental goals because they do not perceive themselves as having sufficient resources to cajole their southern counterparts into

---

7. Austria's tropical timber legislation, adopted in June 1992 and withdrawn in December 1992 in the face of a threatened trade boycott by the ASEAN nations, is the best example of this genre of trade action. For the background on this case, see Sucharipa-Behrmann (1993). France is moving more cautiously and in cooperation with timber-producing countries to develop an ecolabeling system for tropical timber (French Ministry of Cooperation 1993; Solagral 1993).

preferred environmental stances.[8] But if peace on this front is to be established, industrialized nations must look for opportunities to provide poorer countries with the incremental funds required to undertake developmental programs in an environmentally benign manner.[9]

Developed countries should look for more carrots, not just to be nice to developing countries, but more fundamentally because sticks cannot be counted on to produce results. Successful programs of environmental protection are almost never undertaken as a result of external threats. The governmental effort required to make an environmental commitment work can only be sustained by domestic political pressures. Governments forced at the point of a trade gun to agree to certain environmental standards may do so—but making such commitments into something more than lip service requires positive incentives.

The difficulty of making economic sanctions stick in general has been well-documented (Hufbauer, Schott, and Elliott 1990). Success in the use of trade restrictions in the environmental realm is equally limited. Too often environmental trade measures result in economic harm but not environmental progress. There are some exceptions to this rule. For example, Iceland bowed out of whaling in the late 1980s under pressure from US trade sanctions, but the consumer boycott of Icelandic fish and other products led by Greenpeace may have been an even more important factor in Iceland's decision. In fact, Mexico has not stopped tuna fishing with dolphin-killing purse seine nets despite the US embargo, although Mexico has no doubt paid a price in lost tuna export earnings in the US market. For those who are interested not in punitive scorekeeping but environmental results, this outcome is not very satisfactory.

There can be no doubt that finding resources for positive incentives presents a serious challenge in today's tight-budget world, making resort to trade penalties appear attractive as a "no cost" option for leverage. But it is equally clear that the use of environmental trade

---

8. The problem, of course, is not really a lack of resources but the priorities that have been selected. The US foreign assistance budget, for instance, exceeds $20 billion. The difficulty in finding funds within this sum for environmental projects is that popular support for spending overseas has fallen, and thus the total foreign aid budget has gone down in recent years. Moreover, large segments of the foreign assistance account are considered politically untouchable (Storm 1993). The fiscal pressure created by the ongoing US federal budget deficit adds to the difficulty of freeing up resources (Hyland 1988).

9. What constitutes "incremental" can become a major issue, as the discussion of the Global Environment Facility in chapter 4 makes clear. Of course, many local problems have global consequences, and thus devoting resources to addressing problems that yield both local and worldwide benefits makes sense. For example, rural development projects and sound agricultural policies have direct local benefits and indirectly help preserve forests and protect biological diversity. Investments in energy conservation also cut national costs while providing global benefits (Petesch 1992). Thus, the concept of incremental costs must be applied flexibly enough not to deter projects that have both substantial global benefits and positive local consequences.

measures is neither really costless nor very effective as an environmental policy tool.

Success in translating international environmental commitments into ecological and public health protection depends on positive incentives, which largely turn on the seriousness of the funding provisions of the particular agreement. The Montreal Protocol provides on important model in this regard. The 1990 London amendments to the protocol committed the parties not only to a full phaseout of chlorofluorocarbons (CFCs) and other ozone-depleting chemicals but also established a $240 million fund to subsidize the transition of developing countries to CFC substitutes. These resources allowed developing countries—led by Mexico—to sign onto the CFC restrictions without fear that their development programs would be set back by the added costs of producing refrigerators and other CFC-dependent products using the more expensive CFC substitutes. Even hesitant China and shrill India have now joined 124 other nations and signed the accord.

There are other reasons for the success of the ozone layer protection efforts: a confined and clearly identifiable issue, the relative certainty of the science, the limited number of producers of the problematic product, the increased availability of CFC substitutes, and the relatively limited economic impact of the phaseout. But the funding mechanism played, and continues to play, a major role in ensuring North-South cooperation. In fact, not only is the existence of the Montreal Protocol Fund an important archetype, the governing structure for the disbursement of funds also provides an important lesson in North-South collaboration. Specifically, ozone layer protection funds are controlled by an executive committee made up of seven developed (donor) countries and seven developing (recipient) countries. Resources are committed only upon a majority vote of both halves of the committee.

Additional multilateral development assistance, perhaps funneled through a Green Fund, offers one obvious generic solution to the environmental funding problem. Indeed, the proposal for a "Green Fund" laid out in chapter 4, supported by a tiny environmental surcharge on worldwide trade and financial flows, would provide a substantial pot of money to address global environmental problems with carrots rather than sticks. Targeted on the incremental cost of pursuing development projects in a manner that minimizes global environmental harms, such resources would be a cost-effective and ecologically valuable way to advance environmental goals and trade liberalization efforts simultaneously. Increased bilateral assistance would be another answer.

Beyond supporting the marginal cost of development strategies with global environmental benefits that would otherwise go unfunded, reliance on foreign aid is not, however, a long-term recipe for success. In the 1970s, tedious UN debates about a New International Economic

Order took place without advancing any realistic ideas for North-South resource transfers. Similar discussions have occurred in the 1980s and '90s, but redistribution of global wealth is still not—and probably never will be—on the political agenda of most countries in the North.

Some officials in the South have expressed the hope that the environment, especially global environmental problems, would provide the leverage that the developing world needs to extract substantial financial transfers from the North. But despite all of the hoopla surrounding the 1992 Earth Summit, at the end of the conference new eco-aid commitments amounted to only a few hundred million dollars a year, far short of the $125 billion per year that Earth Summit coordinator Maurice Strong estimated would be required to put developing countries on an ecologically sound and sustainable path to economic growth. The very limited success of the Global Environment Facility in attracting contributions provides further support for the conclusion that other means of providing new resources to developing countries should be explored.

Trade Not Aid

History suggests that the most significant and sustained source of funding for developing-country environmental investments will be the developing countries themselves. Notwithstanding the attention paid to the concept of sustainable development over the last several years, concrete programs to integrate environmental needs and economic aspirations have not emerged.[10] Top policy priority should therefore be given to establishing the underpinnings—trade liberalization, debt relief, investment reform, and adoption of market-based economic policies—for sustained worldwide economic development, which would generate resources for, among other things, environmental protection.

Most countries in the South see trade as an important avenue to economic growth.[11] At the Earth Summit in Rio, the world community agreed that:

> States should co-operate to promote a supportive and open international economic system that would lead to economic growth and sustainable development in all countries, to better address the problems of environmental degradation. (Rio Declaration, Principle 12)

---

10. The Winnipeg-based International Institute for Sustainable Development recently issued (Shaw and Cosbey 1994) a set of "trade and sustainable development principles" designed to help advance this integration process.

11. Part IV of the GATT on trade and development already calls on the developed world to provide less-developed countries with special treatment and not to "expect reciprocity for commitments made by them in trade negotiations to reduce or remove tariffs and other barriers to the trade of less-developed countries."

Agenda 21 (chapter 2), the Rio conference's major substantive output, expands on the assumption that trade is a necessary element of sustainable development and an important force for the promotion of environmental objectives in developing countries. It specifically calls on the nations of the world to promote "sustainable development through trade liberalization."

At the same time, the Earth Summit set ambitious global environmental goals and advanced the notion that environmental costs should be internalized as an important element of what makes development sustainable. But by failing to match these good intentions with any plan to generate the necessary resources for developing countries, the Earth Summit may actually have exacerbated trade and environment tensions. In particular, the summit's confirmation of the importance of environmental goals has emboldened environmentalists who want to punish those who do not meet high standards, regardless of the lack of available resources. Rising expectations for environmental action in the North, combined with little progress in identifying the financial means of achieving environmental advances in the South, may therefore have increased the pressure to impose trade restrictions on developing countries when they fail to meet developed-country environmental aspirations.

Finding New Carrots

Commodity Agreements

The paucity of creative thinking about how to overcome this disconnect between environmental ambitions and resources is troubling. A number of new ideas are, however, beginning to emerge. For example, some commentators (e.g., Arden-Clarke 1992a; Taylor 1993; Kisiri 1992) have argued for commodity agreements to shore up the prices developing countries receive for their exports and to provide them with adequate resources to internalize environmental costs.[12] The logic of this approach to economic growth in the South derives from the recognition that many developing countries are heavily dependent on export earnings from primary products such as timber, cocoa, or bauxite ("Poor Relations," *The Economist*, 16 April 1994, 76). Most of these commodity exports go to industrialized countries. More significantly, real commodity prices have fallen sharply in recent years. In the 1980s alone, nonoil commodity prices dropped 50 percent, exacerbating cost pressures and making attention to environmental issues more difficult (Mensink 1991).

---

12. Dawkins (1994) provides a broad critique of current North-South trade, identifying "imbalances" in the balance of trade, terms of trade, "price-cost" ratio, and "social/ ecological" accounts.

As Charles Arden-Clarke (1992a) of the World-Wide Fund for Nature has observed: "Low revenue capture and the loss of export earnings represented by this decline in commodity prices is costing developing countries more than money. It is contributing to the destruction of their environment and preventing development on the basis of sustainable use of natural resources." Henk Kox of the Free University of Amsterdam (1993 and 1992) has proposed the creation of International Commodity-Related Environmental Agreements (ICREAs) to address this problem (see also Linneman et al. 1993). Under Kox's scheme, an "environmental premium" would be paid on all sales of unprocessed products as part of globally negotiated commodity agreements. Kox sees ICREAs responding to the need to boost developing-country incomes, with OECD countries footing the bill, and to provide a source of funds to support pollution control and resource management investments in the commodity-producing developing countries. The revenues raised would go into an environmental fund, administered by an ICREA Secretariat and paid out to commodity-exporting developing countries upon implementation of environmental management plans.

Dartmouth College's Konrad von Moltke (1992) has called for a similar scheme of "mutual tariffs" to encourage environmental cost internalization and the development of sustainable production practices. Under von Moltke's proposal, tariffs would be imposed either by commodity exporters to fund their environmental activities or by importers against any commodity exporter that fails to impose export tariffs. This importer action, in the absence of an exporter program to collect duties, would protect exporters that are internalizing costs with their own tariffs. While acknowledging the difficulties of implementing this mutual tariff proposal, von Moltke argues that the alternatives—internationally agreed and enforced environmental policies or massive North-South subsidies—are even more difficult to achieve.

The idea of creating incentives for appropriate resource management and the adoption of pollution control techniques and of having a fund to support these activities is attractive. The ICREA or "mutual tariff" proposals, however, face serious practical obstacles, not the least of which is the UN Conference on Trade and Development's (UNCTAD) long history of failed commodity agreements.[13] Specifically, there is little reason to believe that efforts to override market-based commodity pricing in the name of environmental progress will be much more successful than past efforts to do so in the pursuit of equity for developing countries.[14]

---

13. Verleger (1993) has detailed the failure of all past commodity price control agreements.

14. Kox's most recent work (1993) on ICREAs shows more flexibility and promise. He suggests, for example, that there might be standard-setting ICREAs that simply define competition but do not interfere with market forces or try to force side payments among parties.

Arden-Clarke (1992a) has advanced a similar concept to facilitate the internalization of environmental costs by developing countries. Arden-Clarke proposes that developed countries levy ecoduties on products entering their markets that do not fully reflect environmental costs but then rebate the import fees to the exporting countries for use in making needed environmental investments. Arden-Clarke foresees the repatriation of funds occurring on the basis of bilateral negotiations that define the specific uses toward which the monies would go.

This idea again gets to the critical issue of resource needs in developing countries. But developing-country exporters are unlikely to be enthusiastic about having their products penalized with import duties, no matter that they can negotiate for the return of the funds collected. In addition, this approach may well be viewed as patronizing and intrusive. The Arden-Clarke scheme would also raise questions of fairness in the calculation of the environmental costs "not internalized" and require broad adherence by the developed world to function smoothly. In addition, implementation of these countervailing ecoduties would either violate the GATT or require an amendment (unlikely to be accepted by developing countries) of the GATT rules on trade restrictions for production processes and methods.

Environmental Trade Preferences

Lyuba Zarsky (1993) argues for "ecological conditionality" on trade combined with "environmental trade preferences" to subsidize pollution control and conservation investments by developing countries. She notes that from an economic point of view one can only be sure free trade will support ecologically sustainable development if "environmental costs and limits are expressly incorporated into the prices and quantities of traded goods" (1993, 51). To soften the blow to developing countries of mandatory environmental cost internalization, Zarsky calls for developing countries to be given preferential tariff reductions and market access if they meet agreed environmental standards. Zarsky would implement her program through an expanded version of GATT's Generalized System of Preferences (GSP) or through resource- or product-specific environmental agreements that provide for tariff reductions tied to specific environmental actions.

Zarsky's proposal has considerable merit and deserves further exploration. It does not require jiggering with commodity markets and relies entirely on the positive incentive of preferential market access to induce developing countries to meet environmental demands. By lowering duties (and increasing profits), Zarsky's trade preferences would generate income streams that would permit developing countries to make the requisite investments in pollution control technologies or integrated resource management programs.

Flexibility is another hallmark of this mechanism. Trade preferences could be negotiated multilaterally or bilaterally. They could also be adopted entirely unilaterally. Because the system does not change prices in the global marketplace and relies purely on rewards for good behavior, not trade penalties for bad deeds, there can be no complaint about unilateral implementation. Such a trade preferences scheme might be especially useful in the context of regional free trade agreements that link more and less developed countries, particularly to facilitate the transition of poorer countries to higher environmental standards as part of a negotiated commitment to upward harmonization. The main problem with Zarsky's proposal is that there may not be many areas left where preferential tariff treatment will be worth much. With a few notable exceptions, such as textiles, industrialized-nation tariffs are already quite low. Thus, consideration should be given to other trade and nontrade preferences that might be made available.

Environment and Resources "Linkage": The Enterprise for the Americas Model

The United States' little-noticed Enterprise for the Americas Initiative (EAI), launched in 1990, offers a possible model for a broader-gauge opportunity to link environmental advances and the availability of new resources to help developing countries establish the economic foundation for truly sustainable development. Under the EAI program, the US government offered to reduce the official debt[15] of Latin American countries that agreed to economic restructuring consistent with International Monetary Fund agreements, opened their markets to foreign investment, and liberalized trade. In addition to writing off part of the foreign government's debt, the US government allowed the borrower to divert a portion of the dollar interest payments owed to the US Treasury into a local-currency trust fund to support environmental projects.[16] Bolivia, Jamaica, Colombia, Uruguay, El Salvador, and Chile have taken advantage of this program to fund millions of dollars of environmental activities.

An expanded version of the EAI might be adopted to bridge the North-South divide over funding for environmental programs and to

---

15. The debts to be written down were specifically those incurred under the US Public Law 480 "food for peace" program, Agency for International Development lending, Export-Import Bank credits, and the US Agriculture Department's Commodity Credit Corporation. Actual implementation of the EAI program has been limited by concerns in Congress and the Office of Management and Budget about the budget impact of writing off debt and losing interest payments. For a good review of the EAI program, see Gibson and Schrenk (1991).

16. In addition to funding the environmental trust accounts, the write-down of foreign debt strengthens the economy of the country, creating new opportunities for US export sales and serving international security interests (Moran 1990).

reduce trade-environment tensions. Specifically, the OECD countries should offer to reduce the official debt of developing countries in return for commitments to participate in global environmental efforts and to move over time to higher environmental standards more broadly. The total debt of the developing world currently stands at approximately $1.1 trillion.[17] Of this amount, about $520 billion is official debt owed to governments and international institutions. Some $44 billion is owed by developing countries to the United States.

Using the EAI model, some portion of this total might be forgiven outright over time in countries that commit to global environmental protection efforts such as ozone layer preservation, biodiversity, oceans protection, and climate change prevention. Some of the interest due on the remaining debt might be conditionally converted into local-currency payments and put into environmental accounts to meet nationally determined environmental needs, contingent upon progress in elevating environmental standards toward international baselines. Moreover, to the extent the EAI reform package helps to stimulate broad-based economic growth, additional resources will be generated, a portion of which might be devoted to environmental projects.

Environmental Conditionality

Conditionality is a word developing countries dislike because it reminds them of harsh IMF economic restructuring programs. But the concept need not resonate negatively. Specifically, if the environmental requirements imposed come with funding, conditionality gives the developing countries an opportunity to advance their environmental protection programs without detracting from economic growth goals.

History's two most sweeping programs of environmental standard setting both build on resource inducements. While enforcing baseline environmental standards, the US federal government has for years provided and continues to provide billions of dollars to the states to help them upgrade water delivery systems, sewage treatment facilities, and other aspects of their environmental infrastructure. Similarly, the European Union's Cohesion Fund has eased the transition to a single European market with common environmental standards through tens of billions of dollars in resource transfers to the poorer states in the Union. The prospect of additional resources takes away much of the sting of conditionality and much of the burden of mandated higher environmental standards. Of course, political support for large-scale financial assistance programs is easier to achieve in the context of a single country or an economic community, with their shared borders

---

17. Debt statistics are from Sewell et al. (1992). Sewell heads the Overseas Development Council, which has also called for debt reduction negotiations.

and common economic and political destiny, than among the international community as a whole.

There are, however, ways to internalize the compensation concept. For example, the NAFTA might be seen as a giant side payment to Mexico to help advance a series of domestic policy reforms aimed at democracy, economic prosperity, political stability—and environmental protection—that will make Mexico a better neighbor for the United States. Certainly, the prospect of NAFTA-generated economic growth and the technical assistance offered by the United States made it easier for Mexico to accept the environmental undertakings required by the NAFTA and the environmental side agreement that accompanies it.

The Role of Multilateral Development Banks

Even if a broad-scale debt-for-environment program or other financial assistance programs were adopted, the environmental resource needs of the South will far outstrip the income that could be made available. Additional funds from other sources will therefore be required. To help fill the gap, the basic lending programs of the World Bank and other multilateral development banks must be redirected to include a significant number of environmental projects. Some progress in this regard has been made, but more needs to be done. Specifically, the development banks need to be more strategic in their approach to the environment. Proposals for an "Earth increment" as part of the recent replenishment of World Bank funds[18] were advanced but not adopted.

More immediately and importantly, environmental considerations should be factored more vigorously into the structure of the World Bank's existing project development and approval process (Petesch 1992). For example, when a loan is proposed to support a new power plant, the project should incorporate appropriate energy efficiency and pollution control technologies. Indeed, care should be taken to ensure that every project with a potential environmental impact (which will be nearly every loan) meets the polluter pays principle and internalizes environmental costs. The bilateral assistance programs of OECD countries should also be expanded to include more environmental projects and better environmental cost internalization in nonenvironmental projects.

Redirecting Foreign Aid

As the world moves into the post–Cold War era, the time is ripe to redirect existing foreign assistance and development programs. The US

---

18. For an explanation of the International Development Association (IDA) and the IDA-10 replenishment see IDA (1993) and Gwin and Bates (1993).

foreign aid program still reflects Cold War priorities and must be updated to meet current needs.[19] The Overseas Development Council has developed an alternative US international affairs budget aimed at promoting sustainable development and funding programs to respond to environmental threats, among other goals (Sewell 1992).

America's foreign assistance program needs to be reinvigorated with a new focus on supporting sustainable economic growth both at home (through export promotion efforts) and abroad, as well as providing resources to support environmental programs that protect the US interest in the planet's ecological health. In fact, the Clinton administration has advanced a major legislative initiative to reform US foreign aid. The Peace, Prosperity, and Democracy Act of 1994 aims to make sustainable development the cornerstone of US foreign assistance and to streamline the functioning of the US Agency for International Development (AID) ("Christopher Lobbying for $3 Billion More in Foreign Aid," *Washington Post*, 7 December 1993, A12).

John Sewell (1992) has called for even more dramatic reform. He would like to see creation of a Sustainable Development Fund to replace current assistance channeled through AID. Sewell argues that US aid should be funneled through existing global environmental programs and US government agencies with technical competence (e.g., EPA, Department of Energy), private entities, voluntary organizations, and international institutions. He believes that such a fund would allow the United States to target its bilateral assistance more effectively and to improve both the efficiency and efficacy of its foreign assistance programs. Moreover, a foreign assistance program that tied in more directly to today's public priorities might well enjoy greater popular and congressional backing—a critical issue since a lack of political support has resulted in a recent drop in America's foreign aid contributions.

Technology Transfers

Another approach to closing the North-South environmental gap should be the diffusion of environmental knowledge and technologies to developing countries to strengthen their efforts to pursue sustainable programs of development (EPA 1992). In many cases, low environmental standards do not reflect a conscious decision to degrade the environ-

19. The Foreign Assistance Act of 1961 is a hodge-podge of 30 distinct goals and 75 "priority" areas of activity. Moreover, as Sewell et al. (1992) note, the United States spends $3.5 billion annually on arms transfers on a concessional basis to non-NATO countries. In addition, the United States spends $0.8 billion per year on economic support funds and foreign military financing for NATO allies. Hundreds of millions of additional dollars a year are spent in support of Radio Free Europe, Radio Liberty, and other US Information Agency propaganda programs that should no longer be funded (see also Storm 1993; "A Foreign Aid of Words, Not Cash," *New York Times*, 5 December 1993, E5).

ment for competitive advantage but rather a lack of capacity to carry out environmental programs. Developing countries often lack the governmental expertise to effectively regulate, and the developing world's private sector frequently wants but does not have access to or cannot afford the latest low-polluting manufacturing technologies. Assistance to southern governments to help design, implement, and enforce pollution control programs will pay big dividends to the developed world not only in improved environmental conditions but also in business opportunities for northern producers of environmental goods and services.

Too often, however, the requests for technology assistance from the South come in the form of demands for access to environmental products on a preferential or noncommercial basis.[20] Veiled threats sometimes lie just behind those calls for "cooperation." Such demands make little sense. Industrialized countries often do not own the technologies in question and thus are in no position to give them away, even if this were something that they wanted to do. More importantly, technology donations have a tendency to be mishandled because the test of economic need and value is missing.

The transfer of environmental technologies is, nevertheless, an important way of advancing environmental quality around the globe. The primary mechanism for broadening access to the latest pollution control equipment must be the provision of resources, particularly the incremental funds developing countries need to purchase the environmental goods and services. Subsidizing only the marginal cost of environmental goods or services—the added expense of undertaking a project using environmentally sound technologies—encourages careful thinking about the solutions proposed to any particular environmental problem and creates an incentive for the recipient country to consider the appropriateness of technologies to their own circumstances.[21]

Another related approach, proposed recently by Carraro and Siniscalco (1994), is North-South cooperation on research and development. Specifically, they argue that developing countries should be encouraged to join global environmental efforts in return for participation in joint R&D efforts. As Miller and Zhang (1994) have noted, the strength of the incentive can be magnified by focusing the collaborative

---

20. See, for example, the debates leading up to Rio Earth Summit and the 1992 Climate Change Convention. Private-sector technology assistance can also play an important role in helping developing nations meet high environmental standards and in reducing trade and environment tensions. For example, the Industry Cooperative for Ozone Layer Protection (ICOLP) has facilitated North-South technology cooperation and joint ventures, enabling a number of developing countries to speed up their shift to ozone-layer-friendly CFC substitutes (ICOLP 1993).

21. Limited budgets provide a further incentive to consider the least-cost approach to solving environmental problems, including consideration of pollution-prevention process redesign as well as "end-of-pipe" solutions.

R&D efforts on pollution abatement technologies, further reducing the costs of complying with emission control requirements.

Country Studies

To maximize the reach of the resources provided, comprehensive country environmental studies should be developed, aimed not simply at cataloging problems but also at developing solutions, setting priorities, and identifying funding mechanisms. According to a 1992 OECD analysis, some 200 country studies were undertaken in 1980–91, addressing environmental problems in more than 100 countries. The 1992 Earth Summit elicited environmental country studies from more than 150 nations. Unfortunately, much of the past work provides little foundation for good policy decisions. As O'Connor and Turnham note (1992), the data presented are too often incomplete or unreliable, and the policy analyses presented are frequently sketchy because of unclear study objectives or the political sensitivity of policy issues.

A worldwide commitment to increased funding for environmental programs should therefore be undergirded by thoughtful country-by-country environmental planning with clear objectives, careful data gathering and quality control, risk-based priority setting, broad issue coverage, public participation and oversight, and rigorous policy analysis. The sustainable development plans and strategies that are being undertaken in many countries to follow through on the Rio commitment to Agenda 21 offer an opportunity to develop systematic and coherent planning. There is, however, no mechanism in place to assure that these reports will be useful.

North-South Partnerships

The call for partnerships between developed and developing countries has become a cliché. Cooperation between or among nations on specific environmental projects nonetheless offers an important additional way of addressing North-South tensions (Wirth 1991). In a surprising number of cases, the failure of developing countries to pursue "proper" environmental policies is not due to bad will but a lack of knowledge about better alternatives or shortcomings in the capacities of their environmental agencies. Environmental training programs sponsored by developed countries are therefore an important way of diffusing knowledge about ecological and public health issues and sharing current thinking about policy solutions to these problems.

A large number of international institutions (including UNEP, UNDP, UNCTAD, OECD, and the US- and EU-sponsored Eastern

European Environmental Center in Budapest, to name just a few) offer environmental training programs. In addition, many countries sponsor training activities. For instance, in the United States, the EPA, the Department of Energy, AID, the Interior Department, the Peace Corps, and many nonprofit and academic institutions provide environmental education opportunities. Unfortunately, there is no overarching coordination of these courses, nor is the training necessarily focused on critical issues or aimed at the countries that need it most. Some effort to manage these activities more systematically and comprehensively would pay dividends in better use of limited environmental training resources and in reduced tensions between industrialized and developing countries.

Joint Implementation

Additional opportunities for North-South partnerships may be found in future international environmental agreements. In fact, the 1992 Climate Change Convention signed at Rio de Janeiro already provides for joint implementation of emission reduction projects. Under this provision, for example, the Netherlands might develop and fund a project to reduce methane emissions from rice paddies in Indonesia. This joint endeavor would allow the Dutch to achieve greenhouse-gas reductions at a cost lower than any project available within their own country (since the environmentally conscious Dutch have already implemented most of the inexpensive ideas for reducing emissions in the Netherlands) and provide resources for an environmental program that Indonesia would otherwise not have been able to afford.

Joint implementation is still a controversial policy tool, especially in the climate change context. Many developing countries, in particular, fear that it offers industrialized nations a way to ''get off the hook'' and to avoid making changes in their energy-intensive economies.[22] Others, however, recognize the potential to create a new mechanism for resource transfers, as well as the economic efficiency of obtaining emissions reductions wherever they are cheapest, thereby maximizing the range of resources available for climate change mitigation.[23] With these virtues in mind, the United States and a few other nations such as Norway are going forward with active efforts to explore joint imple-

---

22. Nevertheless, a growing number of developing countries support joint implementation efforts. Both Mexico and Poland spoke out in favor of joint implementation at the August 1993 meeting of the International Negotiating Committee on Climate Change.

23. For an interesting theoretical analysis of the potential for the use of ''emissions trading'' as a way of subsidizing the South's participation in global environmental efforts, see Diwan and Shafik (1992).

mentation programs and to develop specific emissions reduction projects.[24]

Just as it took time for the climate change policy community to recognize the analytic validity of the comprehensive approach to climate change (Stewart and Wiener 1992)—allowing countries to reduce emissions of whichever greenhouse gases they find it most cost-effective to control—the value of joint implementation will inevitably grow. The logic of obtaining greenhouse-gas emissions reductions wherever they can be most cheaply found is overwhelming. The developing world will certainly come to realize the potential that lies in opening a new channel for resources and technology from the North. The key to making joint implementation really work is getting the public in the developed world to understand that domestic environmental protection can often be provided most efficiently in the context of global problems such as climate change by investing in emissions controls overseas.

Stretching Dollars

In light of the difficulty of getting the governments of the North to ante up money for environmental projects in developing countries for which the South cannot or does not want to pay, innovative thinking about new funding mechanisms is urgently needed. Ensuring that the available money is well-spent must be another top priority. Unless and until a Green Fund of the sort proposed in chapter 4 is adopted, resources for environmental investments will have to be eked out of existing sources and stretched through creative policy programs. Unfortunately, as long as the resources available fall short of the needs, some nations (led by the United States) will be tempted to use trade restrictions to force other countries to reorder their environmental spending priorities, thus creating trade and environment disputes.

---

24. Joint implementation is an important element of the Clinton administration's Climate Change Action Plan announced in October 1993 (Executive Office of the President 1993).

Greening the GATT: Specific Steps

Whether or not a Global Environmental Organization is created, the General Agreement on Tariffs and Trade must be updated to reflect environmental considerations. In the absence of a new international environmental institution to work in tandem with the GATT, the policy void the GATT must fill will be greater, thus requiring more substantial changes in its rules and procedures to inculcate environmental values and to permit the GATT to reconcile competing trade and environmental goals. Because the environment was not part of the charge laid out at Punta del Este in 1986, the recent Uruguay Round negotiations did not advance the trade and environment agenda very far. Talk has already begun, however, about a Green Round or "green negotiations" to be undertaken soon.[1]

There are several approaches that might be pursued in "greening" the GATT. First, the "environmental" provisions of Article XX could be entirely replaced or supplanted with a new environmental code. It might, however, be difficult to achieve agreement on such radical surgery to the GATT. It is therefore worth considering how existing GATT language might be reinterpreted to build new environmental sensitivity into the international trade regime. This chapter explores both the environmental overhaul and the softer "reinterpretation" options.

---

1. At the April 1994 GATT ministerial meeting in Marrakesh formally concluding the Uruguay Round of negotiations, the GATT parties committed to a "trade and environment work programme," seen by many countries as laying the groundwork for actual negotiations. A number of agendas for this group have been put forward, including NRDC-FIELD (1994); Shaw and Cosbey (1994); Prudencio and Hudson (1994); BirdLife (1994); and Esty (1994b).

A Green Round Agenda

Despite the broad commitment to sustainable development evinced at the 1992 Rio Earth Summit, negotiations to update the GATT along environmental lines are likely to be contentious. Indeed, the European Union's chief trade negotiator, Sir Leon Brittan, has cautioned against "fashionable and politically correct" trade policies, arguing that efforts to green the GATT could be a pretext for protectionism (*Financial Times*, 18 January 1994, 6). The issues to be addressed are complicated and politically charged.

As recent trade and environment debates in the context of the Uruguay Round and at the Organization for Economic Cooperation and Development have demonstrated, serious differences exist between the United States and the European Union over the unilateral use of trade restrictions and other issues. OECD countries also have widely varying views about the need to make GATT procedures more open to nongovernment organizations—a top US priority. The divide between the industrialized world and developing countries may be even more significant, as the differences go to the heart of how GATT should accommodate competing development and environment concerns and when low environmental standards constitute an unfair basis on which to establish a competitive advantage in world trade.

Underlying these conflicts are deep issues of philosophy and political theory, raising questions about the appropriate trade-off (if any) between economic growth and environmental protection, the changing nature of sovereignty, the use of power in the international realm, the optimal structure for democratic decision making, and the proper role of interest groups in governmental processes. These questions have no easy answers, and merging disparate views on these matters into a common program for building environmental concerns into the international trading system will require extraordinary diplomacy.

What follows is a package of reforms designed to steer a middle course between the Scylla of blind environmentalism and the Charybdis of narrowly focused trade liberalization. It encompasses both procedural reforms and substantive changes in GATT rules, and it tries to identify appropriate mechanisms for GATT evolution.

Procedural Reforms

Good trade policymaking requires an understanding of environmental issues. Even the most ardent advocates of free trade concede that liberalizing trade in goods that cause pollution, either in their production or consumption, leads to greater environmental degradation and possibly reduced social welfare unless appropriate environmental policies such as pollution taxes are in place (Anderson 1992a). Thus environmental analysis should accompany efforts to open markets, and such analysis should advance policies to mitigate environmental stresses that trade liberalization might cause. To ensure that such programs are developed, trade negotiations with possible environmental consequences need to have procedures for environmental analysis built into them. More importantly, since a commitment to transparent processes is the mother's milk of environmentalists and an essential element of sound environmental policymaking, a GATT procedural reform effort that creates opportunities for participation by environmental (and other) interests in trade policymaking, builds understanding of trade goals and decision processes, and creates mechanisms for the airing of divergent views will go a long way toward making peace between the trade and environmental communities.

Environmental Assessments

To ensure that trade negotiators are aware of environmental issues related to their work, a comprehensive environmental impact analysis should be undertaken at the outset of any trade negotiation with elements likely to have environmental effects. Such an assessment need not attempt to model in detail all of the potential environmental ramifications of liberalized trade but should provide negotiators with a general sense of the environmental interests at stake and alternative ways of addressing the issues identified.[2] Specifically, the assessment should recommend environmental policy reforms that might be adopted alongside trade commitments to maximize the chances that movement toward freer trade will at least not harm the environment and, to the extent possible, will actually benefit the environment.

For example, in examining the Uruguay Round of GATT negotiations, some analysis of the environmental impacts of agricultural subsidies would have been useful. Indeed, recognition that heavily subsidized farmers often resort to environmentally harmful, chemical-intensive

---

2. The US National Environmental Policy Act (NEPA), as currently structured, does not provide a very useful environmental impact assessment model for trade negotiations. The NEPA environmental impact statement process generally takes too long and requires far too much detail to be valuable in the trade negotiation setting. Under US law, moreover, environmental impact studies are not required until after a government agency's action is final. But in the trade context, it makes no sense to wait to do the analysis until after a trade agreement has been concluded. The information is of much greater utility during the course of the negotiations when something can be done about the issues raised. NEPA assessments are also subject to interminable judicial reviews, which would not fit with the pace of trade negotiations. To ensure that environmental considerations are factored in to future US trade negotiations, NEPA should be amended to provide a special process for environmental assessments of prospective trade agreements.

production practices might have given added impetus to the efforts to reduce US and EU agricultural subsidies. Similar broad-scale analysis of the environmental implications of trade liberalization in textiles, services, and intellectual property and the opportunities for environmental advances through reform of the subsidies rules, dispute resolution procedures, and other issues would have been potentially valuable.[3] The analysis should not focus solely on trade effects but should also encompass environmental policy advances that could be or should be moved in parallel with trade liberalization.

Completing an environmental assessment at an early stage in the trade negotiation process would highlight for negotiators the sweep of ecological and public health issues potentially affected by freer trade. The goal should be to give the negotiators a sense of the broader policy context of the trade agreement on which they are working. Draft analyses should be made available for public comment in every jurisdiction participating in the negotiation.[4] A final environmental assessment should then be produced that responds to the most significant criticisms leveled at the draft and specifies environmental policy options to consider in the trade liberalization process. If the negotiations take an unexpected turn, provision should be made to reopen the environmental review to evaluate any new issues raised.

Such environmental assessments could be separately undertaken by each country participating in a liberalization negotiation. But efficiency and consistency of analysis argues for a single assessment with national contributions to the common effort. Although the GATT should add environmental experts to its staff to facilitate the compiling of environmental assessments, the credibility of the assessments would be enhanced by having the work done by an outside organization with recognized technical competence and independence.[5]

Although flawed in some important respects, the 1992 NAFTA environmental review, undertaken by the Office of the US Trade Representative (and updated in 1993) in conjunction with the US Environmental Protection Agency and other federal agencies, offers a useful starting

---

3. The Miami-based North-South Center has undertaken an interesting study of the environmental implications of extending the NAFTA to Venezuela, demonstrating an informative and manageable methodology for environmental trade reviews.

4. Although many countries do not share "work in progress" during trade negotiations, a more open process is the norm in the environmental realm. For example, drafts of the 1992 Climate Change Treaty, the recent Biodiversity Convention, and Agenda 21 adopted at the Earth Summit were all released for review in draft by nongovernment organizations.

5. The outside experts might be found in an international organization such as United Nations Environment Programme (UNEP) but might also be drawn from nongovernment organizations or the private sector. National authorities should participate as well, coordinating their work through the assigned international body.

point for trade-negotiation environmental assessments.[6] Specifically, the February 1992 *Review of US-Mexico Environmental Issues* spelled out the history of environmental cooperation between the two countries; reviewed current pollution, conservation, and public health programs; discussed environmental enforcement policies and practices; provided background on the proposed trade agreement; laid out alternative scenarios for economic growth and development under the NAFTA; and spotlighted potential environmental impacts of the trade agreement. The review covered the full sweep of possible issues, including border pollution impacts, air quality, water pollution, toxic chemicals, solid waste management, chemical emergency response needs, wildlife and endangered species protection, and public health matters. The review paid particular attention to environmentally sensitive economic sectors such as transportation, agriculture, energy, and investment. Demographic patterns and migration flows also were examined.

The NAFTA review concluded with specific recommendations on how to mitigate potentially negative NAFTA environmental effects, such as attempting to shift Mexican economic development away from the border region to avoid further stress on already overburdened ecosystems such as the Rio Grande River and streamlining customs procedures that cause border-crossing delays and add to air pollution problems in cities such as El Paso and Brownsville. The report also highlighted opportunities to improve the environment through expanded trade—for example, reducing barriers to the export of clean-burning natural gas.

Although it was an important precedent, demonstrating that environmental reviews of trade agreements are possible, the review missed several opportunities to expand the NAFTA environmental dialogue and therefore should not be seen as a completely model environmental assessment. Notably, USTR failed to publish the review in the *Federal Record*, thereby ignoring the usual US government requirements for notice and comment on a public document. Moreover, the review lacked a second traditional element of public review processes: a rundown on the policy alternatives available to respond to each of the potential environmental issues identified. Finally, USTR chose not to publish responses to the significant concerns raised in public comments, a useful procedural device for ensuring that government officials take seriously the criticisms put forward. Future environmental reviews of trade agreements would benefit from these additional steps.

Some trade experts worry that environmental analyses will bog down trade negotiations or burden trade negotiators with extraneous concerns. But, in fact, the opposite result is more likely. By carefully examining possible environmental issues—and excluding misplaced concerns that some environmentalists now attribute to trade liberalization—such

---

6. For a critique of the NAFTA environmental review, see Esty (1994a).

assessments will facilitate serious consideration of the real environmental issues and help to avoid having the agreement hampered by nonissues.

Negotiations

Environmental standards often must be set in the absence of complete data and in the face of scientific uncertainties. Thus sound environmental decision making depends on constant reevaluation driven by scientific advances and a flexibility to update policy choices in response to new information. In this context, a transparent policy development process that gives access to the critical data to as many people as possible maximizes the chances that important new correlations will be uncovered quickly and that new thinking will be brought to bear on the policy problems at hand.

Trade negotiators might learn to draw more on open processes. Broader dissemination of information would, in some aspects of trade policymaking, defuse tension and improve decision making. For example, where choices must be made in the absence of good data, greater public participation in the decision process would be helpful. At the very least, better public understanding of the policymaking process would help to shore up recognition of the value of trade liberalization and the work of the GATT. Broader dissemination of GATT materials would also put interested parties on more equal footing. Currently, certain groups have access to inside information and others do not, creating a sense of unfairness that is harmful to the GATT's legitimacy and reputation for impartiality.[7]

Creating a more transparent trade policy development and negotiating process offers another point of congruence between environmentalists and free traders. True liberal traders, unencumbered by the demands of specific national industries, support more open processes. They recognize that sunshine can help prevent protectionist "rent seekers" or other narrow interests from hijacking the policy process.

Of course, public participation is not always a good thing. Too often public access really means interest group access. Operating in the name of the "public," special interests may be able to manipulate outcomes for their own benefit. Ironically, environmentalists often overlook this fact and, in demanding public participation in GATT decision making, thus ignore the reality that they are creating opportunities for other nongovernment organizations, including business and industry representatives, to shape the policy process. Trade negotiations invariably

---

7. For example, a recent series of reference volumes on the Uruguay Round, produced by the Washington law firm of Stewart & Stewart (Terence P. Stewart 1993), extensively cites restricted GATT documents.

involve making concessions that hurt certain groups but bring counter-concessions that benefit the broad national interest. This give-and-take is sometimes better done away from the glare of those whose privileged treatment is traded away and who, if given notice of their impending loss, might bring political pressure to bear to reverse the course of the negotiations.[8] It is therefore important to distinguish between general access to information and the ability of special interests—whether environmental or business-oriented—to manipulate decisions. In particular, while GATT reform to ensure better public understanding of the trade liberalization process is essential, government negotiators should not be stripped of the power—facilitated by confidential meetings—to advance national needs at the expense of special interests.

Dispute Resolution

No area of GATT activity has attracted more criticism from an environmental perspective than dispute settlement (e.g., von Moltke 1993). Part of the problem derives from the structure of the GATT dispute settlement process. Specifically, trade/environment cases generally arise when one party challenges some aspect of another's environmental policies or standards. The party defending its environmental program almost invariably sees itself on the defensive. This creates the impression that trade principles are being used to attack environmental values. This impression is strengthened by the GATT requirement that the defending party justify deviations from basic free trade obligations by reference to the narrowly interpreted exceptions in GATT Article XX.

Some of these concerns are overdone. For example, the fact that in almost all cases the party with the trade interest at stake is the challenger should be of no real concern. To the contrary, since a party whose trade position has been impaired must call for GATT dispute settlement, the "burden of going forward" is placed on those who have trade interests, not environmental interests, at stake.

Other environmentalists' questions about the GATT dispute settlement process are, however, more serious. For example, the reliance on closed-door reviews by panels of trade experts fails to produce results with much public support or legitimacy, particularly if the dispute turns on questions outside the competence of the trade experts who sit on the panels. In truth, the secretive nature of the process reflects not evil intentions but the formalistic world of international mediation and the origins of dispute settlement as another forum for negotiation. How-

---

8. Of course, if trade negotiators are captured by special interests, then the give-and-take can result in harm to the broad public interest. In fact, it is for this reason that many dyed-in-the-wool free traders, like environmentalists, prefer open procedures that smoke out rent-seeking behavior by narrow interests.

ever, the evolution over time of the dispute panel mechanism toward a quasi-judicial structure has rendered the traditional secrecy outmoded. GATT would benefit from a new dispute settlement process that reflects basic elements of due process, transparency, and institutional neutrality. Although some first steps to improve the efficiency and efficacy of the dispute settlement procedures were taken in the Uruguay Round agreement, a number of additional opportunities for progress remain.

Specifically, to maintain its perceived legitimacy and its role as a cornerstone of the management structure of international relations, the trade regime would benefit from putting to rest environmentalist suspicions that the GATT deck is inappropriately stacked against the environment. It should further dispel the impression that its dispute procedures are unfair, dominated by insiders, and manipulated by multinational corporations. As a starting point, the GATT should open up its dispute settlement process. All panels should meet in public when receiving evidence and should be required to publish their decisions as soon as they are issued.[9] All written submissions to panels should be available to the public.[10] Environmental groups and other nongovernment organizations should be allowed to make written submissions on any issue under review.[11] As in the negotiation context, public participation in the dispute settlement process need not be and should not be unlimited. Dispute settlement efforts should be made more transparent by providing access to information, but safeguards should be developed to prevent interests with narrow perspectives—be they environmental groups or industry representatives—from exploiting the process. Specifically, governments should remain free to discuss pending disputes in private, with an eye toward settlement of the cases outside the formal panel process.

National and international environmental standards should be presumed to be valid and legitimate until shown to be otherwise. Thus, the burden of proof should be placed on the country challenging an environmental trade measure. To ensure balanced consideration of compet-

---

9. Currently, dispute panels meet entirely in private and do not publish their decisions until after the GATT Council has endorsed the panel's report. Of course, information is often leaked, indicating it is available ahead of time to those who know where to look for it. Under the new WTO rules, panel decisions will not be voted upon by the GATT Council unless a "negative consensus" emerges to block a panel report.

10. The Uruguay Round agreement on dispute settlement calls on parties to release non-confidential summaries of their written submissions to dispute panels. But this half-way measure is not adequate.

11. The US Supreme Court's process of accepting "friend of the court" briefs might be used as a model for the GATT. The Supreme Court accepts submissions from any party, subject to established page and subject limitations. Law clerks screen all of the materials, but the justices review and take seriously only those that add substance to the debate at hand.

ing trade and environmental values and to prevent the thinking of panelists from being dominated by GATT perspectives (as opposed to broader conceptions of social welfare, including environmental considerations), all GATT dispute panels addressing environmental issues should include members from outside the traditional pool of trade experts residing in Geneva and working in the missions to the GATT.

Whenever environmental issues underlie a dispute, the panel should receive technical support from scientific or environmental experts at the request of any party or the panel itself. The Uruguay Round amendments to the dispute settlement procedures make some small steps in this direction by giving GATT panels easier access to scientific or technical experts. But the text fails to provide parties to disputes with an opportunity to insist that panelists obtain outside expert advice. Nor does the Uruguay Round resolution open the dispute settlement process to nongovernment observers or submissions from environmental or business groups.

Environmental Staffing and the WTO

The GATT needs to solidify its commitment to the environment by bolstering the staff resources it devotes to ecological and public health issues and by institutionalizing its environmental outreach efforts. Three people out of a total GATT staff of more than 200 currently carry the environment portfolio. This permits the GATT Secretariat to support periodic meetings of the GATT Environmental Measures and International Trade (EMIT) group and to do limited gathering, distillation, and distribution of trade and environment materials.

This modest commitment of resources does not allow the GATT to monitor and participate in all the ongoing environmental negotiations concerning climate change, ozone layer protection, biodiversity, forest management, Global Environment Facility restructuring, and other issues. As a result, environmental negotiators continue to debate the use of trade mechanisms in support of their efforts with little of the sensitivity to trade concerns that GATT experts might provide. Nor does the current level of staffing enable the GATT to develop in-house environmental expertise so that the international trade regime can thoughtfully address emerging trade-environment linkages such as ecolabeling or packaging restrictions.

Ironically, most environmental groups opposed the best prospect for institutionalizing an environmental focus in the GATT: the new World Trade Organization (WTO). Designed to replace the existing GATT structure and to enhance GATT's ability to manage international economic relations, creation of the WTO could provide new resources that would allow the GATT to expand its environmental work and to play a leadership role in integrating trade and environmental policymaking.[12] Under a WTO, the international trade regime may be able to expand its work with the negotiators of international environmental agreements to ensure that trade enforcement mechanisms are properly structured and that parties to existing agreements apply trade restrictions in a manner that produces optimal environmental outcomes with minimal trade disruption. An expanded environment division would furthermore broaden GATT's capacity to coordinate with other international institutions such as the UN Environment Programme, the UN Conference on Trade and Development, and the UN Development Programme.

As part of the WTO structure, the GATT parties have agreed to set up a Committee on Trade and Environment, designed to provide an ongoing forum for consideration of environmental matters. Unfortunately, the new committee's work program is vague and largely focused on the concerns of the trade world about environmental regulations becoming an obstacle to freer trade. For example, the terms of reference call for "surveillance of trade measures used for environmental purposes"—hardly a neutral starting point for integrating trade and environmental policymaking. The work, moreover, is aimed at a report to be delivered in two years rather than at negotiating actual changes to the GATT's rules and procedures.

The emergence of the WTO should be used to expand the trade world's outreach efforts to both government environmental officials and nongovernment organizations. Specifically, following the example of the OECD's Business and Industry Advisory Committee, the GATT should organize one or more environmental advisory committees made up of nongovernment organizations—environmental groups, business organizations, and policy institutes—interested in the trade and environment linkage. These advisory committees would provide the GATT Secretariat in particular and the international trade community more generally with insight into new developments in the environmental realm. New lines of communication and a more participatory GATT process would go a long way toward assuaging the process-oriented environmental community's concerns about freer trade.

As this study has stressed, full reconciliation of trade and environmental goals requires changes not only to the trade regime but also to environmental policymaking. Thus, consideration should be given to setting up an Intergovernmental Panel on Trade and Environment (IPTE) outside the GATT to help advance an environmental policy reform agenda for other institutions in parallel with the GATT environ-

---

12. Appendix A explains the GATT's role as a contract and not a formal international organization and how the GATT was meant to be replaced with the ITO, an actual international body. Leelanda de Silva (1993) provides a critical review of the Uruguay Round evolution toward a WTO.

mental program. Drawing on environmental experts, international law-yers, resource economists, scientists, and public health and ecological risk analysts, an IPTE could build an analytic foundation for the strengthening and restructuring of environmental regulation at both the national and international levels and help a consensus to form on direc-tions and modalities for reform. The work of the Intergovernmental Panel on Climate Change, which provided a foundation for global action to address the greenhouse effect, demonstrates the potential efficacy of such an approach.

Broadening the trade and environment dialogue would be of enor-mous benefit to the international trading system—relieving the GATT of the sole burden of advancing ideas for making environmental protection and trade liberalization more mutually reinforcing. It would reinforce the notion—which is a fundamental conclusion of this study—that the trade and environment issue is as much or more a problem of environ-mental policymaking as one of trade policymaking. In fact, an IPTE might serve as a forerunner to a full-fledged global environmental organization.

Greening the GATT will require both changes in long-standing pro-cedures and an investment of additional resources. Aside from shifting the burden of proof in dispute settlement cases, the modifications to current GATT practices outlined above would not require any amend-ment to the actual GATT text. The GATT could therefore move forward quite quickly with a procedural reform package and, in doing so, make major environmental progress. Given the environmental community's emphasis on process, these changes would go a considerable distance toward bridging the gap between free traders and environmentalists.

Substantive GATT Reform

Greening the GATT's substantive rules will require a more complicated process of change than that outlined above. Although the GATT is for-mally a contract and not a treaty or international organization, its rules as applied through the 1947 Protocol of Provisional Application have binding treaty status (Jackson 1969; Jackson 1992a).[13] But because the GATT was meant to have been replaced by the International Trade Organization as embodied in the 1948 Havana Charter, which was never approved by the US Congress, it suffers from structural problems that GATT expert John Jackson (1990) describes as "birth defects." Promi-nent among these shortcomings is the difficulty of amending the GATT.

---

13. In fact, the Vienna Convention on the Law of Treaties makes no distinction between a contractual agreement such as the GATT and other kinds of treaties. Thus, although it was never ratified by the US Congress, the GATT, under international law, is a treaty. For a more complete history of the GATT's evolution, see appendix A.

Although some of these problems will be addressed by the evolution of the GATT into the WTO, many of these issues will remain under the WTO structure.

Ways to Change the GATT

There are a number of provisions for changing GATT rules.[14] GATT Article XXX expressly provides for amendments to the GATT. Amendments to central GATT principles (Articles I and II) require a unanimous vote of all GATT parties; other articles may be amended by a two-thirds majority. However, with more than 120 countries in the GATT, achieving unanimous consent has become very difficult. In fact, the GATT has never been revised through an Article XXX unanimous amendment. Even a two-thirds vote is nearly impossible to obtain since one-third of the GATT parties do not participate in day-to-day GATT meetings.[15] Moreover, Article XXX provides that any country that disagrees with an amendment may decline to be bound by it. Thus, amendment of the GATT is not an attractive vehicle for change.

GATT parties may, by two-thirds vote (which must reflect a majority of the total GATT membership), waive GATT obligations. The Article XXV waiver provision offers a flexible mechanism for changing GATT rules and has been successfully used in the past to ratify preferential tariffs for developing countries under the Generalized System of Preferences (GSP), the US-Canada automotive agreement, and the US Caribbean Basin Initiative (Jackson 1993, 106). Waivers, however, only serve to lift (temporarily or permanently) GATT requirements;[16] they cannot create new obligations. Article XXV can also be read to permit the adoption by majority vote of new rules "facilitating the operation and furthering the objectives" of the GATT. But as Jackson notes, this provision could easily be abused and has never been used to establish new GATT obligations.

Acting under Article XXV authority, GATT parties are also free to issue interpretations of existing rules. This provision would permit, for instance, the GATT parties to expand the reach of the environmental provisions of Article XX. A number of countries have argued for such an

---

14. The entire discussion that follows draws on Jackson's analysis of GATT reform options, prepared for the EPA, reproduced in Jackson (1992a). The WTO Charter contains some new and not-yet-fully explained clauses concerning future WTO amendments.

15. Only two-thirds of the GATT parties have established membership in the GATT Council, the organization's regular forum for decision making (Jackson 1993).

16. Under the WTO, the strictures on waivers become more severe. For example, an end date must be stipulated at the time a waiver is granted.

interpretation to address the most pressing trade and environment problems.[17]

Reinterpretation of existing rules and practices by dispute panels offers another flexible method for integrating environmental concerns into the international trading system. Some analysts of the trade-environment linkage believe that recent GATT panel decisions have given an overly narrow interpretation to GATT's existing environmental provisions and that future panels could undo the damage by reading broader protection for natural resources into the current language (e.g., Housman and Zaelke 1992a; Charnovitz 1993c). This mechanism is, however, inherently ad hoc and dependent on issues being raised in a dispute among GATT parties. Moreover, there are only limited opportunities to instruct panels as to how they should decide cases, making this approach unreliable as the basis for comprehensive GATT reform.

Another relatively flexible method of changing the GATT is to negotiate a side agreement or code. This technique was used in the Tokyo Round of GATT negotiations to establish subsidies and dumping codes. The advantage of such codes is the opportunity to create out of whole cloth significant new obligations rather than trying to tinker with existing language. The disadvantage is that a code is binding only on the parties that accept it. Indeed, to eliminate the problem of "GATT *a la carte*," under the WTO, members must subscribe to all GATT agreements, including the existing codes. Nevertheless, a new environment code that attracted a significant number of initial members (perhaps a majority of the 24 OECD countries and some number of newly industrialized nations) could have an important impact—setting the bounds of environmental behavior within the international trade regime.

A final way of changing the GATT would be to replace it entirely with a new treaty. This sort of sweeping reform is probably only available once a generation. Unfortunately for those with environmental interests, such a reconfiguration of the GATT will take place in the context of establishing the World Trade Organization called for by the Uruguay Round agreement. But fundamental changes to incorporate new environmental provisions are not a component of the Uruguay Round reforms.

Key Substantive Changes

Any update of the GATT's environmental provisions must cover a number of substantive issues, including GATT's interaction with international environmental agreements; standards for judging the legitimacy

---

17. The Nordic countries, in particular, have developed a proposed interpretation of Article XX, designed to expand and define the basis for environmental exceptions to the GATT (interview with Swedish GATT delegate Mikael Lindstrom, 17 May 1993).

of environmental trade measures, including, most notably, restrictions on production processes and methods; Article XX and its trade-environment balancing tests; and development of a scale of approved trade measures to be employed in response to defined environmental injuries. Other matters such as how to manage environmental policy-based competitiveness, the harmonization of environmental standards—including the appropriate bases for ecodumping penalties—and rules governing environmental subsidies should be on a longer-term agenda.

International Environmental Agreements

Fear that GATT rules might be used to override the trade provisions of international environmental agreements is one of the core trade concerns of environmentalists (French 1993b; Charnovitz 1993b).[18] For instance, the commitment of parties to the Montreal Protocol not to trade in products containing chlorofluorocarbons (CFCs) with nonparties to the protocol is seen by many observers as an essential element of the success of the ozone-layer protection accord. In particular, the threat of trade restrictions has all but eliminated free riders, who might have undermined the agreement. It has also ensured that 126 countries have signed onto the phaseout of chemicals that destroy the ozone layer, ensuring that no country and no company obtains a competitive advantage in the global marketplace by continuing to use CFCs rather than shifting to the more expensive substitute chemicals.

Similar concerns exist about the GATT undercutting the trade-based enforcement mechanisms of the Basel Convention regulating the export of hazardous waste and the CITES agreement on trafficking in endangered species. Environmentalists anticipate, moreover, that future agreements to protect the planet's ecological resources will also rely on trade provisions to ensure broad participation and to deter noncompliance. They therefore want some assurance that the international trade regime will respect the trade controls built into future environmental agreements.

Most GATT experts argue that the GATT would not likely interfere with the imposition of trade measures consistent with a widely supported international environmental agreement (Eglin 1993a). But they concede that there is ambiguity over how a GATT party should handle conflicting obligations under the trade regime and international environmental agreements (Jackson 1992a; GATT 1992b). Notably, the GATT Secretariat's own trade and environment analyses cast doubt on the GATT compatibility of the trade provisions of the Montreal Protocol,

---

18. This concern can also be seen in the press release issued by the Environmental Defense Fund and World-Wide Fund for Nature at the Tokyo G-7 Summit on 8 July 1993.

particularly vis-à-vis nonparties to the environmental agreement (GATT 1992b; Eglin 1993a).

The 1969 Vienna Convention on the Law of Treaties suggests that, as a matter of international law, where treaty obligations conflict (and the subject matter of the two instruments is the same), the more recently established obligation prevails. This would perhaps suggest that, between parties to both agreements, the 1987 Montreal Protocol takes precedence over 1947 GATT obligations. But there is a reasonable argument that the Vienna Convention principle of priority does not apply because these treaties are not on the same subject. Moreover, adoption of the WTO arguably makes the trade obligation the more recent, perhaps permitting it to leapfrog into dominance.

Given this confusion and the importance of the issue to environmentalists, it would be useful for the GATT to recognize expressly existing international environmental agreements and to "bless" them in some way (see appendix D for a list of multilateral environmental agreements with trade provisions). One way of doing this would be through a waiver naming the "protected" agreements, although under the new WTO rules, waivers are meant to be strictly temporary. Alternatively, the GATT parties could issue an interpretation of Article XX referencing specific international agreements. In addition, the list could be appended to a new environmental code or included in an amendment to Article XX.

GATT acceptance of a treaty should establish that actions taken in accordance with that treaty meet the basic test of environmental legitimacy, thus providing a presumption of justification to those using trade measures against parties in noncompliance.[19] In fact, GATT Article XX(h) provides a precedent for GATT acceptance of trade restrictions imposed under international conventions, in this case pursuant to commodity agreements.

A new GATT provision blessing international environmental agreements should also specify that a country's status as a party or nonparty to an agreement does not figure in the GATT's presumption of environmental legitimacy for actions taken pursuant to recognized international agreements. As chapter 6 notes, parties must not be permitted to benefit from nonparticipation in global environmental efforts. Free traders should share this concern about free riding, as similar risks of "beggar-thy-neighbor" behavior plague the international trading system.

It would also be useful to have GATT officials participate in environmental treaty negotiations so that trade interests could be woven into the agreements from the start. Coordinated trade and environmental policymaking—including the specification of not only standards but

---

19. Whether the specific actions taken are reasonable would remain an issue and should be judged according to the circumstances presented.

appropriate trade remedies for noncompliance and perhaps even compliance evaluation mechanisms within the environmental agreement—minimizes the chances of a later GATT conflict over enforcement.

The parallel policy—having environmental officials participate in trade negotiations—should also become standard practice. The presence of EPA officials on a number of the NAFTA negotiating teams offers both a precedent for adding environmental officials to trade negotiations and a first data point suggesting that the inclusion of environmental negotiators will improve the handling of environmental issues in the resulting agreement.

Environmental Legitimacy

The centerpiece of any environmental face-lift for the GATT must be new rules defining and governing environmental legitimacy. The most straightforward way to ensure that environmental variables are added into the GATT calculus would be through adoption of the three-pronged test outlined in chapter 5, substituting new language for the relevant portions of Article XX. Similar results could also be accomplished through adoption of a new environment code. If these more comprehensive reform options were to be foreclosed, substantial progress could still be made by reinterpreting current GATT provisions.

Specifically, the GATT must move beyond the existing distinction between trade restrictions on like products and those on production processes. A new environmental legitimacy test that focuses on the nature and location of the environmental injury at issue and that applies without regard to the product-process distinction would accomplish this important step. The same result could be achieved by redefining ''like product.'' If products made using different processes were deemed to be unlike, trade restrictions could be applied to goods produced using environmentally unacceptable methods without changing the existing structure of GATT rules. For example, if a semiconductor made using CFCs were deemed not to be like a semiconductor made without CFCs, trade restrictions on the environmentally harmful semiconductor would be GATT-consistent and would uphold the Montreal Protocol.

A similar advance could be made by reinterpreting the Article XX reference to ''where similar conditions prevail.'' Again, if differences in production processes were deemed to create different conditions, restrictions on products from countries with inadequate environmental controls on production could be found GATT-consistent. Both Petersmann (1991b) and Baker (1993) have offered elaborations on this approach.

Evolution toward acceptance of restrictions based on production processes is already evident. Notably, the European Community's 1992 submission to the GATT Environmental Measures and International Trade (EMIT) group implies support for trade restrictions where production processes pose a "serious risk for the global environment." Furthermore, the Uruguay Round text updating the 1979 Technical Barriers to Trade Agreement suggests that technical regulations may specify "product characteristics or *their related processes and production methods* [emphasis added]," thus establishing a basis for incorporating process characteristics into the definition of like product. Austria's EMIT summary paper (1993, S-7) analyzing the GATT trade and environment debate, goes so far as to suggest that Article XX could be "construed to justify not only product related but also production related measures if they are necessary to protect human, animal or plant life or health (or the environment)." Thus, GATT reform to countenance trade restrictions aimed at environmentally harmful production processes seems achievable.

While there appears to be growing support for refining GATT rules to reach production processes and methods, thereby breaking down the hard-and-fast prohibition against trade restrictions that have extraterritorial or extrajurisdictional application, a second traditional GATT rigidity—a blanket proscription of unilateral trade actions—will be harder to overcome. As chapter 6 argued, however, unilateralism is to some extent unavoidable in the absence of a functioning multilateral environmental organization. The GATT parties should therefore accept the inevitability of some elements of unilateralism and instead of adhering to a pretense of barring all unilateral actions, strive to establish a system of checks and balances to manage the unilateral use of environmental trade measures. Specifically, by overseeing and condoning "unilateral" actions in support of internationally agreed environmental standards or in response to significant transboundary or global environmental harms, the GATT would strengthen its ability to control environmental trade measures and discourage abuses. An acknowledgment of the validity of certain forms of "multilateral unilateralism" would enable the GATT to save its powder for egregious cases of unilateral action aimed at harms with no physical spillover effects outside the country targeted by extraterritorial trade restrictions.

Even these limited elements of unilateralism could be eliminated if a functioning international environmental regime were created. Thus, the best way to get beyond the intractable unilateralism issue would be to establish a Global Environmental Organization, or at least some international body able to make effective environmental injury judgments.

Article XX Revisions

The Austrian paper cited above hints at another important GATT reform: the addition of the word "environment" to Article XX. The current focus on human, animal, or plant life or health is too narrow and overlooks important ecological resources such as the atmosphere and other elements of the global commons. Thus, if Article XX is to be amended, as opposed to being replaced, the addition of the words "or the environment" to the definitional list of legitimate policy goals in Article XX(b) would be important. Again, a redefinitional fix might also be possible. Notably, the Article XX(b) reference to human, animal, or plant life and health might be interpreted as covering the global commons.

Article XX's balancing test must also be restructured, if not replaced entirely. The current reading of the word "necessary" as mandating the least GATT-inconsistent environmental policy choice available fails to give sufficient deference to the judgments of national politicians and officials concerning environmental goals and the means of pursuing them.[20] Specifically, this imbalance creates an inappropriately high hurdle for establishing the GATT consistency of environmental policies since there are almost always policy mechanisms available that would be less inconsistent with the GATT. The question is, are these policies available and effective?

To establish a more neutral test for weighing the burden on commerce of environmental trade measures, some measure of policy flexibility and a nod in the direction of political reality needs to be folded into Article XX. Thus the pivotal word "necessary" should be reinterpreted to mean "not *clearly* disproportionate in relation to the putative environmental benefits and in light of equally effective policy alternatives that are reasonably available."

Scale of Trade Measures

To facilitate trade and environment dispute resolution and to make clear the consequences of environmentally irresponsible behavior, the GATT should establish a scale of trade measures and an illustrative list of environmental injuries that would justify various trade sanctions or restrictions. This list should facilitate analysis of whether a trade measure invoked in support of environmental policies is justified. Although no precise formula can readily be produced and case-by-case judgments will still be required, guidelines would give countries employing trade measures some sense of what remedy is appropriate given the injury they are suffering. Clear rules would make it harder for countries to plead ignorance about their obligations, thereby sharpening the incentive for environmental responsibility and decreasing the need for the actual use of trade actions. In addition, countries faced with trade

---

20. See the *Thai Cigarette* and *Tuna-Dolphin* GATT cases in appendix C and the discussion of the "necessary" test in chapters 2 and 5.

restrictions would be able to gauge whether the measures imposed against them were disproportionate to the harm and thus whether their GATT challenge would be likely to succeed.

Uruguay Round Advances

The recent Uruguay Round of GATT negotiations did little to resolve the plethora of environmental issues now facing trade negotiators. As noted earlier, the GATT parties meeting at Marrakesh in April 1994 to conclude the Uruguay Round did commit to further discussions aimed at building greater environmental sensitivity into the international trading system. The Marrakesh Declaration contains a work program that demonstrates an appreciation of the importance of the environment as a trade issue and roughs out a course for future GATT reform.

The GATT parties must move quickly to advance the dialogue on the green trade agenda. Putting off serious discussions of environmental issues until the start of a new round of GATT negotiations (which might not begin until the end of century) would be seen as dodging a critical if difficult subject. Specifically, the GATT parties need to clarify the vague language of the Ministerial Declaration on Trade and Environment and establish an analytic foundation for negotiations aimed at "greening" the GATT. Some of the items that should be listed as priority topics:

- establishing procedures for environmental assessments of trade agreements;

- building greater transparency into GATT negotiations to assure the requisite environmental input;

- restructuring GATT dispute settlement procedures;

- sanctifying the trade measures used to enforce international environmental agreements;

- broadening the scope of GATT's environmental provisions (particularly Article XX);

- refining the disciplines imposed on national environmental standards;

- clarifying the bases on which environmental trade measures may be used to discipline environmentally inadequate production processes and methods;

- defining appropriate bounds for unilateral trade actions in support of environmental policies;

- developing guidelines for ecolabeling and packaging requirements.

Getting agreement on GATT refinements to respond to these topics will not be easy. Failure, however, to address the issues at all invites even more serious long-term problems (Esty 1994b). Confusion and uncertainty themselves harm trade and make doing business internationally more difficult. In addition, lacking clear support and guidance from the GATT for environmental trade measures, a number of countries (most notably the United States) will be tempted to act unilaterally, using trade restrictions to reinforce their own priority environmental policies and programs. If, on the other hand, effective multilateral procedures are agreed upon and faithfully implemented, forbearance should be the rule.

Finally, the GATT's very existence and ability to contribute to the management of international economic affairs depends on its perceived legitimacy. GATT's legitimacy, in turn, depends upon an ongoing political judgment in major trading countries (especially the United States) that the institution is upholding important public values and balancing appropriately competing policy goals. A sense that GATT's rules or procedures have lost their balance and are insufficiently attentive to environmental considerations could therefore be very damaging to GATT's credibility and institutional standing.

10

Summary and Conclusions

Trade liberalization and environmental protection share a common aim: enhancing social welfare by improving the quality of life. In striving for the common goal, considerable conflict inevitably arises over differences in approaches and emphases. Nevertheless, as this study has stressed, the scope for reducing the tension between trade and environmental policy is also considerable.

Environmental issues have grown in prominence on both the domestic and international policy agendas, and today the environment competes with trade and other long-standing issues of high politics for public attention. Moreover, global environmental problems—ozone layer depletion, loss of biodiversity, climate change, the spread of radiation, deforestation, and protection of the global commons (the oceans, Antarctica, and outer space)—have revealed the ecological interdependence of the planet. These issues, inherently worldwide in scope, cannot be confined by political boundaries. They spill across borders and sometimes engulf the entire Earth.

These pollution spillovers and the potentially global environmental consequences of the actions of others mean that no country has complete environmental independence. Indeed, to maintain control today over the quality of one's own environment requires worldwide cooperation; it also demands a more refined understanding of the realities of political sovereignty. The international trading system and the rules and obligations embedded in the General Agreement on Tariffs and Trade (GATT) and the future World Trade Organization (WTO), which take as their foundation traditional assumptions about sovereignty, must be updated to reflect these global realities. In an ecologically interdependent world, each country's right to decide for itself how to exploit the natural resources within its borders and how much waste to dump into the air, water, or onto the land must be reconciled with the environmental needs of others in the shared ecosystem and the global aspiration for sustainable economic growth.

Integrating new issues into an established policy discipline is always difficult, and the effort to build environmental considerations into the international trading system has proved to be no exception. In this case, the task has been made more complicated by the lack of consensus on how best to protect the environment or on optimal regulatory strategies.

Just as environmental issues are increasingly shaping trade policy, the economic interdependence of the world is influencing the dynamics of environmental policy. The linkage between trade liberalization and environmental protection is manifested in several ways. Domestic environmental matters, such as local air and water pollution control and waste management, have taken on an international cast because of their implications for the economic competitiveness of firms and countries. Not only do businesses complain about having to compete with companies from countries with less stringent environmental requirements, environmentalists argue that these competitiveness concerns weigh down the environmental policy debate in high-standard countries and result in "political drag" that makes it difficult to raise standards in the face of much less strict pollution control mandates elsewhere.

A broad array of "trade and environment" problems have emerged in the last several years. Some of the conflicts derive from misunderstandings between the trade and environmental camps, reflecting two communities with different traditions, values, and modes of operation, although neither side is monolithic. Other frictions reflect deeper differences over philosophical assumptions and substantive priorities.

But the battle lines need not become entrenched. Both sides of the trade and environment debate seek to improve the efficiency of resource use and to add to worldwide social welfare. Both free traders and environmentalists would like to deter one nation from irresponsibly shifting burdens to another or from one generation to the next. And both communities face a constant threat from special interests that seek to twist the policy process to their own advantage at the expense of the broader public good. Most importantly, policy choices are available that can make trade liberalization and environmental protection mutually compatible and minimize the extent of disputes.

Two Bridges

This study identifies two core concepts that can bridge the gap between the policy goals of trade liberalization and environmental protection.

First, most free traders and most environmentalists recognize the benefits of having environmental regulations that internalize the cost of ecological or public health damage into the prices consumers and producers pay. Adherence to a polluter pays principle or other cost-internalization strategies can harness market forces in the cause of environmental protection by creating incentives to use scarce resources carefully and to minimize pollution. At the same time, such incentive-based environmental regulations (by avoiding the technology-specific mandates of traditional command and control regulations) reduce the scope for conflict with market access rules and other aspects of the international trading system.

Second, both trade liberalization and environmental protection in the global context require carefully structured collective action among nations to avoid shortsighted and ultimately self-defeating policy outcomes such as "beggar-thy-neighbor" economic policies and "free riding" on the environmental efforts of others. The cooperation required to overcome these collective-action problems is most effectively engendered through international regimes based on mutual forbearance and adherence to common, overarching principles. The GATT provides such a regime to facilitate collaboration in support of freer trade, centered on the concept of nondiscrimination in the treatment of trade partners. The environment needs a comparable structure, built on a commitment to the polluter pays principle.

The polluter pays principle and an international regime to reinforce it provide two bridges for integrating trade and environmental policymaking. Neither alone would be sufficient to reconcile trade and environmental interests. In fact, a key to the success of the GATT as a management structure for international economic relations is the presence of a common ideology—market-based capitalism—which all participants in the system accept and which guides the parties in times of dispute. For a comparable system of environmental cooperation to be established, there needs to be a central policy idea—and cost-internalizing environmental regulation seems the most likely candidate—around which countries can rally and which then can be embodied in an international regime. The guiding ideology would define the bounds of acceptable environmental behavior and provide a link to other elements of the international system, particularly the rules and procedures of the trade regime.

Economic and Political Policy Failures

The necessity of collective action in the environmental realm derives from a series of market failures that must be addressed through government regulation or intergovernmental cooperation. First, environmental amenities such as fresh water and clean air are collective goods and are thus underprotected by the free market in the absence of government intervention to make prices reflect social rather than private (or single-country) costs and benefits. Domestically, environmental regulation is often far from optimal; internationally, it is almost nonexistent.

Second, market prices frequently do not include ecological externalities—i.e., pollution spillovers. If environmental costs were fully internalized in the prices that producers and consumers face, market forces would work to efficiently ration the Earth's natural resources and to prevent the overuse of the planet's biosphere as a waste dump.

Third, time lags and threshold effects characterize many environmental issues. As a result, environmental problems often do not become apparent until long after the harm has begun to accrue. These delayed impacts create an intergenerational market failure as political leaders succumb to the temptation to defer hard choices and to avoid paying contemporaneously for environmental costs.

The economic system failures combine to make it difficult to get sound, long-term environmental policies that fully internalize environmental costs adopted. While a strict regime of getting environmental prices right would not prevent all trade and environment disputes, it would dramatically narrow the zone of conflict.

Unfortunately, adherence to the polluter pays principle, which aligns the interests of free traders and environmentalists, is politically hard to achieve. Putting a price on pollution is fraught with value judgments. Moreover, cost internalization is a difficult environmental strategy to sell politically. The benefits of properly pricing environmental amenities are widely spread across society and thus hard to see, so those who would benefit are rarely motivated to speak out.

In contrast, polluters and the beneficiaries of subsidized access to timber, water, minerals, or other natural resources are very well aware of their stake in environmental policy debates. More importantly, they are generally well-organized and willing to invest sizable financial resources in the political process to defend the privileges they enjoy. Thus, while the polluter pays principle sounds attractive in theory, getting the US Congress (or legislatures anywhere in the world) to enact the requisite cost-internalizing policies is not an easy row to hoe. Indeed, the asymmetry between the political visibility and clout of special interests and the lack of organization and activity of the general public in defense of its environmental aspirations is a defining characteristic of the US system of interest-group democracy and an element of political life in many nations.

Ironically, liberal traders face a similar political problem. They seek to contain protectionist pressures from domestic rent-seeking interests and to overcome noncooperative economic policy postures through a structured program of collective action with other countries. In fact, the central goal of the now 50-year-old international trading system is the prevention of international economic policy breakdowns of the sort that occurred in the 1930s to the detriment of all nations.

These similarities of circumstance—benefits that are widely dispersed across society, exposure to counterproductive political pressures from domestic special interests, the risk of system failure, and the need for an international regime to reinforce cooperative behavior—should make free traders and environmentalists natural allies and should make the GATT a model for environmentalists.[1] Notably, the architects of the postwar international order recognized the ever-present risk of political failure with regard to trade liberalization. They comprehended the need to construct safeguards against the reemergence of protectionist policies. They further understood that the origins of the downward economic spiral that led to World War II lay not in international strife but in domestic politics that pushed economic policies toward noncooperative stances vis-à-vis trade partners. Most dramatically, they determined that the solution to these stresses lay in reinforcing domestic political structures with an international regime, based on mutual commitments to long-term, economically sound policy principles.

The system they created—the GATT, now evolving into the WTO—has given strength to what Robert Hudec of the University of Minnesota describes as the "better angels of our nature" in trade policymaking (speech to the International Symposium on Trade and Environment, Minneapolis, 10 November 1993). In elevating the commitment to freer trade above the din of day-to-day domestic politics, the GATT casts an almost constitutional aura over the goal of more open markets. The internationalization of trade-liberalizing principles, as embodied in the GATT rules of mutual forbearance, therefore provides a barricade against protectionist political influence and has played a key role in securing 50 years of unprecedented prosperity and relative peace.

In harshly attacking the GATT, environmentalists have thus been, at least in some respects, barking up the wrong tree. They have narrowly looked to a "greening" of the GATT—the building of environmental values into the substantive rules and procedures of the international trading system—as the central means for making trade and environmental policies mutually supportive. In doing so, they have largely ignored the policy failures that stymie efforts to adopt sound, incentive-based environmental programs that could be much more easily integrated with freer trade goals.

Free traders, on the other hand, found the right tree but stopped barking upon reaching it. They identified the need to reform environ-

---

1. There is, however, a difference in circumstances that must be highlighted: the Great Depression and the subsequent world war revealed the collective-action problem in international economic relations. No such global crisis has yet demonstrated the need for international cooperation in the environmental realm.

mental policies in general and the necessity of internalizing environmental costs in particular as a key to the resolution of the trade-environment conundrum. But the trade community has largely failed to understand or take seriously the political difficulty of getting appropriate environmental policies adopted.

GATTing the Greens

A fundamental conclusion of this book is that, rather than tearing down the GATT, environmentalists ought to view the international trade regime as a model for how to overcome political resistance to optimal environmental policies, particularly the internalization of environmental costs. Indeed, free traders and environmentalists should be able to commit to the principle of cost internationalization in dealing with environmental harms and to recognize the value of an international regime to support this goal. They should then work together to achieve both through a Global Environmental Organization (GEO). In fact, a GEO designed to respond to the collective-action problems plaguing environmental protection efforts and charged with coordinating a comprehensive international response to environmental challenges would do more for the quality of the environment worldwide than any program of "greening" the GATT could ever accomplish.

Like the GATT, a GEO would provide a bulwark against domestic pressures that undermine long-term thinking and make sensible policies hard to achieve. Such a body could serve as an honest broker in transnational environmental disputes, assessing risks and benefits from environmental threats and allocating costs and cleanup responsibilities. Just as the GATT built on the core concept of nondiscrimination as a means to trade liberalization, a GEO would establish guidelines, centered on the polluter pays principle, to promote international cooperation in addressing environmental matters and the integration of economic and environmental policy goals.

A GEO would provide, moreover, an institutional counterweight and counterpart to the GATT. Environmental aspects of trade disputes could be delegated to the GEO, with the GATT adopting the GEO's conclusions as it now accepts balance of payments judgments from the International Monetary Fund. This would shelter the GATT from charges that, in handling environmental matters, it has overreached its technical competence and accepted legitimacy. It would also reduce the need for a complete environmental makeover of the GATT itself.

Of course, skepticism abounds concerning the value of a new international organization, particularly an environmental body. Nevertheless, the existing international environmental management structure is not working. In fact, there is no single institution, *a la* GATT in the trade realm, charged with coordinating international environmental policy-making. Thus, decisions are made and strategies set on an ad hoc, issue-by-issue, agreement-by-agreement basis, with separate secretariats staffing each effort. The UN Environment Programme (UNEP) has responsibility over some issues but so too do the UN Commission on Sustainable Development, the UN Development Program (UNDP), the Global Environment Facility (GEF), and a number of other organizations. The result is policy chaos—and a lack of systematic attention to international environmental issues.

The central problem is that no existing organization has a mandate or the resources to coordinate worldwide efforts to protect the environment. As a result, no single body has the combination of technical competence, capacity, policy vision, and authority to work across issues—determining risks, setting priorities, identifying synergies, assessing options, examining related problems, and rationalizing programs and budgets.

Despite these obvious shortcomings and a growing recognition that the global response to some issues (e.g., deforestation, loss of biodiversity, and climate change) has been haphazard, ineffective, and not very cost-efficient, the prospects of a GEO being established any time soon appear slim. Thus, if trade and environmental policies are to be made more mutually supportive in the short run, attention must be paid to environmental reform of existing institutions, particularly the GATT.

Greening the GATT

Even if a GEO is created (and certainly in the absence of such an institution), GATT rules and procedures will have to be updated to accommodate environmental values. Environmentalists have many gripes about the GATT and the international trading system, but four fundamental issues repeatedly emerge:

■ Trade leads to economic growth which, without environmental safeguards, causes pollution.

■ GATT rules are unbalanced, giving more weight to market access than to environmental protection.

■ Free traders try to prevent the use of trade sanctions and restrictions as leverage to enforce international environmental agreements and to discourage transboundary or global pollution spillovers.

■ Countries with lax environmental standards can obtain a competitive advantage in the global marketplace at the expense of the environment.

The first issue is really not about trade but rather about economic growth generally. The solution therefore lies not in "trade and environment" policymaking but in basic environmental regulation to address pollution harms. As environmentalists are increasingly discovering, harnessing market forces—notably the polluter pays principle—offers a powerful tool for making economic development environmentally sound and sustainable. Incentive-based regulations also minimize the clash with trade liberalization and thus support economic growth, which in turn produces new resources that can be devoted to environmental protection.

The second issue, concerning the environmental sensitivity and balance of GATT rules, reflects the environmentalists' "defensive" agenda—their desire not to have legitimate environmental programs trumped or overridden by trade principles and priorities. The central challenge is to separate high environmental standards (which the GATT should generally not touch) from protectionism in green garb (which the GATT should condemn). Beyond smoking out hidden protectionism, a balance must be struck between the commercial advantages of uniform standards and easy market access on the one hand, and the environmental and economic benefits of regulatory diversity (that is, standards tailored to local conditions and preferences) on the other.

The third issue raises the prospect of trade actions being used "offensively" to penalize countries whose environmental standards are deemed too low. The GATT currently is asymmetric. It provides for assessments that an environmental standard is, in some sense, "too high" and a burden on trade flows. But no comparable provision exists to allow a determination that an environmental standard is "too low" and is burdening other countries with pollution externalities. Such judgments are needed to determine whether a nation is "free riding" rather than participating in efforts to address transboundary or global environmental problems and, in doing so, perhaps reducing its manufacturing costs and obtaining an unfair trade advantage.

Environmentalists recognize the need for policy mechanisms to overcome the collective-action problem that underlies the market failures relating to environmental harms and, specifically, to enforce international environmental agreements. They also recognize that countries that externalize environmental costs through transboundary or global pollution may benefit competitively.

Trade restrictions can be used to address both of these problems. For example, the threat of trade restrictions has induced about 130 countries to sign the Montreal Protocol and its phaseout of CFCs and other chemicals harmful to the ozone layer. The protocol's trade provisions also ensure that no country will be tempted to try to gain a competitive advantage in the global marketplace by using CFCs rather than more expensive substitutes in the production of refrigerators, semiconductors, or other products that once were made with CFCs.

The fourth issue—addressing the perceived competitive advantages of lax environmental standards—also involves the use of trade measures as environmental leverage. But the harm at which these environmental trade measures are aimed may be localized in the target countries—not transboundary or global. This distinction is critical. Environmental trade measures with extraterritorial impacts (i.e., affecting behavior outside the country imposing the measure) can quite readily be justified if they reinforce internationally agreed standards or are aimed at transboundary or global pollution spillovers.

Environmental trade measures aimed at purely foreign harms are harder to justify. Nevertheless, there are a number of reasons for seeking changes in the environmental behavior of foreign countries and companies regarding their own "local" environmental programs. "Psychological spillovers"—the distress caused by knowing that others are mistreating animals or the environment—is one prominent reason. Competitiveness concerns and "political drag" are other potential bases for intervention.

Harmonization or convergence of differing environmental standards would help to address these concerns. But any such efforts must be undertaken multilaterally to succeed. Dealing with these issues unilaterally risks undermining the trade system, undoing the substantial economic benefits it provides, and failing, in all likelihood, to advance environmental goals as well.

In sum, the first environmental concern is really not about trade. The second and third issues are real and should be addressed. The fourth critique reflects serious concerns but should be handled through multilateral negotiations, not through unilateral trade measures.

To better accommodate environmental considerations, the GATT needs a new balancing test for settling trade and environment disputes, replacing the general exceptions that relate to public health and resource conservation laid out in GATT Article XX. The existing GATT rules distinguish inappropriately between product standards (e.g., auto emissions requirements, pesticide safety standards) and regulations aimed at production processes or methods (e.g., CFC bans, tuna fishing practices). In an ecologically interdependent world, *how* a foreign product is made can be more environmentally significant than *what* imported goods show up at the border. A product's global or transboundary environmental impact should therefore be open to review within the GATT structure. Article XX, as currently interpreted, makes no accommodation for such regulation.

Article XX also requires that an environmental policy with trade effects employ the "least trade-restrictive" means available to achieve the desired goal in order to be GATT-legal. While this standard of review could serve as an efficiency guide to policymakers, as employed today, it gives too little deference to national decisions about how to pursue environmental goals. The GATT needs a more refined approach to evaluating clashes between environmental policies and trade principles.

The experience of the United States (and the European Union) with environmental federalism—that is, in balancing an interest in freer trade among the states with the right of each jurisdiction to set its own environmental standards—provides a useful starting point for this endeavor. Using the US commerce clause jurisprudence as a base, this study argues for adoption of a three-pronged test to weigh competing trade and environmental claims. In particular, when a challenge has been made to the use of trade restrictions in support of an environmental program, a review panel would examine:

- the intent or effect of the challenged policy or regulations;
- the legitimacy of the underlying environmental policy or claim of environmental injury;
- the justification for the disruption to trade.

Regulations that intentionally discriminate against foreign products may constitute blatant protectionism and should be subject to careful scrutiny. Strict scrutiny should also be applied to requirements that have a disproportionate effect on imported products—perhaps indicating that the "environmental" standard was surreptitiously designed as a hidden trade barrier.

The second prong of the new balancing test for trade and environment disputes—the environmental legitimacy or injury examination—represents an entirely new concept for the GATT. It recognizes two fundamental bases for establishing the legitimacy of environmental policies with trade effects:

- multilateral agreement; or
- environmental injury to the country imposing trade measures.

This second prong provides a basis for separating "real" environmental programs from those in protectionist guises.

Internationally agreed standards offer the most secure foundation for environmental trade measures. To the maximum extent possible, nations should be encouraged to obtain multilateral support for any environmental program with an impact on trade.

In the absence of a multilateral agreement that expressly sanctions trade measures to combat noncompliance, the legitimacy of an environmental policy should be judged by reference to the presence of a bona fide environmental issue or injury and the nexus of the party using the trade measures to the environmental harm they wish to stop. In this context, a claim of legitimacy implicitly derives from the general commitments not to cause transboundary or global environmental harm that are embedded in the Stockholm and Rio Declarations and in customary international law. The bona fides of an environmental claim should be established by the scientific underpinnings of the policy in question and the significance of the harm addressed. The significance of an environmental injury should be calculated by reference to the importance of the species or ecosystem at risk, the strength of the scientific analysis of harm, the speed at which the harm is occurring, the irreversibility of the potential damage, and the breadth of the threatened harm.

In cases where the use of environmental trade measures rests on the implicit multilateral obligations found in the Stockholm and Rio Declarations, the connection of the party imposing environmental trade measures to the injury should be a central factor in the legitimacy assessment.[2] This study separates five possible "locations" of environmental harms:

- domestic
- transboundary
- global
- foreign resulting in a loss of global "positive externalities"
- foreign

Countries should have the greatest leeway to use regulatory policies with trade effects when addressing environmental problems that arise within their own territories.[3] Thus, domestic environmental regulations such as product standards should be given considerable deference, as they currently are under existing GATT rules.

Policies designed to curb transboundary pollution should also be generally considered legitimate insofar as they respond to established violations of international law—that is, multilaterally determined norms. Trade actions penalizing a neighboring country polluting a shared waterway therefore might well be appropriate. Environmental trade measures aimed at harm to the global commons affecting the sustainability of an important species or ecosystem should also benefit from a presumption of legitimacy based on the established international obligation not to cause such harm.

---

2. Ultimately, the environmental injury test should work like the injury assessment under the antidumping or countervailing duty provisions of established trade laws. Specifically, countries make a unilateral judgment about their injuries but do so against a backdrop of internationally agreed norms.

3. Nondiscriminatory policies should, of course, be employed where effective and available. The second-prong test of environmental injury, however, is meant to focus on the legitimacy of the policy ends in question. The appropriateness of the means chosen to pursue a particular environmental goal are evaluated under the third prong of the three-part test enunciated above.

The most difficult cases are those in which the direct harm per se affects only a foreign country but there are indirect negative effects on others, or, as economists would say, a loss of positive externalities. For example, deforestation directly affects the country whose trees are cut or burned, causing erosion and other local environmental damage. But the loss of forests also has climate change and biodiversity impacts that affect other countries. In such cases, if outsiders who benefit from (but do not pay for) the "positive externalities" demand the forests' preservation, there is a strong argument for them to compensate the country with the forest.

Environmental trade measures that attempt to address an injury that is entirely "local" to a foreign country should not be considered legitimate if undertaken unilaterally. This study argues, however, that nations should always retain the right, in a "soft" sense, to impose unilateral trade restrictions in support of their own environmental policies or values so long as they are willing to compensate those whose trading opportunities are impaired.

Once the legitimacy of an environmental policy has been established, the remaining question—and the third prong of the proposed trade and environment balancing test—is whether the trade remedy chosen to support the policy is appropriate. The severity of the measure applied should vary with the significance and locus of the environmental harm. Respecting the prior determination of environmental legitimacy, the chosen trade restriction should generally be accepted as long as the burden imposed on trade is not clearly disproportionate to the environmental benefits to be obtained in light of alternative policies that are reasonably available and equally effective.

In sum, this study argues that the bar on "extrajurisdictional" trade measures—which is not actually in the GATT text but has been read into Article XX by GATT dispute panels—should be softened. It also suggests that a more refined analysis of unilateral trade actions is needed. Environmental trade measures are most appropriate where internationally agreed standards have been violated and a multilateral institution (preferably a new Global Environmental Organization) responds to the noncompliance. But recognizing the absence of such a multilateral process, this study calls for GATT acceptance of two forms of "multilateral unilateralism"—that is, unilateral trade measures taken:

- to reinforce multilaterally agreed standards;

- to respond to significant global or transboundary pollution spillovers.

The first case of "multilateral unilateralism" involves actions that have in effect been multilaterally condoned by the setting of an international standard. Thus, for example, US trade measures taken against Norway for whaling in violation of the International Whaling Commission's moratorium would be justified. The second case—involving trade restrictions imposed in response to serious pollution spillovers—also can be seen as multilaterally condoned by dint of the internationally recognized obligation not to cause transboundary or global environmental harm. In both cases, there should be multilateral review of such unilateral actions (by a future GEO or the GATT) to ensure the appropriateness of the measure imposed.[4]

In addition to these substantive changes in the rules of international trade, GATT (and future WTO) procedures would benefit from being made more transparent. Open processes would enable environmental interests to advance their views and to better understand the outcome of trade procedures. More openness would also help liberal traders in their battle to avoid protectionist contortions of the trading system.

Future trade agreements, moreover, should be set in a broader policy context by means of environmental impact assessments done at the start of any negotiation with an identifiable potential impact on public health or ecological issues. Such assessments need not be exhaustive modeling efforts. In this regard, US environmental impact statement procedures under the National Environmental Policy Act (NEPA) are *not* a useful guide. Instead, trade assessments should focus on highlighting for negotiators at an early stage the environmental sensitivities related to the issues they will address and on identifying environmental policy advances that should accompany trade liberalization. In the GATT Uruguay Round negotiations, for example, some analysis of the environmental impact of agricultural subsidies would have been useful—as a guide for both trade and environmental policymakers. The "big-picture" environmental impacts of investment liberalization, government procurement, and other issues also might have been productively addressed in this manner.

Environmental groups and other nongovernment organizations should be permitted to submit statements of their views on issues under GATT review or which are the subject of dispute resolution procedures. The dispute settlement process should be made generally more transparent, with evidence taken in public and panel reports made public as soon as they are completed. Where GATT disputes involve environmental issues, technical or scientific experts should be available at the request of any party or the dispute panel itself, and the GATT should make greater efforts to include environmental experts as panel members.

---

4. Where a review concludes that the trade action taken exceeded the bounds of legitimacy, derived from a mistaken judgment that the target country was in violation of international standards or norms, or was clearly disproportionate to the environmental harm in question, the nation imposing the environmental trade measure would be called upon to modify or withdraw its measure. If the nation imposing trade penalties were to refuse to conform to the judgment of the multilateral review, it should be asked to pay compensation or to accept retaliatory withdrawal of trade benefits by others.

Next Steps

The environment was not on the agenda for the Uruguay Round of global trade talks. Thus, reform of the GATT will require new negotiations. Although there is likely to be some sense of fatigue after the halting process of bringing the Uruguay Round to a conclusion, there is considerable urgency in moving forward on an environmental update of the international trading system. The thrust from the environmental community in the United States and around the world to build environmental considerations into the rules and procedures of the GATT is likely to continue unabated. The legitimacy of the international trading system will, moveover, be in some question until peace can be mediated between the trade and environment camps.

The next series of battles over trade and the environment may well emerge from efforts by the US Congress to address competitiveness concerns arising with regard to imports from countries with lax environmental standards or practices, even when the environmental harm has only a local impact. Unilateral imposition of countervailing ecoduties will not, however, improve the trade or environmental situation. Multilaterally negotiated, baseline environmental standards (rather than strict harmonization) offer better prospects for protecting both natural resources and the benefits of open markets. A serious commitment to the implementation of the polluter pays principle would be a significant starting point—and a big step toward a more comprehensive international environmental regime. GATT rules regarding border tax adjustments and subsidies should also be refined to reflect environmental considerations.

North-South Issues

North-South conflicts will further complicate the process of making trade and environmental policymaking mutually reinforcing. Developing countries are deeply suspicious of the industrialized countries' environmental motives, fearing that the OECD countries will use environmental regulations as an excuse to block access to their markets. They also object to being told how to manage their own natural resources and how they should balance competing environment and development goals. In addition, they take exception to international environmental mandates that require them to spend limited resources on the North's environmental priorities such as climate change and ozone layer depletion, particularly when industrialized-country emissions have largely been responsible for these problems.

A central reason for North-South trade and environment disputes is the reliance by certain countries, particularly the United States, on "sticks" (trade measures) to advance their environmental policy goals rather than "carrots" (financial or technical assistance) to coax developing countries into joining international environmental efforts. To foster resolution of global environmental conflicts, new strategies for getting resources to developing countries for environmental investments must be developed.

Ideally, a worldwide system of pollution fees on global environmental harms should be implemented. But the administrative difficulties with such a system of "green fees" are probably insuperable in the near future. A Green Fund financed by a 1/100 of 1 percent tax on trade and capital flows would be another answer. Although also subject to administrative complexities, such a tax would generate $15 billion to $20 billion per year and would go a long way toward shifting decision making in developing countries to reflect the worldwide costs and benefits of possible environmental protection projects rather than simply the national or private cost-benefit calculus. This would mean, for instance, that new Chinese power plants could be built in a more energy-efficient way (i.e., having the lowest possible emissions of greenhouse gases), with the world reaping substantial environmental benefits.

Much of the analytic work in defining the incremental costs of projects with global environmental benefits has already been undertaken by the Global Environment Facility. In fact, the GEF—a partnership among the World Bank, UNEP, and UNDP—provides an existing institutional structure with carefully negotiated governance provisions, financial controls, and administrative safeguards. It offers a solid base on which to build an expanded effort to fund an optimal level of global environmental protection.

Finding mechanisms to promote strong and sustainable growth in the economies of the developing world offers another approach to generating resources for environmental investments in developing countries. The US Enterprise for the Americas Initiative—with its environmental funds tied to market reforms, debt reduction, investment policy reforms, and trade liberalization—provides a concrete example of how a linked package of economic and environmental programs might work in practice. Identifying additional trade concessions that could be offered in return for enhanced environmental commitments should also be explored.

Conclusion

The trade and environment status quo cannot be maintained. Despite the durability of Mother Nature, blind adherence to traditional notions of sovereignty and the pursuit of narrow national interests lead inevitably to the externalization of environmental costs and the strengthening of incentives for unsustainable resource use. Such outcomes in turn could ultimately lead to environmental crises. A coordinating body to manage the worldwide response to environmental issues in general, and to promote adherence to the polluter pays principle in particular, would help to protect the planet from the "tragedy of the commons."

Although there is great mistrust of any idea that seems akin to world government, in an ecologically interdependent world, carefully drawn international environmental rules and a supporting multilateral authority are necessary to achieve a successful collective response to the market failures that afflict environmental policymaking and threaten the biosphere's long-term vitality. The world community has responded to problems raised by interdependence with international organizations in a variety of contexts, including the IMF to coordinate international monetary policy and the GATT to support freer trade. There is no reason policy coordination in the environmental realm should be given less consideration.

The optimal approach to making trade and environmental policies work to mutual advantage is therefore the establishment of a Global Environmental Organization. With a properly defined mandate, such a body could reconcile trade and environment disputes with the GATT, advance environmental cost internalization, facilitate international environmental agreements—including the creation of baseline environmental standards—and coordinate funding for developing-country efforts to upgrade their environmental programs.

With an environmental body working alongside it, the GATT would need only modest changes to accommodate today's environmental priorities. Without a GEO (and recognizing the difficulty of creating any such organization in the foreseeable future), a comprehensive restructuring of GATT's environmental posture will be necessary to permit the GATT to reconcile internally competing trade and environmental goals.

In any case, the GATT (or WTO) reform agenda proposed here would help to ensure that society gets the benefit of both trade liberalization and environmental protection. As applied, the rules proposed would guide the GATT toward greater recognition of environmental concerns. They would unequivocally permit, for instance, the use of trade restrictions to enforce international environmental agreements such as the Montreal Protocol phaseout of CFCs and other chemicals harmful to the ozone layer.

The rules proposed would also steer the United States and other countries away from reliance on unilateral trade measures to advance environmental values toward more trade-friendly and environmentally effective multilateral efforts. Thus, in the tuna-dolphin case, for example, unless the dolphins in question were named an endangered species or there were other scientific justification, the United States would be notified it had overstepped the bounds of mutual respect necessary to maintain international harmony. This would not prohibit a US embargo on Mexican tuna but would let the United States know it needed to gain broader international concurrence on its dolphin protection program, to adopt less trade-disruptive policy tools such as ecolabels, or to measure the depth of its dolphin protection commitment against the trade losses for which Mexico would be entitled to compensation.

The 50th anniversary of the Bretton Woods Conference has generated major reviews of the international organizations set up to manage world affairs in the aftermath of World War II. In following through on these studies, current world leaders have a chance to look forward, to establish mechanisms that address 21st-century global challenges, and to respond to today's political and economic policy failures before they devolve into crises. We must all hope that it does not require the ecological equivalent of World War II to spur initiatives to restructure global environmental management and to make trade and environmental policies work together.

Appendix A:
A Brief History of the GATT

Origins of the GATT

Between the world wars, many nations sought to gain advantage economically by manipulating the terms of their international trade using tariffs (fees on imported goods), quantitative restrictions on imports (quotas), and other trade-disrupting measures. The United States, for instance, responded to the economic slowdown of 1929 by enacting the Smoot-Hawley tariff bill in 1930. In passing this legislation, the US Congress intended to give domestic producers an advantage over competition from imported goods, and in doing so lift the United States out of economic stagnation. By raising tariffs on dutiable items to an average of 52 percent, however, the tariff bill provoked retaliation from the major trading partners of the United States. The new, higher tariffs contributed to a rapid collapse of world trade, and this helped to tip the world's major economies into crisis.

Recognizing the folly of the Smoot-Hawley legislation, the US Congress adopted the Reciprocal Trade Agreements Act of 1934. This statute granted the president broad powers to liberalize trade between the United States and other nations with "reciprocal agreements," including tariff cuts of up to 50 percent.[1] While trade increased moderately in the following years, it did not reach precrash levels. Irreparable damage

---

1. For more details on the origins and development of the GATT see Jackson (1969 and 1992b).

had been done to the international economic structure, helping to create the conditions for war in Europe and the Pacific.

Envisioning an International Trade Organization

Hoping to avert the pattern of economic mismanagement that led to political disaster, the Allied war leaders committed to a new postwar world order that would "bring about the fullest collaboration between all nations in the economic field" (Atlantic Charter, 14 August 1941). The British and the Americans, in particular, began to focus on creating new international institutions to help manage global economic relations, picking up President Woodrow Wilson's proposal for a World Trade Board as part of the League of Nations structure. At the Bretton Woods Conference in 1944, the Allied leaders agreed to set up an International Bank for Reconstruction and Development (IBRD or World Bank) and the International Monetary Fund (IMF). The World Bank's mission was to finance postwar development and reconstruction. The IMF was designed to stabilize exchange rates and official balances of payments. The leaders also agreed on the need for a new institutional structure to reduce obstacles to international trade and to promote mutually advantageous commerce.

Building on this commitment, the United States prepared a proposal for an International Trade Organization (ITO) in December 1945. The ITO was designed to liberalize and oversee international trade, extending America's Reciprocal Trade Agreements program on a multilateral basis.

The World Bank and IMF were set up with relatively little controversy. The debate over the ITO, however, proved to be much more contentious. The delegates to the ITO negotiations became more reserved about committing themselves to free trade obligations and more insistent on exceptions and safeguards from the potential rigors of trade liberalization. Lawmakers in the United States, in particular, seemed reluctant to cede sovereignty to an international organization. Thus, the ITO proposal agreed upon in Havana in November 1947, known thereafter as the Havana Charter, was less binding and less clearly trade liberalizing than the institution that had seemed imperative only three years before at Bretton Woods.

Pending ratification of the ITO proposal, delegates at the Havana Conference adopted an interim measure committing the participants to certain basic principles of international trade. While the ITO required legislative ratification as a treaty, this document, the General Agreement on Tariffs and Trade (or GATT) was adopted at the conference and subsequently accepted by the United States as an executive agreement not requiring congressional approval. The GATT came into force on 1 January 1948 and was expected to provide a temporary framework for trade liberalization efforts pending passage of the ITO.

From ITO to GATT

But the ITO was not to be. Slow postwar growth, concerns about the surrender of US sovereignty to an international institution, and lackluster support from the business community undermined congressional momentum for a new trade organization. The Truman administration quietly withdrew the ITO proposal in 1950 without a congressional vote ever having been taken. The worldwide politics of the situation was clear. The United States was the driving force behind the ITO, and without American support creation of the organization was not possible.[2]

The GATT was never intended to stand alone without the ITO. It possessed no enforcement mechanisms, no codified rules, and no administrative structure to guide its operations (Jackson 1969, 50). In fact, while accepting the obligation of the United States to abide by the GATT as an executive agreement, the US Congress never formally approved the GATT and has at times even explicitly distanced itself from the regime (Diebold 1952, 28; cited in Schott 1990, 28). The GATT has nevertheless persisted and is today the defining agreement behind the international trade regime that has guided trade relations for nearly 50 years.

GATT Principles

While the agreement is a somewhat complex document including 38 articles and appended tariff schedules, the GATT's most fundamental principle can be boiled down to a single concept: nondiscrimination—or more simply, do unto others as you would have them do unto you. The nondiscrimination obligation has two key components: most-favored nation status and national treatment.

- The most-favored nation provision (Article I) requires each signatory to treat imported products from any other contracting party no less favorably than "like" products imported from another GATT member country. In particular, tariff reductions extended to one trading partner must be applied to all GATT parties.

---

2. Further comment on the significance of the failure of the ITO to materialize can be found in Schott (1990, 24–28). Destler (1992) provides a thorough analysis of American trade politics.

- The national treatment provision (Article III) mandates that imported products be treated no less favorably than "like" domestically produced goods once they enter the country of importation. The only valid exception to this obligation is that nations may maintain (but not raise) tariffs on imported goods.

The GATT has two other central provisions: tariffication and consultation.

- Under the tariffication obligation (Article XI), GATT parties are obligated to convert all trade barriers to tariffs. This conversion of quotas, nontariff barriers, and other trade restrictions is intended to produce the most transparent possible trade regime (with any remaining barriers to international commerce visible) and make it easier to reduce remaining barriers through negotiated rollbacks of tariffs.

- The GATT consultation provision (Article XXII) requires parties to try to settle through consultation and negotiation any trade dispute that may arise.

The remainder of the GATT agreement supports these four imperatives. The larger goal is to keep trade liberalization moving forward toward ever-lower tariff barriers and greater market access.

GATT: Administrative Structure

As a result of its provisional roots, the GATT is not a formal international organization and thus has a relatively lean structure. Its secretariat, located in Geneva, Switzerland, includes about 200 professional staff officials and is led by a director general and three deputy directors general.

The GATT's formal political organ is the Session of Contracting Parties, attended by high-level officials from each GATT signatory, or contracting party. This is the overseeing and steering body of the GATT, and it usually meets once a year. Since 1960, a Council of Representatives, composed of delegates from each member state, has met eight or nine times a year to address GATT business.

The focused efforts of the GATT are carried out through committees, including the Trade Negotiating Committee, which orchestrates multilateral negotiations in rounds. GATT also serves as an arbiter in trade disputes between and among members. Dispute settlement efforts are carried out by three-person panels of impartial trade experts appointed by the director general to hear specific disputes. These panels, supported by the GATT staff, review written submissions by the parties to the dispute and hear oral presentations. The panel then issues a recommendation to the GATT Council, which must ratify the panel's proposal in order for it to become an official GATT decision.[3]

ITO Redux: The World Trade Organization

The Uruguay Round of GATT negotiations created a World Trade Organization (WTO) to serve as an umbrella administration for the GATT and other elements of the international trading system. As such, the GATT will be subsumed within the WTO but will continue to exist as the structure of rules for international merchandise trade, alongside separate regimes to cover services trade and intellectual property protection.

The Uruguay Round outcome embodied in the WTO also reflects major changes in the dispute settlement process—for example, speeding up the time for resolving disputes and eliminating the opportunity for any single member to prevent panel decisions from being adopted by the GATT Council. It also mandates that all parties accept all the GATT codes and modifies the traditional decision-making rules (making complete consensus a less strict requirement).

The WTO will be directed by a ministerial conference of participants, which will meet at least every two years. A WTO Council will manage day-to-day responsibilities of the organization as well as forming dispute settlement panels as needed. Like the GATT currently, all matters of major WTO importance will require consensus, although a spectrum of less unanimous votes are applicable for other business.

The Rounds

The main GATT business of lowering trade barriers has been accomplished in periodic, usually multiyear "rounds" of negotiations among all parties. With the recent conclusion of the Uruguay Round, eight rounds have been completed:

- Geneva (1947). The 23 founding GATT nations established the first GATT tariff schedules, regulating goods in 20 categories. Tariff reductions covering 45,000 items and $10 billion in trade—half the total value of world trade at the time—were agreed upon.

- Annecy (1949). In this round, 13 nations exchanged 5,000 tariff reductions.

---

3. After the Uruguay Round amendments are ratified, panel decisions will become final without GATT Council approval unless a consensus forms *against* adoption (the reverse of current procedures). This means, significantly, that parties found to be in violation of their GATT obligations by a panel will no longer be able to block the decision against them from being accepted.

- Torquay (1950–51). This round resulted in a 25 percent overall decrease in tariffs, achieved with 8,700 tariff concessions among 38 parties.

- Geneva (1956). Twenty-six countries agreed to a relatively modest package of tariff cuts totaling $2.5 billion.

- Dillon (1960–62). Twenty-six contracting parties lowered tariffs on about $5 billion of trade in goods. Agreement was reached on 4,400 items.

- Kennedy (1964–67). Far more successful than its predecessors, the Kennedy Round implemented a formula for achieving deep, across-the-board tariff cuts of 35 percent among the 62 participants in a wide range of sectors. Together with separate agreements on textiles and an antidumping code, the round covered $40 billion worth of trade. It failed, however, to make progress on agricultural issues or to set up a framework for augmenting trade with less-developed nations, as some had proposed.

- Tokyo (1973–79). Ninety-nine parties liberalized $300 billion worth of global trade. Weighted average tariffs in the most industrialized markets declined from 7 percent to 4.7 percent. Preferential arrangements to assist developing nations through trade measures were adopted. In addition, the antidumping code was revised, and subsidies, government procurement, and a number of sector-specific codes were developed and implemented.

- Uruguay (1986–93). The most recent round included 117 participants and achieved broad gains in liberalization despite a sometimes grueling seven-year negotiation. Twenty-eight separate accords were concluded, covering among other things agriculture, textiles, services, intellectual property, and foreign investment. Significant attention was devoted to nontariff barriers, including efforts to draft better rules for assessing technical barriers and standards, liberalization of government procurement, and new rules to facilitate dispute settlement. The parties agreed to form a World Trade Organization (WTO), creating a formal international body to support the GATT.

Appendix B:
Scale of Trade Measures (from Most to Least Restrictive)

Trade Sanctions

Trade sanctions, as noted in chapter 4, target "innocent" products in an effort to change another country's environmental standards or practices. Trade sanctions are a subset of the broader category of economic sanctions, which may involve a variety of means of exercising power internationally to induce modification of another party's behavior. Sanctions are potentially very disruptive to trade, although their impact varies widely depending on multiple political and economic variables, such as the degree of dependence in the targeted nation on the restricted goods. An example of a sanction imposed for environmental purposes would be the US ban on imports of Japanese pearls designed to pressure Japan into joining the International Whaling Commission's moratorium on whaling.

Hufbauer, Schott, and Elliott (1990) have compiled a very complete history and discussion of the use of economic sanctions, including trade actions. These authors conclude that sanctions are often not effective. More importantly, some of the key factors that must be present to make sanctions work (e.g., parallel efforts by other countries) are often lacking in the trade and environment context, particularly where the United States imposes environmental trade measures unilaterally.

In the environmental community, however, there is a broad-based belief that trade sanctions are an effective deterrent against international misbehavior. Proponents of the use of, or at least threat of, sanctions point to successes in forcing Iceland out of whaling, ending Japanese drift-net fishing and protecting sea turtles from shrimpers in the Gulf of

Mexico, among other accomplishments. An honest appraisal of the use of sanctions in the environmental context would also include some less successful case examples. For instance, Japan refused for many years to give up whaling, despite facing sanctions under the US Pelly amendment.

Import Bans on Environmentally Harmful Products

Trade bans[1] targeted on specific environmentally harmful products might be based on concerns about the products' effect on public health (e.g., restrictions on pesticides that have not been proved safe for use on food) or ecological resources (e.g., restrictions on eggshell-softening DDT). Bans have also been employed—contrary to GATT dictates—on products based on how the goods were produced. The US ban on Mexican tuna caught with dolphin-killing purse seine nets is an example of such a production process–based trade ban. Another example of such restrictions imposed on a product because of environmentally unsound production methods is the EC's ban on the sale of furs caught in leg-hold traps.

Many environmental trade bans are not even noticed but simply define the terms on which products may enter a market. For example, car makers know that to sell their vehicles in the United States they must meet US emissions control requirements. Nonconforming cars may not be imported. Thousands of similar environmental laws and regulations channel commerce in countries all over the world, almost always without much controversy. In this sense, trade bans—particularly those aimed at product characteristics—are often successful.

Environmentally based trade bans generally become an issue only if they are used as a "sword" to try to change behavior extraterritorially (i.e., addressing production processes of foreign entities outside the country employing the trade measure) or if they are structured in ways that disproportionately affect imported rather than domestic products.

Import Restrictions (Short of a Trade Ban)

Countries have an infinite number of ways to slow the importation of disfavored products. In one infamous case, France required all Japanese videocassette recorders to enter the nation through the small customs office at Poitiers, resulting in a severe limitation on the number of units able to enter the country. In the environmental realm, Denmark's efforts

---

1. This discussion focuses on import bans only. For a discussion of export restrictions and bans see the note at the end of this appendix.

to control solid waste by banning the sale of beer and soft drinks except in returnable glass bottles was upheld as a legitimate trade restriction by the European Court of Justice in a landmark 1988 case.[2] Germany's new packaging law—requiring all merchants to take back the packaging materials in which their products are sold—offers another example of a nonban import restriction with a potentially serious impact on trade flows.

Differential Tariffs or Taxes

Charging different fees for products depending on their environmental characteristics or qualities is another way of influencing trade to advance an environmental agenda. Ontario's environmental levies (10 cents per can) on nonrefillable beer containers, aimed at encouraging reuse of bottles to cut waste, recently provoked an angry response by US brewers, who tend to use (easily recycled) aluminum cans. In reviewing ways to bring the US Marine Mammal Protection Act into compliance with the GATT tuna-dolphin decision, the US government in 1992 considered introducing legislation to amend the act to replace the ban on all Mexican tuna with a fee of several dollars per can on tuna caught using dolphin-unsafe fishing methods. At least some US government officials thought that such a scheme would be GATT-legal since it would permit, in a strict sense, all Mexican tuna to enter the United States. The extra fee for dolphin-unsafe tuna would have applied nondiscriminatorily to US as well as Mexican producers. Moreover, Mexican fishermen using dolphin-safe methods would have been able to import their tuna without any differential cost burden.

Labeling Requirements

Labeling requirements provide another trade measure that can be used to give market favor to environmentally sound products (or to disfavor environmentally harmful goods). In fact, the US tuna ban in the infamous tuna-dolphin case had very little practical effect on Mexican tuna exports to the United States because the demand for Mexican tuna had collapsed as a result of commercial and consumer pressures, intensified by the US tuna packers voluntary dolphin-safe labeling scheme. The market for tuna lacking the dolphin-safe label almost completely dried up, despite the price premium consumers had to pay for the dolphin-safe product.

---

2. Appendix C provides more details on the *Danish Bottles* case in establishing the boundaries of legitimate import restrictions. Kromarek (1990) and Clark and Barrett (1991) also analyze this case.

Considerable attention has also been given to ecolabeling schemes in the context of efforts to protect tropical rain forests. Under pressure from Malaysia and other ASEAN countries, Austria in 1992 dropped a plan to label all tropical timber imports as either "sustainably" grown or not. The Netherlands and France are now developing sustainable timber labels, but these efforts face considerable hurdles in determining what really constitutes sustainable forestry and in overcoming developing-country suspicions that these environmental programs are really meant to block their access to markets in favor of northern timber producers.

Environmentalists have underused the power of consumer-driven market forces. In addition to the success in driving dolphin-unsafe tuna out of the US market, a well-orchestrated boycott of Icelandic products forced Iceland to give up whaling in the late 1980s. Why more efforts have not been undertaken to channel consumer spending to environmentally preferable products through such GATT-consistent, voluntary ecolabeling schemes remains something of a mystery.

A number of countries, including 22 of the 24 OECD countries, have launched voluntary, multicriteria (i.e., focused on the overall environmental impact of the products in question, including air and water pollution effects, toxic exposures, and waste issues) ecolabeling programs designed to highlight green products to the consumer (Salzman 1991). Germany's Blue Angel program, in existence since 1978, has labeled 3,600 products in 64 categories. Canada's Environmental Choice program has been another leader in this field, with labels for dozens of product categories, including diapers, paints, batteries, and household appliances. The Nordic Council (Norway, Sweden, and Finland) also has a well-developed program of ecolabels. The European Community launched a Europe-wide labeling scheme in 1993 with labels on two products: washing machines and dishwashers. Two US nongovernment efforts to launch ecolabel programs, Green Seal and Scientific Certification Systems (SCS), have run into considerable difficulties. The US Environmental Protection Agency's more narrowly focused Energy Star program, addressing the energy efficiency of computers and other office equipment, has been rather more successful. See box 5.5 for a further discussion of labeling.

Environmental Education

Another potentially powerful, and GATT-legal, trade tool is environmental education. By providing information to producers and consumers about the environmental qualities of products, it is often possible to influence purchasing decisions and to promote environmentally preferable goods. Of course, what constitutes "preferable" remains a matter of opinion and can lead to complaints that decisions about favored products are influenced by commercial interests as well as ecological or public health principles.

Education efforts may include labeling programs but are often broader. For example, the EPA Energy Star energy-efficiency program targeted computer producers, convincing them to build energy-saving "sleep" functions into their machines. After abandoning its ecolabel for tropical timber, Austria launched an educational campaign, working with tropical timber producers to develop better sustainable forestry management practices.

One can conceive of other cases where an educational effort might have offered an appropriate trade response to a perceived low-level environmental harm. For example, rather than banning Mexican tuna, the United States (or US environmental groups) could have worked to help Mexican fishermen develop dolphin-safe tuna fishing methods or tried to persuade the Mexican public or Mexican environmental groups to push their own government to end the use of purse seine nets.

Technology Transfers

The transfer of environmentally sound technologies or practices offers an effective way to influence the behavior of another country whose environmental performance is considered to be substandard. Thus, one of the central elements of France's sustainable tropical timber initiative is outreach to timber producers in key developing countries with a goal of helping them obtain cutting-edge (quite literally!) technologies and sawmill techniques (French Ministry of Cooperation 1993). Requests for technology assistance are often part of developing-country requests, made in conjunction with their commitment to participate in an environmental protection program. Some international agreements (e.g., the Montreal Protocol) include explicit technology assistance provisions.

Carraro and Siniscalco (1994) have argued for the use of cooperative research and development as an inducement to get developing countries to join international environmental agreements. Miller and Zhang (1994) have observed that the inducement is even more powerful if the joint R&D is focused on pollution abatement technologies related to the agreement in question, lowering the cost of compliance. Whatever the form, technology cooperation offers a GATT-consistent measure that will be seen as a positive incentive by those whose environmental performance needs to be improved.

Financial Assistance

The easiest and most straightforward way to get another party to go along with an environmental program is to pay them to do it. This

GATT-consistent, positive incentive is infrequently used because of limited funds among those who might pay (i.e., the OECD countries). Nevertheless, there are a number of examples of financial assistance being used to promote better environmental performance. The most notable case is the $240 million fund set up under the Montreal Protocol to help developing countries acquire CFC substitutes and to facilitate their phaseout of CFCs and other ozone layer–damaging chemicals. Austria also used financial contributions to smooth out the flap caused by its plan to label tropical timber.

There is, of course, some danger that financial inducements will create a problem of "moral hazard," in which countries will refuse to do things they would have done anyway (and may have good reasons to do for their own sake) until they are compensated for their actions. This danger is particularly pronounced in the climate change area, where countries often have a number of "no regrets" actions they could undertake (improving energy efficiency, reducing unwarranted energy consumption subsidies, etc.) that will pay positive returns regardless of the benefits in reducing greenhouse gas emissions. One can argue that countries should not have to be subsidized to take these actions. But, in at least some cases, these "easy" investments with positive returns are not funded because competing development opportunities promise higher rates of return. Thus, the danger of moral hazard may be overstated.

Diplomatic Warnings

Diplomatic consultations are often part of the process of resolving trade-environment disputes. For instance, the United States sent Mexico several strongly worded diplomatic notes prior to imposing the tuna trade ban. The GATT often facilitates diplomatic exchanges in an attempt to head off full-blown trade conflicts. Such consultations should be mandatory before trade actions are taken.

Running counter to the diplomacy trend is the impatience of some environmental groups, especially in the United States. These groups see diplomacy as a waste of time and want to move quickly to squeeze environmental bad actors in the vice of trade restrictions or sanctions. US laws—such as the Marine Mammal Protection Act (MMPA; 16 U.S.C. §§1361–1407, ELR Stat. MMPA 011–028) and the Pelly amendment (22 U.S.C. §1978a [1990])—often add to the pressure by confining the US government's diplomatic options and time frame flexibility in conservation disputes. The Supreme Court has, however, ruled in *American Cetacean Society v. Baldrige* (768 F.2d 426; 15 ELR 20877; 247 U.S. App. D.C. 309) that the certification under the Pelly amendment—that is, the identification of a nation as diminishing the effectiveness of an international conservation agreement as a prelude to possible sanctions—is discretionary. However, in *Earth Island v. Mosbacher* (929 F.2d 1449), another court concluded that the government had failed to uphold the MMPA and ordered the trade ban on Mexican tuna.

There is, moreover, a push in Congress to make trade retaliation in general and environmental trade measures in particular mandatory under certain circumstances. This legislative thrust has arisen in response to the belief that the executive branch (under both Republicans and Democrats) is too willing to compromise and is not tough enough on "unfair" actions by US trade partners. The danger, unfortunately, is that Congress often has a narrow view of the problem at hand and is not required, as the president is, to manage all of the many facets of foreign affairs on a daily basis. Moreover, congressional dictates often reflect narrow interests (especially when a small group feels strongly about an issue and others do not care very much one way or another) rather than the broad needs of the country as a whole.

Informal Consultations

Informal consultations can often be used to manage trade and environmental conflicts and produce amicable settlements of even difficult matters. In fact, dozens of minor issues do arise each year, and many are worked out through informal discussions. For example, the United States and the European Community worked out an acceptable resolution to the 1990 crisis over the presence of residues of procymidone, a pesticide not yet tested or approved, in French and Italian wines coming into the United States. The US Environment Protection Agency and the Food and Drug Administration agreed to an expedited review of procymidone, and the European Community agreed to hold back wines with procymidone residues until the review was done (see *Procymidone in Wine* case in appendix C). The advantage of low-key intergovernmental consultation is that it allows technical experts to work with their counterparts in other countries and to address problems before they become politicized.

Note on Export Restrictions

Although inappropriate to the foregoing analysis because they are not aimed at inducing a change in behavior abroad, export restrictions focused on environmental harms present another category of trade action. Such export restrictions come in two distinct varieties. The first kind is designed to protect a domestic processing industry. Examples of this sort would include limitations or bans on raw log exports designed to force sawmilling to be done in the country where the logs originate.

Canada's "landing" requirements for salmon and herring caught in Canadian waters, designed to ensure that fish processing would occur in Canada, present a second type of export ban—and one that was found to be GATT-illegal (appendix C). In such circumstances, the ban often has little to do with environmental protection and much more to do with job protection.

The second type of export ban is designed to protect foreign buyers of environmentally unsound products. One major category of export bans is aimed at protecting importing countries from environmental "bads" such as toxic or radioactive waste, which they cannot adequately regulate the disposal of and which the importing company may well not handle properly. As chapter 8 discusses, such export bans are controversial. Some developing countries insist on having trade in "domestically prohibited goods" (such as chemicals or pesticides that are not permitted to be sold in the producing country) banned. Other countries find such controls paternalistic. Rather than feeling protected by exports bans, they see their sovereignty being eroded, as others make environmental policy choices for them. These concerns are especially acute where a product (such as antimosquito pesticides used to combat malaria) has no application in the developed world and thus can be banned with little worry but may be of great value to developing countries facing different public health conditions and choices.

Appendix C:
Key Trade and Environment Cases

US Court Cases

Dean Milk Co. v. Madison 340 US 349 (1951)

The town of Madison, Wisconsin, passed a regulation requiring milk sold in the city to be processed and bottled at an approved facility within five miles of downtown Madison. Milk producers outside of this exclusive zone challenged the statute as an unlawful barrier to interstate commerce. The Supreme Court held that the statute was facially neutral because it affected Wisconsin producers outside Madison and producers in other states equally, but noted that the effect of the Madison regulations was blatantly discriminatory in favor of local producers. The Court further held that a facially neutral statute with discriminatory impact must address a legitimate local interest to be justified.

In the absence of any local interest other than protection for Madison milk producers, the Court struck down the Madison bottling regulations. In doing so, the Court established that facially neutral statutes with discriminatory effects merit strict scrutiny in balancing the interests of commerce against local (e.g., environmental) benefits.

Huron Portland Cement Co. v. Detroit 362 US 440 (1960)

In *Huron*, the constitutionality of the city of Detroit's air pollution controls was questioned as they applied to boilers powering cement trans-

This appendix draws on the analyses of Housman and Zaelke (1992b), Brown Weiss (1992), and, especially, Geradin (1993a).

port ships engaged in interstate commerce on Lake Erie. Although the ships were licensed and approved by the federal government, Detroit claimed the right to require them to be refit with cleaner engines if they chose to put in at the Port of Detroit. The Supreme Court held in favor of Detroit because the city's purpose (air pollution abatement) did not overlap with the federal government's objective in its regulatory scheme (assurance of seaworthiness).

The *Huron* finding shows that while the federal government has a special interest in protecting interstate commerce under the Constitution's commerce clause, the Supreme Court will give deference to the states to address local health, safety, and environmental interests.

Pike v. Bruce Church 397 US 137 (1970)

In this seminal case, the state of Arizona challenged the Bruce Church cantaloupe farming company for violating a state regulation prohibiting the shipment of unpackaged fruit out of state. Arizona argued that its regulation was necessary to improve and maintain state quality and health standards. The Supreme Court found that Arizona's interest in locally packaging and inspecting the fruit was minimal and did not outweigh the regulation's burden to interstate commerce.

In *Pike*, the Court sets out a three-part balancing test to weigh a state's interests against the federal objective of safeguarding interstate commerce:

- Is the statute evenhanded? (That is, does it discriminate against out-of-state goods?)

- Is the statute rationally related to a legitimate state objective—such as environmental protection?

- Are the burdens to interstate commerce excessive? (Could the objective be achieved through less onerous means?)

Palladio v. Diamond 321 F. Supp. 630 (S.D.N.Y.) (1971)

In this case, a federal district court examined whether New York's prohibition on commerce in goods made from certain reptilian species was preempted by the less stringent 1969 federal Endangered Species Act, which did not cover the reptiles in question. The court upheld the New York law, declaring that states are entitled to take a more cautious approach than the federal government with regards to preserving a species. The court noted that extinct species "like lost time, can never be brought back."

American Can v. Oregon Liquor Control Commission 517 P.2d 691 (1972)

Oregon enacted a law requiring deposits on glass beer and soft drink containers and prohibiting the use of detachable pull-top cans. The American Can Company challenged the ban as an unnecessary burden on interstate commerce.

After examining the environmental intentions and likely economic effects of the ban, the Supreme Court did not find interstate commerce to be threatened sufficiently to go through the *Pike* weighing process. The Court specifically concluded that conserving the beauty of the state of Oregon and protecting public health from discarded containers defied balance against narrow economic interests of the beverage container industry. This case stands for the proposition that when the local interests pursued by the state are substantial, the burden of proof falls heavily on those who are opposing environmental legislation to demonstrate a significant and unnecessary disruption to trade.

Procter and Gamble v. Chicago 421 US 978 (1975)

In *Procter and Gamble v. Chicago*, the Supreme Court refined the three-part test constructed in *Pike* and extended its application directly to environmental policy. The city of Chicago banned detergents using phosphates, which enter water systems and contribute to the growth of algae. The Procter and Gamble Company protested that the ordinance was a hindrance to their interstate trade because they would be forced to market different formulas of detergent in different localities.

The Supreme Court ruled in favor of the ban. The Court found the burden on interstate commerce to be slight and affecting only one company and held that when the impact on commerce was so limited, the party opposing the state's intentions must bear the burden of proving the statute unnecessary.

Philadelphia v. New Jersey 437 US 617 (1978)

The State of New Jersey enacted a statute that banned the import of most solid or liquid waste originating outside the state's boundaries. The city of Philadelphia argued that this was discriminatory and a hindrance to interstate commerce. The Supreme Court found that the New Jersey ban was discriminatory on its face and thus should face strict scrutiny with regard to whether the putative local benefit of the statute justified the ban and its deleterious effects on commerce. The Court held that New Jersey's objective of slowing the flow of garbage into its landfills, although legitimate, did not require discrimination on the basis of the origin of garbage. The Court concluded that other means of achieving this end were available, such as reducing the flow of all garbage, intrastate as well as interstate. The disruption to commerce was, therefore, held to be was constitutionally barred.

Minnesota v. Clover Leaf Creamery Co. 449 US 456 (1981)

The state of Minnesota banned the retail sale of milk in nonreturnable, nonreusable plastic containers, while accepting the use of containers made of other materials such as cardboard. The state justified its ban on the need to reduce solid waste. Applying the *Pike* analysis, the Court upheld the ban, finding that it was nondiscriminatory in its impact upon interstate and intrastate commerce, the putative local environmental gains justified the interference in trade, and no less-restrictive alternative existed that could achieve the same ends as effectively.

Silkwood v. Kerr-McGee Corp. 464 US 238 (1984)

The Supreme Court examined a state court's award of punitive damages to a woman injured by an accidental release of plutonium from a nuclear power plant that was in compliance with federal regulations. The Court held that in the area of nuclear safety, the federal government regulatory regime preempted states from promulgating more stringent nuclear standards than the federal requirements.

Chemical Waste Management v. Hunt 112 S.Ct. 2009 (1992)

Alabama passed a law setting fees for the disposal of hazardous wastes, with an extra charge for the disposal of hazardous wastes generated out of state. An Alabama waste disposal facility brought suit, challenging the differential fees as an unnecessary impairment of interstate trade.

The Court, following the *Philadelphia v. New Jersey* rationale, held the act to be discriminatory on its face and in its effect. Alabama claimed a compelling local interest in regulating waste and protecting the health of its citizens from the danger of hazardous waste. The Court rejected this claim and concluded that the burden of proof with regard to local environmental benefits, and the nonavailability of less trade-disruptive alternative measures to achieve those benefits, falls upon the state in cases of facially discriminatory measures.

Oregon Waste Systems v. Department of Environmental Quality Slip Opinion 93-70 (1994); 1994 US Lexis 2659.

The state of Oregon, concerned about the flow of out-of-state wastes into its landfills, imposed a surcharge on refuse from other states entering

Oregon. Oregon Waste Systems, a waste handler, objected to the fees, which made the cost of using Oregon landfills for out-of-state wastes triple that charged for in-state refuse. The company argued that the discriminatory treatment of out-of-state waste was a hindrance to its interstate commercial business and a violation of the Constitution's commerce clause.

As in the *Chemical Waste Management v. Hunt* case, the Supreme Court found against the two-tier fee system, noting that "if a restriction on commerce is discriminatory, it is virtually per se invalid." Oregon failed to convince the Court that disposing out-of-state wastes cost more than in-state garbage. The Court also rejected Oregon's claim of environmental intent, writing: "Even assuming that landfill space is a 'natural resource' a state may not accord its own inhabitants a preferred right of access over consumers in other states to natural resources located within its border."

European Union (European Community Pre-1994) Cases

Commission v. Italy 91/79, 1980 E.C.R. 1099 (1973)

In this early test of the European Community's authority to deal with environmental issues, Italy claimed that it did not have to comply with Community Directive 73/404, requiring detergents to be biodegradable, because the environment was not within the competence, or authority, of the Community.

Finding for the Community, the European Court of Justice (ECJ) rejected the Italian position on two grounds. First, the Court concluded that the directive sought, aside from protecting the environment, to eliminate trade barriers resulting from differences in individual member-state laws, thereby justifying the directive under Article 100 of the EEC Treaty, which provides the basis for forging a common market. Second, the Court noted that environmental provisions themselves could be justified under Article 100. In its decision, the Court stated: "Provisions which are made necessary by considerations relating to the environment and health may be a burden upon the undertakings to which they apply and if there is no harmonization of national provisions on the matter, competition may be appreciably distorted." Thus, the European Community has long recognized the importance of environmental standards as an element of competitiveness policy that must be coordinated to ensure trade flows smoothly.

The finding that Article 100 provided the basis for environmental action was significant, moreover, because, unlike other provisions of the Treaty of Rome, Article 100 allows action to be taken with a qualified majority of the member states instead of the unanimity otherwise required.

Cassis de Dijon 120/78; 1979 E.C.R. 649, 662 (1979)

West Germany banned the importation of certain low-alcohol beverages, including Cassis de Dijon liqueur, on the purported basis of public health. Such drinks, Germany argued, fostered a more permissive attitude toward the consumption of alcohol and were deceptive to consumers accustomed to higher-proof products. Furthermore, the Germans claimed the banned imports were at a comparative advantage over domestic beverages because tax rates for liquors were tied to the percentage of alcohol they possessed. Importers of Cassis de Dijon challenged the ban as an unfair restriction on trade before the European Court of Justice.

The Court had to consider the relationship between Article 30 and Article 36 of the EEC Treaty. Article 30 specifically establishes a prohibition against quantitative restrictions on imports among member states, including measures with an effect equivalent to trade restrictions—nontariff barriers. Article 36 offers exceptions to Article 30 for purposes of public policy, security, or morality; the protection of health and life of humans, plants, and animals; and the protection of national heritage and property. While the environment is not explicitly mentioned and Article 36 is meant to be interpreted strictly, the Court concluded that the relationship between the environment and human, animal, and plant health is sufficient to merit the use of Article 36 exceptions for environmental purposes.

In applying Article 36, the Court developed a "rule of reason" analysis. The Court adopted a balancing test weighing the means and the ends of an environmental measure against its impact on trade. Applying this proportionality test, the Court struck down the ban, finding that the banned beverages posed no real health threat to consumers, that Germans routinely watered down their alcoholic beverages, and that if the German objective were the protection of public health, less-intrusive measures were available, such as labeling requirements.

The adoption of a balancing test established that disparities in national laws for the sake of protecting public goods were legitimate and to be expected until full harmonization of standards could be accomplished within the common market. While this case specifically addressed health measures, subsequent decisions have extended the *Cassis* precedent to include environmental measures and established the "rule of reason" and proportionality analysis as the basis for adjudication of cases involving environmental regulations with trade effects.

Gilli 788/79, 1980 E.C.R. 2071 (1980)

Italy banned the sale of all vinegar except wine vinegar, arguing that the measure was necessary to protect its consumers. The European Court of

Justice struck down the ban on the grounds that it lacked proportionality. Specifically, the Court concluded that the Italian rules served no necessary interest, protecting neither the health standards nor commercial quality of the Italian market. In the absence of a proportional relationship between the intrusion of the trade measure and the advantages to public health, the statute was deemed to be unnecessarily disruptive to trade.

Waste Oils 240/83, 1984 E.C.R. 531 (1984)

The European Court of Justice was asked to examine whether the Council Directive 75/439/EEC of 16 June 1975 was consistent with the Community's commitment to free trade. The directive suggested a system of waste oil collection including exclusive zones for collectors of waste oils, approval of collection firms, and indemnification of collectors.

While the Court explicitly endorsed free trade and the free market system, it provided that trade had to be subject to limits derived from other central objectives of the Community, including protection of the environment. Based on this analysis, the Court upheld the directive.

Together with the *Cassis de Dijon* case, this finding created a clear mandate for integrated environmental protection programs within the Community and provided the legal basis for excepting environmental policies from the prohibitions against interference in intra-Community trade laid out in Article 30 of the EEC Treaty.

Danish Bottles E.Comm.Ct.J.Rep. 4607, 54 Comm.Mkt.L.R. 619 (1988)

Denmark implemented regulations governing containers for beer, soda, lemonade, and gaseous mineral waters. Denmark justified the regulation as necessary to minimize excess packaging waste. Under this regulation, containers had to be collectable and reusable through a system of deposit and return, which effectively ruled out materials other than glass. In addition, the regulations required that manufacturers use only container shapes and sizes approved by the Danish government. These bottle standards were justified as necessary to facilitate reuse.

Foreign companies opposed the Danish regulations because relative to plastic or metal, glass containers increased shipping weight and thus costs for foreign producers; transportation costs made it more difficult for foreign producers to reclaim and refurbish containers; and mandated container shapes meant less opportunity to differentiate a foreign product from domestic ones through distinctive bottle design.

The Danish bottle regulations were challenged in the European Commission as an unnecessary restriction on the free flow of goods, contrary to Article 30 of the Treaty of Rome. After pressure from the Community, the Danish government responded with small changes to its statutes, allowing alternative bottle designs for limited volumes of foreign product—3,000 hectoliters per year, or enough for products being test marketed. These changes, however, did not satisfy the Commission, which proceeded to investigate and then ask the European Court of Justice for a ruling on the Danish regulations.

The Court first addressed the deposit-and-return system and accepted it as a necessary element of Denmark's legitimate objectives, noting that environmental protection was a primary objective of the European Community. In doing so, the Court appears to have made the purpose of the legislation the primary factor in determining the legitimacy of environmental regulations—with almost no regard to whether the means chosen to pursue a legitimate environmental end burdened trade. Applying a stricter test of proportionality to the volume limit on beverages in unapproved bottle designs, the Court rejected the Danish claims, holding that mandating types of bottles would be unnecessarily disruptive to trade in proportion to the added environmental benefits.[1]

Titanium Dioxide 1991 E.C.R. 2867

The European Court of Justice was asked by the European Commission to annul a Council directive, 89/249, regarding reduction and cleanup of wastes from the titanium dioxide industry on the grounds that the directive was improperly based on Article 130(s) (addressing regulations involving shared EC and member state competency and therefore requiring unanimity of the member states) of the Single European Act instead of Article 100(a) (addressing matters concerning the European single market and thus requiring a qualified majority, not unanimity, for action). The Court found that the directive was inherently concerned with both environmental protection and fair competition, meaning that it involved both the articles, but insofar as the articles prescribed different rules and procedures, they could not both inform the question. The Court held that in borderline cases between Article 130(s) and 100(a), Article 100(a) rules and procedures (giving greater scope to the interest of European integration) trump Article 130(s) and are appropriate. Because many cases can be considered borderline in this sense, this decision positioned the Community to exercise more decisive action on environmental matters than it could have otherwise.

It is notable, however, that the European Court of Justice contradicted the *Titanium Dioxide* reasoning and ruled that Article 130(s) predominates in borderline cases in *Commission v. Council*, Case C-155/91.

---

1. Kromarek (1990) and Clark and Barrett (1991) provide more details and an analysis of this case.

Scottish Red Grouse (1991)

The Netherlands established unilateral measures, including prohibitions on trade, to protect the red grouse, a bird found only in Scotland. The European Court of Justice rejected this extrajurisdictional effort to use trade measures to affect environmental conditions in another country. Though not as well known as the GATT tuna-dolphin case, this EC case enunciates the same principle of opposition to the use of environmental trade measures aimed at changing behavior outside the jurisdiction imposing the restrictions.

Belgian Waste 2/90, Commission v. Belgium ECJ 9 July 1992

The European Court of Justice was asked by the European Commission to determine the legality of a universal ban on waste importation promulgated by the Walloon region of Belgium.

Although the Court rejected the Belgian position that waste was not to be considered a product because it might not have intrinsic commercial value, the Court nonetheless upheld the ban under a rule of reason analysis. The Court found that waste importation could be given extraordinary treatment because the flow of wastes could pose a future environmental danger, if not a present one. The Court further held that with regard to dangerous waste, specific European Community regulations had already been established. The Belgian ban could continue only to the extent that it was consistent with the Community's regulations.

The case has been sharply criticized by EC legal experts for failing to apply the concept of proportionality developed in the *Cassis de Dijon* case and to weigh the environmental benefits of the Walloon ban against the trade burdens on EC commerce. From a trade perspective, this appears to be a serious omission, given the likelihood that waste policy alternatives existed that would have allowed Walloon region to meet its environmental objectives with less interference to international commerce.

The General Agreement on Tariffs and Trade (GATT)

Belgian Family Allowances GATT, BISD 1 Supp. 59 (1953)

Belgium placed a 7.5 percent excise tax on imported goods purchased by government agencies in cases where the exporting country did not have a social program of family allowances such as Belgium had established.

The tax was intended to offset the competitive effect of Belgium's potentially higher social charges on businesses. Goods from nations that had a similar allowance system were exempted from the levy.

The Belgian tax was challenged before a GATT dispute panel, which determined that it was inconsistent with Belgium's GATT Article I most-favored nation obligations. The panel differentiated between taxes applied to products, which would be GATT-consistent, and taxes applied to the conditions attendant to the manufacture of a product, which are GATT-illegal. This analysis sets out the basic GATT rule that like products may not be treated differentially on the basis of the production process or methods by which the products were obtained or manufactured.

Canada-US Tuna GATT, BISD 29 Supp. 91 (1982)

In a dispute between the United States and Canada relating to jurisdiction over Pacific fisheries, Canada seized 19 US fishing vessels operating within its 200-mile Exclusive Economic Zone. The United States responded with a total ban on Canadian tuna and tuna products. Canada challenged the ban before a GATT dispute panel. The United States responded that the ban was justified under GATT Article XX(g) as a measure to conserve an exhaustible natural resource.

The GATT panel first noted that the American action did not constitute a "disguised restriction on international trade" because the United States had announced the ban as a trade measure publicly. The panel, however, went on to find that the US measure was not "primarily aimed at" environmental protection as required for an Article XX(g) exception. The panel based this finding on the fact that the US ban applied to all species of tuna, including those not in danger of depletion, and because the United States had taken no steps to restrict domestic tuna consumption commensurate with its efforts to restrict imports of tuna from Canada.

Superfund GATT, BISD 34 Supp. 136 (1987)

The US Superfund Act of 1986 provided for excise taxes on imported petroleum and products produced with petroleum. Canada, Mexico, and the European Community brought a GATT case against the United States on the grounds that differential tax rates on imported and domestic petroleum and on petroleum-based products violated the principle of national treatment for foreign goods to which the United States was bound under GATT Article III. The United States argued that the resulting differential was competitively insignificant and that the higher taxes were for an entirely benign purpose (cleaning up hazardous waste sites).

The panel reasoned that the objective to which tax receipts will be applied is irrelevant to the GATT consistency of the tax and that all taxes must meet national-treatment requirements. Examining whether the Superfund Act levies on petroleum and products made from petroleum were higher for imports than for domestic goods, the panel found the tax on imported petroleum to be higher, thus unacceptable, and the tax on imported products of petroleum to be comparable, and therefore acceptable under GATT Article III. The United States refined its law to be consistent with this ruling.

Canada—Herring and Salmon GATT, BISD 35 Supp. 98 (1988)

Canada issued statutes prohibiting the export of unprocessed herring, herring roe, and pink and sockeye salmon, requiring that these fish first be landed in Canada for processing. The United States brought the case before a GATT panel, arguing that the export ban was inconsistent with GATT Article XI:1, which prohibits members from banning the free flow of goods to another member. Canada claimed exemption from this prohibition under two GATT exceptions: Article XI:2(b), permitting export prohibitions for the purposes of ensuring quality or regulations relating to the international marketing of a good, and Article XX(g), permitting measures relating to the protection of a natural resource.

The panel found against an Article XI:2(b) exception to Canada's GATT obligations, noting that unprocessed fish, the object of the Canadian ban, was not the target of marketing or promotion. In examining the Article XX(g) exemption, the panel found that a trade measure must have a "primary aim" relating to conservation and include comparable restrictions on domestic consumption and production. In the opinion of the panel, neither of these criteria was met in the Canadian ban. Canada accepted the panel's findings and pledged to lift its export prohibition. Soon after doing so, however, further prohibitions replaced the unprocessed herring regulations.

Thai Cigarettes GATT Doc. DS10/R (1990)

The government of Thailand placed an import ban, quantitative restrictions, and discriminatory internal taxes on imported cigarettes, citing the need to protect the health of Thai citizens. The United States argued that comparable obstacles to commerce were not imposed on the Thai state tobacco monopoly, and a GATT panel was formed at the request of the United States. The panel found against Thailand and its claim of an Article XX(b) exception to its GATT obligations, declaring that the Thai measures were not necessary to achieve the stated objective of protecting public health, in that there were less GATT-inconsistent means of achieving the established policy goal available, such as advertising bans or labeling restrictions.

In rejecting Thailand's trade measures, the GATT panel interpreted Article XX(b) of the GATT strictly, defining necessary to mean that no other less GATT-inconsistent policies were available that the contracting party could be reasonably expected to employ instead of the chosen trade measures.

Tuna-Dolphin GATT Doc. 21/R (3 September 1991)

The US Marine Mammal Protection Act (P.L. 92–522, 86 Stat. 1027), enacted in 1972, requires the US government to take steps to curtail the incidental killing of marine mammals by commercial fishermen, both domestic and foreign. Specifically, the MMPA instructs the secretary of commerce to prohibit the importation of tuna products from countries whose dolphin kill ratio (dolphin deaths per net dropped) exceeds that of US fisherman beyond a certain margin. In 1988, believing that dolphins in the Eastern Tropical Pacific Ocean were being killed by foreign tuna fisherman in violation of the law, Earth Island Institute, a California-based environmental group, sued to enforce the congressional mandate (*Earth Island v. Mosbacher*, 929 F.2d 1449, 1991). A federal judge agreed that the government was failing to uphold the law and ordered Mexican tuna imports banned from the United States.

Mexico argued that its right to sell tuna in the United States had been violated and asked for a GATT dispute settlement panel to adjudicate the matter. In September 1991, the panel concluded that the United States was in violation of its GATT obligations. Specifically, the panel found that:

- the US ban violated GATT Article III's national treatment requirement, which preempts trade measures based on production practices;

- the US kill-ratio standard was inappropriate because it was retroactively determined based on the number of dolphins killed by American fishermen in any given year—and thus uncertain until after the fact;

- the US ban could not be justified under GATT Article XX(b) for actions necessary to protect human or animal life or Article XX(g) for the conservation of exhaustible natural resources and that these exceptions could not be applied unilaterally or extrajurisdictionally;

- the United States was justified in using its ''dolphin safe'' tuna labeling program because the program had no discriminatory effects.

Though the tuna-dolphin panel's finding has not been adopted by the GATT Council, and so technically has no value as a GATT precedent, the case is seen as indicative of GATT decision-making priorities and has provoked heated debate over the fairness of GATT resolution of trade and environment conflicts.[2]

Tuna Dolphin II (May 1994)

Unhappy that Mexico refused to push its GATT victory in the tuna-dolphin case through to ratification by the GATT Council, the European Community brought its own challenge to the US Marine Mammal Protection Act and specifically to the "secondary embargo" provision of the US statute. This provision bars tuna imports to the United States from any country engaging in tuna trade with an embargoed country such as, in this case, Mexico. Several European countries import tuna from Mexico. The case raises similar questions as the first tuna-dolphin case about the right of a nation to impose environmental trade measures unilaterally and extrajurisdictionally. In again finding the US tuna ban to be GATT-illegal, the Tuna Dolphin II panel rested its conclusion not on the extraterritorial element of the US trade restrictions but on their unilateral nature.

CAFE Standards (1994)

The United States imposes penalties under the 1975 Energy Policy and Conservation Act on auto manufacturers whose fleetwide fuel economy averages do not meet Corporate Average Fuel Economy (CAFE) mileage standards. The law now requires a tax to be paid on cars from fleets averaging less than 27.5 miles per gallon. The measure appears to apply equally to foreign and domestic producers. But the exclusion of light trucks from the rules, the methodology used to determined the fleetwide average mileage, and the fact that a number of European automakers sell only in the large-car (low mileage) market makes the CAFE rules discriminatory in effect. Claiming that this measure, like the petroleum tax of the 1980s, is trade protection masquerading as environmentalism, the European Union challenged the CAFE law before a GATT panel.

Gas Guzzler (1994)

Under the US Energy Tax Act of 1978, a "gas guzzler" tax was established. The act imposed a scale of fees on passenger vehicles with less

---

2. For a more complete analysis, see Housman and Zaelke (1992b).

than a mandated fuel economy level (22.5 miles per gallon currently). Depending on how far from the standard the offending vehicle is, a tax of $1,000 to $7,000 is levied upon it. The tax does not apply to certain categories of vehicles such as light trucks or vans.

While the fees are nondiscriminatory on their face—they apply equally to foreign and domestic vehicles—the European Community has challenged them as GATT-illegal in their effect. As in the *CAFE Standards* case, the Europeans have brought a GATT case, arguing that the law in its application is arbitrary and has a disproportionate effect on foreign producers.

Venezuelan Reformulated Gasoline (1994)

Under the requirements of the 1990 US Clean Air Act, oil companies must reformulate the gasoline they sell in the parts of the United States with air quality problems. The law specifically requires refiners to reduce a variety of smog-causing contaminants in their gasoline from a baseline determined by their products' composition in 1990. In December 1993, EPA issued regulations permitting American refiners to establish their baseline using actual data or several alternative methodologies for reconstructing their fuel composition. Foreign producers, lacking actual data on their fuel composition, were required to use the US refining industry average level of contaminants as their baseline.

Venezuela protested that these EPA Clean Air Act regulations were discriminatory and inconsistent with GATT-mandated national treatment and threatened to bring a GATT challenge against the United States. American refiners of gasoline insisted that they had been saddled with extraordinary costs to meet new air pollution regulations and that foreign producers that face less stringent environmental requirements should not be given a competitive advantage or any right to sell "dirty" fuel in the United States.

To avoid a GATT dispute proceeding, the Clinton administration reopened the EPA rule-making process and proposed revised clean fuels regulations to permit Venezuela to export the same volume of reformulated gasoline to the United States that it had in 1990 using the alternative methodologies available to US companies to determine its baseline level for reducing contaminants. In response, Venezuela dropped its GATT challenge.

United States–European Union Cases

Beef Hormones (1989)—Unresolved

After allegations that bovine growth hormones had caused deformities in babies, the European Community banned all use of growth hormones in beef sold in Europe. US exports of beef to Europe consist mainly of beef offal; the meat itself is sold mainly in the US market. Because beef and offal production are inseparable, American cattlemen were faced with either using hormones to maintain beef quality while abandoning the profitable European offal market ($145 million per year), or else eschewing hormones and being saddled with lesser quality, hormone-free beef at home. In the absence of scientific evidence showing a danger from hormones, the United States saw the European regulations as unnecessarily trade-distorting and potentially as disguised protectionism.

The United States threatened to raise the issue in the GATT, arguing that there was no real scientific or health basis for a hormone ban and that the putative benefits to the Europeans were out of line with the disruption to trade. In February 1989, an interim compromise was struck, whereby the Europeans submitted their policy to a scientific panel and doubled the US high-quality beef quota, while the United States agreed to abide by the ban for the time being.[3]

Procymidone in Wine (1990)

Wine growers in Europe widely use the fungicide procymidone, produced by the Sumitomo Company of Japan, on their grape vines. Because procymidone is not approved for use in the United States, the detection of residue from the fungicide in wine imported from Europe into the United States led to a US ban on all procymidone-tainted wine. The European Community threatened to challenge this disruption to their wine trade, arguing that the residue posed no threat to health and was being used as a nontariff barrier to trade.

Normally, the US Environmental Protection Agency requires a lengthy study to establish acceptable levels of a pesticide residue before registering it for use. Recognizing and explicitly citing the trade-related significance of the ban on European wines, EPA Administrator William Reilly accelerated the process of granting a temporary standard for procymidone once its safety had been established.

US-Canada Free Trade Agreement Cases

Landing Requirements for Pacific Salmon and Herring, Final Report of the US-Canada FTA Panel, 19 October 1989

Following the finding of a GATT panel (BISD 35 Supp. 98 [1988]) against Canada's ban on the export of unprocessed herring and salmon, Canada

---

3. Froman (1989) provides more details on this case.

pledged to implement the GATT decision. However, at the same time as Canada lifted its export ban, it introduced new regulations requiring all roe herring, pink and sockeye salmon (species in the previous ban), and coho, chum, and chinook salmon (species not in the previous ban) caught commercially in Canadian waters to be landed in Canada prior to export. The United States complained that the effect, if not the intent, of the regulations was to restrict Canadian exports and put US fish processors at a disadvantage to their Canadian competitors. The United States took the case to a US-Canada Free Trade Agreement (FTA) panel, which had to decide whether the landing requirement was prohibited under GATT Article XI and, if so, whether the measure was entitled to an exception under GATT Article XX(g). Both GATT articles had been incorporated into the FTA.

The panel, using a test of whether the measures would have a materially greater impact on exports and exporters than on domestic sales, found that the effect of the Canadian landing requirement was indeed a quantitative restriction, prohibited in Article XI. The panel rejected Canada's claim under Article XX(g), reasoning that if the economic burdens of the trade measure fell as heavily upon Canadian producers as they fell on foreigners, the measure would not have been taken. Furthermore, the panel concluded that the conservation benefits of the measure could be achieved in a less trade-distorting way.

Lobster Case, Final Report of US-Canada FTA Panel, 25 May 1990

The United States enacted an amendment to the Magnuson Fishery Conservation and Management Act setting minimum size requirements for domestic or imported lobsters sold in the United States. The regulations were meant to ensure that US lobster stocks would be able to reach sexual maturity and breed, thus sustaining the viability of the industry. The prohibition on imports of undersized lobsters (almost entirely from Canada) was meant to prevent American lobster dealers from fraudulently selling undersized US lobsters as Canadian lobsters; to reduce the lure of the illegal American market for undersized lobsters; and to assuage the fear of US lobstermen that they would be at a comparative disadvantage in competing against unrestricted Canadian lobstermen.

Canada, justifying its continued harvesting of smaller lobsters on the grounds that Canadian lobsters reach sexual maturity at a smaller size due to the colder waters of Canada's lobster beds, challenged the legitimacy of the US action as a GATT-illegal trade restriction. The Canadians further argued that the differences between US and Canadian lobsters made a US appeal to Article XX(g), relating to the conservation of exhaustible resources, unjustified.

After detailed scrutiny of GATT Articles III and XI, which are incorporated into the US-Canada Free Trade Agreement (FTA), a majority of the panel (formed under FTA auspices) found the American lobster size requirements to be a legitimate standard under GATT Article III. The final statement of the panel did not even mention the Canadian claim that their lobsters matured at a smaller size, thus failing to address the conservation issue and the related question of regulating extraterritorial process and production methods.

Softwood Lumber (1986 to present)

This case was initiated in 1986 and continues today in a third iteration. At issue are the stumpage fees charged by the government of Canada for the right to cut timber on government lands and the question of whether low fees constitute a subsidy to Canadian lumbermen. On its face, the case involves mainly issues of competitiveness and the definition and scope of subsidy regulations. But while American timber interests—the originators of the case—did not cite environmental reasons for opposing the Canadian practice of cheap timber-rights sales (for fear of facing a backlash of environmental scrutiny at home), environmentalists have paid close attention to the case.

The softwood lumber dispute has underscored the seriousness of competitiveness concerns related to environment and natural resource issues. This matter has also highlighted the complexity of trying to internalize environmental costs—in this case, ensuring that timbering practices adhere sustainable yield rates.

Ultra-High Temperature Milk USA-93-1807-01 (1991)

In December 1991, the commonwealth of Puerto Rico revoked the license of the Lactel Company of Quebec, Canada, to import and sell ultra-high temperature milk, which is heat treated and sealed to extend its shelf life. The stated justification for this action was to meet local safety and quality standards, as mandated by Puerto Rico's accession to the US National Conference on Interstate Milk Shipments (NCIMS), a standard-setting organization governing milk sales in the 50 US states.

After attempts at consultation were unsuccessful, Canada requested dispute resolution under the US-Canada Free Trade Agreement (FTA). The panel noted that parties to the FTA had a right to promulgate technical standards but that the FTA explicitly recognized the danger of protectionism in the guise of standards. Though Canada ascribed a broad set of unfair practices to Puerto Rico, including prohibited quantitative restrictions, internal discrimination, illegal domestic protection, failure to consult in good faith, and the use of other than the least trade-restrictive measure under GATT Article XX, the panel found only one argument valid: Puerto Rico's trade measure had nullified and impaired the benefits Canada could reasonably have expected to achieve under the FTA.

The panel recognized that the facts of the case turned on the equivalency of Quebec's milk inspection procedures. Though the panel noted that UHT milk had been exported from Canada to Puerto Rico without incident for 14 years, it nevertheless accepted Puerto Rico's right to raise its milk standards as a legitimate goal without regard to the necessity or proportionality of the regulations.

Ontario Beer Case (1993 to present)

The Canadian province of Ontario enacted beer regulations governing both beer containers and distribution. While the statutes applied to both domestic and imported products, American beer producers argued that the container regulations requiring a 10-cent levy on all metal beer cans were discriminatory in effect because most American beer is sold in cans, thus subject to the levy, while Canadian beer is largely bottled in glass.

Claiming that the measures had a legitimate environmental purpose (to facilitate container reuse) and were therefore justified under international obligations, Canada refused to remove the regulations. A compromise was achieved focused on improving distribution access for American beer, without the removal of the levy for nonglass containers. The market-access targets of the compromise have not been reached, however, and the conflict continues to flare.

Appendix D: Multilateral Environmental Agreements with Trade Provisions

Agreements in Force

Convention Relative to the Preservation of Fauna and Flora in their Natural State, 1933

The objective of this agreement is to preserve the natural fauna and flora of the world, particularly of Africa, by means of national parks and reserves, and by regulation of hunting and collection of species. The convention prohibits the import and export of trophies unless the exporter is given a certificate permitting export. Parties shall take measures to control and regulate in each of their territories the internal import and export of trophies acquired in a manner not in accord with national law (Article 9).

Convention on Nature Protection and Wildlife Preservation in the Western Hemisphere, 1940

The objectives of this convention are to preserve all species and genera of native American fauna and flora from extinction and to preserve areas of extraordinary beauty, striking geological formation, or aesthetic, historic, or scientific value. The convention provides for issuance of export permits to regulate trade in protected species (Article 9). Parties are countries in the Western Hemisphere.

This appendix has been adapted, with permission, from the *Trade and Environment Report* (GATT 1992b).

International Convention for the Protection of Birds, 1950

The objective of this accord is to protect the populations of birds, and particularly migratory birds, from extinction. The convention prohibits the import, export, transport, offer of sale, or sale of any live or dead birds killed or captured during the protected season (Article 3) and eggs, or their shells, or broods of young birds in the wild state during the breeding season (Article 4). Parties are 10 countries in Western Europe.

International Plant Protection Agreement, 1951

The objectives of this agreement are to maintain and increase international cooperation in controlling pests and diseases of pests and plant products and to prevent their introduction and spread across national boundaries. Parties to the agreement are required to regulate very strictly the import and export of plants and plant products, where necessary, through prohibitions, inspections, and destruction of consignments (Article 6).

Plant Protection Agreement for the South East Asia and Pacific Region, 1956

The objective of this accord is to prevent the introduction and spread of diseases, insect pests, and other enemies of plants. Under the agreement, each party shall use its best endeavors to apply with respect to the importation of any plants from anywhere outside the region prohibition, certification, inspection, disinfection, disinfestation, quarantine, destruction or other measures as may be recommended by the Plant-Protection Committee for the South East Asia and Pacific Region (Article III). This agreement arose out of the International Plant Protection Agreement of 1951.

Convention on Conservation of North Pacific Fur Seals, 1957

The objective of this convention is to achieve maximum sustainability of the fur seals of the North Pacific Ocean. The convention prohibits the import and delivery into and the traffic within a party's territory of skins taken in the North Pacific Ocean, except those taken by the United States or Russia on rookeries, those taken for research purposes or by native populations, or those confiscated or inadvertently captured (Article VIII). Parties are Canada, Japan, the United States, and Russia.

Agreement Concerning the Cooperation in the Quarantine of Plants and Their Protection against Pests and Diseases, 1959

The objective of this treaty is to prevent the introduction and spread of diseases, insect pests, and other enemies of plants. Under the agreement, parties apply uniform phytosanitary regulations for the import, export, and transit of consignments of vegetable matter dispatched from one country to another (Article 4). Parties are states in Central and Eastern Europe and the former Soviet Union.

Phytosanitary Convention for Africa, 1967

The objective of this agreement is to prevent the introduction and spread of diseases, insect pests, and other enemies of plants. Each party shall control the import of plants and apply prohibition, quarantine, certification, or inspection measures for any plant, plant material, seed, or packing material the Organization of African Unity considers necessary. The agreement arose out of the International Plant Protection Agreement of 1951 and supersedes the Phytosanitary Convention for Africa South of the Sahara, 1954.

African Convention on the Conservation of Nature and Natural Resources, 1968

The objective of this convention is the conservation and managed development of the soil, water, flora, and fauna of the African continent. The convention provides that, for all species, a party shall regulate trade in the transport of specimens or trophies and shall do so in such a manner as to prevent their illegal capture or killing. Trade in trophies and transport of specimens of protected species[1] shall be subject to a standard authorization, additional to that required for the hunting, killing, capture, or collection; which indicates the destination; which shall not be given unless they have been legally obtained; and which shall be examined before export. Parties to the convention will require presentation of the necessary authorization for the import and transit of such specimens or trophies and confiscate illegally exported specimens or trophies (Article IX). All members of the Organization of African Unity are parties to the agreement.

---

1. Species in Class A are completely protected; species in Class B are protected but may be hunted, killed, captured, or collected under special authorization granted by the competent authority (Article VIII).

European Convention for the Protection of Animals during International Transport, 1968

The objective of this accord is to safeguard from suffering, as far as possible, animals in transport. Each party to the convention shall apply its provisions governing the international transport of animals (Article I).

Benelux Convention on the Hunting and Protection of Birds, 1970

The objective of this convention is to harmonize regulations on the hunting and protection of wild birds. In the case of traffic with third countries, the convention provides that the export, import, and transit of live or dead game shall be governed by the regulations in force in the partner countries in which such operations take place (Article 6) and that the export, import, and transit of all live or dead birds and of their eggs and young shall be permitted only with prior authorization from the partner countries in which such operations take place (Article 9). Parties are Belgium, Luxembourg, and the Netherlands.

Convention on International Trade in Endangered Species (CITES), 1973

The objective of this well-known convention is the protection of endangered species. Under the convention, trade of species threatened with extinction (listed in its appendix I) and trade in species that may become endangered unless trade is strictly regulated (listed in its appendix II) are authorized by export and import permits approved by the scientific authorities of the parties concerned (Articles III and IV). Species that a party identifies as being subject to regulation within its own jurisdiction and as requiring international cooperation to control trade (listed in the convention's appendix III) are subject to an export permit authorized by the scientific authority of the party (Article V). Article XXII permits a party to exempt itself from the requirements of the convention with regard to a specific species listed in appendices I, II, or III. Provisions also regulate trade between a party and a nonparty to the convention.

CITES builds on a long history of controlling trade in endangered species through the issue of export permits. It adds the twist of requiring an import permit for an export permit to be issued in order to prevent circumvention to nonparties.

Agreement on the Conservation of Polar Bears, 1973

The objectives of this agreement are to prohibit the capture and killing of polar bears and to protect the ecosystems of which the bears are a part.

The agreement prohibits the exportation from or importation and delivery into, and traffic within, a party's territory of polar bears or any part or product thereof taken in violation of the agreement (Article V).[2] Parties are Canada, Denmark, Norway, the United States, and Russia.

Convention for the Conservation and Management of the Vicuña, 1980

This convention's objective is the conservation and management of the vicuña. The export of fertile vicuña semen or other reproductive material is prohibited except to member countries for research and/or repopulation (Article 4). Parties are four Latin American states.

ASEAN Agreement on the Conservation of Nature and Natural Resources, 1985

The objective of the agreement is to promote joint and individual state action for the conservation and management of the natural resources of the ASEAN region. Parties are to regulate trade and the possession of species recognized as endangered by the parties.

International Code of Conduct on the Distribution and Use of Pesticides (UN Food and Agricultural Organization), 1985

The code's objective is to identify potential hazards in the distribution and use of pesticides, to establish standards of conduct, and to define responsibility for those involved in the regulation and use of pesticides. The provisions of the code require a system of prior informed consent specifying that: exporters notify importing states prior to the export of restricted pesticides; and that exporting nations notify importing nations of their domestic pesticide restrictions. In addition, the code covers the testing, labelling, packaging, storage, disposal, distribution, and advertising of pesticides in international trade.

Montreal Protocol on Substances That Deplete the Ozone Layer, 1987

The objective of the protocol is to reduce the production and use of ozone-depleting substances, particularly a class of chemicals known as chlorofluorocarbons, or CFCs. The 1987 agreement addressed controlled substances, products containing controlled substances, and products

---

2. Polar bears are listed in appendix II of CITES, which means that the export of bears and other listed animals must be limited to a level that is not detrimental to the species.

produced using controlled substances. It calls for trade restrictions against nonparties. The 1990 London amendments committed the parties from developed countries to a full phaseout of CFCs as of 2000; developing countries were given an additional 10 years to complete the CFC phaseout. The 1992 Copenhagen amendments further speed the phaseout of ozone layer–depleting chemicals, including the elimination of CFC production by 1996.

Convention for the Prohibition of Fishing with Long Drift Nets in the South Pacific, 1989

The objective of the agreement is to curtail through regional cooperation the depletion of South Pacific marine resources, especially stocks of albacore tuna, resulting from the unregulated use of long drift nets. Parties to the agreement are to prohibit transshipment, landing, processing, import, or export of drift net catches, whether processed or unprocessed, within their jurisdiction. Furthermore, parties must restrict port access and servicing facilities for vessels engaged in drift net fishing and must prohibit the possession of drift nets aboard any fishing vessels within their fisheries jurisdictions. Parties are 14 nations of the South Pacific region, including two extraregional nations with local protectorates: France and the United States.

Basel Convention on the Control of Transboundary Movements of Hazardous Wastes and Their Disposal, 1989

The objectives of the agreement are to limit the transboundary movement of hazardous waste among party countries, to set up notice and consent procedures, to define the scope of the agreement, and to define what constitutes illegal traffic and the responsibilities of the parties. Categories of wastes are defined in annex I and characteristics of hazardous wastes in annex III. In addition, a party may define as, or consider to be a hazardous waste, other substances in its domestic legislation.

Parties may prohibit the import of hazardous wastes for disposal. The central requirement of this agreement is a system of prior informed consent, committing parties to the convention not to export hazardous wastes to another party unless the state of import consents in writing. Parties to the accord agree not to allow the export of hazardous waste to a party if it has reason to believe that the waste will not be disposed of in an environmentally sound manner. Trade in hazardous wastes with nonparties is prohibited (Article 4).

Illegal traffic in hazardous wastes is also subject to a duty to reimport if an improper waste shipment is uncovered. The agreement leaves open the definition of hazardous waste.

Amended London Guidelines for the Exchange of Information on Chemicals in International Trade, 1989

The objective of the agreement is to increase the sound management of chemicals through the exchange of scientific, technical, economic, and legal information on the movement of chemicals in international trade in order to better protect human health and the environment at the global level. The guidelines provide a mechanism for importing countries to formally record and disseminate their policies regarding trade-restricted chemicals. They provide an outline of shared responsibilities of importing and exporting countries.

Appendix E

Table E1 Matrix of appropriate unilateral trade measures by locus and significance of environmental harm[a]

Locus of harm (vis-à-vis country imposing trade measures)	Rapid, major, certain, irreversible harms (serious)	Less rapid, major, certain, or reversible harms (moderate)	Least certain, slower, reversible, or narrower harms (limited)
Domestic	Bans	Bans	Bans
Transboundary	Sanctions	Sanctions[b,c]	Import restrictions[b]
Global	Sanctions	Bans[b,c]	Labeling[c]
Foreign with positive externalities	Sanctions[d]	Bans[b,c,d]	Labeling[c,d]
Foreign	Labeling[c,d]	Labeling[b,c,d]	Labeling[c,d]

a. Measures in each cell represent the most severe action that ought to be taken; in each case, this or any less-restrictive measures could be employed.

b. Severe measures justified only after less trade-intrusive measures have been tried and failed.

c. If international standards have been adopted, more serious restrictions might be justified.

d. Unilateral actions should be taken only under extraordinary circumstances.

References

Ackerman, Bruce, and William Hassler. 1981. *Clean Coal/Dirty Air*. New Haven: Yale University Press.

Ackerman, Bruce, and Richard B. Stewart. 1988. ''Reforming Environmental Law: The Democratic Case for Market Incentives.'' *Columbia Journal of Environmental Law* 13, no. 171.

Adede, A. O. 1992. ''International Environmental Law from Stockholm to Rio: An Overview of Past Lessons and Future Challenges.'' *Environmental Law and Policy* 22, no. 2.

Aman, Alfred C. Jr. 1993. ''The Earth as Eggshell Victim: A Global Perspective on Domestic Regulation.'' *Yale Law Journal* 102, no. 8 (June).

Anderson, Kym. 1992a. ''Agricultural Trade Liberalization and the Environment: a Global Perspective.'' *World Economy* 15, no. 1: 153–72.

Anderson, Kym. 1992b. ''Effects on the Environment and Welfare of Liberalizing World Trade: The Cases of Coal and Food.'' In Anderson and Blackhurst, *The Greening of World Trade Issues*. Ann Arbor: University of Michigan Press.

Anderson, Kym. 1992c. ''The Standard Welfare Economics of Policies Affecting Trade and the Environment.'' In Anderson and Blackhurst, *The Greening of World Trade Issues*. Ann Arbor: University of Michigan Press.

Anderson, Kym. 1993. *Economic Growth, Environmental Issues and Trade*. Centre for Economic Policy Research Discussion Paper 830. London: CEPR.

Anderson, Kym, and Richard Blackhurst, eds. 1992a. *The Greening of World Trade Issues*. Ann Arbor: University of Michigan Press.

Anderson, Kym, and Richard Blackhurst. 1992b. ''Trade, the Environment and Public Policy.'' In Anderson and Blackhurst, *The Greening of World Trade*. Ann Arbor: University of Michigan Press.

Anderson, Patrick. 1989. ''The Myth of Sustainable Logging: The Case for a Ban on Tropical Timber Imports.'' *The Ecologist* 19, no. 5: 166–8.

Arden-Clarke, Charles. 1991. *The GATT: Environmental Protection and Sustainable Development*. World Wide Fund for Nature Discussion Paper. Gland, Switzerland: WWF (June).

Arden-Clarke, Charles. 1992a. *South-North Terms of Trade, Environmental Protection and Sustainable Development*. World Wide Fund for Nature Discussion Paper. Gland, Switzerland: WWF.

Arden-Clarke, Charles. 1992b. *The GATT Report on Trade and the Environment: A Critique*. World Wide Fund for Nature Discussion Paper. Gland, Switzerland: WWF (March).

Arden-Clarke, Charles. 1993a. "An Action Agenda for Trade Policy Reform to Support Sustainable Development: A United Nations Conference on Environment and Development Follow-Up." In Durwood Zaelke, *Trade and the Environment: Law, Policy and Economics*. Washington: Island Press.

Arden-Clarke, Charles. 1993b. "Environment, Competitiveness, and Countervailing Measures." *OECD Papers on Competitiveness*. Paris: OECD.

Arnold, Frank. 1993. "Life Cycle Doesn't Work." *The Environmental Forum* 10, no. 5 (September/October): 18–23.

Austria, GATT Delegation. 1993. *Submission to EMIT Group*. Unpublished GATT Submission on GATT and International Environmental Agreements. GATT Doc TRE/W/19 (1 October). Geneva: Austrian GATT Mission. Reprinted in *Inside US Trade*, 15 October 1993.

Baker, Betsy. 1992. "Eliciting Non-Party Compliance with Multilateral Environmental Treaties: US Legislation and the Jurisdictional Bases for Compliance Incentives in the Montreal Ozone Protocol." *German Yearbook of International Law* 35.

Baker, Betsy. 1993. "Protection, Not Protectionism: Multilateral Environmental Agreements and the GATT." *Vanderbilt Journal of Transnational Law* 26, no. 3 (October).

Barcelo, John J. III. 1994. "Countervailing Against Environmental Subsidies." *Canadian Business Law Journal*. Forthcoming.

Barrett, Scott. 1990. "The Problem of Global Environmental Protection." *Oxford Review of Economic Policy* 6, no. 1.

Barrett, Scott. 1992. "Strategic Environmental Policy and International Trade." CSERGE Working Paper GEC 92–19. London: University College London and University of East Anglia.

Barrett, Scott. 1993. "Strategy and Environment." *Columbia Journal of World Business* 27 (Fall/Winter).

Batra, Ravi. 1993. *The Myth of Free Trade*. New York: Macmillan.

Baucus, Max. 1991. "Protecting the Global Commons: the Nexus between Trade and Environmental Policy." Speech delivered to the Institute for International Economics (30 October).

Baucus, Max. 1994. "From the Uruguay Round to the Green Round." Speech delivered to the Washington State Council on International Trade (13 January).

Baumol, William, and Wallace Oates. 1975. *The Theory of Environmental Policy*. Englewood Cliffs, NJ: Prentice-Hall.

Bayard, Thomas O., and Kimberly Ann Elliott. 1994. *Reciprocity and Retaliation in Trade Policies*. Washington: Institute for International Economics. Forthcoming.

Benedick, Richard. 1991. *Ozone Diplomacy: New Directions in Safeguarding the Planet*. Cambridge, MA: Harvard University Press.

Bennett, Graham, and Barbara Verhoeve. 1994. *Environmental Product Standards in Western Europe, the US and Japan: A Guidebook*. Arnhem, Netherlands: Institute for European Environmental Policy.

Bergsten, C. Fred. 1971. "Crisis in US Trade Policy." *Foreign Affairs* 49, no. 4 (July): 619–35.

Bergsten, C. Fred. 1990. "The World Economy After the Cold War" *Foreign Affairs* 69, no. 3 (Summer): 96–112.

Bergsten, C. Fred. 1992. "The Primacy of Economics." *Foreign Policy* 87 (Summer): 3–24.

Bergsten, C. Fred. 1993. "Trade Policy: Apocalypse Now?" *International Economic Insights* 4, no. 6 (November/December): 37–8.

Bergsten, C. Fred, and Edward M. Graham. 1994. *The Globalization of Industry and National Governments*. Washington: Institute for International Economics. Forthcoming.

Berlin, Isaiah. 1969. "Two Concepts of Liberty." In *Four Essays on Liberty*. London: Oxford University Press.

Berlin, Kenneth, and Jeffrey M. Lang. 1993. "Trade and the Environment." *The Washington Quarterly* 16, 4: 35–51.

Bhagwati, Jagdish. 1993a. "The Case for Free Trade." *Scientific American* (November): 42–9.

Bhagwati, Jagdish. 1993b. "The Demands to Reduce Domestic Diversity among Trading Nations." Unpublished paper developed for Ford Foundation project. New York: Columbia University.

Bhagwati, Jagdish. 1993c. "Trade and the Environment: The False Conflict?" In Durwood Zaelke, *Trade and the Environment: Law Economics and Policy*. Washington: Island Press.

Bhagwati, Jagdish, and Hugh T. Patrick, eds. 1990. *Aggressive Unilateralism: America's 301 Trade Policy and the World Trading System*. Ann Arbor: University of Michigan Press.

Bhagwati, Jagdish, and T. N. Srinivasan. 1993. "Trade and Environment: Does Environmental Diversity Detract from the Case for Free Trade?" Photocopy, Yale University.

BirdLife International. 1994. *The World Trade Organisation Environment Work Programme*. Special Report. Cambridge, UK: BirdLife International (March).

Birdsall, Nancy, and Andrew Steer. 1993. "Act Now on Global Warming—But Don't Cook the Books." *Finance & Development* (March): 6–8.

Black, Dorothy J. 1992. "International Trade v. Environmental Protection: The Case of the U.S. Embargo on Mexican Tuna." *Law and Policy in International Business* 24 (Fall): 123–56.

Blackhurst, Richard. 1992. "International Trade and Domestic Environmental Policies in a Growing World Economy." In Anderson and Blackhurst, *The Greening of World Trade*. Ann Arbor: University of Michigan Press.

Blackhurst, Richard, and Arvind Subramanian. 1992. In Anderson and Blackhurst, *The Greening of World Trade*. Ann Arbor: University of Michigan Press.

Blazejczak, Jürgen. 1993. "Environmental Policies and the Decision of Enterprises to Migrate." Paper prepared for OECD workshop on Environmental Policies and Industrial Competitiveness (28 January). Paris: Organization for Economic Cooperation and Development.

Bodansky, Daniel. 1991. "Scientific Uncertainty and the Precautionary Principle." *Environment* 33 (September).

Bonner, Raymond. 1993. "Crying Wolf Over Elephants." *New York Times Magazine* (7 February): 17

Botkin, Daniel. 1990. *Discordant Harmonies: A New Ecology for the Twenty-First Century*. New York: Oxford University Press.

Bowles, Ian A., and Glenn Prickett. 1994. *Reframing the Green Window: An Analysis of the GEF Pilot Phase Approach to Biodiversity and Global Warming and Recommendations for the Operational Phase*. Discussion Paper. Washington: Conservation International and the National Resources Defense Council.

Bramble, Barbara J., and Gareth Porter. 1992. "Non-Governmental Organizations and the Making of US International Environmental Policy." In Hurrell and Kingsbury, *The International Politics of the Environment*. New York: Oxford University Press.

Brandts, J., and C. de Bartolome. 1988. *Social Insurance and Population Uncertainty: Demographic Bias and Implications for Social Security*. C.V. Starr Center Economic Research Report #88–05 (February). New York: New York University.

Brisson, Inger. 1993. "Packaging Waste and the Environment: Economics and Policy." *Resources, Conservation and Recycling* 8: 183–292.

Brown, Lester R. 1988. *State of the World: 1988*. New York: W. W. Norton & Company.

Brown, Lester R. 1992. *State of the World: 1992*. New York: W. W. Norton & Company.

Brown, Lester R. 1993. *State of the World: 1993*. New York: W. W. Norton & Company.

Brown, Lester R. 1994. *State of the World: 1994*. New York: W. W. Norton & Company.

Brown, Lester R., Christopher Flavin, and Sandra Postel. 1991. *Saving the Planet: How to Shape an Environmentally Sustainable Global Economy*. New York: W. W. Norton & Company.

Brown, William. 1990. "Trade Deals a Blow to the Environment." *New Scientist* (10 November).

Brown Weiss, Edith. 1984. "The Planetary Trust: Conservation and Intergenerational Equity." *Ecology Law Journal* 2: 495.

Brown Weiss, Edith. 1989. *In Fairness to Future Generations: International Law, Common Patrimony, and Intergenerational Equity*. New York: Transnational Press.

Brown Weiss, Edith. 1992. "Environment and Trade as Partners in Sustainable Development." *American Journal of International Law* 86 (October): 700–35.

Brown Weiss, Edith. 1993a. "Environmentally Sustainable Competitiveness: A Comment." *Yale Law Journal* 102, 8 (May).

Brown Weiss, Edith. 1993b. "International Environmental Law: Contemporary Issues and the Emergence of a New World Order." *Georgetown University Law Journal* 81, no. 3 (March): 675.

Brown Weiss, Edith, Daniel Barstow Magraw, and Paul C. Szasz. 1992. *International Environmental Law: Basic Instruments and References*. New York: Transnational Publishers.

Buchanan, James, and Gordon Tullock. 1971. *The Calculus of Consent*. Ann Arbor: University of Michigan Press.

Cairncross, Frances. 1992. *Costing the Earth*. London: Business Books Ltd.

Cairncross, Frances. 1993. "An Analysis of Greening World Trade." Transcript of a recorded documentary for BBC Radio, tape no. TLN308/93VT1008.

Cameron, James, and Julie Abouchar. 1991. "The Precautionary Principle: A Fundamental Principle of Law and Policy for the Protection of the Global Environment." *Boston College International and Comparative Law Review* 14.

Cameron, James, Paul Demaret, and Damien Geradin, eds. 1994. *Trade and the Environment—The Search for Balance*. London: Camercon (May).

Canada, GATT Delegation. 1993. "Submission to GATT EMIT Group." Unpublished Submission on GATT and Trade and Environment Issues. GATT Doc TRE/12 (July). Geneva: Canadian GATT Mission.

Cannon, James S. 1990. *The Health Costs of Air Pollution: A Survey of the Studies Published 1984–89*. A report prepared for the American Lung Association. Washington: American Lung Association.

Carlin, Alan. 1990. *Environmental Investments: The Cost of a Clean Environment*. Environmental Protection Agency, Office of Policy, Planning and Evaluation Paper EPA-230-12-90-084. Washington: EPA (December).

Carlin, Alan. 1992. *The United States Experience with Economic Incentives to Control Environmental Pollution*. Report prepared for the EPA. Washington: EPA.

Carnegie Commission. 1993. *Risk and the Environment: Improving Regulatory Decision Making*. Report of the Commission. New York: Carnegie Commission (June).

Carraro, C. and D. Siniscalco. 1994. "Policy Coordination for Sustainability." In Goldin and Winters, *The Economics of Sustainable Development*. Cambridge, UK: Cambridge University Press. Forthcoming.

Caves, Richard, Jeffrey Frankel, and Ronald Jones. 1990. *World Trade and Payments: An Introduction*. London: Scott, Foresman.

Centre for Economic Policy Research (CEPR). 1993. *Making Sense of Subsidiarity: How Much Centralization for Europe?* London: CEPR.

Chapman, Duane. 1992. *Potential Impact on the US Economy and Selected Industries of the North American Free Trade Agreement*. Monograph SP 92–19. Cornell, NY: Cornell University Department of Agricultural, Resource, and Managerial Economics.

Charnovitz, Steve. 1991. "Exploring the Environmental Exceptions in GATT Article XX." *Journal of World Trade* 25, no. 5 (October).

Charnovitz, Steve. 1992a. "Reconsidering the Debate on GATT and the Environment." Paper presented at a conference on International Trade and Sustainable Development, Ottawa, Centre for Trade Policy and Law, Carleton University, 14 May.

Charnovitz, Steve. 1992b. "The Regulation of Environmental Standards By International Trade Agreements." *International Environmental Reporter* (25 August).

Charnovitz, Steve. 1992c. "GATT and the Environment: Examining the Issues." *International Environmental Affairs* 4, no. 3 (Summer).

Charnovitz, Steve. 1993a. "Achieving Environmental Goals Under International Rules." *Reciel* 2, no. 1: 45–52.

Charnovitz, Steve. 1993b. "The Environment vs. Trade Rules: Defogging the Debate." *Environmental Law* 23, no. 2: 475–517.

Charnovitz, Steve. 1993c. "Environmental Harmonization and Trade Policy." In Durwood Zaelke, *Trade and the Environment: Law, Policy and Economics*. Washington: Island Press.

Charnovitz, Steve. 1993d. "Environmental Trade Measures and Economic Competitiveness: An Overview of the Issues." Paper prepared for OECD Workshop on Environmental Policies and Industrial Competitiveness, Paris, 28 January.

Charnovitz, Steve. 1993e. "Environmental Trade Measures: Multilateral or Unilateral?" *Environmental Law and Policy* 23, no. 3.

Charnovitz, Steve. 1993f. "Environmentalism Confronts GATT Rules." *Journal of World Trade* 27, no. 2 (April): 37.

Charnovitz, Steve. 1993g. "NAFTA: An Analysis of its Environmental Provisions." *Environmental Law Reporter* 23: 10067.

Charnovitz, Steve. 1993h. "A Taxonomy of International Trade Measures." *Georgetown International Environmental Law Review* 6, no. 1 (Winter): 1.

Charnovitz, Steve. 1994a. "The Green Trade Debate." Overseas Development Council Policy Focus 1–94 (March). Washington: ODC.

Charnovitz, Steve. 1994b. "NAFTA's Social Dimension: Lessons from the Past and Framework for the Future." *International Trade Journal* 8, no. 1 (Spring): 39–72.

Charnovitz, Steve. 1994c. "Trade and the Environment: Four Schools of Thought." *Ecodecision* (January): 23–24.

Charnovitz, Steve. 1994d. "The World Trade Organization and Environmental Supervision." *International Environmental Reporter* 17, no. 2 (26 January): 89.

Charnovitz, Steve. 1994e. "No Time for NEPA: Trade Agreements on a Fast Track." *University of Minnesota Journal of Global Trade* (Summer). Forthcoming.

Chayes, Abram. 1991. "Managing the Transition to a Global Warming Regime, or What to do til the Treaty Comes." In *Greenhouse Warming: Negotiating a Global Regime*. Washington: World Resources Institute.

Chayes, Abram, and Antonia Handler Chayes. 1991. "Compliance Without Enforcement: State Behavior Under Regulatory Treaties." *Negotiation* 7, no. 311.

Clad, James C., and Roger D. Stone. 1993. "New Mission for Foreign Aid." *Foreign Affairs* 72, no. 1 (Winter): 197.

Clark, John, and Matthew B. Arnold. 1993. "The Danish Bottles Case: Commission of the European Communities v. Kingdom of Denmark." In *The Greening of World Trade*. EPA Report no. EPA 100-R-93-002. Washington: EPA.

Clark, John, and Scott Barrett. 1991. *The Danish Bottles Case*. London Business School Case Study. Washington: Management Institute for Environment and Business.

Cline, William R. 1992. *The Economics of Global Warming*. Washington: Institute for International Economics.

Cline, William R. 1993. "Give Greenhouse Abatement a Fair Chance." *Finance & Development* (March): 3–5.

Clinton, Bill. 1992. "Expanding Trade and Creating American Jobs." Speech by Governor Bill Clinton, North Carolina State University, Raleigh, NC (4 October).

Clinton, Bill. 1993. Speech by the President in NAFTA Bill Signing Ceremony. Mellon Auditorium, Washington (8 December).

Clough, Michael. 1994. "Grass-Roots Policymaking." *Foreign Affairs* 73, no. 1 (January/February): 2.

Coase, Ronald. 1960. "The Problem of Social Cost." *Journal of Law and Economics* 3.

Cobb, Joe. 1994. *A Guide to the New GATT Agreement*. Heritage Backgrounder Paper no. 985 (5 May). Washington: The Heritage Foundation.

Committee on Science, Engineering, and Public Policy, National Academy of Science. 1991. *Policy Implications of Greenhouse Warming*. Washington: National Academy Press.

Competitiveness Policy Council (CPC). 1992. *First Annual Report to the President & Congress*. Washington: CPC (March).

Congressional Budget Office (CBO). 1990. *Carbon Charges as a Response to Global Warming: the Effects of Taxing Fossil Fuels*. Washington: CBO (August).

Congressional Research Service (CRS). 1973. *A Legislative History of the Water Pollution Control Act Amendments of 1972*. Serial No. 93-1. Washington: CRS.

Cooper, Richard N. 1968. *The Economics of Interdependence: Economic Policy in the Atlantic Community*. New York: McGraw-Hill Book Company.

Cooper, Richard N. 1972. "Trade Policy is Foreign Policy." *Foreign Policy*, no. 9 (Winter): 18–37.

Cooper, Richard N. 1985. "International Economic Cooperation: Is It Desirable? Is It Likely?" *American Academy of Arts and Sciences Bulletin* 39, no. 2 (November): 11–35.

Cooper, Richard N. 1992. "United States Policy Towards the Global Environment." In Hurrell and Kingsbury, *The International Politics of the Environment*. New York: Oxford University Press.

Cowhey, Peter F., and Jonathan D. Aronson. 1993. "A New Trade Order." *Foreign Affairs* 72, no. 1 (Winter): 183.

Crookston, Peter. 1994. "The Shetland Islands, One Year After the Oil Spill." *Travel and Leisure* (February).

Cullen, Robert. 1993. "The True Cost of Coal." *Atlantic Monthly* (December): 38.

Cummings, Christopher A., and Matthew B. Arnold. 1993. "The Montreal Protocol Case." In *The Greening of World Trade*, EPA Report no. EPA-100-R-93-002. Washington: EPA.

Daly, Herman E. 1993. "The Perils of Free Trade." *Scientific American* (November): 51.

Daly, Herman E., and J. B. Cobb Jr. 1989. *For the Common Good*. Boston: Beacon Press.

Daly, Herman E., and Kenneth N. Townsend, eds. 1993. *Valuing the Earth: Economics, Ecology, Ethics*. Cambridge, MA: MIT Press.

Dasgupta, Partha. 1990. "The Environment as a Commodity." *Oxford Review of Economic Policy* 6, no. 1 (Spring): 51–67.

Davies, J. Clarence (Terry). 1970. *The Politics of Pollution*. New York: Pegasus.

Davies, J. Clarence (Terry). 1994. "Reforming Federal Environmental Laws." In William K. Reilly, *Environment Strategy America: 1994–1995*. London: Campden Publishers, Ltd.

Davis, Lester A. 1992. *U.S. Jobs Supported by Merchandise Exports*. US Department of Commerce, Economics and Statistics Administration. Research Series OMA-1-92 (April). Washington: Department of Commerce.

Davison, Ann. 1993. "Changing Western Consumer Lifestyle." Paper presented at conference on Striking a Green Deal, Brussels, European Parliament (7–9 November).

Dawkins, Kristin. 1994. "Balancing: Policies for Just and Sustainable Trade." Institute Paper. Minneapolis: Institute for Agriculture and Trade Policy.

Day, David. 1987. *The Whale War*. San Francisco: Sierra Club Books.

Dean, J. M. 1992. "Trade and the Environment: A Survey of the Literature." In Patrick Low, *International Trade and the Environment*. World Bank Discussion Paper 159. Washington: World Bank.

Demaret, Paul. 1993. "Environmental Policy: The Emergence of Trade-Related Environmental Measures (TREMs) in the External Relations of the European Community." In M. Maresceau, *The European Community's Commercial Policy after 1992: The Legal Dimension*. Norwell, MA: Kluwer Publishers.

Destler, I. M. 1992. *American Trade Politics: Systems Under Stress*. 2nd ed. Washington: Institute for International Economics.

Diamond, Peter. 1977. "A Framework for Social Security Analysis." *Journal of Public Economics* (December).

Diamond, Peter, and Michael Rothschild, eds. 1978. *Uncertainty in Economics*. New York: Academic Press.

Diebold, William Jr. 1952. *The End of the I.T.O.* Essays in International Finance 16. Princeton: International Finance Section, Princeton University (October).

Diwan, Ishac, and Nemat Shafik. 1992. "Investment, Technology and the Global Environment: Towards International Agreement in a World of Disparities." In Patrick Low, *International Trade and the Environment*. World Bank Discussion Paper 159. Washington: World Bank.

Dixit, Avinash, and Barry Nalebuff. 1991. *Thinking Strategically*. New York: W. W. Norton.

Dixon, R. K., S. Brown, R. A. Haughton, A. M. Solomon, M. C. Trexler, and J. Wisniewski. 1994. "Carbon Pools and Flux of Global Forest Ecosystems." *Science* 263 (14 January): 185–90.

Dornbusch, Rudiger, and James M. Poterba, eds. 1991. *Global Warming: Economic Policy Responses*. Cambridge, MA: MIT Press.

Dower, Roger C., and Mary Beth Zimmerson. 1992. *The Right Climate for Carbon Taxes: Creating Economic Incentives to Protect the Atmosphere*. World Resources Institute Report. Washington: WRI (August).

Downs, Anthony. 1957. *An Economic Theory of Democracy*. New York: Harper & Row.

Drucker, Peter. 1994. "Trade Lessons from the World Economy." *Foreign Affairs* 73, no. 1 (January/February): 99.

Dubos, René. 1981. *Celebrations of Life*. New York: McGraw-Hill.

Dunoff, Jeffrey L. 1992. "Reconciling International Trade with Preservation of the Global Commons: Can We Prosper and Protect?" *Washington and Lee Law Review* 49, no. 4 (Fall): 1407–54.

Dunoff, Jeffrey L. 1994. "Institutional Misfits: The GATT, the ICJ, and trade/environment disputes." *Michigan Journal of International Law* 15, no. 4. Forthcoming.

Durning, Alan Thein. 1993. *Saving the Forests: What Will It Take?* Worldwatch Paper 117. Washington: Worldwatch Institute (December).

Edelman, Paul S. 1990. "The Oil Pollution Act of 1990." *New York Law Journal*, 7 September, 3.

Eglin, Richard. 1993a. "GATT and Environment." *Ecodecision* (March).

Eglin, Richard. 1993b. "International Economics, International Trade, International Environmental Protection." *Wirtschaftspolitische Blatter* 4, no. 3.

Eglin, Richard. 1993c. "International Trade and the Environment." Unpublished paper presented at University of Fribourg conference on International Trade and the Environment (May).

Ehrlich, Paul. [1968] 1972. *The Population Bomb*. New York: Ballantine Books.

El-Ashry, Mohamed. 1993. "Funding for Global Environmental Concerns." *Ecodecision* (March).

Elliott, E. Donald, Bruce A. Ackerman, and John C. Millian. 1985. "Toward a Theory of Statutory Evolution: The Federalization of Environmental Law." *Journal of Law Economics and Organization* 1, no. 2 (Fall).

Emerson, Peter M., and Alan C. Nessman. 1994. *Integrating Environmental Protection and North American Free Trade*. Paper prepared for Australian Agricultural Economics Society 38th Annual Conference, Victoria University, Wellington, New Zealand, 7–11 February. Available from Environmental Defense Fund (EDF), Austin, Texas.

Engel, Ronald, and Joan Gibb Engel, eds. 1990. *Ethics of Environment and Development*. Tuscon: University of Arizona Press.

Environment Canada. 1992. *North American Free Trade Agreement: Canadian Environmental Review*. Canadian Government Report. Ottawa: Environment Canada (October).

Environmental Protection Agency (EPA). 1987. *Reducing Risk*. Washington: EPA.

Environmental Protection Agency (EPA). 1990a. *Environmental Investments: The Cost of a Clean Environment*. Washington: EPA.

Environmental Protection Agency (EPA). 1990b. *Reducing Risk: Setting Priorities and Strategies for Environmental Protection*. EPA Science Advisory Board. Washington: EPA.

Environmental Protection Agency (EPA). 1991a. "Integrated Environmental Plan For The Mexico-U.S. Border Area." Working draft. Washington: EPA (1 August).

Environmental Protection Agency (EPA). 1991b. *Permitting and Compliance Policy: Barriers to US Environmental Technology Innovation*. Report and Recommendations of the Technology Innovation and Economics Committee. Doc. no. EPA 101/N-91/001. Washington: EPA (January).

Environmental Protection Agency (EPA). 1992. *Improving Technology Diffusion for Environmental Protection*. Report and Recommendations of the Technology and Economics Committee. Doc. no. EPA 130-R-92-001. Washington: EPA.

Environmental Protection Agency (EPA). 1993a. *Regulatory Impact Analysis*. Stratospheric Protection Division Report. Washington: EPA.

Environmental Protection Agency (EPA). 1993b. *Transforming Environmental Permitting and Compliance Policies to Promote Pollution Prevention: Removing Barriers and Providing Incentives to Foster Technology Innovation, Economic Productivity, and Environmental Protection*. Report and Recommendations of the Technology Innovation and Economics Committee. Doc. no. EPA 100-R-93-004. Washington: EPA.

Esty, Daniel C. 1993a. "Integrating Trade and Environmental Policymaking: First Steps in the NAFTA." In Durwood Zaelke, *Trade and the Environment: Law, Economics and Policy*. Washington: Island Press.

Esty, Daniel C. 1993b. "Rio Revisited: Turning the Giant's Head." *Ecodecision* (September): 90–91.

Esty, Daniel C. 1993c. "GATTing the Greens: Not Just Greening the GATT." *Foreign Affairs* 72 no. 5 (November–December).

Esty, Daniel C. 1994a. "Making Trade and Environmental Policies Work Together." *Aussenwirtschaft* [Swiss Review of International Economic Relations] (April).

Esty, Daniel C. 1994b. "Toward a Greener GATT." *International Economic Insights* 5, no. 2 (March/April): 17–20.

Esty, Daniel C., and Jamison Koehler. 1993. *Restructuring the Global Environment Facility*. Overseas Development Council Policy Focus Papers 1. Washington: ODC.

European Community. 1992a. "Proposal for Directive on the Introduction of a Tax on Carbon Dioxide Emissions and Energy." Com(92)226. *The Official Journal of the European Community* C196 (3 August).

European Community. 1992b. "Submission to EMIT Group." Unpublished GATT Submission to the EMIT Group. GATT Doc. TRE/W/5 (17 November). Geneva: EU GATT Mission.

European Community. 1992c. *Report of the Committee on External Relations on Environment and Trade*. European Parliament Doc. A3-0329/92 (3 November). Brussels: European Union.

European Community. 1993. "Growth, Competitiveness, Employment: The Challenges and Ways Forward into the 21st Century." Commission of the European Communities White Paper COM(93) 700 Final (December). Brussels: European Union.

European Parliament. 1994. "Opinion of the Committee on the Environment, Public Health and Consumer Protection for the Committee on External Economic Relations on Recommendations of the European Parliament to the Commission Concerning the Negotiations in the Trade Negotiations Committee of GATT on an Agreement on a Trade and Environment Work Programme." EU Doc. PE 208.088/fin (23 February).

Executive Office of the President. 1993. "Climate Change Action Plan." Presidential report, available in reprinted form from the US Department of Energy.

Feketekuty, Geza. 1993. "The Link Between Trade and Environmental Policy." *Minnesota Journal of Global Trade* no. 2 (Summer): 171–205.

Fishbein, Bette K. 1994. *Germany, Garbage, and the Green Dot: Challenging the Throwaway Society*. New York: Inform, Inc.

Fletcher, Susan, and Mary Tiemann. 1992. *Environment and Trade*. Congressional Research Service Report to Congress no. IB92006. Washington: Congressional Research Service, Environment and Natural Resources Policy Division.

Folke, Carl, ed. 1994. *International Trade and Environment*. Special Issue of *Ecological Economics* 9, no. 1 (February).

France, Ministry of Cooperation. 1993. "Vers un Eco-Label des Bois Tropicaux." Communiqué (12 May).

French, Hilary F. 1991. "The EC: Environmental Proving Ground." *Worldwatch* (November/December): 26–33.

French, Hilary F. 1992. *After the Earth Summit: The Future of Environmental Governance*. Worldwatch Paper 107. Washington: Worldwatch Institute (March).

French, Hilary F. 1993a. *Costly Tradeoffs: Reconciling Trade and the Environment*. Worldwatch Paper 113. Washington: Worldwatch Institute (March).

French, Hilary F. 1993b. "The GATT: Menace or Ally?" *World Watch* (September/October).

Frey, Bruno S. 1984. "Public Choice and Global Politics." *International Organization* 38, no. 1 (Winter): 199–223.

Froman, Michael B. 1989. "International Trade: The United States–European Community Hormone Treated Beef Conflict." *Harvard International Law Journal* 30, no. 2 (Spring): 549–56.

Gallup International Institute. 1992. "The Health of the Planet Survey." Washington: Gallup International Institute (May).

Gaines, Sanford. 1991. "The Polluter-Pays Principle: From Economic Equity to Environmental Ethos." *Texas International Law Journal* 26, no. 3 (Summer).

Gardner, Richard N. 1992. *Negotiating Survival: Four Priorities after Rio*. New York: Council on Foreign Relations.

General Agreement on Trade and Tariffs Secretariat. 1990. "Brussels Draft." GATT Document MTN.TNC/W/35/Rev. 1. Geneva.

General Agreement on Trade and Tariffs Secretariat. 1992a. "Dunkel Text." GATT Document MTN.TNC/W/FA. Geneva.

General Agreement on Trade and Tariffs Secretariat. 1992b. *International Trade 1990–91*, vol. 1. Geneva.

General Agreement on Trade and Tariffs Secretariat. 1992c. *Trade and Environment Report*. Geneva.

General Agreement on Trade and Tariffs Secretariat. 1993a. *GATT Analytical Index: 1993*. Geneva.

General Agreement on Trade and Tariffs Secretariat. 1993b. "Final Act Embodying the Results of the Uruguay Round of Multilateral Trade Agreements." GATT Document MTN/FA. Geneva.

General Agreement on Trade and Tariffs Secretariat. 1994. *Trade and Environment: Final Uruguay Round Ministerial Decision*. Forthcoming GATT Document. Geneva.

General Accounting Office (GAO). 1990. *Report on the Furniture Finishing Industry*. Washington: GAO.

General Accounting Office (GAO). 1992. *Environmental Protection Issues*. Washington: GAO.

General Accounting Office (GAO). 1993. *Pesticides: A Comparative Study of Industrialized Nations' Regulatory Systems*. Report GAO/PEMD-93-17. Washington: GAO.

Gephardt, Richard A. 1992. Address on the status of the North American Free Trade Agreement before the Institute for International Economics (27 July).

Geradin, Damien. 1993a. "Free Trade and Environmental Protection in an Integrated Market: A Survey of the Case Law of the United States Supreme Court and the European Court of Justice." *Florida State University Journal of Transnational Law and Policy* 2 (Summer): 141–97.

Geradin, Damien. 1993b. "Trade and Environmental Protection: Community Harmonization and National Environmental Standards." *Yearbook of European Law* 13.

German Chamber of Industry and Commerce in the United Kingdom. 1992. *The New German Packaging Law*. Seminar Papers. London: German Chamber (13 July).

Gibson, J. Eugene, and William J. Schrenk. 1991. "The Enterprise for the Americas Initiative: A Second Generation of Debt-for-Nature Exchanges—With an Overview of

Other Recent Exchange Initiatives." *George Washington Journal of International Law and Economics* 25, no. 1.

Goldin, Ian, and Alan Winters, eds. 1994. *The Economics of Sustainable Development*. Cambridge, UK: Cambridge University Press. Forthcoming.

Goldman, Patti. 1992a. "The Legal Effects of Trade Agreements on Domestic Health and Environmental Regulations." *Journal of Environmental Law and Litigation* 7: 11–56.

Goldman, Patti. 1992b. "Resolving the Trade and Environment Debate: In Search of a Neutral Forum and Neutral Principles." *Washington and Lee Law Review* 49, no. 4 (Fall): 1279–98.

Goldman, Patti, and Richard Wiles. 1994. *Trading Away US Food Safety*. Occasional Report (12 April). Washington: Public Citizen.

Goodland, Robert. 1992. "The Case that the World Has Reached Limits." In Goodland et al., *Environmentally Sustainable Development: Building on Brundtland*. Paris: United Nations Educational, Scientific and Cultural Organization.

Goodland, Robert, Herman Daly, Salah El Serafy, and Bernd Von Droste. 1992. *Environmentally Sustainable Development: Building on Brundtland*. Paris: United Nations Educational, Scientific and Cultural Organization.

Gore, Albert Jr. 1992. *Earth in the Balance: Ecology and the Human Spirit*. Boston: Houghton Mifflin.

Goulet, Denis. 1990. "Development Ethics and Ecological Wisdom." In Engel and Engel, *Ethics of Environment and Development*. London: Belhaven Press.

Graham, Edward. 1993. "Multinational Enterprise and Competition Policy." *International Economic Insights* 4, no. 4 (July/August).

Gray, Wayne B., and Ronald J. Shadbegian. 1993. *Environmental Regulation and Manufacturing Productivity at the Plant Level*. National Bureau of Economic Research Working Paper No. 4321. Cambridge, MA: NBER (April).

Gregory, Michael. 1992. "Environment, Sustainable Development, Public Participation and the NAFTA: A Retrospective." *Journal of Environmental Law and Litigation* 7: 99–173.

Greve, Michael S., and Fred L. Smith, eds. 1992. *Environmental Politics: Public Costs, Private Rewards*. New York: Praeger.

Grossman, Gene M., and Alan B. Krueger. 1993. "Environmental Impacts of a North American Free Trade Agreement." In Peter M. Garber, *The Mexico-US Free Trade Agreement*. Cambridge, MA: MIT Press.

Grunwald, Joseph, and Kenneth Flamm. 1985. *The Global Factory: Foreign Assembly in International Trade*. Washington: Brookings Institute.

Gwin, Catherine, and Lisa Bates. 1993. *The Potential of the IDA-10*. Overseas Development Council Policy Focus 1993-02. Washington: ODC.

Haas, Peter M., Robert O. Keohane, and Marc A. Levy, eds. 1993. *Institutions for the Earth: Sources of Effective International Environmental Protection*. Cambridge, MA: MIT Press.

Hahn, Robert W. 1993. "Toward a New Environmental Paradigm." *Yale Law Journal* 102: 1719.

Hahn, Robert W., and Kenneth R. Richards. 1989. "The Internationalization of Environmental Regulation." *Harvard International Law Journal* 30, no. 2 (Spring): 421–46.

Hahn, Robert W., and Robert N. Stavins. 1992. "Economic Incentives for Environmental Protection: Integrating Theory and Practice." *AEA Papers and Proceedings* 82, no. 2: 464–67. Washington: American Economic Association (May).

Haigh, Nigel, and Frances Irwin. 1990. *Integrated Pollution Control in Europe and North America*. Washington: The Conservation Foundation.

Hajost, Scott. 1990. "The Challenge to International Law and Institutions." *EPA Journal* 16, no. 4 (July/August): 23–24.

Handl, G. 1991. "Environmental Security and Global Change: The Challenge to International Law." *Yearbook of International Law* 1: 3–33.

Hardin, Garrett. 1968. "The Tragedy of the Commons." *Science* 162: 1243–48.

Harvard Law Review. 1974. "State Environmental Legislation." *Harvard Law Review* 87, no. 8 (June): 1762–85.

Harwell, Christine C., Rexene Hanes, Miguel Acevedo, Mark A. Harwell, and Andrés Serbín. 1994. *Free Trade and The Environment: A Prospective Analysis and Case Study of Venezuela*. Miami: University of Miami North-South Center.

Hauser, Heinz, and Madeleine Hösli. 1991. "Harmonization or Regulatory Competition in the EC (and the EEA)?" *Aussenwirtschaft* 46 (October): 269.

Hernandez, Maria Christina. 1993. "Green Protectionism: Does the End Justify the Means?" Paper presented at conference on Striking a Green Deal, Brussels, European Parliament, 7–9 November.

Hittle, Alex. 1992. "Trade and the Environment at an Impasse." *The Environmental Forum* 9, no. 4: 26.

Hoel, Michael. 1991. "Global Environmental Problems: The Effects of Unilateral Actions Taken by One Country." *Journal of Environmental Economics and Management*, 20, no. 1 (January): 55–70.

Hoffman, Stanley. 1978. *Primacy or World Order?* New York: McGraw-Hill.

Hoffman, Stanley. 1990. "The Case for Leadership." *Foreign Policy* 81: 20.

Housman, Robert. 1992. "A Kantian Approach to Trade and the Environment." *Washington and Lee Law Review*, 49, no. 4: 1373–88.

Housman, Robert. 1994. *Reconciling Trade and the Environment: Lessons from the North American Free Trade Agreement*. Environment and Trade Series Paper No. 3. Geneva: United Nations Environment Programme (UNEP).

Housman, Robert, Paul Orbuch, and William Snape. 1993. "Enforcement of Environmental Laws Under a Supplemental Agreement to the North American Free Trade Agreement." *Georgetown International Environmental Law Review* 5, no. 3 (Summer): 593–622.

Housman, Robert, and Durwood Zaelke. 1992a. *Trade, Environment, and Sustainable Development: A Primer*. CIEL-US Environmental Law Paper. Washington: Center for International Environmental Law (February).

Housman, Robert, and Durwood Zaelke. 1992b. "The Collision of the Environment and Trade: The GATT Tuna/Dolphin Decision." *Environmental Law Reporter* (April).

Hudec, Robert. 1975. *The GATT Legal System and World Trade Diplomacy*. New York: Praeger Publishers.

Hudec, Robert. 1989. "Thinking About the New Section 301: Beyond Good and Evil." In Jagdish Bhagwati, *Aggressive Unilateralism: America's 301 Trade Policy and the World Trade System*. Ann Arbor: University of Michigan Press.

Hudec, Robert. 1993. "Circumventing Democracy: The Political Morality of Trade Negotiations." *New York University Journal of International Law and Politics* 25, no. 2 (September/October): 401–12.

Hudson, Stuart. 1992. "Trade, Environment and the Pursuit of Sustainable Development." In Patrick Low, *International Trade and the Environment*. Washington: The World Bank.

Hudson, Stuart. 1993. "North American Free Trade Agreement." *Ecodecision* (March).

Hudson, Stuart, and Rodrigo J. Prudencio. 1993. *The North American Commission on Environment and Other Supplemental Environmental Agreements: Part II of the NAFTA Package*. Discussion Paper. Washington: National Wildlife Foundation (4 February).

Hufbauer, Gary Clyde. 1989. "Beyond GATT." *Foreign Policy* 77: 64.

Hufbauer, Gary Clyde, and Kimberly Ann Elliott. 1994. *Measuring the Costs of Protection in the United States*. Washington: Institute for International Economics.

Hufbauer, Gary Clyde, and Jeffrey J. Schott. 1992. *North American Free Trade: Issues and Recommendations*. Washington: Institute for International Economics.

Hufbauer, Gary Clyde, Jeffrey J. Schott, and Kimberly Ann Elliott. 1990. *Economic Sanctions Reconsidered*. Washington: Institute for International Economics.

Hufbauer, Gary, and Joanna Shelton Erb. 1984. *Subsidies in International Trade*. Washington: Institute for International Economics.

Hurrell, Andrew, and Benedict Kingsbury, eds. 1992. *The International Politics of the Environment*. Oxford: Clarendon Press.

Hyland, William G. 1988. "Setting Global Priorities." *Foreign Policy* 73: 22.

Iglesias, Enrique V. 1992. "The Delicate Balance between Environment and Development: The Latin American Experience." In Üner Kirdar, *Change: Threat or Opportunity?* New York: United Nations Publications.

Ikegawa, Jima. 1993. "NAFTA: How Will It Affect U.S. Environmental Regulations?" *The Transnational Lawyer* 6, no. 1: 225–53.

Industry Cooperative for Ozone Layer Protection (ICOLP). 1993. "Environmental Technology Cooperative Projects: Some Operating Guidelines." Washington: ICOLP.

Inman, B. R., and Daniel F. Burton Jr. 1990. "Technology and Competitiveness." *Foreign Affairs* 69, no. 2: 116.

Intergovernmental Panel on Climate Change (IPCC). 1990. *Scientific Assessment of Climate Change*. New York: World Meteorological Organization and United Nations Environment Programme.

International Development Association (IDA). 1993. "Investing in the Future." Report on the status of programs. Washington: World Bank (IDA).

International Institute for Sustainable Development. 1994. *Trade and Sustainable Development Principles*. Winnipeg: IISD.

Irwin, Frances H. 1992. "An Integrated Framework for Preventing Pollution and Protecting the Environment." *Environmental Law* 22, no. 1.

Jackson, John. 1969. *World Trade and the Law of GATT*. New York: Bobbs-Merrill Co.

Jackson, John. 1990. *Restructuring the GATT System*. London: Royal Institute of International Affairs.

Jackson, John. 1992a. "World Trade Rules and Environmental Policies: Congruence or Conflict?" *Washington and Lee Law* Review 49, no. 4 (Fall): 1227–78.

Jackson, John. 1992b. *The World Trading System: Law and Policy of International Economic Relations*. Cambridge MA: MIT Press.

Jackson, John. 1993. "Changing GATT Rules." In Environmental Protection Agency, *The Greening of World Trade*. Washington: EPA (February).

Jaffe, Adam B., Steven Peterson, Paul R. Portney, and Robert N. Stavins. 1994. *Environmental Regulation and International Competitiveness: What Does the Evidence Tell Us?* Resources for the Future Discussion Paper 94-08. Washington: RFF.

Japan. 1994. Report by Ambassador Ukawa (Japan), chairman of the Group on Environmental Measures and International Trade, to the 49th Session of the Contracting Parties. Geneva: General Agreement on Trade and Tariffs Secretariat.

Johnson, Pierre Marc, and Andre Beaulieu. 1994. "NAFTA's Green Opportunities." *Journal of Environmental Law and Practice* 1, no. 5 (March/April): 5–15.

Johnstone, John W. 1994. "Superfund Makes Strange Bedfellows." *Eco* (January).

Kalt, Joseph. 1988. "The Impact of Domestic Environmental Regulatory Policies on US International Competitiveness." In A. Michael Spence and Heather A. Hazard, *International Competitiveness*. Cambridge, MA: Ballinger Publishing Company.

Kelly, Katherine M. 1992. "Declaring War on the Environment: The Failure of International Environmental Treaties During the Persian Gulf War." *American University Journal of International Law and Policy* 881: 921.

Kennedy, Paul. 1993. "*Preparing for the Twenty-First Century: Winners and Losers.*" The New York Review of Books (11 February): 33–44.

Khor, Martin. 1994. *Trade and Environment: A Conceptual Note*. Third World Network Paper. Penang: TWN.

Kimble, Lee A. 1992. *Forging International Agreement: Strengthening Inter-governmental Institutions for Environment and Development*. World Resources Institute report. Washington: WRI.

Kindleberger, Charles. 1981. "Dominance and Leadership in the International Economy—Exploitation, Public Goods and Free Riders." *International Studies Quarterly* 25.

Kirdar, Üner, ed. 1992. *Change: Threat or Opportunity?* New York: United Nations Publications.

Kirgis, F. L. 1972. "Effective Pollution Control in Industrialized Countries: International Economic Disincentives, Policy Responses, and the GATT." *Michigan Law Review* 70: 901.

Kirton, John, and Sarah Richardson. 1992. *Trade, Environment and Competitiveness.* Ottawa: National Round Table on the Environment and the Economy.

Kisiri, Marwa J. 1992. "International Trade and Environment: An Additional Non-Tariff Barrier Against the Developing Countries' Trade?" *World Competition* 16, no. 1.

Klabbers, Jan. 1992. "Jurisprudence in International Trade Law: Article XX of GATT." *Journal of World Trade* 26, no. 2: 63–94.

Komoroski, Kenneth S. 1988. "The Failure of Governments to Regulate Industry: A Subsidy Under the GATT?" *Houston Journal of International Law* 10: 189.

Kopp, R. J., P. R. Portney, and D. E. DeWitt. 1991. *International Comparisons of Environmental Regulation.* Discussion Paper. Washington: Resources for the Future.

Kox, Henk. 1992. "The Non-Polluter Gets Paid Principle for Third World Commodity Exports." *European Journal of Development Research* 3, no. 1.

Kox, Henk. 1993. "International Agreements to Deal with Environmental Externalities of Primary Commodity Exports." Paper presented at conference on Striking a Green Deal, Brussels, European Parliament, 7–9 November.

Kozloff, Keith Lee, and Roger C. Dower. 1993. *A New Power Base: Renewable Energy Policies for the Nineties and Beyond.* Washington: World Resources Institute.

Kromarek, Pascale. 1990. "Environmental Protection and the Free Movement of Goods: The Danish Bottles Case." *Journal of Environmental Law* 2, no. 1: 89–107.

Krugman, Paul R. 1994. "A Dangerous Obsession." *Foreign Affairs* 73, no. 2 (March/April): 28–44.

Krugman, Paul R., and Maurice Obstfeld. 1991. *International Economics.* New York: Harper-Collins.

Lal, Deepak. 1993. "Trade Blocs and Multilateral Free Trade." *Journal of Common Market Studies* 31, no. 3 (September): 349–58.

Lallas, Peter L. 1993. "NAFTA and Evolving Approaches to Identify and Address 'Indirect' Environmental Impacts of International Trade." *Georgetown International Environmental Law Review* 5, no. 3 (Summer).

Lallas, Peter L., Daniel C. Esty, and David J. Van Hoogstraten. 1992. "Environmental Protection and International Trade: Toward Mutually Supportive Rules and Policies." *The Harvard Environmental Law Review* 16, no. 2 (Fall).

Lalonde, Brice. 1993. *Pour Une Injection Écologique dans les Règles du Commerce International.* Report to the prime minister on international commerce and protection of the environment. Paris: Ministry of the Environment (December).

Lang, Tim, and Colin Hines. 1993. *The New Protectionism.* New York: The New Press.

Lang, Winfried. 1993. "International Environmental Agreements and the GATT: The Case of the Montreal Protocol." *Wirtschaftspolitische Blätter* 3, no. 4.

Lardy, Nicholas R. 1994. *China in the World Economy.* Washington: Institute for International Economics.

Lee, Thea. 1992. "NAFTA and the Environment: A Critique of Grossman and Krueger." Background Reading for Trade and Environment Workshop of the Center for International Environmental Law and The Pew Charitable Trusts, 30 October.

Leonard, H. Jeffrey. 1988. *Pollution and the Struggle for the World Product.* Cambridge, UK: Cambridge University Press.

Leonard, H. Jeffrey. 1989. *Environment and the Poor: Development Strategies for a Common Agenda.* US-Third World Policy Perspectives, no. 11. Washington: Overseas Development Council.

Levien, Lawrence David. 1972. "A Structural Model for a World Environmental Organization: The ILO Experience." *George Washington Law Review* 40: 464.

Linneman, H., H. L. M. Kox, C. M. van der Tak, and A. P. M. de Vries. 1993. *Preliminary Conditions for International Commodity-Related Environmental Agreements: Results of a Pre-Feasibility Study.* Free University of Amsterdam Monograph (January).

Lipstein, Robert. 1993. "It's Time to Dump the Dumping Laws." *International Economic Insights* (November/December).

London, Caroline. 1993a. "Environnement et GATT." *Ecodecision* (March).

London, Caroline. 1993b. *Environnement et Stratégie de l'Entreprise.* Rennes, France: Collection Ecoplanete, Editions Apogée.

Lönngren, Rune. 1992. *International Approaches to Chemicals Control: An Historical Overview.* Stockholm: Chemicals Inspectorate of Sweden.

Low, Patrick, ed. 1992. *International Trade and the Environment.* World Bank Discussion Paper 159. Washington: World Bank.

Low, Patrick. 1993a. "Trade and the Environment: What Worries the Developing Countries?" *Environmental Law* 23, no. 2.

Low, Patrick. 1993b. *Trading Free: The GATT and U.S. Trade Policy.* New York: The Twentieth Century Fund.

Low, Patrick, and Alexander Yeats. 1992. "Do Dirty Industries Migrate?" In Patrick Low, *International Trade and the Environment.* World Bank Discussion Paper 159. Washington: World Bank.

Lowi, Theodore. 1969. *The End of Liberalism: Ideology, Policy and the Crisis of Public Authority.* New York: Norton & Co.

Lucas, R. E. B., D. Wheeler, and H. Hettige. 1992. "Economic Development, Environmental Regulation and the International Migration of Toxic Industrial Pollution: 1960–1988." In Patrick Low, *International Trade and the Environment.* World Bank Discussion Paper 159. Washington: World Bank.

MacNeill, Jim, Pieter Winsemius, and Taizo Yakushiji. 1991. *Beyond Interdependence: The Meshing of the World's Economy and the Earth Ecology.* New York: Oxford University Press.

MacKenzie, James J., Roger C. Downs, and Donald D. T. Chen. 1992. *The Going Rate: What it Really Costs to Drive.* World Resources Institute Report. Washington: WRI (June).

Magraw, David. 1994. "Environment and Trade: Talking Across Cultures." *Environment* (March).

Mahathir bin Mohamad, Honorable Dr. Datuk Seri (Prime Minister of Malaysia). 1992. Speech given at UN Conference on Environment and Development, Rio de Janeiro 13 June.

Mani, Muthukumara S. 1993. "The Impact of Trade Policy on the Environment." Unpublished Paper. College Park, MD: University of Maryland, Department of Economics.

Margulies, Rebecca L. 1993. "Protecting Biodiversity: Recognizing International Intellectual Property Rights in Plant Genetic Resources." *Michigan Journal of International Law* 14, no. 2 (Winter): 322.

Mashaw, Jerry L. 1989. "The Economics of Politics and the Understanding of Public Law." *Chicago-Kent Law Review* 65, no. 123.

Mathews, Jessica Tuchman. 1989. "Redefining Security." *Foreign Affairs* 68, no. 2: 162.

Mathews, Jessica Tuchman. 1991. *Preserving the Global Environment: The Challenge of Shared Leadership.* New York. Norton.

Mayhew, David. 1974. *Congress: The Electoral Connection.* New Haven: Yale University Press.

McKibben, Bill. 1989. *The End of Nature.* New York: Random House.

McKinsey and Company. 1991. *The Corporate Response to the Environmental Challenge.* New York: McKinsey & Co.

Mead, Walter Russell. 1992. "Bushism Found." *Harper's* 285 (September): 37–45.

Meadows, Donella H. 1972. *The Limits to Growth.* New York: Universe Books.

Mendelsohn, Robert, William D. Nordhaus, and Daigee Shaw. 1992. *The Impact of Climate on Agriculture: A Ricardian Approach.* Cowles Foundation Discussion Paper No. 1010 (5

February). New Haven: Cowles Foundation for Research in Economics at Yale University.

Mensink, Rens. 1991. "The Role of UNCTAD in Relation to Environment and Trade." Paper prepared for the International Working Group on Environment and Trade on the Future of UNCTAD. Washington: Environment and Development Resource Centre (November).

Meyer, Carrie A. 1993. *Environmental and Natural Resource Accounting: Where to Begin?* World Resources Institute Issues in Development Paper. Washington: WRI (November).

Mhlanga, Liberty. 1993. "Concerns of Less Developed Countries." In Williamson, *Agriculture, the Environment, and Trade: Conflict or Cooperation?* Washington: International Policy Council on Agriculture and Trade.

Miller, Marcus, and Lei Zhang. 1994. "A Discussion of Carraro and Siniscalco's *Policy Coordination for Sustainability*." In Goldin and Winters, *The Economics of Sustainable Development*. Cambridge, UK: Cambridge University Press.

Mintzer, Irving M., ed. 1992. *Confronting Climate Change: Risks, Implications and Responses*. Cambridge, U.K.: Cambridge University Press.

von Moltke, Konrad. 1992. "Free Trade and Mutual Tariffs: A Practical Approach to Sustainable Development." *Ecodecision* (June).

von Moltke, Konrad. 1993. "Dispute Resolution and Transparency." In *The Greening of World Trade*. Pub. No. EPA 100-R-93-002. Washington: EPA.

Moore, Curtis, and Alan Miller. 1994. *Green Gold: Japan, Germany, the United States and the Race for Environmental Technology*. Boston: Beacon Press.

Moran, Theodore H. 1990. "International Economics and Security." *Foreign Affairs* 69, no. 5: 74.

Moss, Ambler. 1993. "Global Trade as a Way to Integrate Environmental Protection and Sustainable Development." *Environmental Law* 23, no. 2.

Myers, Norman. 1989. "Environment and Security." *Foreign Policy* 74: 23.

Myers, Norman. 1992. "The Anatomy of Environmental Action: The Case of Tropical Deforestation." In Hurrell and Kingsbury, *The International Politics of the Environment*. New York: Oxford University Press.

National Academy of Sciences. 1991. *Policy Implications of Global Warming*. Washington: National Academy Press.

National Commission on the Environment. 1993. *Choosing a Sustainable Future* (The Train Commission Report). Washington: Island Press.

National Research Council. 1992. *Global Environment Change: Understanding the Human Dimensions*. Washington: National Academy Press.

Natural Resources Defense Council (NRDC). 1994. "Green Reform of the World Trading System: A Framework for Action." Press Release. New York: NRDC.

New Zealand. 1992. "Submission to GATT EMIT Group." Unpublished Submission on GATT and Trade and Environment Issues. GATT Doc. Geneva: New Zealand GATT Mission.

Nicolaïdis, Kalypso. 1993. "Mutual Recognition Among Nations: The European Community and Trade in Services." Ph.D. dissertation. Cambridge, MA: Harvard University.

Nordhaus, William. 1992. "An Optimal Transition Path for Controlling Greenhouse Gases." *Science* 258 (20 November).

Nordic Group. "Submission to GATT EMIT Group." Unpublished Submission on GATT and Trade and Environment Issues. GATT Doc. Geneva: Nordic GATT Office.

Nye, Joseph S. 1992. "What New World Order?" *Foreign Affairs* 71, no. 2 (Spring): 83.

O'Connor, David, and David Turnham. 1992. *Managing the Environment in Developing Countries*. Paris: Organization for Economic Cooperation and Development.

O'Riordan, Tim, and James Cameron, eds. 1994. *Interpreting the Precautionary Principle*. London: Cameron May Books.

Oates, Wallace E., and Paul R. Portney. 1992. "Economic Incentives and the Containment of Global Warming." *Eastern Economic Journal* 18, no. 1: 85–98.

Oates, Wallace E., Paul R. Portney, and Karen Palmer. 1993. *Environmental Regulation and International Competitiveness: Thinking About the Porter Hypothesis.* Resources for the Future Discussion Paper #94-02. Washington: RFF.

Odhiambo, Ojijo. 1993. "Constraints to a Just Global Trading System: A Southern Perspective." Paper presented at conference on Striking a Green Deal, Brussels, European Parliament, 7–9 November.

OECD Chemicals Group. 1993. "The OECD Chemicals Programme." Paris: OECD Chemicals Group.

Office of Technology Assessment (OTA). 1991. *Changing By Degrees: Steps to Reduce Greenhouse Gases.* OTA Report OTA-O-483. Washington: US Government Printing Office (February).

Office of Technology Assessment (OTA). 1992. *Trade and Environment: Conflicts and Opportunities.* OTA Report OTA-BP-ITE-94. Washington: US Government Printing Office (May).

Olson, Mancur. 1965. *The Logic of Collective Action: Public Goods and the Theory of Groups.* Cambridge, MA: Harvard University Press.

Organization for Economic Cooperation and Development (OECD). 1972. "Guiding Principles Concerning International Economic Aspects of Environmental Policies." Paris, 26 May.

Organization for Economic Cooperation and Development (OECD). 1975. *The Polluter Pays Principle: Definition, Analysis, Implementation.* Paris.

Organization for Economic Cooperation and Development (OECD). 1991. "Environmental Costs and Industrial Competitiveness." DSTI/IND(91)46. Paris, 22 October.

Organization for Economic Cooperation and Development (OECD). 1992. "Statement of the Business and Industry Advisory Council." Paris, November.

Organization for Economic Cooperation and Development (OECD). 1993a. *Life Cycle Management Conference Papers.* Paris, July.

Organization for Economic Cooperation and Development (OECD). 1993b. *Assessing the Effects of the Uruguay Round.* Paris, October.

Organization for Economic Cooperation and Development (OECD). 1994a. *Export Promotion and Environmental Technologies.* OECD Environment Monograph 87. Paris.

Organization for Economic Cooperation and Development (OECD). 1994b. "Summary Report of the Workshop on Life-Cycle Management and Trade." Paris.

Organization for Economic Cooperation and Development (OECD). 1994c. *The Environmental Effects of Trade.* Paris.

Ostry, Sylvia. 1990. *Governments & Corporations in a Shrinking World.* New York: Council on Foreign Relations.

Overseas Development Council. 1989. *Environment and the Poor: Development Strategies for a Common Agenda.* Washington: ODC.

Palmer, Geoffrey. 1992. "New Ways to Make International Environmental Law." *American Journal of International Law* 86: 259.

Palmeter, David. 1993. "Environment and Trade: Much Ado About Little." *Journal of World Trade* (June): 55–70.

Pasurka, Carl A., and Deborah Vaughn Nestor. 1992. *Trade Effects of the 1990 Clean Air Act Amendments.* Washington: EPA.

Patterson, Eliza. 1992. "GATT and the Environment—Rule Changes to Minimize Adverse Trade and Environmental Effects." *Journal of World Trade* 26, no. 3 (June).

Paye, Jean-Claude. 1994. "Merciless Competition: Time for New Rules?" *International Economic Insights* 5, no. 1 (January/February): 21–23.

Pearce, David W., and R. Kerry Turner. 1989. *Economics of Natural Resources.* London: Harvester-Wheatsheaf.

Pearce David W., Anil Markandya, and Edward Barbier. 1989. *Blueprint for a Green Economy.* London: Earthscan.

Pearce, David, and R. Kerry Turner. 1990. *Economics of Natural Resources and the Environment.* Baltimore: Johns Hopkins Press.

Pearce, David W. 1991. "The Role of Carbon Taxes in Adjusting to Global Warming." *Economic Journal* 101: 138–48.

Pearce, David W., and Jeremy Warford. 1993. *World Without End: Economics, Environment, and Sustainable Development*. New York: Oxford University Press.

Pearson, Charles. 1985. *Down to Business: Multinational Corporations, the Environment, and Development*. Washington: World Resources Institute.

Pearson, Charles. 1994. "Testing the System: GATT + PPP = ?" *Cornell International Law Journal* 27 no. 3 (Summer). Forthcoming.

Pearson, Charles, and Robert Repetto. 1993. "Reconciling Trade and Environment: The Next Steps." In *The Greening of World Trade*. Washington: US EPA National Advisory Committee for Environmental Policy and Technology.

Pedersen, William F. 1994a. "Limits to Market-Based Approaches to Environmental Protection." *Environmental Law Reporter* 24, no. 4: 10173.

Pedersen, William F. 1994b. "Protecting the Environment: What Does that Mean?" *Loyola of Los Angeles Law Review* (Spring).

Peltzman, Sam. 1976. "Toward a More General Theory of Regulation." *Journal of Law and Economics* 19.

Percival, Robert V., Alan S. Miller, Christopher H. Schroeder, and James P. Leape. 1992. *Environmental Regulation: Law, Science, and Policy*. Boston: Little, Brown and Company.

Perot, Ross. 1993. *Save Your Job, Save Our Country: Why NAFTA Must Be Stopped—Now!* New York: Hyperion.

Petersmann, Ernst-Ulrich. 1991a. *Constitutional Functions and Constitutional Problems of International Economic Law*. Fribourg, Switzerland: University Press.

Petersmann, Ernst-Ulrich. 1991b. "Trade Policy, Environmental Policy and the GATT." *Aussenwirtschaft* 46: 197–221.

Petersmann, Ernst-Ulrich. 1992. "National Constitutions, Foreign Trade Policy, and European Community Law." *European Journal of International Law* 3, no. 1: 1–35.

Petersmann, Ernst-Ulrich. 1994. "Why Do Governments Need the Uruguay Round Agreements, NAFTA and the EEA?" *Aussenwirtschaft* 49 (March): 31–55.

Petesch, Patti L. 1992. *North-South Environmental Strategies, Costs, and Bargains*. Overseas Development Council Policy Essay no. 5. Washington: ODC.

Pezzey, John. 1988. "Market Mechanisms of Pollution Control: 'Polluter Pays,' Economic and Practical Aspects." In R. Kerry Turner, *Sustainable Environmental Management*. Boulder, CO: Westview Press.

Pigou, Arthur Cecil. 1918. *The Economics of Welfare*. London: Macmillan and Co.

Pinchot, Gifford. [1947] 1987. *Breaking New Ground*. Washington: Island Press.

Plofchan, Thomas K. 1992. "Recognizing and Countervailing Environmental Subsidies." *International Law* 26: 763.

Porter, Gareth, and Janet Brown. 1991. *Global Environmental Politics*. Boulder, CO: Westview Press.

Porter, Gareth, with Inji Islam. 1992. "The Road from Rio: An Agenda for US Follow-up to the Earth Summit." Washington: Environmental and Energy Study Institute.

Porter, Michael. 1990. *The Competitive Advantage of Nations*. New York: Free Press.

Porter, Michael. 1991. "America's Green Strategy." *Scientific American* (August).

Porter, Michael, and Claas van der Linde. 1994. "Towards a New Conception of the Environment-Competitiveness Relationship." Unpublished working paper. Harvard University.

Postel, Sandra. 1992. "Denial in the Decisive Decade." In Lester Brown, *State of the World: 1992*. New York: W. W. Norton & Company.

Postiglione, A. 1990. "A More Efficient International Law on the Environment and Setting Up an International Court for the Environment Within the United Nations." *Environmental Law* 20.

Poterba, James M. 1991. "Tax Policy to Combat Global Warming: on Designing a Carbon Tax." In Dornbusch and Poterba, *Global Warming: Economic Policy Responses*. Cambridge, MA: MIT press.

Primo Braga, Carlos Alberto. 1992. "Tropical Forests and Trade Policy: The Case of Indonesia and Brazil." In Patrick Low, *International Trade and the Environment*. Washington: World Bank.

Prudencio, Rodrigo J., and Stuart J. Hudson. 1994. "The Road to Marrakech: An Interim Report on Environmental Reform of the GATT and the International Trade System." Washington: National Wildlife Foundation (25 January).

Ramphal, Shridath. 1990. "Third World Grievances." *EPA Journal* (July/August).

Rapaport, R. A., N. R. Urban, P. D. Capel, J. E. Baker, B. B. Looney, S. J. Eisenreich, and E. Gorham. 1985. "'New' DDT inputs to North America—atmospheric deposition." *Chemosphere* 14, 1167–73.

Rawls, John. 1971. *A Theory of Justice*. Cambridge, MA: Harvard University Press.

Reilly, William K. 1990. *The Green Thumb of Capitalism*: *Policy Review*. Washington: Heritage Foundation (Fall).

Reilly, William K. 1994. "Risky Business: Life, Death, Pollution, and the Global Environment." Speech delivered at Stanford University, Stanford, California, 12 January.

Repetto, Robert. 1993a. "Trade and Environment Policies: Achieving Complimentarities and Avoiding Conflicts." *WRI Issues and Ideas* (July). Washington: World Resources Institute.

Repetto, Robert. 1993b. "A Note on Complimentarities Between Trade and Environmental Policies." In *The Greening of World Trade*, 78 (Pub. No. EPA 100-R-93-002). Washington: EPA.

Repetto, Robert. 1994. "High (and Low) Priority Trade and Environment Issues Facing the WTO." Paper delivered at the US/EU Roundtable on the Environment and Trade, The Hague, Netherlands, 27 January.

Repetto, Robert, W. Magrath, M. Wells, C. Beer, and F. Rossini. 1989. *Wasting Assets: Natural Resources in the National Income Accounts*. Washington: World Resources Institute.

Repetto, Robert, Roger C. Dower, Robin Jenkins, and Jacqueline Geoghegan. 1993. *Green Fees: How a Tax Shift Can Work for the Environment and the Economy*. WRI Paper Series. Washington: World Resources Institute (November).

Revesz, Richard L. 1992. "Rehabilitating Interstate Competition: Rethinking the 'Race-to-the-Bottom' Rational for Federal Environmental Regulation." *New York University Law Review* 67 (December): 1210.

Richardson, J. David. 1993. *Sizing Up US Export Disincentives*. Washington: Institute for International Economics.

Richardson, Sarah, ed. 1993. *Shaping Consensus: The North American Commission on the Environment and NAFTA*. Workshop Report. National Round Table on the Environment and the Economy, Ottawa, Canada (7 April).

Rizopoulos, Nicholas X., ed. 1990. *Sea-Changes*. New York: Council on Foreign Relations.

Roberts, Adam, and Benedict Kingsbury. 1993. *United Nations, Divided World: The UN's Role in International Relations*. Oxford: Oxford University Press.

Roe, David. 1989. "Toxic Chemical Control Incentives." *Economic Development Quarterly* 3, no. 3 (August).

Roessler, Freider. 1992. "The Constitutional Function of the Multilateral Trade Order." In Hilf and Petersmann, *National Constitutions and International Economic Law*. Norwell, MA: Kluwer.

Roht-Arriaza, Naomi. 1992. "Precaution, Participation, and the 'Greening' of International Trade Law." *Journal of Environmental Law and Litigation* 7: 57–98.

Roper Organization. 1992. *The Green Gauge Report*. New York: Roper.

Rose-Ackerman, Susan. 1981. "Does Federalism Matter? Political Choice in a Federal Republic." *Journal of Political Economy* 89.

Runge, Ford. 1994. *Freer Trade, Protected Environment*. New York: Council on Foreign Relations Press.

Runnalls, David, and Aaron Cosbey. 1992. *Trade and Sustainable Development: A Survey of the Issues and a New Research Agenda*. Winnipeg: International Institute for Sustainable Development.

Sagoff, Mark. 1988. *The Economy of the Earth*. Cambridge, UK: Cambridge University Press.

Salzman, James. 1991. *Environmental Labelling in OECD Countries*. Paris: OECD.

Sand, P. 1991. "Lessons Learned in Global Environmental Governance." *British Columbia Environmental Affairs Law Review* 18: 213.

Sand, Peter H. 1980. "The Creation of Transnational Rules for Environmental Protection." In Bothe, M., *Trends in Environmental Policy and Law*, IVCN Environmental Policy and Law Paper No. 15: 311–20.

Schmidheiny, Stephan. 1992. *Changing Course: A Global Business Perspective on Development and the Environment*. Cambridge, MA: MIT Press.

Schneider, Stephen. 1976. *The Genesis of Strategy: Climate and Global Survival*. New York: Plenum Press.

Schoenbaum, Thomas. 1992. "Agora: Trade and Environment." *The American Journal of International Law* 86 (October): 700–28.

Schott, Jeffrey J. 1990. *Completing the Uruguay Round*. Washington: Institute for International Economics.

Schuck, Peter. 1981. "The Politics of Regulation." *Yale Law Journal* 90.

Schumacher, E. F. 1973. *Small Is Beautiful*. New York: Harper and Row.

Sebenius, James K. 1991. "Negotiating a Regime to Control Global Warming." In World Resources Institute, *Greenhouse Warming: Negotiating a Global Regime*. Washington: WRI.

Sebenius, James. K. 1992. "Challenging Conventional Explanations of International Cooperation: Negotiation Analysis of the Case of Epistemic Communities." *International Organization* 46 (Winter).

Sewell, John, Peter M. Storm, and contributors. 1992. *Challenges and Priorities in the 1990s: An Alternative U.S. International Affairs Budget*. ODC Paper Series. Washington: Overseas Development Council.

Shabecoff, Phil. 1993. *A Fierce Green Fire*. New York: Hill and Wang.

Shaw, Nevil, and Aaron Cosbey. 1994. *Positioning GATT's Trade and Environment Work Programme to Support Sustainable Development*. Occasional report. Winnipeg: International Institute for Sustainable Development (March).

Shrybman, Steven. 1988. "Selling Canada's Environment Short: The Environmental Case Against the Trade Deal." Unpublished paper. Toronto: Canadian Environmental Law Association.

Shrybman, Steven. 1989. "International Trade and the Environment: An Environmental Assessment of Present GATT Negotiations." unpublished paper. Toronto: Canadian Environmental Law Association.

Shrybman, Steven. 1990. "International Trade and the Environment: An Environmental Assessment of the General Agreement on Tariffs and Trade." *The Ecologist* 20, no. 1: 30–1.

Shrybman, Steven. 1993. "It's Resources, Stupid!" Paper presented at conference on Striking a Green Deal, Brussels, European Parliament, 7–9 November.

de Silva, Leelanda. 1993. "A Curate's Egg: An Assessment of the Multilateral Trade Organization." Paper presented at conference on Striking a Green Deal, Brussels, European Parliament, 7–9 November.

Silver, Cheryl. 1990. *One Earth, One Future: Our Changing Global Environment*. Washington: National Academy Press.

Sistema Económica Latinamericano (SELA). 1992. "Trade, Environment and the Developing Countries." SP/CL/8.0/ Di no. 2 (September).

Smith, Joel, and Dennis Tirpak, eds. 1989. *The Potential Effects of Global Climate Change on the United States*. Pub. No. EPA-230-05-89-050. Washington: EPA.

Snape, Richard. 1992. "The Environment, International Trade and Competitiveness." In Anderson and Blackhurst, *The Greening of World Trade Issues*. Ann Arbor: University of Michigan Press.

Sohn, Louis B. 1973. "The Stockholm Declaration." *Harvard International Law Journal* 14: 423.

Solagral. 1993. "Commerce et Environment." Monograph. Paris: Solagral Institute (8 June).

Solomon, Robert. 1977. *The International Monetary System 1945–1976*. New York: Harper and Row.

Sorsa, Piritta. 1991. "GATT and the Environment: Basic Issues and Some Developing Country Concerns." Paper presented at World Bank Symposium on International Trade and the Environment, 21–22 November.

Sorsa, Piritta. 1992. "GATT and Environment." *World Economy* 15, no. 4: 115–33.

Speth, James Gustave. 1992. "A Post-Rio Compact." *Foreign Policy* 88: 145.

Sprinz, Detlef, and Tapani Vaahtoranta. 1994. "The Interest-Based Explanation of International Environmental Policy." *International Organization* 48 (Winter).

Smith, Fred L. 1992. "Environmental Policy at the Crossroads." In Greve and Smith, *Environmental Politics: Public Costs, Private Rewards*. New York: Praeger.

Stavins, Robert N., ed. 1988. "Project 88: Harnessing Market Forces to Protect our Environment." Public document released by the offices of Senators Timothy Wirth and John Heinz. Washington: US Senate (December).

Stevens, Candice. 1993a. "A GATT for the Environment: Options for a Multilateral Environmental Organization." *Ecodecision* (March).

Stevens, Candice. 1993b. "The OECD Principles Revisited." *Environmental Law* 23.

Stewart, Richard B. 1977. "Pyramids of Sacrifice? Problems of Federalism in Mandating State Implementation of National Environmental Policy." *Yale Law Journal* 86: 1196.

Stewart, Richard B. 1990. "Madison's Nightmare." *University of Chicago Law Review* 57, 335.

Stewart, Richard B. 1992. "International Trade and Environment: Lessons From the Federal Experience." *Washington and Lee Law Review* 49, no. 4 (Fall): 1329.

Stewart, Richard B. 1993a. "The NAFTA: Trade, Competition, Environmental Protection." *The International Lawyer* 27 (Fall): 751–64.

Stewart, Richard B. 1993b. "Environmental Regulation and International Competitiveness." *Yale Law Journal* 102 (June): 2039.

Stewart, Richard B., and Jonathan B. Wiener. 1992. "A Comprehensive Approach to Global Climate Policy: Issues of Design and Practicality." *Arizona Journal of International and Comparative Law* 9: 83.

Stewart, Terence P. 1993. *The GATT Uruguay Round: A Negotiating History 1986–1992*. Kluwer: Norwell, MA.

Stigler, George J. 1971. "The Theory of Economic Regulation." *Bell Journal of Economics* 2.

Stokes, Bruce. 1991. "Greens Talk Trade." *National Journal* (13 April).

Stone, Roger D., and Eve Hamilton. 1991. *Global Economics and the Environment*. New York: Council on Foreign Relations Press.

Storm, Peter M. 1993. *The US Foreign Aid Budget: Is the Well Running Dry?* Overseas Development Council Policy Focus no. 5. Washington: ODC.

Strong, Maurice. 1992. "Required Global Changes: Close Linkages between Environment and Development." In Üner Kirdar, *Change: Threat or Opportunity?* New York: United Nations Publications.

Subramanian, A. 1992. "Trade Measures for Environment: A Nearly Empty Box?" *World Economy* 15, no. 1: 135–52.

Sucharipa-Behrmann, Lilly. 1993. "Eco-labelling Approaches for Tropical Timber: The Austrian Experience." Presentation to OECD Workshop on Life Cycle Management, Paris (July).

Susskind, Larry. 1994. *Environmental Diplomacy: Negotiating More Effective Global Agreements*. New York: Oxford University Press.

Taylor, Ronnie. 1993. *Positive Incentives, Sustainable Commodity Production and the OECD*. Friends of the Earth Discussion Paper. London: Friends of the Earth.

Tinbergen, Jan. 1952. *On the Theory of Economic Policy*. Amsterdam: North Holland Press.

Tobey, James A. 1990 "The Effects of Domestic Environmental Policies on Patterns of World Trade: An Empirical Test." *Kyklos* 43 no. 2 (May): 191–209.

Tobin, James. 1978. "A Proposal for International Monetary Reform." *Eastern Economic Journal* 4 (July/October): 3–4.

Topping, John. 1992. "Likely Impact of Global Warming on Developing Countries." In Üner Kirdar, *Change: Threat or Opportunity?* New York: United Nations Publications.

Trisoglio, Alex, and Kerry ten Kate. 1993. "Systemic Integration of Environment and Trade." *Ecodecision* (March).

Tucker, Stuart K. 1992. "Equity and the Environment in the Promotion of Nontraditional Agricultural Exports." In Sheldon Annis, *Poverty, Natural Resources, and Public Policy in Central America*. Washington: Overseas Development Council.

Tullock, Gordon. 1989. *The Economics of Special Privilege and Rent Seeking*. Norwell, MA: Kluwer Academic Publishers.

Turner, R. Kerry. 1988. *Sustainable Environmental Management*. Boulder, CO: Westview Press.

United Nations. 1974. Charter of Economic Rights and Duties of States. General Assembly Res. 3281.

United Nations. 1992a. *Agenda 21: The United Nations Programme of Action from Rio*. New York: UN.

United Nations. 1993. *World Economic Survey 1993: Current Trends and Policies in the World Economy*. Publication no. E/1993/60. New York: UN.

UN Food and Agricultural Organization (UNFAO). 1993a. *Forest Resources Assessment 1990: Tropical Countries*. FAO Forestry Paper 112. Rome: FAO.

UN Food and Agricultural Organization (UNFAO). 1993b. *World Review of High Seas and Highly Migratory Fish Species and Straddling Stocks*. UNFAO Fisheries Circular No. 858 (preliminary version). Rome: UNFAO.

US Council for International Business (USCIB). 1992. "Policy Statement on an Integrated Approach to Environment and Trade Issues and the GATT." New York: USCIB (May).

US Council for International Business (USCIB). 1993. "Policy Statement on International Environmental Agreements and the Use of Trade Measures to Achieve Their Objectives." New York: USCIB (December).

US Council for International Business (USCIB). 1994. "Policy Statement on Constraints on the Unilateral Use of Trade Measures to Enforce Environmental Policies." New York: USCIB (April 8).

US Government Interagency Environmental Policy Group. 1994. Interagency memo on trade and environment. Unreleased document, on file with the author (February).

US International Trade Commission (USITC). 1988. *Forklifts from Japan Antidumping Investigation*. USITC Publication No. 2082. Washington: USITC.

US International Trade Commission (USITC). 1991. *International Agreements to Protect the Environment and Wildlife*. USITC Publication No. 2351. Washington: USITC (January).

US International Trade Commission (USITC). 1994. *Metallurgical Coke: Baseline Analysis for the U.S. Industry and Imports*. USITC Publications No, 2745. Washington: USITC (March).

US Trade Representative. 1992. *Review of U.S.-Mexico Environmental Issues*. Washington: USTR (February).

US Trade Representative. 1993a. *NAFTA Supplemental Agreements: North American Agreement on Environmental Cooperation*. Washington: USTR (13 September).

US Trade Representative. 1993b. *The NAFTA: Report on Environmental Issues*. Washington: USTR (November).

Van Houtven, George L., and Maureen L. Cropper. 1994. "When Is a Life Too Costly to Save? The Evidence from Environmental Regulations." *Resources* 114 (Winter): 6–10.

Vander Stichele, M. 1992. "GATT, UNCTAD, UNCED, and Trade Related Issues." *International Coalition for Development Action (ICDA) Update*. Brussels: ICDA.

Verleger, Philip K. 1993. *Adjusting to Volatile Energy Prices*. Washington: Institute for International Economics.

Vester, Frederic. 1993. "Systems Thinking and the Environment." *The McKinsey Quarterly* 2.

Waldron, J. 1987. "Can Commercial Goods Be Human Rights?" *European Journal of Sociology* 17.

Westbrook, David A. 1991. "Environmental Policy in the European Community: Observations on the European Environment Agency." *Harvard Environmental Law Review* 15: 257–73.

Whalley, J. 1991. "The Interface Between Environmental and Trade Policies." *Economic Journal* 101, no. 405: 180–89.

Wiemann, Jürgen. 1992. *Environmentally Oriented Trade Policy: A New Area of Conflict between North and South?* German Development Institute Paper. Berlin: GDI (September).

Wildavsky, Aaron. 1988. *Searching for Safety*. New Brunswick, NJ: Transaction Books.

Williams, Maurice J., and Patti L. Petesch. 1993. *Sustaining the Earth: Role of Multilateral Development Institutions*. Washington: Overseas Development Council.

Williamson, Caroline T., ed. 1993. *Agriculture, the Environment and Trade: Conflict or Cooperation?* Washington: International Policy Council on Agriculture and Trade.

Wilson, Edward O. 1992. *The Diversity of Life*. Cambridge, MA: Harvard University Press.

Wirth, David. 1989. "Climate Chaos." *Foreign Policy* 74: 3.

Wirth, David. 1991. "Legitimacy, Accountability, and Partnership: A Model for Advocacy on Third World Environmental Issues." *Yale Law Journal* 100, no. 8: 2645–66.

Wirth, David. 1992a. "The International Trade Regime and the Municipal Law of Federal States: How Close a Fit?" *Washington and Lee Law Review* 49, no. 4 (Fall): 1389–1401.

Wirth, David. 1992b. "A Matchmaker's Challenge: Marrying International Law and American Environmental Law." *Virginia Journal of International Law* 32, no. 2 (Winter): 377–420.

World Bank. 1992a. *World Bank Development Report 1992: Development and the Environment*. Washington: World Bank.

World Bank. 1992b. *The World Bank and the Environment*. Washington: World Bank.

World Bank. 1993a. *Terms of Reference: Evaluation of the Global Environment Facility Pilot Phase*. Report of the GEF Administrator. Washington: World Bank.

World Bank. 1993b. *Toward an Environmental Strategy for Asia*. World Bank Discussion Paper no. 224. Washington: World Bank.

World Commission on Environment and Development. 1987. *Our Common Future*. Oxford: Oxford University Press.

World Resources Institute (WRI). 1989. *The Crucial Decade: The 1990s and the Global Environmental Challenge*. World Resources Institute Report. Washington, January.

World Resources Institute (WRI). 1991. *Greenhouse Warming: Negotiating a Global Regime*. Washington, January.

World Resources Institute (WRI). 1994. *World Resources 1994–95*. Washington.

Wyden, Ron. 1992. "Using Trade Agreements to Protect the Environment." *Journal of Environmental Law and Litigation* 7: 1–5.

Young, M.D. 1994. "Ecologically-Accelerated Trade Liberalisation: A Set of Disciplines for Environment and Trade Agreements." *Ecological Economics* 9: 43–51.

Zarsky, Lyuba. 1993. "Environmental Trade Preferences and the Transition to 'Green Trade.'" *Ecodecision* (March): 51–2.

Zaelke, Durwood, Robert Housman, and Paul Orbuch. 1993. *Trade and the Environment: Law, Policy and Economics*. Washington: Island Press.

Zaelke, Durwood, Robert Housman, and Gary Stanley. 1993. "Frictions Between International Trade Agreements and Environmental Protections." In *The Greening of World Trade*, Pub. No. EPA 100-R-93-002. Washington: Environmental Protection Agency.

Index

Eglin, Richard, 39, 102, 145, 164, 176, 218, 219
El-Ashry, Mohamed, 87
Elliott, Kimberly Ann, 25n, 57, 73n, 76n, 132, 133n, 144, 168n, 190, 249
El Serafy, Salah, 11n
Emissions, 12, 12n, 12f, 16
    developing country shares, 187n
    fixed limits, 14–15
    inventories, 78
    reductions, 23, 203
    trading, 202n, 202–203
Endangered species, trade in, 130. *See also* CITES
Energy conservation, investment in, 190n
Energy pricing, 22
Energy taxes, 23
Enterprise for the Americas Initiative (EAI), 196n, 196–197
Environment
    education about, 201–202, 252–253
    global problems, 15b, 17–19, 225
    interest in, 9–14
    intergenerational aspect of problems, 68, 228
    international management of, 77–78
    limits of, 13
    threshold effects, 11, 12f, 13, 228
    trade conflict origins, 9–34
Environmental agreements. *See* International environmental agreements
Environmental conditionality, 197–198
Environmental Defense Fund (EDF), 28n, 218n
Environmental federalism, 111–113, 234
Environmental harms
    bona fides of 118–121, 142
    categories of, 121–122
    domestic, 121
    foreign, 121–122, 125–126
    global, 121, 124–130
    incidental, 121
    locations, 235
    nexus to, 121–127
    purely domestic, 122
    purely foreign, 122, 126–127
    transboundary, 121, 123–124
    valuation of, 128n
Environmental impact assessments, 207–210, 237
Environmental imperialism. *See* Ecoimperialism
Environmental injury test, 233, 234–235, 235n
Environmental policy efficacy of, 190
Environmentalists, 3b,9, 36–37, 229
    challenge to free trade, 42–46
    defensive agenda, 3, 232
    divisions among, 28
    ends and means dispute, 14–17
    GATT-specific critique, 52–54
    offensive agenda, 3, 232
    pragmatic, 61
    trade perspectives, 2, 13
    trade propositions, 2–6, 42–46
Environmental legislation, 73n, 73–74, 77, 92, 105b
Environmental measures. *See* Environmental standards
Environmental Measures in International Trade GATT (EMIT) Group, 106n, 145, 220–221
Environmental organizations
    anti-NAFTA, 28n

    influence of, 76, 76n
    membership in, 9–10
    pro-NAFTA, 28n
    regional, 83–84
Environmental policy
    ad hoc, 92, 92n
    convergence with trade policy, 54–59, 63–69, 225–227
    corporate sensitivity to, 23
    economic and political failures, 227–230
    efficacy of, 14–15, 190
    elements of, 40–41
    essential principles for, 81, 81n
    legitimacy of, 117–127, 220–221, 234–235
    moral basis for, 119n, 119–120, 120n, 166
    precautionary approach, 41, 118n
    public participation in, 172n, 172–173
    recommendations, 153–154, 178–179
    relating to conservation test, 49b
    US, 37
Environmental protection, 24
    aim of, 225
    benefits of, 73
    market failure, 79
    political failure, 73–75
    programs, 6
    prosperity and, 64
    trade liberalization congruence, 65–69
    trade liberalization linkage, 226–227
    trade resources for, 63–65
    US, 161
Environmental Protection Agency (EPA), 14, 19, 20, 81, 110, 160, 165, 187, 199
    asbestos ban, 101, 101n
    Energy Star program, 252, 253
    environmental education, 202
    environmental risk list, 188
    informal consultations, 255
    operating budget, 165n
Environmental regulations, 14–16. *See also* Environmental standards, Cost internalization, Polluter pays principle
    authorities, 109
    command and control, 14
    competitiveness effects, 160n
    diversity, 43
    domestic, 101, 228
    GATT-consistent, 102
    in high-standard countries, 51n
    implementation of, 19–20
    integrated approach, 92, 92n
    international, 228
    market-based, performance-oriented, 17
    precautionary approach, 81
    reformulated gasoline, 44n
    trade liberalization threat to, 100–105
Environmental standards, 45. *See also* Environmental regulations, International trade-environment balancing test
    appropriateness test, 127–130, 128n
    assimilation of, 2
    baseline, 140
    CAFE, 45
    clear disproportionality test, 127–130
    commerce clause (US), 113–114
    as competitiveness factor, 5–6
    compliance, 148–151
    convergence or harmonization of, 172n, 172–174, 179, 233

NEPA. *See* National Environmental Policy Act
Netherlands
  contributions to GEF, 87
  energy taxes, 23
  environmental taxes, 23, 162*n*
  joint implementation efforts, 202
  pollution, 54
  sustainable timber labels, 252
New International Economic Order debates, 191–192
New Zealand GATT Statement, 19 November 1992, 106*n*
NGOs. *See* Nongovernment organizations
Nicolaïdies, Kalypso, 175
No-growth environmental view, 54
Nongovernment organizations (NGOs), 26*n*, 27
Nordhaus, William, 19*n*, 40, 88*n*
Nordic Council
  ecolabeling, 252
  interpretation of Article XX, 217*n*
North American Commission on Environmental cooperation, 176
North American Free Trade Agreement (NAFTA), 1–2, 27–32, 35–36, 74*n*, 165*n*, 187
  environmental effects, 42–43
  environmental provisions, 28, 165
  environmental review, 208–209
  environmental side agreements, 28, 176, 176*n*
  environmental support for, 28*n*
  standards chapter, 119*n*
North-South Center, 208*n*
North-South relations, 25–26, 181–183, 185–188, 193–203
  assistance and development programs, 198–199
  commodity agreements, 193–195
  compensation disputes, 30–31
  competitiveness, 159*n*
  country studies, 201
  environmental conditionality, 197–198
  environmental trade preferences, 195–196
  environment and resources linkage, 196–197
  multilateral development banks, 197–198
  partnerships, 201–202, 202–203
  resource transfers, 189–192
  technology transfers, 199–201
  trade, 192–193
  trade and environment disputes, 238–239
Norway
  ecolabeling, 252
  joint implementation efforts, 202–203
  US trade restrictions against, 140–141
  whaling violations, 236–237
Nye, Joseph S., 27

Oates, Wallace, 66, 88*n*, 159, 160
Obstfeld, Maurice, 44*n*, 159*n*
Ocean pollution, 17*n*
O'Connor, David, 201
Odhiambo, Ojijo, 182
Office of Technology Assessment (OTA), 20
Oil spills, 11, 112
Olson, Mancur, 73*n*, 79*n*
O'Neill, Thomas P., Jr., 140*n*
Ontario Beer Case, 274
Openness of GATT procedures, 211, 211*n*
Oregon Waste Systems v. Department of Environmental Quality, 115*n*, 260–261

Organization for Economic Cooperation and Development (OECD), 16, 21*b*, 78, 81, 114*n*, 159, 160, 171, 177*n*
  bilateral assistance programs, 198
  Chemicals Group, 178
  commitment to polluter pays principle, 177
  country studies, 201
  environmental training program, 201–202
  joint experts group on trade and environment, 37*n*
  no equalization of costs principle, 177
  US relations, 7, 206
O'Riordan, Tim 41*n*
Ostry, Sylvia, 20, 75
Outer space, protection of, 12*n*
Overseas Development Council, 197*n*, 199
Ozone layer
  depletion of, 17, 18, 41
  protection of, 191

Packaging restrictions, 102, 182, 188
Palladio v. Diamond, 113, 258
Palmer, Geoffrey, 159, 160
Palmeter, David, 63, 70, 164
Paradigms, clash of, 37–39
Patrick, Hugh T., 25*n*
Patterson, Eliza, 99, 171
Paye, Jean-Claude, 156
Peace, Prosperity, and Democracy Act, 199
Peace Corps, 202
Pearson, Charles, 16, 27*n*, 66, 67, 99, 168
Pedersen, William F., 17
Pelly amendment, 254
Percival, Robert V. 37*n*
Performance standards, 175, 175*n*
Perot, Ross, 35–36, 155
Pesticides, 186
  circle of poison, 109, 109*n*, 186
  international residue guidelines, 173*n*
  safety standards, 103*b*
Petersmann, Ernst-Ulrich, 76, 96, 112*n*, 220
Petesch, Patti L., 86*n*, 90, 190*n*, 198
Philadelphia v. New Jersey, 113, 259–260
Photosynthesis, 126*n*
Phytosanitary Convention for Africa, 277
Pigou, Arthur, 67
Pike v. Bruce Church, 113, 114, 258
Pinchot, Gifford, 10*n*, 74, 184*n*
PL 92–522. *See* Marine Mammal Protection Act
Plant Protection Agreement for the South East Asia and Pacific Region, 276
Political Drag 23, 107*n*, 126–127, 156, 162–163, 162*n*
Political failure
  of environmental policy, 73–75, 227–230
  of trade policy, 73–75, 75–77
Political spillovers, 107*n*, 162–163. *See also* Political drag
Polluter pays principle, 17, 38, 38*n*, 58, 80, 170, 179, 227, *See also* Cost internalization
  convergence on, 176–178
  implementation of, 65–69, 66*n*, 227, 228
  market failure, 70–71
  policy implications, 69–70
Pollution, 11*n*, 11–13, 12*n*, 12*f*, 16, 16*n*, 54, 225
  income and, 64, 65*f*
  prevention of, 81
  spillovers, 225, 228. *See also* Spillovers

Pollution control, 41
  costs, 159, 160–161
  fees, 239
  laws, 13
  policies, 235
  victim pays scheme, 84–85
Population growth, 11n, 43
Porter, Gareth, 27n, 40
Porter, Michael, 157n, 159, 160
Portney, Paul R., 88n, 159, 160
Positive externalities, loss of, 125–126
Postel, Sandra, 11
Postiglione, A., 83n
Poterba, James M., 88n
Poverty, 183, 184
Precautionary principle, 41, 41n, 81
Prickett, Glenn, 87n
Primo Braga, Carlos Alberto, 189
Prison labor, 119n, 166
Process standards, 44n, 51, 104
Procter & Gamble v. Chicago, 114, 259
Procymidone in Wine US–EU case, 271
Production subsidies, 170n
Production processes and methods, 44n, 51, 104
Products, GATT focus on, 49–51, 104, 139, 233
Product standards, 44n, 51
Project 88, 88n
Property rights, 13, 68
Prosperity and environmental protection, 64, 65f
Protocol of Provisional Application, 215
Prudencio, Rodrigo, J., 99, 205n
Psychological spillovers, 107n, 119, 233
Public goods, 67, 79, 227–228. *See also*
  Collective-action problems
Public participation, in environmental decision
  making, 172n, 172–173

Quality of life issues, 10

Radioactivity, spread of, 12n
Ramphal, Shridath, 183
Rawls, John, 80n, 97n
Reason, rule of, 100n
Reformulated gasoline regulations, 44n
Regulations. *See* Environmental regulations
Rents, monopoly, 45
Repetto, Robert, 44n, 65, 66, 70, 88n, 99, 168
Research and development, North-South
  cooperation on, 200–201
Revesz, Richard L., 22, 156n, 161
Richards, Kenneth R., 10, 19
Richardson, J. David, 21
Richardson, Sarah, 159
Rio Conference. *See* Earth Summit
Rio Declaration on Environment and
  Development, 98n, 105b, 123n, 124n, 141n,
  143–144, 183, 192, 193
Roberts, Adam, 90
Roe, David, 134
Roessler, Freider, 39n
Roht-Arriaza, Naomi, 81n
Roosevelt, Franklin Delano, 166
Roper Organization, 10n
Rose-Ackerman, Susan, 73n
Rothschild, Michael, 40
Rule of reason, 100n

Sagoff, Mark, 37
Salzman, James, 252
Sanitary and phytosanitary (SPS) standards,
  49, 50b, 119n
Scandinavian countries, contributions to GEF,
  87
Schmidheiny, Stephan, 10n, 11, 27, 65
Schneider, Stephen, 18, 41n
Schoenbaum, Thomas, 102
Schott, Jeffrey J., 21b, 57, 132, 133n, 190, 245n,
  249
Schrenk, William J., 196n
Schuck, Peter, 76n
Scientific Certification Systems (SCS) labels,
  252
Scottish Red Grouse EC case, 265
Sea turtles, protection for, 249–250
Security, national, 25n
SELA. *See* Sistema Económica Latinamericano
Sewell, John, 197n, 199
Shabecoff, Phil, 74n
Shadbegian, Ronald J., 160n
Shafik, Nemat, 202n
Shaw, Daigee, 19n
Shaw, Nevil, 192n, 205n
Sheehan, Jack, 22n
Shrybman, Steven, 47, 104
Sierra Club, 28n
Silkwood v. Kerr-McGee Corp., 260
Siniscalco, D., 200, 253
Sistema Económica Latinamericano (SELA), 99
Smith, 51n, 85n
Smith, Joel, 19
Snape, Richard, 176
Softwood Lumber, US-Canada FTA case, 273
Solagral Institute, 189n
Solidarity Fund, 88n
Solomon, Robert, 75n
Sorsa, Piritta, 99
South. *See also* North-South relations
  support for trade regime status quo, 181–183
Sovereignty, 56–58, 93, 105b. *See also* Ecological
  interdependence
Soviet Union, environmental history, 10
Special interests, 73, 73n, 74, 77, 77n
Speth, James Gustave, 25, 26n
Spillovers
  political, 107n, 162–163
  pollution, 46, 51–53, 55, 66, 82, 86, 96, 225,
  228
  psychological, 107n, 119, 233
Sprinz, Detlef, 79
SPS standards. *See* Sanitary and phytosanitary
  standards
Standards. *See also* Environmental standards
Stanley, Gary, 101
Stavins, Robert N., 16, 88n
Steer, Andrew, 40
Stevens, Candice, 81n, 177n
Stewart, Richard, 22, 52n, 65, 106, 112, 161, 203
Stewart, Terence P., 210n
Stockholm Declaration, 105b, 123n, 124n, 141n
Storm, Peter M., 190n, 199n
Strategic behavior in standard setting, 157,
  157n *See also* Competitiveness
Strong, Maurice, 86, 86n, 183, 192
Strong GATT rights, 118, 124
Subramanian, A., 107n, 140n

Other Publications from the
Institute for International Economics

POLICY ANALYSES IN INTERNATIONAL ECONOMICS Series

1 The Lending Policies of the International Monetary Fund
   John Williamson/*August 1982*
                    ISBN paper 0-88132-000-5   72 pp.

2 "Reciprocity": A New Approach to World Trade Policy?
   William R. Cline/*September 1982*
                    ISBN paper 0-88132-001-3   41 pp.

3 Trade Policy in the 1980s
   C. Fred Bergsten and William R. Cline/*November 1982*
   (out of print)   ISBN paper 0-88132-002-1   84 pp.
   Partially reproduced in the book *Trade Policy in the 1980s.*

4 International Debt and the Stability of the World Economy
   William R. Cline/*September 1983*
                    ISBN paper 0-88132-010-2   134 pp.

5 The Exchange Rate System, Second Edition
   John Williamson/*September 1983, rev. June 1985*
   (out of print)   ISBN paper 0-88132-034-X   61 pp.

6 Economic Sanctions in Support of Foreign Policy Goals
   Gary Clyde Hufbauer and Jeffrey J. Schott/*October 1983*
                    ISBN paper 0-88132-014-5   109 pp.

7 A New SDR Allocation?
   John Williamson/*March 1984*
                    ISBN paper 0-88132-028-5   61 pp.

8 An International Standard for Monetary Stabilization
   Ronald I. McKinnon/*March 1984*
                    ISBN paper 0-88132-018-8   108 pp.

9 The Yen/Dollar Agreement: Liberalizing Japanese Capital Markets
   Jeffrey A. Frankel/*December 1984*
                    ISBN paper 0-88132-035-8   86 pp.

10 Bank Lending to Developing Countries: The Policy Alternatives
   C. Fred Bergsten, William R. Cline, and John Williamson/*April 1985*
                    ISBN paper 0-88132-032-3   221 pp.

11 Trading for Growth: The Next Round of Trade Negotiations
   Gary Clyde Hufbauer and Jeffrey J. Schott/*September 1985*
                    ISBN paper 0-88132-033-1   109 pp.

12 Financial Intermediation Beyond the Debt Crisis
   Donald R. Lessard and John Williamson/*September 1985*
                    ISBN paper 0-88132-021-8   130 pp.

13 The United States-Japan Economic Problem
   C. Fred Bergsten and William R. Cline/*October 1985, 2d ed. January 1987*
   (out of print)   ISBN paper 0-88132-060-9   180 pp.

BOOKS

SPECIAL REPORTS

FORTHCOMING

Reciprocity and Retaliation in US Trade Policy
Thomas O. Bayard and Kimberly Ann Elliott

The Globalization of Industry and National Governments
C. Fred Bergsten and Edward M. Graham

Managing the World Economy: Fifty Years After Bretton Woods
Peter B. Kenen, editor

**The Political Economy of Korea–United States Cooperation: The
Bilateral, Asia Pacific, and Global Dimensions**
C. Fred Bergsten and Il SaKong, editors

International Debt Reexamined
William R. Cline

Trade, Jobs, and Income Distribution
William R. Cline

Overseeing Global Capital Markets
Morris Goldstein and Peter Garber

Foreign Direct Investment in the United States, Third Edition
Edward M. Graham and Paul R. Krugman

Global Competition Policy
Edward M. Graham and J. David Richardson

Currencies and Politics in the United States, Germany, and Japan
C. Randall Henning

Toward a Pacific Economic Community?
Gary Clyde Hufbauer and Jeffrey J. Schott

Western Hemisphere Economic Integration
Gary Clyde Hufbauer and Jerrey J. Schott

Measuring the Costs of Protection in Japan
Yoko Sazanami, Shujiro Urata, and Hiroki Kawai

The Uruguay Round: An Assessment
Jeffrey J. Schott

The Case for Trade: A Modern Reconsideration
J. David Richardson

The Future of the World Trading System
John Whalley, in collaboration with Colleen Hamilton

Estimating Equilibrium Exchange Rates
John Williamson, editor

For orders outside the US and Canada please contact:

Longman Group UK Ltd.
PO Box 88
Harlow, Essex CM 19 5SR
UK

Telephone Orders: 0279 623925
Fax: 0279 453450
Telex: 817484

Canadian customers can order from the Institute or from either:

RENOUF BOOKSTORE
1294 Algoma Road
Ottawa, Ontario K1B 3W8
Telephone: (613) 741-4333
Fax: (613) 741-5439

LA LIBERTÉ
3020 chemin Sainte-Foy
Quebec G1X 3V6
Telephone: (418) 658-3763
Fax: (800) 567-5449